STEVENS AT THE AGE OF SEVENTY-FOUR

From a photograph by Matthew B. Brady in the possession of the
United States Signal Corps

Old Thad Stevens
A STORY OF AMBITION

By
Richard Nelson Current
ASSISTANT PROFESSOR OF
HISTORY AND POLITICAL SCIENCE
RUTGERS UNIVERSITY

Madison
THE UNIVERSITY OF WISCONSIN PRESS
1942

Printed in the United States of America

Sept 13 '78
43-52549

Foreword

BEWIGGED, clubfooted, sarcastic Old Thad Stevens was the imperious kind of man whom few could love but to whom none could be indifferent or lukewarm. He was conspicuous as an extremist politician in an age of political extremes, when an irrepressible conflict was carried from the forum to the battlefield and back to the forum again. To Americans of the eighteen-sixties, disagreeing violently as they did in politics, he was at once a saint, albeit a tarnished one, and a fiend. To millions of Northerners he seemed no less than an avenging angel of the Lord; to millions of Southerners, many of whom thought Damn Thad Stevens was his name just as they thought damyankee one word, he seemed an agent of the devil out of hell.

If his contemporaries disagreed so widely, it is not surprising that writers after his death have come to no common conclusion about the merit and meaning of his career. The epitaph he composed for himself gives "Equality of man before his Creator" as the guiding principle of his life. Taking this as their starting point and working backward, the biographers of Stevens have concluded that he was essentially a great "leveler" or "egalitarian." They have accepted as their theme his own rationalization of his life. Others have gone to the opposite extreme and have found motivations in his affection for his mulatto "housekeeper," which, they imply, gave him an unreasoning passion for vengeance on all Southern whites. None has taken adequately into account the simple fact that he was, above everything else, a man of politics seeking always to get and exercise the powers of public office.

The present biography offers a more complete and, it is hoped, a better balanced view than has heretofore been given of the greatest dictator Congress has ever had. The aim has been not to debunk him but to paint a realistic and unretouched portrait, to tell a straightforward story that would harmonize the contradictory aspects of his amazing personality. Stevens was a colorful person, but he was much more human and less odd than he often pretended to be. His public actions were determined not so much by mysterious motives as by frustrated personal ambitions and an understandable and outspoken desire to keep his party in power and make it a vehicle for industrialists like himself. Though called a Radical in politics, he was by no means an economic radical, and he did his part in bringing about the Age of Big Business that followed his death. When all is said and done, however, enigmas still remain, as they must in the life of any man, which no biographer has the magic to resolve.

The book is based on a careful reinterpretation of source material already familiar to historians and on a thorough exploration of other material hitherto unused and much of it hitherto unknown. Among the sources previously unworked by writers on Old Thad may be mentioned the numerous and highly interesting Stevens letters in the Simon Cameron Papers, those in the Edward McPherson Papers, and many of those in the Stevens Papers themselves, all in the Library of Congress. There are also numbers of hitherto unused Stevens manuscripts in collections in the library of Dartmouth College, the library of the Historical Society of Pennsylvania, and the Pennsylvania State Library, and in private hands. Not only the metropolitan newspapers but also, for the first time, the journals of Lancaster itself have been finely combed. On Stevens as an ironmaster the data left by the manager of his ironworks and made available to the author have been pertinent and revealing. The abundant anecdotal mythology that has clustered about the name of Stevens has been used cautiously and sparingly.

The author acknowledges his debt to Professor William B. Hesseltine, of the University of Wisconsin, who first showed him the need for a new Stevens biography and whose teachings conditioned the point of view from which it was written; to Mr. T. Fred. Woodley, of Bangor, Pennsylvania, who kindly allowed him to use materials in private possession; to Miss Mira L. Dock, of

Fayetteville, Pennsylvania, who helped him with the ripe wisdom of her more than four score years; to Professor Robert Fortenbaugh, of Gettysburg College, who put him on the track of information he otherwise would never have found; to Mr. F. A. Gorham, of the *Lancaster Intelligencer-Journal*, who graciously opened the files of that newspaper to him; to Mr. M. Luther Heisey, of the Lancaster County Historical Society, who generously provided cuts for illustrations; to his brother Ira Current, of Binghamton, New York, who prepared the map of the Stevens country; and to his wife, Rose Bonar Current, who gave invaluable assistance as typist and stenographer at various stages of the manuscript's development.

R. N. C.

New Brunswick, New Jersey
October, 1942

Illustrations

Contents

OLD THAD STEVENS

*I can scarce restrain myself from giving vent to a
just Indignation, in severe Complaints: But an Historian must tell things truly as they are, and leave
the descanting on them to others.*—Bishop Bur-
net's History of His Own Time (*London, 1734*).

I. Out of the Rough Paths

ONE day in 1827 two Pennsylvania lawyers strolled, one of them with a limp, down a lane leading away from the town of York. They had been arguing a case in the courthouse and were killing time while the jury was out. Coming to a fence, they climbed to the top rail and sat down together, to talk.

Inevitably their conversation turned to politics. For nearly three years, ever since the election of John Quincy Adams, many Americans had talked of little else. Few had not heard of the "corrupt bargain" between Adams and Henry Clay. Of course Federalists of the old school laughed off the stories of a bargain or refused to believe, at any rate, that it had been corrupt. The followers of Andrew Jackson, on the other hand, shouted that their hero had received more votes than any of his opponents in 1824 and would have been president had not Clay swapped off his own backing to Adams in return for the office of secretary of state. They would put Jackson in the White House yet!

About such matters the two lawyers spoke as they sat upon the rail fence. Both had been known as Federalists, but it was not too late to forget the past, if that seemed the wise thing to do. They were young men, in their thirties; their careers were yet to be made. And so the handsomer of the two, whose name was James Buchanan, turned to his companion and suggested that he join the campaign to vindicate the wrong done Jackson and make him president. The other, he with the clubfoot, wore an habitual pout which seemed to say that, whatever the proposal, he would be against it. How, on this occasion, did Thaddeus Stevens reply?[1] It took him only a moment to decide. Yet, in a truer sense, he had been all his life making up his mind.

[1] This account of the meeting between Stevens and Buchanan is based upon Alexander H. Hood's "Thaddeus Stevens," in Alexander Harris, ed., *A Biographical History of Lancaster County* (Lancaster, 1872), 576–577.

About thirty-five years before, on April 4, 1792, he had been born at Danville, a frontier settlement in northern Vermont. Thither, on the military road through the woods, poor Massachusetts folk like Joshua and Sarah Stevens had wandered, soon after the Revolutionary War opened up the Green Mountain country to those with a strong spirit and a longing for better things. There, perhaps, was to be found the new life, the divine air of freedom, which men throughout the world sought hopefully in those revolutionary days. On the tongues of freedom-loving men were famous names that symbolized the quest, names like that of Thaddeus Kosciusko, the Polish hero who had fought with American colonists against the British foe. And Thaddeus was the name that Joshua and Sarah Stevens chose for the second of their four sons.[2]

As a boy Thad was sickly as well as congenitally lame. This lameness, this differentness, this inescapable cross set him off from others and circumscribed his early life. Boys and girls snickered and mimicked his hobbling gait, and the older folk were sure that the Stevens boy would never amount to much. Certainly he would never be fit to wrest a livelihood from a hardscrabble farm on the hills about the upper Connecticut.

Joshua Stevens could lend no helping hand, nor was he any credit to a son's pride. He had proved to be no such strong soul as the frontier called for. At Danville he farmed a bit and cobbled a while and surveyed at times, but only as a rough-and-tumble fighter did he succeed. He could throw any man in Caledonia County, it was said. He could drink with the best of them, too. As the years passed he wandered off on sprees that lasted longer and longer, and finally forgot to come home at all.

Sarah Stevens was a quite different person. A Baptist, she feared God and kept His commandments. Yet she had her moments of intoxication, too, when words and music from the hymnal would float into her consciousness. "We've no abiding city here," she

---

[2] "Joshua Stephens and Salley [sic], his wife, their children: Joshua Stephens, Jun., Born December 23, 1790; Thaddeus Stephens, Born April 4th, 1792; Abner Morrill Stephens, Born June 4th, 1794; Alanson Stephens, Born March 22, 1797." Records of Births, Deaths, and Marriages, Book 1, p. 261, in the Town Clerk's Office at Danville, Vermont. Note the spelling of the surname.

could sing when the going was hardest. "This may distress the worldly mind, but should not cost the saint a tear who hopes a better rest to find." Sarah Stevens did not, however, evade the duties of this earth. She labored unceasingly and hard to provide schooling for her boys, especially for the second eldest, the crippled one. Book learning he would need, for she planned for him a career as minister of the Gospel and servant of the Lord. "Thaddeus," she would in after years remind him, "you have been taught the Scriptures from a child, which is able to make you wise unto Salvation."[3]

Young Thad adored his mother. Her skirts sheltered him from an inclement world. He followed her about on the daily round of chores, on her visits to the neighbors, everywhere she went. But as he grew older he began to conceive ambitions of his own. Once, at the age of twelve, having gone with his mother to spend a few days with relatives in Boston, he gazed in awe at the stately dwellings on Beacon Hill. How wonderful to live there, to be like those people! Boyishly he then and there resolved to get rich somehow, some day, to get as rich and become as important as the Brahmins of Boston.

At the backwoods school in Vermont, meanwhile, he had taken readily to his lessons. He soon discovered that in the classroom he could best the other boys, even if he were no match for them when it came to driving off the bears and wolves that prowled about the log schoolhouse all winter long. When he had done with the three R's, his mother moved with her brood from Danville to the neighboring town of Peacham, so that he might attend the county academy there. College she also planned for him, with what money she could scrape together and he could earn by teaching during his vacations and they could borrow from relatives or friends. So, late in the autumn of 1811, he bade her good-by and set out down the Connecticut Valley for Hanover, New Hampshire, where stood the white-walled halls of Dartmouth. Once a

[3] Sarah Stevens to Stevens, July 20, [——] and April 27, 1830, in the Thaddeus Stevens Papers, Library of Congress; Hood, "Thaddeus Stevens," in Harris, *Biographical History of Lancaster County,* 568, 572–573; Samuel P. Bates, *Martial Deeds of Pennsylvania* (Philadelphia, 1875), 981; obituary of Stevens in the *New York Tribune,* August 14, 1868.

mission school for Christianizing the wild Indians, Dartmouth was now an academic outpost that served to temper the incipient radicalism of frontiersmen's sons. Here they learned the arts of speech-making and word-jugglery, the beauties of the Greek and Latin tongues, and the propriety of the Federalist point of view in American politics. Here eighteen-year-old Thaddeus Stevens found himself suddenly alone, separated from his mother for the first time in his life.[4]

At Hanover he found it hard to adjust himself to living with young men of his own age. He had few vices; he could not afford them. But neither did he have the virtues that would have made him popular. His roommate despised him. Thad was a "tolerable" student and an "uncommon" debater, in his roommate's opinion, but a poor sport and deeply envious of the scholars who made better marks. Soon his resentment found an outlet in some devilry or other. The college authorities expelled him for what appears to have been a rather serious offense, though he protested to an aunt that all his "affairs" had been "made much worse" than they were. Refusing to go home in shame, he resolved never to see his mother again. But ultimately he relented, turned homeward, attended Burlington College (later the University of Vermont) for a time, and finally was readmitted to Dartmouth.[5]

Once again he suffered the snubs of his classmates at Hanover, when they passed him by in choosing members of Phi Beta Kappa. Of those who were so honored, he remarked acidly: "Those fawning parasites ... must flatter the nobility, or remain in obscurity; ... they must degrade themselves by sycophancy, or others will

[4] Hood, "Thaddeus Stevens," in Harris, *Biographical History of Lancaster County*, 570–572. See also an undated and unsigned memorandum relating to Stevens' collegiate career in the Stevens Papers, vol. 16.

[5] Stevens to Mrs. Smith (his aunt), March 26, [1812?], in the Stevens Papers; Joseph Tracy to the Reverend Dr. Smith, August 19, 1868, manuscript in the library of Dartmouth College. Tracy, who had been a roommate of Stevens at college, refused to furnish a biographical sketch for the *Dartmouth* (a college publication) when he was asked to do so at the time of Stevens' death. "In the first place," Tracy explained in his letter of August 19, 1868, "I have not had time to investigate his history since leaving College; and in the second place, I would not honestly write such a sketch as it would be convenient, at present, to publish in the Dartmouth."

not exalt them." He assuaged his sense of persecution by imagining himself to be a politician in the days of ancient Rome. In his reverie the exclusive fraternity men wore the robes of "patricians"; he remained, as he proudly confessed, only one of the "poor plebeians."[6]

Whatever his role in this dream world, in the world of fact the impecunious son of Sarah Stevens was growing up to be no doctrinaire friend of the common man. Quite the contrary. His commencement oration proved to be, of all things, an elaborate and ingenious argument to justify the "acquisition and unequal distribution of wealth." Civilization itself, the young orator declared, had grown out of the desire of human beings for material gain. Equality? Only in the poverty of barbarism could men hope to be equals. Was the objection heard that the rich were given to "debauchery, intemperance, and idleness"? There was, perhaps, some truth in that. But "if the lofty mansion sometimes becomes the habitation of costly excess, the hovel and the cabin are as frequently poluted by the gratification of baser passions."[7] The rightness of eschewing the "baser passions," the sanctity of seeking after material goods! Young Thad had spoken as a true son of his mother, whose Calvinism he had taken to heart, and as a true son of his alma mater, which stood as a fortress against the "leveling" doctrines of Thomas Jefferson and the like.

After his graduation Thaddeus might have become a preacher, as his mother wished, or a teacher, as in fact he did for a year, at Peacham Academy. But this was a means, not an end. At Peacham he divided his time between Academy Hill and the downtown office of "Judge" John Mattocks, with whom he assiduously "read law." Mattocks was not only the leading lawyer but also the biggest banker of the county and a Federalist influential in the politics of Vermont. Personally he was ruddy-faced, rotund, and jolly, and had a reputation for helping out deserving youths. His

[6] Stevens to Samuel Merrill, January 5, 1814, in *Lancaster County Historical Society Papers*, 10 (1906): 396–401.

[7] A manuscript of Stevens' commencement speech, written in his own hand and indorsed "Conference by Sen[r] Stevens for next commencement—July 9, 1814," is in the library of Dartmouth College.

Federalism was contagious, like his laugh. Young Thad could hardly help making comparisons unfavorable to his own father, who, like a good Jeffersonian Republican, had joined the army in the War of 1812 and, according to rumor, had died in action. Thad remembered him only to forget.[8]

The budding lawyer might have remained at home to practise there and, eventually, to succeed the kindly judge. As his twenty-first birthday came and went, he noted with a trace of wistfulness the "newly licensed copulations . . . more humano" of his contemporaries who, two by two, were marrying and setting up housekeeping in Peacham town. But he seemed reluctant to join them, though he did not lack a certain interest in the fairer sex—if one may so interpret the warning he gave an acquaintance, who had gone out from Peacham to Pennsylvania, to beware of "the invincible charms of those fair Dutch wenches, with their dozen pair of petticoats." A mere joke, an insignificant remark? Perhaps. Or was Thad, as psychologists might say, identifying himself with his friend? And if so, was he giving unconscious expression to a fear or to a wish? He himself had much to attract a woman, so far as appearance went: broad shoulders and a handsome face, an attractively curved and sensuous mouth, fine teeth and a wholesomely clear complexion, and waving chestnut hair above his bright grey eyes. Yet—and this darkened his whole personality—he had a deformed foot!

Whether he felt that at home his past was too much with him, or whether his strong feeling for his mother subtly impelled him to leave, it is impossible to say. At any rate, he was ripe for the first opportunity to get out of Vermont. "If you think I could be sure of employment in Pennsylvania," he wrote in 1814 to his acquaintance, who had already left, "I should like very well to come into those parts." A year or so later he arrived in York, Pennsylvania, to become "preceptor" in the academy there, the position which his friend had resigned.

[8] Hood, "Thaddeus Stevens," in Harris, *Biographical History of Lancaster County*, 570–572; A. M. Hemenway, *The Vermont Historical Gazetteer: A Magazine Embracing a History of Each Town* (5 vols., Burlington, Vermont, 1867–91), 1:367–370.

"I cannot forbear reflecting on the partiality of Fortune," young Thaddeus had written. "Some she compels to crawl in the rough paths of indigent obscurity, while others she leads along the easy road to wealth and eminence." From northern Vermont to southern Pennsylvania was a long stride out of the rough paths, but Stevens had not yet quite reached the easy road. At York he read law for a year while teaching in the academy, as he had done at Peacham. To those in York who took the trouble to notice him at all, he seemed serious-minded and diligent but hard to deal with, now shy, now sharply outspoken, wholly devoid of personal charm. His own defects of personality were to be, perhaps, the largest obstacle in the road that lay ahead. A more tangible obstruction was a ruling of the local bar requiring prospective lawyers to spend at least a year in full-time study of the law. That rule disqualified young Stevens, reading law only in his spare time. And so, one summer day in 1816, he got on his horse, rode across Mason and Dixon's line, and took his bar examination at Bel Air, Maryland, where the requirements were less strict. Indeed, all that was asked of Stevens was that he list the legal authorities he had read, provide each of the examiners with a bottle of wine, and play cards with them (and lose) for most of a night! Having thus passed his examination in Maryland, he was qualified, as a matter of professional courtesy, to practise in Pennsylvania as well. He hung out his shingle in Gettysburg, a likely looking town of a thousand people, about the size of the Peacham he had left a year before.[9]

At first the Yankee newcomer had no luck in Gettysburg. The half dozen lawyers of the place treated him as a poacher upon their hunting ground. Only the scraps were left for him—collection cases so petty that, even had his fee been one hundred per cent, the effort would hardly been worth his while. In despair, he was about to give up and try again somewhere else when a local

[9] Stevens to Samuel Merrill, January 5, 1814, in *Lancaster County Historical Society Papers*, 10 (1906): 396–401; Hood, "Thaddeus Stevens," in Harris, *Biographical History of Lancaster County*, 570–575; Bates, *Martial Deeds of Pennsylvania*, 982; Alexander Harris, *A Review of the Political Conflict in America...Comprising Also a Résumé of the Career of Thaddeus Stevens* (New York, 1876), 15–18.

tragedy changed the course of his fortunes. One fine summer day, in a field near Gettysburg, a crazed farmhand turned on a fellow worker and nearly decapitated him with a scythe. So obvious was the murderer's guilt and so great the shock to the community that cautious lawyers thought twice about accepting his case. But there was one young attorney who had nothing to lose. He took the case, made an ingenious plea of insanity, and lost the verdict but won a considerable fee and considerable fame. Thereafter business came to Stevens faster than he could handle it. In a few years he was known throughout several counties as "a lawyer of much cunning and adroitness, and of considerable celebrity."[10]

As he prospered during the eighteen-twenties Stevens did not hoard his earnings but invested them in the best of existing speculations, real estate. He bought the choicest property in town, the lot and red-brick building on the corner of the square, or "diamond," where not so many months before he had opened his office as an almost penniless stranger who could hardly pay his rent. Farm after farm he bought, timberland by the hundreds of acres, and lands in the neighboring South Mountain, which were honeycombed with iron ore. He staked a partner in the charcoal-iron business at Maria Furnace ("likely to prove a valuable concern for this section of the country," remarked the optimistic *Adams Sentinel* of Gettysburg) while he busied himself with the law. By 1827, less than a dozen years after his arrival, Thaddeus Stevens owned more taxable property than any other man in town.[11]

[10] *Pennsylvania Reporter* (Harrisburg), March 23, 1830. A record of the trial (Commonwealth *v.* Hunter, October term, 1817) may be found in a Minute Book of the Criminal Court which is preserved in the Adams County Courthouse, Gettysburg.

[11] Records of Deeds in the Adams County Courthouse, especially vol. H, p. 461; J, 330; M, 190; N, 126; Q, 13; and U, 331; *Adams Sentinel* (Gettysburg), February 18, 1829; Thomas F. Woodley, *Thaddeus Stevens* (Harrisburg, 1934), 28–29; [Mira L. Dock], "Thaddeus Stevens as an Ironmaster," in the *Philadelphia Times,* July 14, 1895; E. McP. [Edward McPherson], "The Maria Furnace Property," in the *Gettysburg Star and Sentinel,* January 13, 1891. I am indebted to Professor Robert Fortenbaugh of Gettysburg College for calling to my attention the articles by McPherson and Miss Dock, which are indispensable for an account of Stevens' experiences in the iron business.

Maria Furnace operated about twelve years, from 1826 to 1838. Originally

In his haste to attain this local "wealth and eminence," he had, as one might expect, shown a more than becoming avidity, a certain propensity to overreach. He had not hesitated to take advantage of his position as a lawyer to further his quest for real estate. Much of it he had got at sheriff's sales—as he did the library and farm of one James Dobbin in 1822. Before this sale, prospective buyers had come to young Stevens for professional advice. One of them was prepared to bid as high as two thousand dollars for the property, until Stevens explained that, what with the liens and all, it would hardly be worth buying. Then, having discouraged rival bidders from attending the auction, he himself stepped in and got Dobbin's books and farm for a mere six hundred and fifty dollars!

Later old man Dobbin sued Stevens, argued his own case (against Stevens, attorney for the defendant), and won from sympathetic local jurors a ruling that he had been made the victim of a "legal fraud." Appealing the case, Stevens was sustained by a higher court, but he could not silence Dobbin and Dobbin's friends. He offered to sell back the property at the price he had paid. He managed to have Dobbin placed in an almshouse, the dotard being under the delusion that he was to remain there as attorney for the Directors of the Poor. But, for all his efforts, Stevens could not shut the old man up. Years later he was still being called upon to explain, to those who had heard the story, that Dobbin was "a half lunatic lawyer" domiciled in the county poorhouse without suspecting that he was a pauper; "he fancies a thousand things which have no existence."[12]

there were four proprietors—Thaddeus Stevens, James D. Paxton, Thomas C. Miller, and John B. McPherson—but two of them, Miller and McPherson, decided after a couple of years that the business was hopeless and sold out to Stevens, who thus became owner of a three-fourths interest. Later Stevens and Paxton equalized their shares. From the beginning, and so long as this partnership lasted, the partners operated under the firm name of "James D. Paxton & Co." The furnace was named "Maria" after Paxton's wife. See the article by Edward McPherson (son of John B. McPherson) in the *Gettysburg Star and Sentinel*, January 13, 1891.

[12] Stevens to J. Wallace, April 22, 1837, manuscript in the Pennsylvania State Library, Harrisburg; Dobbins [*sic*] v. Stevens, in Thomas Sergeant and William Rawle, Jr., reporters, *Reports of Cases Adjudged in the Supreme Court of Pennsylvania, 1814–1828* (17 vols., Philadelphia, 1818–29), 17:13–15;

Whatever the merits of his course in the Dobbin affair, Stevens was long afterward to feel twinges of conscience over a similar matter. In this instance, in a kind of deathbed repentance, he rectified the wrong. "I bought John Schurtz's property at Sheriff's Sale much below its value," he wrote in 1867, in a codicil to his will. "I only want my own—."[13]

Other quirks of personality made Gettysburg's wealthy bachelor the kind of person who was sure to be gossiped about. Homeless, without a family, boarding at a hotel, he traveled much in solitary ways. Often he would ride off into the mountains at the west of town and gallop over rocks and through thickets (for he had long since cast off the sickliness of his boyhood), to the mystification of mountaineers who caught a glimpse of the strange lone horseman. Or he would lose himself in reading—he owned a large library, from which he lent so freely that now and then he had to advertise for the return of borrowed books. Or, inveterate gambler that he was, he would pass his idle hours at cards with a small circle of cronies. Gossip had it that he enjoyed other, less innocuous, diversions. One story connected the name of the crippled bachelor with the death of a colored girl whose body, *enceinte,* had been found in a roadside ditch.

Yet for all his peculiarities and for all the stories that gathered around his head, Thaddeus Stevens became the friend of respectability in Gettysburg. As lumbering stages and creaking wagons wakened the sleepy village of 1816 into the busy growing town of 1827—it was well located at the point where the turnpikes from Philadelphia and Baltimore joined on their way to Pittsburgh—it was possible for individuals to rise from the ranks, as Stevens rose. True, discernible class lines remained; at the bottom of the social structure even in 1827 was a handful of black slaves, not yet freed under the gradual-emancipation act. But the associations of Stevens were not with the lowly. His closest intimate was John

Dobbin v. Stevens, in a Minute Book containing records of the Circuit Court, especially under the dates April 1, 1833, and April 17, 1834, in the Adams County Courthouse; William M. Hall, *Reminiscences and Sketches, Historical and Biographical* (Harrisburg, 1890), 26–27.

[13] The will, including the codicil, was published after Stevens' death in the *New York Tribune,* August 19, 1868.

B. McPherson, the local banker, and he himself served as counsel for the bank and member of its board of directors.[14] He was an ironmaster, a landlord of thousands of acres, a leader of the professional class, which included preachers, whose business it was to justify the ways of God, and lawyers, to justify the ways of man. His associations were, naturally, with the well-to-do and propertied men, and it was their ways he had most frequent occasion to justify.

And so, when legal affairs brought him back to York in 1827, and a fellow lawyer asked him to come to the support of Andrew Jackson, Stevens did not hesitate to reply. He could confess an interest in politics. In a small way he was himself a politician, for he had several times been a member of the town council of Gettysburg, and from a distance he had watched the goings and comings of politicians in the national scene. Unstayed by ties of home and family, he would, inevitably, desire a larger role of his own in politics. But not as a follower of Andrew Jackson. Jackson embodied the antithesis of Stevens' social point of view. Jacksonians in Pennsylvania were frontiersmen, small farmers, roughhanded artisans of the cities; in short, largely the rabble, the ragtag and bobtail of society. To Stevens they must have represented a degradation of the Jeffersonian dogma, which to him would have seemed none too good at best. As between the Jeffersonian opinion that the tree of liberty should be regularly watered by the blood of its devotees and the Hamiltonian view that the people, sir, is a great beast—he now had an opportunity to indicate his choice. He told Buchanan he could not join the Jacksonian party.

[14] Hood, "Thaddeus Stevens," in Harris, *Biographical History of Lancaster County,* 576 ff. The following advertisement appeared in the *Adams Sentinel* (Gettysburg), March 11, 1829: *"BORROWED BOOKS!* Those persons who have in their possession, any *BOOKS,* known to be the property of the Subscriber, are requested to return them; and, if any have borrowed Books, the owner of which is unknown (as many have gone abroad without his name) he will, if possible, establish his claims to ownership. *T. STEVENS."*

II. The Archpriest of Antimasonry

ANDREW JACKSON, victor of New Orleans, won an even greater victory at the polls in 1828. In proportion as his horny-handed followers were joyous, his conservative opponents, men like Thaddeus Stevens, were gloomy. This was no ordinary political event such as had occurred once every four years, willy-nilly, in earlier, politer days. It was the beginning of a revolution, no less.

The enemies of Jackson and of revolution had no early prospect of checking him and the headlong rush of events. His fame was a magnet which attracted many diverse elements of the population without polarizing the others into a unified opposition. True, even after 1828, there were Federalist organizations which remained intact in many localities. Federalism, however, promised little as a philosophy by which the foes of Jackson might win votes. And so far as the political debut of Stevens was concerned, it was particularly futile to pin any hope to the party in Adams County, Pennsylvania, governed as it was by old-line Federalists whom he could not hope to oust. What new and compelling issue could he and other opponents of Jackson find that would offset the magnetism of the hero's name?

A possible answer to this question came opportunely out of western New York. In 1826 a citizen of Batavia, named William Morgan, had been about to publish a book purporting to expose the secrets of Freemasonry, when he mysteriously disappeared. To democratic Americans the secret and exclusive Masonic order had long been suspect; and now the friends of Morgan, convinced that vengeful Masons had done away with him, started rumors which spread until thousands in New York state were honoring him as a martyr to the cause of human rights. Aiding to revive old suspicions, thwarted politicians were not slow to capitalize upon the new unpopularity of the lodge. Soon the crowds at torchlit rallies were singing, to the tune of *Auld Lang Syne:*

> *Should Morgan's murder be forgot,*
> *Or Masons' grip and sign;*
> *Should Morgan's murder be forgot,*
> *Or Masons' dark design?*
>
> *The Masons' dark design we know,*
> *The Masons' bloody grip and sign;*
> *We'll lend a hand to crush to earth*
> *The Masons' bloody shrine.*[1]

In Pennsylvania, Stevens took a lesson from the excitement to the north. The people of his own commonwealth were divided among sects numerous and diverse: Moravians, Mennonites, Dunkers, Quakers, and Scotch-Irish Presbyterians; but they had one thing in common, their hatred of secrecy, oaths, ceremonials, and anything that smacked of high church. To all of them a crusade against Freemasonry would have a sure appeal. And Stevens found the idea not only convenient in politics but also congenial to his soul. Freemasons were later to allege that they had blackballed him from their society and that he had turned against them in revenge. Had they known it, they might have pointed out that the Phi Beta Kappa fraternity (then a true "secret society") had rejected him at Dartmouth and he had resented it from the bottom of his heart. They could have gone on to show that the Masonic Lodge was now the object of the hatred he had once bestowed upon the college fraternity. Whatever the inner workings of his mind, he soon espoused the creed that "Free-Masonry is inconsistent with pure morals, true religion, and the permanent existence of Liberty; and that the only means by which it can be suppressed, is by opposing it *politically.*"[2]

[1] From *Infidelity Unmasked,* 1:31 (June 19, 1831), an Antimasonry and anti-slavery magazine published at Cincinnati.

[2] From a speech delivered by Stevens at Hagerstown, Maryland, in 1831 and published in *Free-Masonry Unmasked; or, Minutes of the Trial of a Suit of*

Some six months after Jackson, a Freemason, had been inaugurated as president, Stevens gathered a number of towns-
people "opposed to secret societies" into the courthouse at Gettysburg. He had advertised the meeting as a purely nonpolitical and
nonpartisan affair, but the town's leading Federalists, taking
alarm, asserted that his real object was "the demolition of old
party landmarks." He justified their fears by proceeding with the
work of razing their ancient edifice. Within a few years they had
to stand aside and see him honored, even by his Jacksonian
enemies, as "the great luminary of Antimasonry in Adams County,
within whose orbit all the lesser planets of the new system revolve
and reflect the light he dispenses."[3]

Such was the political "eminence" which by 1830 he had won
in addition to his standing as one of the richest men in Gettysburg.
To measure the progress he had made since leaving Vermont, he
could have taken the positions of his three brothers as bench
marks. None of them had gone far. Alanson, who had been a
wayward youth, was still in Vermont, living the life of "poverty
and obscurity." Also in Vermont, at Peacham, was Morrill, who
vicariously enjoyed the more exciting life of Thaddeus. "Be
pleased to write us a long letter and lett us know all the politicks,"
Morrill would request, though he could not offer much news in
return: "I have the same old coat and hat, begin work the same
time of day, and let my moderation be known to all men, except
when upon Antimasonry, then I go the whole hog." Brother
Joshua, the eldest, had got as far as Indianapolis and had "means
of living tolerably comfortably" there, with his "little office of
Associate Judge," but he confessed to Thaddeus an unhappy

*Common Pleas of Adams County, Wherein Thaddeus Stevens, Esq., was
Plaintiff, and Jacob Lefever, Defendant,* published by R. W. Middleton (Gettysburg, 1835), iv–xiii. For the background of Antimasonry in Pennsylvania,
see Charles McCarthy, *The Antimasonic Party: A Study of Political Antimasonry in the United States, 1827–1840* (*Annual Report of the American
Historical Association,* 1902, vol. 2, Washington, 1903), 427–432. On Stevens'
alleged personal motives for joining the Antimasonic party, see Alexander
Harris, *A Review of the Political Conflict in America ... Comprising Also a
Résumé of the Career of Thaddeus Stevens* (New York, 1876), 35.

[3] *Adams Sentinel* (Gettysburg), September 2, 1829; *Pennsylvania Reporter*
(Harrisburg), March 23, 1830.

plight. The "poisonous effluvia" of Indiana had made him ill. "Besides being sick," he complained, "I was so unfortunate as to make a bad bargin by which I lost about four hundred & fifty which was a considerable of a Loss to me." It would not have been "a considerable of a Loss" to Thad.

As in his brothers' letters, so in his mother's there was an eager interest in Thaddeus' political affairs, but also a note of concern for the health of both his body and his soul. Recently he had suffered an attack of "brain fever," which had left him utterly bald, and thereafter he usually wore a reddish brown wig, a poor imitation of the natural chestnut hair he had lost. To her convalescent son Sarah Stevens explained wistfully: "I feel that I should be exceeding glad to make a visit to you and Joshua to see where you live, but I desire to submit to Him that governs all events." Though he was lost to the ministry, she persisted in seeing Thaddeus as a man carrying on the work of God. "My son," she wrote, with more earnestness than orthographical accuracy, "we hear that you are ingaged in the anti misonick cause, I think it a good cause, but a dangerous won, because it creates enemyes. The Loard has, I trust begun to cause Satin kingdom to fall to the ground."[4]

Of the truth of his mother's words, that Antimasonry would make "enemyes," Stevens soon had ample proof. In the summer of 1831 he spoke to a rally of Antimasons in Hagerstown, Maryland, where he repeated and embellished the popular charges against members of the lodge, including the accusation that their ritual amounted to a kind of black mass in which they drank libations from a human skull. The Jacksonian newspaper of Gettysburg, the *Compiler*, reported the event with a communication from one of his hearers in Maryland:

The meeting was addressed by a Mr. Stevens, from your State; a stout man, about 40 years of age, with a bald head, and lame. . . . Of his speech it is enough to say, that it was a compound of the vilest slanders, barefaced falsehood, and pandemoniac malignity, that ever fell from the lips of any man . . . . He and those of his Yankee kindred who sent him here,

[4] Letters to Stevens from Joshua Stevens, October 16, 1829, Sarah Stevens, April 27, 1830, and Morrill Stevens, May 11, 1830, in the Thaddeus Stevens Papers, Library of Congress.

must have presumed largely upon the ignorance and stupidity of the
Marylanders.... We are not so easily duped.... If they talk to us of
crimes and murder, we must *know* that they have no blood in their
skirts.... Those must not come, in whose wake is heard the wail of the
widow and the orphan, or rioting in the spoils of the unfortunate.

The writer could make himself understood in Gettysburg with
words that in themselves were vague—"by inuendoes, and in-
tangibile insinuations," as Stevens complained—for the accusations
of murder and despoliation were meaningful enough to readers
familiar with the stories of a seduced Negro wench and of one
James Dobbin. Stevens replied by suing the editor of the *Compiler*
for libel. He succeeded in having the editor jailed, but the latter's
friends boasted that the governor—George Wolf, a Freemason
and a Jacksonian Democrat—would free the prisoner within a
week. Stevens soon had another crime of Freemasonry to add to
a list already long. Against his libeler he continued to press civil
proceedings, and by turning the case into an investigation of
political favoritism among Freemasons he gained a good deal of
publicity far beyond the borders of Pennsylvania.[5]

Thus Stevens had become a person whom other leaders of the
Antimasonic party in the nation could not ignore when they
gathered at Baltimore in September, 1831, to make nominations
for their first presidential campaign. This proved to be a historic
event, the forerunner of all national nominating conventions. To
Stevens, however, the occasion brought nothing but disappointment. An aspiring president-maker, he had selected Judge John
McLean of the Supreme Court as a likely candidate and had
found the judge willing to "condescend." But when the roll was
called at Baltimore, Stevens learned to his chagrin that McLean
had reconsidered and now declined to run. He nevertheless insisted upon McLean and had a considerable following; for a
time it appeared that the convention would "explode." During
most of one night William H. Seward, who was sharing a hotel
room with Stevens in Baltimore, pleaded with him to yield.

[5] Stevens to George Wolf, August 24, 27, 1831, manuscripts in the Pennsylvania State Library, Harrisburg; Stevens to J. S. Shriver, July 14, 1832,
manuscript in the possession of Mr. T. Fred. Woodley, Bangor, Pennsylvania;
Free-Masonry Unmasked, xiii–xiv.

Finally he came to the support of the convention favorite, William Wirt.[6]

In the campaign of 1832 Stevens worked loyally for Wirt. Against the opposition of two such formidable figures as Henry Clay (the "National" Republican) and Andrew Jackson (the "Democratic" Republican), however, the Antimasons could win for their candidate only the seven electoral votes of Vermont. After this rebuff Antimasonry rapidly ceased to be a significant political force in most of the states, but in Pennsylvania, thanks to Stevens, it remained alive. Out of the unsuccessful campaign he had gained experience and a wider reputation; out of his practice of the law, also, he had acquired an education in dealing with human volitions in conflict. And so, when he himself became a candidate and in 1833 was elected to the Pennsylvania House of Representatives (to be re-elected six times within a decade), he was a politician already well prepared for whatever tasks might come.

Pennsylvania's capital, Harrisburg, was only a small town, but during the winter months the hurly-burly of politicians stirred up an atmosphere which rendered it important "even in the eyes of the nation."[7] A traveler approaching from Gettysburg, before he entered upon the long-roofed bridge spanning the Susquehanna, could see the capitol facing him upon high ground, the central domed hall flanked by two separate and as yet unconnected wings. Across the river and up wide State Street came the new representative from Gettysburg, to take his place in the "eyes of the nation" and to meet the Democrats, including state senator James Buchanan and Governor George Wolf, on more nearly equal terms.

Soon business men, bankers, and Jackson-haters in general recognized an able minority leader in the bewigged gentleman from Adams County, who would sit in the Hall of Representatives with his deformed foot propped up, defiantly, on the edge

[6] Frederick W. Seward, ed., *William H. Seward: An Autobiography from 1801 to 1834 with a Memoir of His Life and Selections from His Letters* (New York, 1891), 89–91; *Niles' Register*, 61:83–85 (October 1, 1831).

[7] *Poulson's Daily American Advertiser* (Philadelphia), December 4, 1834.

of his desk. When he rose to speak, the galleries were packed; crowds of visitors eagerly awaited the sarcasms of the new-found orator, who had a way of "combining the most cutting satire with the sweetest words in the world," as one newspaperman put it. For Governor Wolf and President Jackson no epithets in all the vocabulary of damnation were too extravagant. The whole tribe of Democrats, Stevens declaimed, were the "veriest vampires," sucking the blood of the people and bankrupting the government; they were "hyenas and jackalls"; like Polyphemus, they gorged themselves upon the corpses of their victims. Ignoring the restraints of parliamentary etiquette, he indulged in "ungentlemanly language" which time and again provoked hot-tempered Democrats to challenge him, though he refused to take part in any except verbal duels. Not all his opponents took his rodomontade so seriously, yet in the minds of many his clubfoot assumed the sinister significance of a cloven hoof.[8]

In his oratorical outbursts Stevens frequently gave mock homage to King Andrew—"him who (by the grace of God) sits on the American throne." In this same spirit the anti-Jacksonians everywhere were shedding the name "National Republican" and beginning to call themselves, more expressively, "Whigs." Their national leader was Senator Henry Clay of Kentucky, "Harry of the West" to the thousands who worshipped him. Their program was his "American System"—protective tariffs, a national bank, and roads and waterways built at federal expense. On these issues Stevens stood with the Whigs, but he was not of them. Jealous perhaps, he despised Clay, asserting as his reason that Clay was insincere. Clay had compromised on the tariff issue in 1833 after South Carolina had "nullified" the law and threatened to secede. In doing so, said Stevens, Clay had "changed his position with his interests, abandoned the American System, laid violent hands on his own child."[9] What was worse, Clay was no true friend of the people; like Jackson, he was a Mason! In the Pennsylvania House Stevens maintained a loose alliance with the Whigs but kept the factional distinction clear.

[8] *Ibid.*, March 6, December 13, 1834; February 27, April 15, 1835.
[9] *Pennsylvania Reporter* (Harrisburg), March 13, 1834.

The evils of Freemasonry he allowed no one to forget. He read petition after petition, urged resolution after resolution, and brought in bill after bill proclaiming that the lodge must be destroyed. He would chill the blood of his listeners "as he moved aside the veil that covered the dry bones" beneath the secrecy of Masonic meetings; then, with a sudden ironic turn, he would titillate them to laughter in spite of themselves. The House, with a sense of humor of its own, granted him a committee to investigate the "evils of Masonry" but at the same time authorized a parallel inquiry into the "political motives and evils of Anti-Masonry." Stevens wished particularly to bring Governor Wolf before his committee and make him reveal how many convicted felons he had pardoned who were "brethren of the mystic tie." Failing in this, he later undertook an even more ambitious "inquisition" of the lodge. Of some hundred prominent Pennsylvanians whom he summoned, more than half appeared, but none would allow himself to be sworn as a witness, despite the chairman's "cold grey eyes and severe look." One of those called, a Reverend W. T. Sproul, was outspoken. "I do not feel at liberty," he said, "to answer any interrogatory where the supposed intention of the interrogator is rather to gratify personal antipathies than to obtain information." "Silence!" interrupted Stevens, slamming his hand down upon the chairman's table. Sproul tried to resume. "Not a word!" Stevens insisted. "You have insulted the Legislature already." He then brought the non-juring Masons before the House to answer for contempt, and again they refused either to swear or to affirm. Finally, tiring of the farce, the House ceased to support him, and his investigation came to an inglorious end.[10]

Not all Stevens' activities were so grotesque and obviously partisan as these attacks upon Freemasonry and Jacksonism. He was to gain his greatest fame, in fact, as a champion of public education. Although some provision had been made for "educating the poor gratis," Pennsylvania was in 1833 without a general

[10] *Pennsylvania House Journal*, 1833–34, 1:454, 647; 2:734–737, 861–874; 1834–35, 1:45–46, 435–436, 513–514, 557–559, 829–830; *Niles' Register*, 49:381–382 (January 30, 1836).

system of public schools. Already, however, workingmen who dreamed that book learning might elevate their children to a higher status, were demanding reform. Many of the better born, foreseeing a threat to property in the rude, unlettered condition of the masses, added their support. The opposition came from taxpayers with less foresight, especially the childless, and from German Lutherans and other sectarians who, already tithed for the maintenance of parochial schools, objected to being taxed for public education besides. The issue could not be drawn along strictly partisan lines. Whigs, Antimasons, and Democrats alike were divided on the question; both Stevens and Governor Wolf were well known as foes of "ignorance." These two men, an outstanding Mason and the leading Antimason, became strange bedfellows, in 1834, in the movement for public schools. Wolf and not Stevens was godfather of the bill introduced in that year, but it was due in no small measure to Stevens' exertions that the bill passed with only a single vote against it.[11]

Did not Stevens fear that his support of the school bill might alienate his German constituents? If he did, he effectively hedged himself by aiding one of their parochial institutions at about the same time. In Gettysburg the Lutherans had founded Pennsylvania College (to be known a century later as Gettysburg College) and with Stevens' help had secured a charter from the state. They then besought the legislature for financial aid. Here they ran against prejudices of the same kind as had bred the Antimasonic excitement; many of the non-Germans professed to fear that sectarian colleges fostered a "clannish spirit." As spokesman for this point of view, an Antimason from Adams County led the opposition to the endowment bill which Stevens introduced in the House. To the pleas for "economy" Stevens replied that "if a bill had been brought into this house to improve the breed of hogs," it would have met with no opposition, but "when a measure was brought forward to improve the breed of men," the scales were produced and "the dollars first laid in!" When the Anti-

[11] Samuel P. Bates, *Martial Deeds of Pennsylvania* (Philadelphia, 1875), 33–34; *Pennsylvania House Journal*, 1833–34, 1:433. Stevens had previously agitated for publicly supported schools in Gettysburg. See Thomas F. Woodley, *Great Leveler: The Life of Thaddeus Stevens* (New York, 1937), 105.

masons of his county threatened to repudiate him, he replied in
an open letter that if necessary he would withdraw to some place
"where the advocates of Antimasonry may be advocates of Knowledge." In actual fact there was little danger that he would lose
more friends at home than he would gain by the bill. After its
passage he could add to his political assets the solid good will of
people of German descent. They thanked him appropriately at
the ensuing "public exercises" of Pennsylvania College and
elected him to the board of trustees, a position he was to keep for
the rest of his life.[12]

Not for this, however, nor for his aid in the passage of the
school law, but as the "savior" of Pennsylvania's system of public
education, was Stevens to be most highly acclaimed. Beset by a
storm of public opinion, the new Senate in 1835 quickly passed
a bill repealing the public school law of 1834. When the bill appeared in the House on April 11, 1835, for its third reading and
final vote, all signs indicated that it would pass that evening—all
signs save possibly one, the fact that Stevens was to speak in its
defense. His speech proved to be a masterpiece: the effect on his
audience was ample testimony of the power of his spoken words.
At once the House amended the repealer into a supplemental bill
strengthening the existing law and, suspending the rules, passed
the amended bill that night. No one questioned that Stevens'
eloquence was responsible for this about-face. It was his speech
that had "stayed the coward-hand of clamor's tools from per-
petrating so foul a blot" as repeal of the school law. So wrote a
newspaper reporter while still under the spell the orator had
cast.[13]

[12] *American Advertiser* (Philadelphia), January 10, 24, 1834; *Pennsylvania
Telegraph* (Harrisburg), January 25, 1834; *Pennsylvania Reporter* (Harrisburg), May 30, 1834.
[13] *Pennsylvania House Journal*, 1834–35, 1:897–899; *American Advertiser*
(Philadelphia), April 13, 1835. Since there were no stenographers in the Pennsylvania legislature in 1835, no record was kept of Stevens' exact words. A
short time after its delivery, however, the speech was reconstructed from
memory and widely published in the newspapers. Hood, "Thaddeus Stevens,"
in Harris, *Biographical History of Lancaster County*, 578. Later the speech
was several times reprinted in pamphlet form. An interesting edition is that
published at Lancaster in 1865, a copy of which is in the Stevens Papers,
vol. 1.

If this effort was evidence of the idealism of Stevens, it was also an admirable stratagem of politics. For 1835 was an election year in Pennsylvania, and upon the issue of public schools the Democratic party of the state was splitting into two parts. One group loyally demanded the re-election of Governor Wolf but privately urged him to yield to the clamor against public education in order to preserve harmony within the party. Another faction nominated a Lutheran minister and teacher named Muhlenberg to run for governor on a platform of opposition to public schools. By siding with Wolf and forcing the issue, Stevens might wedge these factions irremediably apart. Thus, perhaps, he could enable his own minority party of Antimasons to elect a governor of the state!

During the campaign in the fall of 1835 Whigs who were Freemasons forgot the abuse they had received from Stevens—whom they now proclaimed "a man who has burst the fetters of obscurity and poverty, and has risen superior to both"—and agreed to support Joseph Ritner, who twice before had been the Antimasonic candidate for governor. Going on the stump for Ritner, Stevens turned the school question to good account. "Knowledge," he declared, "is the only foundation on which republics can stand. Let those who would govern through ignorance—who would make the poor man's children vassals and servants to do homage to the rich—join the sooty ranks of that Cimmerian tribe whose chieftain's black banner bears the dark inscription, '*Muhlenberg and no free schools.*' " Having thus disposed of one of the Democratic candidates, Stevens dismissed the other, Wolf, as a Freemason and hence of course a conspirator against the people's liberties.[14]

When the Whigs and Antimasons won the election and Joseph Ritner was inaugurated as governor, Stevens was prepared to become the mayor of the Pennsylvania palace. He, more than Ritner, enjoyed a reputation as the "great Antimasonic leader" in the state and might therefore expect to handle "Joseph the Farmer," who was supposedly a simple-hearted man. After six years devoted to the career of people's friend, Stevens had at last reached a springboard from which to jump into the waters of national

---

[14] *American Advertiser* (Philadelphia), May 8, July 27, 1835; *Pennsylvania Reporter* (Harrisburg), October 2, 1835.

GETTYSBURG'S EMINENT BACHELOR

At the age of thirty-eight. Engraved by John Sartain from a portrait
painted by Jacob Eichholtz. This halftone reproduction by courtesy
of the Lancaster County Historical Society.

politics and, mayhap, make a resounding splash. Indeed, some
of the Pennsylvania Antimasons began to mention him as their
candidate for vice president, or even president, in the approaching national campaign of 1836. To heighten his eligibility for
the nomination, he coveted the privilege of refusing a position
in Ritner's cabinet. But the governor-elect, revealing an unexpected independence, used the patronage to strengthen his own
hand. He passed Stevens by and threw his support to William
Henry Harrison, the aging hero of the Battle of Tippecanoe, for
president, and Francis Granger of New York for vice president.
When Pennsylvania Antimasons, following Ritner's lead, nominated these two at Harrisburg in December, 1835, the man from
Adams County stomped out of the convention hall and began
to demand a new ticket composed of Daniel Webster and, presumably, himself. He hoped to undo the work of the Harrisburg
gathering at the subsequent national convention, but the Pennsylvania Whigs ratified the nominations of the Pennsylvania Antimasons—as much "to put down Thaddeus S." as "to put up
General Harrison"—and the Whig and Antimasonic parties of the
nation were later to follow suit.[15]

Stevens was henceforth at outs with Governor Ritner, but he
remained a leader of the state House of Representatives. Early
in 1836 he joined with the Whigs and the Ritner faction of Antimasons to carry out a project that was too important to be
thwarted by factional politics, namely, to induce the Commonwealth of Pennsylvania to recharter the Bank of the United States,
which Democrats had long decried as "that whore of Babylon"
and against which President Jackson had declared a war unto

[15] *American Advertiser* (Philadelphia), December 7, 29, 1835; *Harrisburg
Chronicle*, December 21, 1835. To one of the adherents of Webster, Stevens
wrote, before the meeting of the Harrisburg convention: "I . . . agree with you
that Harrison is not the man to be elected if *we* had the appointment, instead
of the people." As for Webster, however, Stevens then professed to believe
"he would not take Pennsylvania from Van Buren." Stevens concluded: "And
if Antimasons are to nominate a man with whom they cannot succeed, they
will nominate a distinctive Antimason so as to keep their party inflexibly
together." Stevens to J. B. Wallace, October 24, 1835, manuscript in the Pennsylvania State Library, Harrisburg. The implication here was that the Antimasonic party should choose between Harrison and Stevens. Evidently, however, Stevens later changed his mind.

the death. The federal charter of the Bank was about to expire, and its stockholders had reason to fear that they were doomed unless they could continue under an act of incorporation from one of the states. The president of the Bank, Nicholas Biddle, himself a Philadelphian, preferred to give the privilege to his own commonwealth. He had given the Whigs and Antimasons his powerful assistance in the campaign of 1835. It was no mere coincidence that, upon the news of Ritner's election, the price of Bank stock had risen several points.

In collaboration with agents of Biddle the leader of the House secretly prepared an act of incorporation which was designed to overcome the "party prejudices and antipathies" of Bank-hating Democrats, who counted a majority in the state Senate. In return for a thirty-year charter the Bank was to pay a bonus of two and a half million dollars into the treasury of the state. Part of this sum was to be allocated to the support of the public school system and thus make possible the repeal of certain taxes, and the rest was to be spent on public works in places where, politically, it would do the most good. As a gesture to those who feared the "money power," Stevens suggested a provision that if the Bank should "interfere with politics," its charter might be repealed. Innocuous though it was, Biddle warned that such a stipulation would cause the charter to be "instantly rejected by the Stockholders"; and so, as a go-between reported to the banker, Stevens "agreed without difficulty to waive the section respecting political interferences, etc."[16]

Disguising the Bank bill with the subtly worded title, "an act to repeal the state tax on real and personal property, and to continue and extend the improvements of the state by rail roads and canals, and for other purposes," Stevens introduced it in the legislature behind the smoke screen of his final "inquisition" of the Masonic Lodge. The House passed it promptly, and immediately rumors of bribery circulated among disgruntled Democrats. In mockery of Stevens' investigation of Freemasonry, one of them

[16] Washington *Globe*, February 3, 1836; Biddle to W. B. Reed, January 15, 1836; J. B. Wallace to Biddle, January 18, 1836, in R. C. McCrane, ed., *Correspondence of Nicholas Biddle Dealing with National Affairs, 1768–1844* (Boston and New York, 1919), 261–262.

suggested a committee "to enquire into the evils of gambling, with power . . . to have before them one *Stevens, a notorious gambler.*" Instead, the gambler himself led a committee packed with members friendly to the Bank who inquired into the stories of bribery. One witness told how he had "put himself among the friends of the bank" for the purpose of discovering bribes but had only found that "if there was anything of the kind, it was so far removed from the bank that there could be no handle made of it," and he "could get nothing more than a bottle of wine and seventeen segars." If they found it hard to prove that anyone had been privately bought, the witnesses clearly demonstrated that Stevens had "offered to bribe" some of the members "publicly in the House." By the same logrolling methods, from outside the Senate, he engineered the Bank bill through the upper chamber.[17]

The chartering of the Bank had an immediate effect not only upon Pennsylvania finances but also upon the "internal improvement" of the state. In the eighteen-thirties the commonwealth was going into the transportation business on a magnificent scale. At public expense it was building a "Pennsylvania System" of turnpikes, railroads, and waterways which was to connect Philadelphia with the interior and enable the metropolis better to compete with Baltimore and New York for the trade of the West. This grand design suffered, however, from the pulling and hauling of local interests which tended to stretch it out of shape. Men with great expectations—men like Stevens, with his ironworks isolated in South Mountain, and his friend McPherson, with investments in real estate in and around Gettysburg—insisted upon the construction of their own pet lines of highway or railroad or canal. These schemes might be irrelevant to the broad plan of the public works but, politically, they were often quite to the point. It was for such enterprises that a large part of the bonus provided by the Bank was to be spent. Stevens' share was two hundred thousand dollars.

This sum was to be used to begin work on a project he had

[17] *Niles' Register,* 49:379 (January 30, 1836); *National Intelligencer* (triweekly edition, Washington), January 23, 1836; *Lancaster Journal,* quoted in the Washington *Globe,* January 22, 1836; *Pennsylvania House Journal,* 1835–36, 1:279; 2:657, 666.

long had in mind. As early as 1831 he had agitated in public meetings for a railroad running south from Gettysburg and connecting
with the proposed Baltimore and Ohio line.[18] A few years later
he and McPherson organized a company to build a road; but the
route they then laid out, instead of following the level valley
of the Monocacy, detoured through the rugged mountains at the
west in such a way as to pass near Maria Furnace. Their surveyor
reported that rail construction over this route would be too costly
to be practicable. Finding that private pocketbooks would not
take the risk, the enterprisers bethought them of the public
purse. As a reward for his interest in the Bank bill, the commonwealth undertook to make a so-called "Gettysburg Extension"
of the Pennsylvania System for Stevens.

This "extension," however, would have no rail connection with
the statewide network unless another line should be built from
Gettysburg eastward or northward. Stevens had already tried to
induce the legislature to make an appropriation for such a connecting link. Failing in that, he had sought a charter for a private
company (every incorporation at that time required a separate
legislative act) and had arranged a swap with several "gentlemen
from Pittsburgh" who agreed to invest in the stock of his company
in return for his offices in persuading the legislature to incorporate
their bank. When the would-be bankers changed their minds, he
had turned to the members from York County, who were planning
a railroad from Wrightsville, on the Susquehanna, to York. They
refused to extend their railroad westward to Gettysburg. Where-
upon Stevens borrowed the draft of their bill (one day shortly
before the famous speech on public schools) and secretly altered

[18] Stevens was the guiding spirit of a group of railroad-minded citizens of
Gettysburg who met in the local courthouse in September, 1831. He and five
others had made a survey for a railroad running from the town to the Maryland boundary. At the meeting in the courthouse, on Stevens' motion, they
presented a report describing the projected route as being "perfectly practicable, at a reasonable expense." Stevens was thereupon made chairman of a
committee to present a petition to the legislature praying for a charter for a
suitable railroad company. Nothing came of this project, however, and the
"Gettysburg Extension" later undertaken by the state of Pennsylvania was to
follow a quite different route. See Samuel Hazard, ed., *The Register of Pennsylvania* (16 vols., Philadelphia, 1828–1836), 8:199 (September 24, 1831).

it to read "Wrightsville, York, *and Gettysburg.*" Noticing the changes in the nick of time, they corrected the draft and said nothing to Stevens. On the last day of the session he helped to hurry the measure through the legislative mill, only to discover, too late, that he had been outtricked. He did not content himself with accusing the York men of "fraud." At the next session, after the passage of the Bank bill, he succeeded in chartering a Wrightsville and Gettysburg R. R. Company which would compete with theirs between the Susquehanna and York. Eventually they had no choice but to combine their enterprise with his and make him the president of the new company.[19]

As head of a railroad corporation Stevens faced the problem of how, when, and where to proceed with selling stock. For help he turned to a banker friend, William D. Lewis of Philadelphia, who was also an official of *"our* rail road." "You know all (money) things," he wrote Lewis. "Then favor me with your good advice and I will reciprocate—such as telling you the price of potatoes, oat straw, or anything in any way." Stevens reciprocated, indeed, and with more than information on the price of oat straw. When Lewis desired a more liberal charter for his bank, Stevens, against the opposition of Governor Ritner, quickly put a suitable reincorporation bill through the House. "About five minutes since," he notified Lewis at the victorious moment, "the bill to which you ref'd with the amendmts you suggested passed the House a first 2d. and 3d. time. We are in a great hurry to go home you see. Our old friend the Govr. is as amiable as ever. 'Lay low.' " The Governor may have seemed docile, but he was only biding his time. On the last night of the session in June, 1836, he sent to the legislature a message vetoing the Lewis bill. Stevens thereupon rose in the House and, as the newspapers mildly put it, "reprobated in very strong terms the conduct of the Executive in holding back the veto to so late an hour."[20]

Thus Ritner tried to reassert his independence of Stevens and

[19] This account is based upon testimony in the *Pennsylvania House Journal,* 1835–36, 2:206–209, 371–372. See also vol. 1, pp. 447–448.

[20] Stevens to Lewis, March 22, May 12, 29, 1836, in the William D. Lewis Papers, Library of Congress; *National Gazette* (Philadelphia), June 21, 1836.

reprove him for his "secession" from the Antimasonic convention in Harrisburg some months before. Stevens confessed that it took "strong nerves" to buck the Ritner faction of the party. Certainly it threatened to ruin his chances of playing an important part in the national election of 1836. Unwilling to go along with the Whigs and Ritner Antimasons in support of Harrison for president, he sulked in his tent and wrote peevishly of his critics: "Those who undertake to manage our affairs better than they have been managed before we got into power, had better beware how they undertake to make Harrisonism a bait of Antimasonry."[21]

It was he himself who ought to have taken care. His persecution of Freemasons had alienated many Masonic Whigs who the year before had been praising him to the skies. As a result he lost even his own campaign for re-election to the legislature as the Democrats swept the polls in the fall of 1836. Only after the October defeats had shown the urgency of harmonious action did he come to the aid of Harrison and the party in November. The election of Martin Van Buren, Jackson's "heir" to the presidency, topping the local disasters as it did, seemed to indicate that Antimasonry had made its last stand even in Pennsylvania.

For Stevens the charm of Antimasonry had worked well but not well enough. In the guise of crusader against the exclusive lodge he could appear before the voters as a leveler of social classes and at the same time serve the political needs of conservative bankers and business men. Charges of corruption he denied, nor were the Democrats able to prove such accusations when, the tables turned, they investigated the recharter of the Bank of the United States. Yet he requested, and was not refused, favors from the president of the Bank, who had it in his power to reward the deserving with easy loans.[22] Whatever its sporadic successes,

---

[21] Stevens to Samuel Shock, September 28, 1836, manuscript in the possession of T. Fred. Woodley, Bangor, Pennsylvania.

[22] *American Advertiser* (Philadelphia), February 13, 20, 27, March 2, 1837. Biddle wrote to Stevens on March 29, 1837: "I received your note on the subject of our friend Mr. Burrowes' request. . . . I now say with pleasure, that Mr. Burrowes may I think rely on obtaining the accommodation he desires." Manuscript in the possession of T. Fred. Woodley.

however, in a larger sense Antimasonry had been for Stevens a failure. For all his spectacular inquisitions of the lodge, he had been unable to make himself so indispensable, as an Antimason, that other party chieftains would reward him with a high position in the federal government. And Andrew Jackson, through his proxy, could still be considered president.

Divided, Antimasons in Pennsylvania had fallen in 1836, though one of their party still held the governor's chair and had two years yet to serve. Wisely Stevens now made his peace with Ritner, and together they began to experiment with a new political cause. When, in his message to the legislature in December, 1836, Ritner assailed the pro-slavery Democrats of the North, it was widely believed that Stevens, now called "the ruler of the Governor," had provided the theme. "Anti-Masonry is defunct in Pennsylvania," one commentator said. "What hobby can, at this time, be so appropriately mounted as the abolition question? Mr. Stevens . . . has been disappointed in the results which he anticipated would accrue to himself from the exhumation of poor Morgan's bones. Now he imagines that political wonders may be accomplished by calling another 'spirit from the vasty deep.' "[23] Previously he had professed to see Freemasonry crawling about as a viper dangerous to democracy; and when the president of Lafayette College requested him *not* to address the Literary Society there, he had written to the students that he had even found "its venomous hissing in the coolness of Academic Shades." Once he had vowed to fight on until he had convinced the people that there was "no other question than Masonry and Anti-Masonry."[24] Now he seemed determined to convince the people that there was no question other than Slavery and Antislavery.

[23] *Pennsylvania Reporter* (Harrisburg), December 30, 1836.

[24] George Jenkins to Stevens, March 2, 1836; Stevens to the Literary Society of Lafayette College, March 19, 1836, in the Edward McPherson Papers, Library of Congress; *Harrisburg Chronicle*, March 10, 1836.

III. A "Caution" to Agrarianism

ANTISLAVERY heroes—whatever may be said of heroes in general—were made, not born. At the time when Thaddeus Stevens migrated from Vermont to a Pennsylvania county bordering on Mason and Dixon's line, he had no strong prejudice against the "peculiar institution" of the South. Indeed, in the very first case the young lawyer of Gettysburg argued before the state supreme court, he defended the property right of a master against a slave's claim to freedom.

A Marylander had leased a chattel, named Charity Butler, to a family whose custom it was to summer in the Pennsylvania mountains and take her along as a nursemaid. When her several sojourns there totaled more than a half year (under the Pennsylvania abolition acts of 1780 and 1788 a slave residing six months in the state was to be declared free), Charity sued for her freedom in the Pennsylvania courts. As attorney for the defendant, her owner, Stevens argued that the lessee had no right to take her outside of Maryland in the first place; certainly he did not "have power to destroy the property of the lessor by removal into another state where the laws divested such property. As to continued residence for six months, it is clear that a slave who happens to come with his master on different visits which may, on adding up the time of their duration, exceed six months, cannot be contemplated by the law." These, the words of a lawyer, not a social reformer, were sufficient to win the case.[1]

This incident occurred in 1821, about a year after the quarrel

[1] Butler et al. v. Delaplaine (October, 1821), in Thomas Sergeant and William Rawle, Jr., reporters, *Reports of Cases Adjudged in the Supreme Court of Pennsylvania, 1814–1828* (17 vols., Philadelphia, 1818–29), 7:378–386.

32

over Missouri had injected the slavery question suddenly into national politics. That quarrel had ended in a compromise: Missouri entered the Union with slaves and Maine without; but wise observers knew that the "Era of Good Feelings" during the presidency of Monroe was now a thing of the past. An alarm had gone off warning of future sectional controversy, an alarm which had wakened Thomas Jefferson "like a fire-bell in the night." For a decade the danger seemed to recede, and then, in 1831, a Boston printer burst forth in fierce denunciation of human slavery and swore he would never be silenced. In the wake of William Lloyd Garrison antislavery societies began to spring up throughout the North. Politicians, however shy of troublesome issues they might be, could not forever turn their eyes aside.

As the summer of 1835 came around—and there was a governor to elect—Stevens made cautious overtures to the slave's new-found friends. At Gettysburg he offered a few remarks on behalf of the abolitionist cause. A little later he hedged himself by giving assistance also to a rival antislavery movement, that of the colonizationists, who were seeking money with which to send free Negroes to colonies in distant lands.[2] This was a program which abolitionists of every stamp condemned as a scheme of Maryland and Virginia slave-breeders to skim off their surplus stock and keep prices up. Certainly, no doctrinaire friend of the Negro could subscribe to colonization and at the same time to abolition.

Before long Stevens had occasion to take a more forthright step. So alarming had the antislavery agitation become, and so insecure the Southern planters' "patriarchal" position at home, that in the fall of 1835 they began to pass legislative resolutions calling upon Northern states to put a damper on "incendiary" speech. A set of such resolutions the legislature of Virginia sent to the government of Pennsylvania, where they were referred to Stevens' judiciary committee. In the midst of his concerns with Antimasonry, banks, and the approaching presidential election, Stevens found time in May, 1836, to give a report to the House. He agreed with the Virginians that Congress had no constitutional power to abolish slavery or the slave trade, either in the District

[2] *Gettysburg Star,* July 27, October 19, 1835.

of Columbia or in the Southern states, but he denied their right to presume to dictate to the lawmakers of a free state.[3]

After his defeat at the polls that fall, Stevens the politician seemed ready to abandon completely the position which Stevens the lawyer had taken in the case of Charity Butler some fifteen years before. In February, 1837, he idled in Harrisburg as delegates of the Pennsylvania Anti-Slavery Society gathered there to hold their annual convention—with the blessings of the Ritner administration, it was said, for Antimasons were about to become abolitionists, "for the purpose of retaining their ill-gotten power." Present at the convention, as a wandering agent of the American Anti-Slavery Society, was the Reverend Jonathan Blanchard (no disciple of Garrison but a convert of Theodore Weld, a less famous but perhaps more important fountainhead of antislavery in the West). Blanchard and Stevens happened to meet and at once became friends. They understood each other. "Mr. Stevens," suggested the preacher, "if you can turn your Anti-Masons into abolitionists, you will have a party whose politics will not bleach out. The slaveholders will not 'possum' like Free Masons, but will die game." This being a conclusion toward which Stevens himself was already moving, he handed Blanchard a roll of bills and said, "Take that, and go down into Adams County and lecture, and if they Morganize you, we'll make a party out of it." A few weeks later, on Washington's Birthday, the Stevens and Ritner wings of the Antimasonic party came together in a public meeting and buried their differences. Abolitionism would perhaps prove to be the platform upon which the party, now reunited, could be remade.[4]

To forestall these plans a number of Democrats calling themselves "Friends of the Integrity of the Union" arranged an anti-abolitionist demonstration in the Harrisburg courthouse. But Stevens appeared in their midst to heckle them. "These abolition-

[3] *Pennsylvania House Journal*, 1835–36, 1:1206–1207.

[4] *Pennsylvania Reporter* (Harrisburg), January 31, 1837; *Poulson's Daily American Advertiser* (Philadelphia), February 27, 1837. For the conversation between Stevens and Blanchard, as the latter long afterward recalled it, see the memoir of Stevens written by Blanchard and published in his religious weekly, the *Christian Cynosure* (Chicago), April 5, 1883.

ists are dangerous men," he mocked. "The danger is that they will get up a flame against this convention as being in favor of the integrity of the chains of the slave, instead of the 'Integrity of the Union.' " In reply to resolutions denying the right of Congress to meddle with slavery, he offered a list of his own, beginning "all men are created equal." All this was the usual stock in trade of abolitionists; but, amid laughter, applause, and hisses, he stole the show from the Democrats. For this and other services to the antislavery cause his recent acquaintance, Jonathan Blanchard, repaid him with publicity. At Blanchard's instance the American Anti-Slavery Society, meeting a few days later in New York, passed resolutions praising Stevens for his "bold, manly, and successful stand" at Harrisburg and for his "manly report" of the previous year, which so "nobly" advocated free speech and a free press as against the "insolent demand of the South."[5]

All at once, by May of 1837, the erstwhile champion of Antimasonry had become a national hero in the eyes of abolitionists. Afterward stories were told of his love for the slave; how he used his legal skill to widen loopholes in the law for the benefit of fugitives; how, that failing, he would take money from his own purse to buy the freedom of hounded black men. All such tales, however, date from a time later than 1837. The quirks of his own personality, which made him feel in some ways an outcast, perhaps predisposed Stevens to sympathy with the oppressed race, but if so, he gave those feelings no forceful public expression until the handwriting had begun to appear on the wall for Antimasons to read.[6]

For the time being at least, Stevens was frankly committed as a radical on the slavery question; but this did not mean that in other matters he had become one of the bolsheviks of his day. He shortly proved himself a stalwart defender of property rights,

[5] *Chambersburg Whig,* May 12, 1837; *Fourth Annual Report of the American Anti-Slavery Society* (New York, 1837), 22, 43–44.

[6] For the opinion of another biographer, who asserts that Stevens was a born abolitionist, antislavery being the innate "bent" of his mind, see James A. Woodburn, *The Life of Thaddeus Stevens: A Study in American Political History* ... (Indianapolis, 1913), 57–59. Woodburn inaccurately dates Stevens' first meeting with Jonathan Blanchard "in the year that Governor Ritner was elected" (1835).

when the question of amending the Pennsylvania constitution
came before the people of the state. Before the constitutional convention of 1837–38 had well begun its sessions, however, a series
of events occurred that damaged some of his material interests and
affected the trend of his thought. That chain of happenings was
the Panic of '37.

Such a disaster had been far from the minds of most Pennsylvanians during the previous winter. Like their fellow Americans
elsewhere, they had been agog, frenzied with prosperity. Wildcat
bankers were furiously printing notes that passed as money and
outdoing each other in granting easy loans; optimistic railroaders
were laying tracks in all directions; enthusiastic canal enterprisers were digging ditches, here, there, everywhere; prices of
land skyrocketed, as did the prices of almost everything else; and,
with a sufficient-unto-the-day philosophy, people forgot that what
went up would probably come down. There were kill-joys, of
course. One of them, at least in his official capacity, was Pennsylvania's governor, who, in his message to the legislature in December, 1836, issued a jeremiad against his people's sins. "A
gambling spirit of speculation is abroad!" he warned. "The great
malady of the times is the desire, which is now so ravenous, of
acquiring wealth without labor."[7]

Did Stevens, who was credited with having inspired the antislavery portions of Governor Ritner's message, also inspire this?
Certainly none was more deeply infected with the gambling
virus than he. Loitering in Harrisburg early in 1837, a politician
without portfolio, he spent his time with men of ideas, men like
the Reverend Mr. Blanchard—and others. One of the others was
James Miles, who had come to the capital from the northwestern
corner of the state. Miles brought with him the contagion of a
speculative fever which, in Erie County, had reached the propor-
tions of an epidemic. A year before, at the news of the recharter
of the Bank of the United States, the price of town lots in the
borough of Erie had doubled overnight, and that had been only
the beginning of a "boom" in land. For the act which reincor-

[7] George E. Reed, ed., *Papers of the Governors, 1832–1845 (Pennsylvania
Archives,* series 4, vol. 6, Harrisburg, 1901), 282–333.

porated the Bank also appropriated a part of the bonus for extending the Pennsylvania Canal from Pittsburgh to Lake Erie.[8] But where would the outlet of the canal be located? at the town of Erie? or elsewhere along the shore? James Miles owned a large tract of land around the mouth of Elk Creek, about fifteen miles to the west of Erie. It was, he thought, an ideal site for a metropolis. Before this dream could come true, however, two things had to be done: first, the canal extension must terminate at Elk Creek; second, the sandbars at the mouth must be dredged out so as to make a harbor. So Miles had gone on a lobbyist's mission to Harrisburg and had succeeded in his quest when he ran upon a pair of Antimasons named Charles Ogle and Thaddeus Stevens.

In March, 1837, the three of them entered into a contract by which Miles agreed to sell to the others a half equity in two hundred acres of land "best suited for the site of a city intended to be located on the same by said Miles, Stevens, and Ogle." Altogether the purchasers were to pay a hundred thousand dollars, but they were to give only five thousand dollars in cash; Miles was to get the rest as his share of the proceeds from the sale of lots in the proposed metropolis. If these seemed easy terms for Stevens and Ogle, it was well enough understood that they could offer other than pecuniary aid. Ogle, a congressman, could perhaps induce the War Department to make a harbor at Elk Creek; and Stevens, assumed to be the power behind the throne in Pennsylvania, would see to it that the canal terminated in the right place. He readily took a chance on the venture, though he had never even seen Miles' property. "The enormous profits which it was hoped, and confidently believed, they would reap from the speculation . . . dazzled the eyes of all parties concerned," a judge of the state supreme court was later to declare.[9]

[8] *Niles' Register*, 49:387 (February 6, 1837); [Benjamin Whitman and N. W. Russell], *History of Erie County, Pennsylvania* (Chicago, 1884), 431.

[9] This account is derived from exhibits, testimony, and court's opinion in the case of Miles *v.* Stevens, in *Pennsylvania State Reports, Containing Cases Adjudged in the Supreme Court*, 3:22–44 (Philadelphia, 1849). Miles had sued Stevens in an effort to collect the five thousand dollars "hand money" which the latter had promised but did not pay.

Meanwhile the rising price of iron encouraged Stevens to invest further in the charcoal-iron business. His Maria Furnace was not yet a profit-making enterprise; its ores produced too brittle castings, and the markets were too hard to reach. The Gettysburg extension of the Pennsylvania Railroad, should it ever be completed, would make Philadelphia and Baltimore more easily accessible. For the betters ores that were required Stevens and his partner, James D. Paxton, had already explored other parts of South Mountain. In 1831 they built Mifflin Forge near the forks of the Conococheague; two years later they rebuilt it after its destruction by fire; and at the beginning of 1837 they were erecting a new and more ambitious furnace near by, named Caledonia after Stevens' native county in Vermont.

Then, in April, the Panic suddenly struck. Maria Furnace, after making the casting for the arch of the new ironworks, soon closed down for good. Caledonia Furnace was pushed to completion against the ebb tide of prosperity, but it was not to yield worth-while profits for years to come.[10] Now that the prospect had become less dazzling, Stevens and Ogle begged off from remitting to James Miles the five thousand dollars they had promised as down payment for their city lots. Stevens intended to visit Erie County during the summer and look the site over but on second thought decided not to go. As he explained to Miles, it seemed inadvisable for him and Ogle to be seen there until after the next session of the legislature. "I have no doubt as to the *final location* [of the canal route]." In the ensuing months the business outlook got no brighter, and Stevens finally suggested that the deal be called off. "He says," Ogle wrote, "the canal will certainly be located on the western route, and an outlet eventually will be made at Elk Creek, but believes the speculation a bad one, although it may turn out otherwise."[11]

With the onset of a full-fledged business depression other men of property, like Stevens, lost the hardy enthusiasm of the specula-

[10] [Mira L. Dock], "Thaddeus Stevens as an Ironmaster," in the *Philadelphia Times*, July 14, 1895.
[11] Stevens to Miles, August 21, 1837; Ogle to Miles, February 12, 1838, in 3 *Pennsylvania State Reports*, 24.

tor and were gripped by timidity, uneasiness, and doubt. As bank failures and bankruptcies multiplied and idle workingmen roamed the streets, a day of judgment seemed at hand for those interested in the maintenance of the status quo. Many of the propertyless who now suffered were blaming their troubles upon the corporations and the banks and were clamoring for reform. Observing the growing tension in the more industrial states of the North, the great leader of Southern thought, John C. Calhoun, had already noted the alarm among the "rich and well born" there. "They begin to feel what I have long foreseen, that they have more to fear from their own people, than we from our slaves." He had convinced himself that there was and always had been "in an advanced stage of wealth and civilization a conflict between capital and labor."[12]

In such an atmosphere of foreboding and discontent the Pennsylvania constitutional convention met at Harrisburg in May of 1837. There the widespread dissatisfaction was to be voiced by the radical Democratic delegates, the "Loco Focos," whose party had sponsored the idea of amending the constitution. Stevens, who had opposed the calling of a convention but had been sent as a delegate from Adams County, was to be the chief spokesman of the men of property who opposed change.

At the outset it appeared that the Whigs and Antimasons together would have a majority of one delegate and that Stevens, as leader of the handful of Antimasons, would be in a position to dictate. Under his lead the Whigs and Antimasons organized the convention by electing their whole slate of officers, from the president on down the list to the most insignificant doorkeeper and sergeant at arms. "The highest state of party discipline I ever saw in my life!" exclaimed a Democrat. And a Whig: "In party tactics and small manoeuvers I have never seen his equal. . . . Who can forget the mingled sarcasm, eloquence, and pathos of his harangue on the assistant doorkeeper? Or who has not delighted with the precision, accuracy, and effect of our evolu-

[12] Calhoun to J. E. Calhoun, February 4, 1834, in J. Franklin Jameson, ed., *Correspondence of John C. Calhoun (Annual Report of the American Historical Association,* 1899, vol. 2, Washington, 1900), 331.

tions under his drill, throughout the election of officers?" But when Stevens sought to discipline the Whigs by reviving the Antimasonic agitation, they felt differently. Then he became a "mad sergeant" mounted on a "ragged hobby" who, "under the fire of the enemy," galloped around disrupting the conservative ranks. "I appeal to my friend from Adams," said the spokesman for the Whigs, "whether we were not sufficiently rebuked at last October's elections for public interference in such concerns."[13] As a result of Stevens' factionalism, the reformers began their work with better than an even chance of success.

He was willing to grant them minor concessions, a Whig journal explained, so as "to conciliate the rage for change and satisfy the desire of those who wish to place everything in the hands of the people."[14] But on important matters he attuned his voice to the ears of propertied men and to them alone. He fought a proposal to extend the suffrage to every man who was free, white, and twenty-one, insisting that only taxpayers ought to be allowed to vote. There was no farmer present, he said, who was not "in favor of giving the Government to the real and substantial part of the community." Another proposal, that the residence requirement for voting be reduced to ten days within a district, Stevens opposed on the grounds that this would give a "vagabond" the rights of a "respectable citizen"—"if he had lodged in a barn in the district for ten days and washed his cravat in a mud hole."

On the subject of Negro suffrage, however, Stevens appeared to be of a different mind. Some of the Negroes and mulattoes of Pennsylvania had acquired property enough to vote and were exercising their right at the polls. But the Democratic delegates at Harrisburg now undertook to write the qualifying word "white" into the constitutional clause which hitherto had enfranchised all taxable adult males. Protesting that God did "out of one clay create all mankind" (except, apparently, the unwashed poor, black and white), Stevens secured for "persons of color" the

[13] John Agg and others, reporters, *Proceedings and Debates of the Convention of the Commonwealth of Pennsylvania to Propose Amendments to the Constitution, Commenced and Held at Harrisburg on the Second Day of May, 1837* (13 vols., Harrisburg, 1837–39), 1:39–40, 63–64; 2:101–103.

[14] *American Advertiser* (Philadelphia), July 1, 1837.

Top: THE BLACKSMITH SHOP AT CALEDONIA
Bottom: STEVENS' LAW OFFICE IN GETTYSBURG
From the *Philadelphia Times,* July 14, 1895

privilege of having their petitions read in the convention and succeeded temporarily in staving off the attempt upon their established rights.

Then he went on to berate the offending Democrats as "apologists" and "sycophants" of slaveholders. He was willing, he said, to concede the constitutional right of Southerners to hold slaves and even to recover their fugitives in Pennsylvania, but he would require a strict conformity with the letter of the constitution and the laws. He would say to the Southern Shylocks, "Take your bond, but take with it not one drop of Christian blood." He concluded his peroration with a challenge—"Are we afraid of the tyrant of the South?"—and sat down with the remark that, as for himself, he felt none of "that sensibility" and none of "that terror" of disturbing the "peace and harmony of the Union" which so many Pennsylvanians had evinced.

However that may have been, he was not so dauntless before the danger of class war within his own state. After he had referred to the Declaration of Independence in justifying the rights of slaves and free Negroes, the Loco Focos in the convention adduced the same brave words in defense of the rights of the common man in the North. As a Philadelphia Democrat put it in a minority report of a committee on banking,

If the principles of the Declaration of Independence are realities . . . not mere words, all corporations are unrepublican and radically wrong. For, the moment that two or more individuals are associated by act of law and endowed with privileges which do not belong to them as individuals, all natural, social, and political equality is destroyed for their advantage, and to the prejudice of the rest of the community. Corporations . . . have become the mere fortresses of property. Property is more equally held and divided in France, than in Pennsylvania. . . . Labor performed for corporations is like the labor of slaves.

Voicing the fright of landed and moneyed men, Stevens urged that this report be kept from publication. "It seems to me," he exclaimed, "that at this particular crisis, of all others, such a document as this ought to be withheld from the public mind. At a time when the whole community is ready for an explosion; when a magazine is laid which a single spark will cause to explode; . . . [it will] perhaps induce mobs to lay violent hands on the institutions of the country, turning the populace loose with inflamed mind." These remarks gave the Loco Focos an opportunity for a little fun at Stevens' expense. One of them said that if the gentleman from Adams County should make a report "concerning the mysteries and mummeries of Masonry," the Democrats would be in favor of letting the people read it. "Are you not afraid," he asked Stevens, "that if you refuse to suffer it [*the bank report*] to be printed, you will give color to the idea that you regard as sacred the rites and mysteries of Mammon?" Another Democrat observed that, as for himself, he had "no terror of mobs" and could not help feeling "somewhat tickled to see the agitation of the gentleman from Adams."

Determined to prevent the possibility of radical reform, Stevens did all he could to discredit the convention and bring it to an untimely end. He stood ready to use Antimasonry as a means of filibustering, threatening that he would "agree to submit the propositions of reform to the people only on condition that a clause in relation to these oaths and secret societies should also be agreed to." As the summer wore on he made much of the impatience of farmers in the convention to get back to their farms, complained of the burdensome expense to taxpayers in maintaining the delegates so long, and prophesied that they would accomplish little of importance anyhow. Time after time he moved for adjournment, *sine die,* or at least until another referendum should give the people a chance to reconsider their desire for change. Finally, in the middle of July, 1837, the convention agreed to adjourn until fall.[15]

The recess gave the delegates, most of whom were, or aspired to be, members of the legislature as well, an opportunity to look to their fences. Using the convention hall itself as a hustings, Stevens had already begun his campaign and, by his defense of business interests was once more drawing Whigs to his support. In Adams County the "substantial portion of the community" were expected to make amends for their defection from him in 1836. "As circumstances tend to draw the line between *Conserva-*

[15] Agg, *Proceedings and Debates of the Convention of the Commonwealth of Pennsylvania,* 1:208, 386–387, 390; 2:108–110, 340–344; 3:685–686, 693–696; *American Advertiser* (Philadelphia), July 1, 17, 1837.

tive and *Loco Foco* principles and candidates throughout the country," said a Whig paper of Baltimore, "we may expect that, with such men as *Stevens* ... for her Conservative candidates, old Adams will give a majority on that side that will be a *caution* to agrarianism."[16]

But in the eyes of many voters the foe of radicals had perhaps compromised himself by experimenting with his own brand of radicalism. In Adams County, where abolitionism was as yet most unpopular and the black population negligibly small, Democrats could seize upon the issue and use it against him. The *Gazette* in neighboring Bedford County exclaimed in disgust, "Thaddeus Stevens!—a man who has taught the *Negroes* to contend for the rights of a white man at the polls." With an eye to the future and to a wider electorate, the champion of the blacks nevertheless persisted. In September he visited John Quincy Adams, lately become the congressional hero of abolitionists for his opposition to the "gag law" against the reading of antislavery petitions. When he returned to Gettysburg he ran upon his friend Jonathan Blanchard, who was tarrying there in the course of an abolitionizing tour. As Blanchard reported a few days later to the American Anti-Slavery Society: "He inquired how much money I had collected, and on being told, handed me fifty dollars for the use of your society. He gave me forty dollars for the same purpose a few months since. His political friends are, many of them, most violent anti-abolitionists, and endeavored to prevent his uttering his mind on any of the topics connected with abolition." Despite their protests, Stevens spoke out boldly in a stump speech. He opposed the admission of Texas, the new-born republic which many slaveholders hoped would soon be a state in the Union, and repeated that he would give the South her "pound of flesh" but no more.[17]

Whatever the merits of abolitionism as against agrarianism, the

[16] Baltimore *Patriot,* quoted in the *American Advertiser* (Philadelphia), September 16, 1837.

[17] Charles F. Adams, ed., *Memoirs of John Quincy Adams* (12 vols., Philadelphia, 1874–77), 9:372–373; *Bedford Gazette,* November 17, 1837; Blanchard to J. Leavitt, September 18, 1837, a letter first published in the *Emancipator* (Washington) and later reprinted in the *National Enquirer* (Philadelphia), October 26, 1837.

re-election of Stevens was not, in fact, to turn upon issues such
as these. In the fall of 1837 the Gettysburg railroad was building,
the work had drawn an influx of laborers from near and far, and
Stevens—if he overlooked the technicalities of the law—could
count upon the contractors' influence and the workingmen's ballots. On election day he thoroughly avenged his previous defeat.
He got more votes than the entire district—Democrats, Whigs, and
Antimasons together—had cast in 1836. Such was the pragmatic
attitude of Stevens the politician toward vagabonds who washed
their cravats, if any, in mud holes![18]

In the interim before the legislature met, Stevens rejoined the
constitutional convention, which had reconvened in Philadelphia
instead of Harrisburg. At this metropolis on the banks of the
Delaware the delegates were closer to the sources of social discontent than they had been in the capital on the Susquehanna,
which by comparison was a sleepy country town. Moreover, a
slight shift in membership had given the Loco Focos, instead of
the Conservatives, a narrow majority in the convention. And
the Democrats, in Pennsylvania as elsewhere in the nation, continued to reflect the class consciousness which had become sharper
as the business depression had deepened since spring. Adapting
to the defense of slavery the views of Southern agrarian philosophers, John C. Calhoun was now to speak out openly in the
United States Senate and argue that the lower class had always
and everywhere been exploited—"there has never yet existed a
wealthy and civilized society in which one portion of the community did not, in point of fact, live on the labor of the other"—
but that the exploited group in the South, the slaves, were better
off than their fellows in the North, the wage earners. When,
against the Loco Foco allies of this champion of the plantation

[18] After the election one of the delegates in the constitutional convention
produced a list of taxables of Adams County to show that no township had
as many legal voters as the votes that Stevens received in it in 1837. This
critic went on to point out that in one township the total number of ballots
cast in 1836 had been 310, of which Stevens got 186; in 1837 the total was
626, of which Stevens got 524. The difference consisted of "votes given by
vagrants and vagabonds such as come from ... Maryland to work on the rail
roads." These figures went unchallenged. Agg, *Proceedings and Debates of
the Convention of the Commonwealth of Pennsylvania*, 5:302–303.

aristocracy, Stevens took his stand as a spokesman for capitalist democracy, loud, bitter, and revealing debates were to be heard in Philadelphia's Music Hall.

As a delegate from rural Adams County, Stevens had to subscribe at least verbally to the necessity of protecting the "interests of the farming classes from the influence of those large manufacturing towns and commercial cities." He even went so far as to quote Thomas Jefferson, the inspiration of the agrarian philosophers; cities were "sores upon the body politic." But, as a Philadelphia Whig retorted, Stevens' legislative career belied these words, for it had been devoted to the encouragement of banks and other corporations, railroads, turnpikes, factories, and all that went to build up the growing urban centers which he professed to contemn. Perhaps the thing he really rued was the fact that the city proletariat voted Democratic.

The excitement began when Democrats threatened to use the constitutional convention to undo the legislation which had chartered the Bank of the United States. One of them suggested that if Northern abolitionists were allowed to go South and arouse the slave against his master, Southern agitators might with equal propriety go North and stir up the workingman against his employer. This suggestion, and indeed the very idea that they could contemplate violating the "vested rights" of bankers, was proof to Stevens that the Loco Focos were plotting a social revolution. It was obvious that they were conspiring "to break down settled principles—and to prepare the public mind, by arraying one class of the community against the other—the rich against the poor—for some violent, illegal, and unjust convulsion, which should rob one portion of the community for the purpose of enriching the other." Everything said in the convention against the Bank was "part and parcel of this levelling doctrine" and "these agrarian feelings." Always in the past revolutionists had begun in just this way, by "arraying the poor against the rich and the laborer against the capitalist."

Did not the gentleman tell us that the southern cotton boys were going to rule us, and did he not threaten that they would send their picture books among us and among all the northern laborers, because the northern laborers were as much slaves to their masters—their employers and the banks—as the southern negroes were to their masters . . . and that these laborers would rise against their masters and the banks and overthrow them? Thus the laborers and mechanics of this free state are to be put upon a level with the shrivelled, lacerated negro of the south. . . . Let those who hold these opinions . . . go form an alliance. It would be . . . an appropriate alliance—between the radical reformers of the north and the lawless nullifiers of the south. If there is a free man on earth, body and soul, it is the bold, fearless laborer and mechanic of the free states.

Again and again Stevens insisted that there was no real antagonism of interest between the laboring and employing groups in the North. What helps business helps everybody; "the whole are never so prosperous as when the bankers and rich men and merchants are all most successful in their business." The existing depression was due to the meddling of misguided politicians, more particularly to Andrew Jackson and his fiscal policies, his war on the Bank. There were no such things as social classes in the North. "Is it an aristocracy of wealth because one man or a set of men are richer than the others?" Stevens demanded. "No, sir. It only makes an inequality of circumstances of gentlemen of the same rank, and no difference of rank unless there was some law passed making those distinctions."

As if to emphasize this legalistic point of view, he urged, when the subject of public education came up, that the school amendment to the constitution be so worded as to remove any implication that poor scholars were wards of the charitable rich. "What do provisions of this kind create? They create one rank composed of the wealth of the land, and another of the plebeians and poor." In thus opposing class distinctions, Stevens laid himself open to charges of inconsistency. "When the subject of suffrage was before the convention," a Democrat now reminded the assembly, "the gentleman from Adams did classify the people of this commonwealth, and brought some of them down to the lowest ebb, and would not agree that they should exercise the rights of citizens of the state." Yet perhaps it was unfair to compare public education with universal suffrage. Education, as Horace Mann later pointed out, would serve as an antidote to the "madness" of agrarianism. By itself, the franchise would merely enable agrarians to give effect to their insanity.[19]

In Philadelphia Stevens was so busy defending the economic system in general and Nicholas Biddle in particular—"the patriotic, the enlightened, the proud-hearted Pennsylvanian"—that he neglected some of his own interests which were being threatened by the Democrats in the legislature, assembled in Harrisburg. On December 18, 1837, while he was absent from his seat in the House and excoriating the class-struggle philosophy of the Loco Focos in Music Hall, his arch-foe in the legislature, Representative Thomas B. McElwee of Bedford County, was securing the passage of an ominous resolution "to examine the route of the Gettysburg rail road." McElwee would now have an opportunity to prove his contention that the railroad was in effect only a private line which the state was building at extraordinary public expense past Stevens' ironworks. Stevens had already sensed the danger that the new legislature, with its Democratic majority, would seek to discontinue the road; but he had hoped to save the project through his influence with the governor and with the board of canal commissioners. He had been able to dictate a part of the commissioners' annual report commending the Gettysburg extension—"This improvement cannot fail to be highly useful to the State"—and urging an appropriation of four hundred thousand dollars so that the contractors would not be put to "great inconvenience and loss" and the workmen would not lose their jobs. Using the same arguments, supplied by Stevens, Governor Ritner appealed to the legislature to grant the sum desired.[20]

---

[19] *Ibid.*, 4:24, 245–247; 5:302–303; 6:154–167. Stevens' attitude on the school question was deeply rooted in the earlier experiences of his life. "I myself have been a teacher in New England," he said, in urging that adults be not excluded from the public schools. "I have taught married men of thirty years of age. I have taught persons of all ages between . . . four and thirty—and it was this very feature which seemed to me to constitute the great beauty of the whole system." Again, insisting that no invidious distinctions be made between rich and poor scholars, he reflected his own background when he protested that "there was no disgrace in being the son of a poor man or a drunkard." *Ibid.*, 5:342–343, 348–349.

[20] *Pennsylvania House Journal*, 1837–38, 1:46; Stevens to E. F. Pennypacker, November 20, 1837, in the Society Collection, Historical Society of Pennsylvania, Philadelphia.

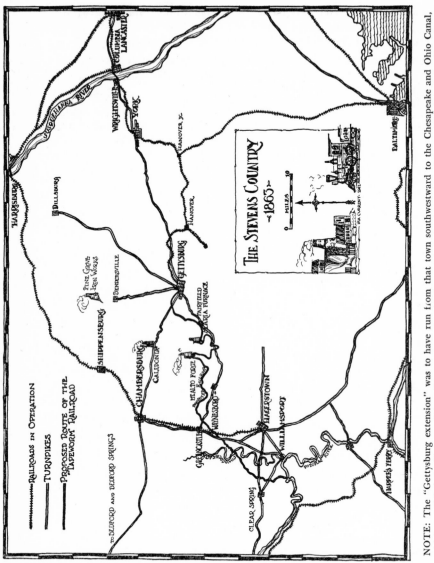

THE STEVENS COUNTRY
~1865~

MILES
0 __ 10

RAILROADS IN OPERATION
TURNPIKES
PROPOSED ROUTE OF THE
TAPEWORM RAILROAD

NOTE: The "Gettysburg extension" was to have run from that town southwestward to the Chesapeake and Ohio Canal, which paralleled the Potomac River. The route as here delineated is derived from the "Map and Profile of the Gettysburg Rail Road, as Surveyed by Order of the Legislature of Pennsylvania, 1839," a copy of which is in the Library of Congress. The railroad running in the other direction, to Wrightsville, was not built until some years later. On the map above,

When, at Philadelphia, Stevens heard of the appointment of McElwee's investigating committee, he hastily sent warning and advice to John B. McPherson of the Gettysburg bank:

The committee to visit our Road will meet at Gettysburg on the 2d day of Jan'y next. Let them all be warned and posted especially our opponents. Be particularly kind to Strohm and Myers [*prominent Whigs of Adams County*] & any other opponent of the road who may be present. I do not know how Baily [*one of the original surveyors of the route*] is, but wish Col. Paxton [*Stevens' partner in the iron business and also a contractor on the road*] would immediately write to him. Let no foolish engineers of the neighborhood be talking. You know how to drug the committee. Speak to Col. Paxton and Clarkson [*superintendent of the work*] as I have not time to write them. We are in the midst of an exciting discussion.[21]

Early in January, 1838, Stevens left the "exciting discussion" at Philadelphia to take up the fight for his railroad on the floor of the House. He had enough influence with the committee on internal improvements to persuade them to introduce only a single general appropriation bill, of which the provision for the Gettysburg road was a part. The Democrats, feigning horror at such "log-rolling," demanded separate appropriation bills. Failing in that, they began a campaign to whittle down the railroad's share. Soon Stevens found that he and his associates had not succeeded in "drugging" the opponents of the road, as Strohm, a Whig, and McElwee, a Democrat, made common cause against him. They charged that he had got up the Wrightsville company as a sinecure for himself, receiving a salary of two thousand dollars for doing nothing, that the track from Wrightsville to Gettysburg would never be laid unless the state paid for it, and that the extension southwestward from Gettysburg would be useless without that link to connect it with the Pennsylvania System. When McElwee, reporting on his investigation, condemned the route as "beginning in the woods and ending nowhere," Stevens amused the House with his reply. The report, he said, "pure fiction" though it was, greatly interested him as literature, for it dealt with American scenery. But as the months went by, his

[21] Stevens to McPherson, December 19, 1837, in the Thaddeus Stevens Papers, Library of Congress.

light-heartedness gave way to pessimism. In March William Mc-Pherson, lately made secretary of the canal board, informed his father with mingled irony and despair that the "real friends of the Governor and the bill have succeeded thus far in cutting it down *so much*. Mr. Stevens was really very much disheartening on Saturday night about the prospects." As finally passed, the bill appropriated only enough to pay for the work already under contract and left the future of the road undetermined.[22]

Meanwhile the banking quarrel had followed Stevens from Music Hall in Philadelphia to the Hall of Representatives in Harrisburg. Bank men and anti-Bank men fought not only with words but also with fists. Stevens once pulled apart two venerable representatives on the steps of the capitol and reprimanded one of them as a father might an unruly boy—"My *son*, my *son*, this is harsh play, though it *is* in sport"—while the crowd which had gathered to watch dispersed chuckling. The Democrats in the legislature were attempting to make such reforms in the banking system as seemed to be called for by the many suspensions and failures that the Panic had occasioned. They would, if they could, have compelled banks (all of which had suspended specie payment) to redeem their notes in silver or gold; would have made stockholders individually liable for the amount of notes issued; would have required banks to sustain the credit of one another in emergencies; and would have forced them to pay all profits over 8 per cent into the treasury of the state. The bankers trusted Stevens to save them from wild legislation of that kind. When they began to doubt his steadfastness, he hastened to reassure Nicholas Biddle himself. "Frightened about the bank bill!" he wrote. "What Solomons in the knowledge of human nature your Phila. gentlemen are!" Yet in the end a "notorious anti-bank bill" passed the House.[23]

In the midst of these legislative fights over bank reform and

[22] W. McPherson to J. B. McPherson, December 23, 1837, and March 26, 1838, in the Edward McPherson Papers, Library of Congress; *American Advertiser* (Philadelphia), 1838: January 6, 11, 20, 25; February 8, 9; March 19.

[23] *American Advertiser* (Philadelphia), January 26, 1838; Stevens to Biddle, February 11, 1838, in the Dreer Collection, Historical Society of Pennsylvania; *Pennsylvania House Journal*, 1837-38, 1:630-632.

the Gettysburg railroad Stevens found some time for his anti-slavery hobby, but he was far less bold than he had been the year before. No longer did he speak, as he had at the "Integrity of the Union" affair, as an out-and-out abolitionist. Cautiously now, when the American Anti-Slavery Society asked permission to use the statehouse, he suggested that agents of both abolition and colonization be heard. He believed that both were "benevolent undertakings," both "honest and respectable," and that "to listen to the sentiments of both, though they came in collision, could do no harm to members but might enlighten them respecting two great enterprises."[24]

While he was making such noncommittal remarks in the legislature, Democrats in the constitutional convention at Philadelphia were reviving their opposition to Negro suffrage. With Stevens absent they succeeded where they had previously failed, and the amended constitution included the word "white" as a qualification of the right to vote. Stevens did not sign the new constitution, but neither did he protest against the wrong done the colored man. The Pennsylvania Anti-Slavery Society, on the other hand, voiced its sense of outrage in an "Address to the People of Color" of the state. "Could fervid eloquence . . . supported by great weight of character . . . have had their accustomed influence, then the deed for your degradation would not have been accomplished," the Negro was told. The friends of the colored man had not stood by him, with the single exception of John Sergeant, president of the convention. Sergeant returned from an absence "just as the vote for the insertion of the word *white*" was closed. Instead of taking a "neutral course," as Stevens had done, he secured permission to have his vote recorded and cast it against the change.[25] The "Address," though it did not mention Stevens by name, was obviously pointed at him.

A few weeks later a bill appropriating large sums to aid several academies and colleges came before the House. Almost everyone expected the members to negative the bill without a second thought. But the representative from Adams County had taken

---

[24] *American Advertiser* (Philadelphia), January 29, 1838.
[25] *National Enquirer* (Philadelphia), March 1, 1838.

the time and trouble to prepare an elaborate address; and though
the March day was sunny and warm outside, the others listened
for a solid hour to his eloquent appeal. In an oration replete with
allusions to the Bible and the Greek and Roman classics he
praised classical learning, not for its usefulness but for "the
effect of liberal and enlarged knowledge upon the spiritual and
immortal portion of man." "It may be true," he confessed, "that
endowed Colleges are only accessible to the rich; but that shows
the necessity of [the state's] endowing them, and thus opening
their doors to the meritorious poor." With unintended irony the
erstwhile frenzied land speculator said: "I have often thought,
and wished, that I was the owner or the trustee of the whole
mountain of Ophir. I would scatter its yellow dirt upon the human intellect." Persuaded for the nonce, his hearers allowed him
to hurry the appropriation bill through the House, on the same
Saturday; but over Sunday they had time to recover from what
a reporter called "the intoxication of the intellectual draughts"
that Stevens had provided, and on Monday they reconsidered and
voted down the bill.[26]

A sponsor of public education, a champion (albeit half-hearted
at times) of the free Negro and the slave, a foe of the exclusive
Freemasonic Lodge, Stevens could claim the votes of freedom-
loving common men. Friend of bankers both great and small,
railroad president and ironmaster, gambler in real estate, defender of business interests in the law courts and out, scourge of
economic radicals and apologist for existing social inequalities in
the North, he demonstrated that he was nevertheless no dangerous
demagogue but a statesman at heart. If he seemed sometimes a
man of many contradictions, that was because his personality,
like everybody's, was anything but simple; and the social trends
of his day, as always, were complex. Yet there was a historical
pattern into which his career fitted, a pattern shifting and often
obscure which was eventually to take the somewhat clearer design
of the American Civil War.

As one of a gifted few who had found the United States truly a

[26] *American Advertiser* (Philadelphia), March 19, 1838; *Pennsylvania House
Journal,* 1837–38, 1:700–709.

land of opportunity in these years of its lusty youth, Stevens had no patience with the less favored many who naïvely and, after the Panic of '37, sometimes angrily persisted in taking with stark literalness the "free and equal" phrase that had attended the birth of the republic. Having risen the hard way to a top rung in his locality, he was in no mood to see others knock down the ladder he had climbed. Confronted in 1837 and 1838 with popular discontent and proposals for drastic reform, he undertook neither to relieve the one nor to temper the other. In his apparent fright he took refuge in a blind and narrow legalism but, conspicuous though he was among the able lawyers in the constitutional convention, he did not distinguish himself as an expert in jurisprudential lore. Lacking the humanitarian impulse, he stood stubbornly for "vested rights" as against what he called "the wild visions of idle dreamers," "the revolutionary and agrarian folly of modern reformers."

In the distant South were men, like frontier-born Calhoun aspiring to be one of the Carolina elite, who in the eighteen-thirties found themselves in an almost identical plight. Just as the outbursts of the Loco Focos in the Pennsylvania constitutional convention of 1837–38 were alarming to Northern men of business, so the demands of slaveless small farmers in the Virginia constitutional convention several years earlier had seemed "incendiary" to the Southern planter class. If laborers in Philadelphia and other Northern cities had begun to affiliate in unions that looked like "conspiracies" in the eyes of the common law, slaves on plantations in Southampton County and elsewhere had found black conspirators, like Nat Turner, to lead them in uprisings. If Northern slums were breeding places of crime and discontent, the Southern back country bred its poor whites who might yet find the energy for revolt. And so men as different as Stevens and Calhoun faced problems that were remarkably alike.

And their solutions were similar too. To avert the danger which from below menaced the "patriarchal" position of the planter, Calhoun and other leaders taught Southerners to cease apologizing for slavery and to boast of it as "a good—a positive good." This pro-slavery argument, ancestor of the doctrine of white supremacy, tended to solidify the chosen race in a common hatred of abolitionists and at the same time to separate the lower classes along the color line, and thus to enable the elite to keep their position according to the ancient maxim of divide and rule. Thus, if no William Lloyd Garrison had ever been born, propagandists in the South would have found it useful to invent one.[27]

Recognizing these similarities between Northern and Southern problems, Calhoun did not at first take an exclusively sectional stand. He hoped to effect a political alliance between the upper classes North and South, the better to deal with their common foe on all fronts. Indeed, his purpose in exposing the class conflict in the industrial regions was to waken Northern men of property to the danger of standing apart from their brothers-under-the-skin in the South. But Stevens, for one, refused to see Calhoun's outstretched hand. When Pennsylvania Democrats, taking their cue from the Southern leaders of their party, denounced the concentrations of property in their state, Stevens replied that there was no "aristocracy of wealth," merely "an inequality of circumstances of gentlemen of the same rank." He then imitated Calhoun's technique by drawing attention to the contradictions in society on the other side of Mason and Dixon's line. But he rejected the possibility of joining with the "well born" of the South. With his antislavery argument he took steps to break up the "appropriate alliance" which, he sarcastically noted, the planter tories were making with the radical workingmen of the North.

If the danger of a social "convulsion," a word that both Calhoun and Stevens used repeatedly, was nearly as great as both of them seemed to think, there was once a possibility that when civil war came to the United States, it would be a true *civil* conflict, a war of the social classes. When the war actually came, of course, class lines were obscured and complicated by geographical lines. This was partly because other leaders of capitalist and planter thought and action eventually sensed the feasibility of turning domestic discontent away from home, as Stevens had done as early as 1837.

[27] See William B. Hesseltine, "Some New Aspects of the Pro-Slavery Argument," *Journal of Negro History*, 21 (1936): 1–14.

For the time being, in 1838, he found it wise to subordinate the slavery issue to more urgent matters of state. When invited to attend the dedication of Pennsylvania Hall, the antislavery "Temple of Liberty" in Philadelphia, he delayed answering for several months and then sent his regrets. In his letter he admitted that the Constitution, in permitting slavery, was incompatible with the Declaration of Independence, but he would content himself with a strict enforcement of the existing law. Again the thought of the slaveholder brought Shylock to his mind: "If his heart exacts the fulfilment of the cruel bond, let him take the pound of flesh, but not one drop of blood." This was nobly said, but it hardly promised an early fulfilment of the prophecy which John Quincy Adams had recently made. "A remarkable man," Adams had noted in his diary in September, 1837, after his abolitionist visitor from Gettysburg had gone. "A remarkable man, likely hereafter to figure in the history of the Union."[28]

[28] Stevens to Samuel Webb, May 4, 1838, in the *Pennsylvania Freeman* (Philadelphia), May 17, 1838; *Memoirs of John Quincy Adams*, 9:372–373.

IV. Out the Window

ABOUT the middle of May, 1838, William McPherson, secretary of the board of canal commissioners, sat in the Canal Room of the capitol writing a letter to his father, head of the Gettysburg bank. He opened the folded sheet to add a postscript: "... Mr. Stevens was this morning elected President of the Board of C. C. I hope this may turn out for the best. I expect a tremendous *buz* for a while." Young McPherson had guessed right about the *buz*, and a few days later, sitting in the same room, he wrote again: "The appointment of Mr. Stevens has thrown the Loco Focos into consternation here. They say it is a *gunpowder* plot to blow them up." And it was, in truth, just that.[1]

The fall elections would decide whether Whigs and Antimasons, through their candidate Joseph Ritner, should continue to enjoy the spoils of office and direct the administration of the state. Their defeat was likely, for success had come to them three years before only through a division in the ranks of the Democrats, now reunited. Yet the Ritner forces had one weapon which might turn the tide. That was the board of canal commissioners, who had charge of all spending on the public works. When the governor placed Thaddeus Stevens on the board, and its members named him president, the object was to give control of the canal funds to the political tactician who could make the best use of them.

The strategy of the Whigs was to have Stevens visit the public works during the summer of 1838 and relet the contracts on roads and waterways then being built. If the jobs were relet at a higher price to sound Ritner men, the Whigs could not only count upon

[1] W. McPherson to J. B. McPherson, May 16, 19, 1838, in the Edward McPherson Papers, Library of Congress.

the support of the contractors but could also take a rebate from them and thus get state aid for their campaign. Preparing for his summer's work, Stevens went first to Caledonia to put his iron business in order. While there, needing money, he dispatched a letter to Nicholas Biddle: "I want the enclosed note discounted —if you are not too much oppressed with being obliged to do all the business of Europe and America both in business and politics, as your *eulogists* say, will you please inform me as early as you can (at Gettysburg) as I leave it on a Missionary tour of a few months, next week—." In June Stevens the missionary set out on horseback, with another of the canal commissioners, to make the rounds of the public works. "They go as you know with a *peculiar* object in view," wrote William McPherson to his father.[2]

Stevens a "missionary!" That was the kind of ironic touch in which he took delight. And more was to come. While stopping at Tunkhannock he penned a letter for the press. "In traversing the Public Works," he wrote, "the Canal Commissioners have seen with regret the great want of literary and moral instruction among the children of the laborers." The children were too far from schools and so temporary ones ought to be set up, or Sunday schools at least. Doubtless "the workmen would be willing to allow the contractors to retain a small monthly sum to defray the expense." Whig papers printed this communication with the comment that "the eminent friend and advocate of universal education, Thaddeus Stevens," was contributing "another lasting benefit to his fellow men."[3]

He could chuckle at the double meaning which the words "moral instruction" might be made to have. Some twenty-four hours later he held a letting of contracts at Tunkhannock and inquired, first of all, into the "moral character" of those making bids. He told a couple of bidders of doubtful morals that "if they would be good Ritner men, he thought they could get work." And so it went throughout his travels along the canals. Whenever a

[2] Stevens to Biddle, May 21, 1838, manuscript in the possession of T. Fred. Woodley, Bangor, Pennsylvania; W. McPherson to J. B. McPherson, June 20, 1838, in the McPherson Papers.

[3] *Bradford Argus*, quoted in *Poulson's Daily American Advertiser* (Philadelphia), August 4, 1838.

bid was made by a contractor whom the commissioners did not know, they inquired into his *"moral character"* or his *"religious principles,"* which meant of course his politics. At one of their stopping places Stevens' fellow traveler suggested that all Democratic applications be sent "end ways." "Mr. Stevens then took a seat at the table," one of the contractors later recalled, "and the bids that were to be registered he put on the table, and threw a large number on the floor." Those who got the contracts had to contribute to a "missionary fund" which went to finance the Whig campaign. Workingmen (who earned from a dollar to a dollar and a half a day) were compelled to bet a part of their earnings on Ritner as a sort of insurance—their votes would certainly follow their bets. To mask the purpose of their contributions, the contractors put their names to a document which read: "We the undersigned agree to pay . . . the sums set opposite our names for the purpose of diffusing useful knowledge among the people."[4] Actually, they hired no schoolmasters and set up no "temporary schools" along the public works. At this particular moment the eminent friend of education had a special kind of useful knowledge to disseminate.

He was full of clever schemes for spreading the propaganda of Whiggery. The banks of Philadelphia, "friendly to the Gov. and anxious to help him and his cause," were planning to resume specie payments at some time during the summer of 1838. Stevens suggested that they inform the governor of the exact day, so that, just beforehand, he could "come out with a *tearing proclamation* commanding them to resume by such and such a day." Many people who held worthless bank notes had blamed the governor and his party for not compelling the banks to redeem them. Now the governor would crack the whip—and the bankers would jump! "This we conceive a bold stroke, and one which must make us votes," William McPherson told his father; "—you see through the object no doubt." About all this young McPherson had his qualms, however, for he was new to the game. "In politics there

---

[4] Testimony of contractors on the public works, given in January, 1839, to a committee of the legislature investigating the activities of the canal commissioners and published in the *Pennsylvania House Journal*, 1838–39, vol. 2, part 2, pp. 4–5, 7, 78–79.

is not too much honesty I find—but the enemy must be fought with their own clubs." Nicholas Biddle, less easily shocked by bold stratagems of politics, sent his congratulations to the Machiavelli of Gettysburg: "You are a magician greater than Van Buren, & with all your professions against Masonry, you are an absolute right worshipful Grand Master."[5]

Meanwhile the Democrats, with their candidate David R. Porter, were by no means silent or inactive in this, the wildest campaign in the history of the state. Ritner they noisily denounced as a "damned Dutch hog," but Stevens was the real villain of their piece. "Thaddeus Stevens is the Governor, and not 'Joseph the Farmer,' " they said, and turned upon his Gettysburg railroad, which was vulnerable to their attacks. Exaggerating the snake-like curves of the route, they made a woodcut which they labeled "the *tapeworm*" or "the Gettysburg *sarpent*" and reproduced it in their papers throughout the state. And if their foes were betting heavily on Ritner, they dared openly to advertise bets of hundreds of thousands of dollars on their own man.[6]

The Whigs granted that it would be a close race, but they were confident of victory. Stevens was promising "a majority for the old farmer of 12 or 1500 *at least*." Reports from various points on the public works gave assurance that "the 'missionaries' in their journeyings by land and water do not forget the *main* object, &...all things look well." Jubilantly young McPherson asked: "What can defeat us?"[7] It was a hot, dry, dusty summer through which the canal commissioners rode—until late in July, when out of nowhere there blew up a violent storm of wind, rain, and hail. The gale tore the roof off a big red-brick barn of Stevens' in Gettysburg and knocked down part of the walls.[8] If this was an omen it went unheeded.

During the month of September, 1838, as election day drew

[5] W. McPherson to J. B. McPherson, June 28, 1838, in the McPherson Papers; Biddle to Stevens, July 3, 1838, in R. C. McCrane, ed., *Correspondence of Nicholas Biddle Dealing with National Affairs, 1768–1844* (Boston, 1919), 315.

[6] *American Advertiser* (Philadelphia), August 31, September 1, 6, 1838.

[7] W. McPherson to J. B. McPherson, June 5, 28, 1838, in the McPherson Papers.

[8] *Adams Sentinel* (Gettysburg), July 30, 1838.

nearer, Stevens made definite plans for the conduct of the canal contractors at the polls. They "must be careful to have *no Porter bosses* on the line"; they "must bring their men up ... and see that they deposited their ballots"; they must "bring their men to the polls at different hours, so that the crowd would not be so great." Nor did the Whigs forget the votes of men not on the public works. With hard times going from bad to worse, they offered a clear-cut issue: "Let the motto of every laboring man be Ritner and Prosperity vs. Porter, Idleness, and Poverty; or Bread, or no Bread."[9]

If the stakes seemed high for the laboring man—bread or no bread—they were far higher for Whig and Antimasonic politicians. In the excitement of the hour Whigs who were Freemasons were again willing to forget, for the nonce, the abuse that Stevens had heaped upon them.[10] For Stevens himself the stakes were highest of all. On the outcome would depend the fate of Biddle's bank and of his own Gettysburg railroad; if the Whigs won, he had reason to believe that they would send him to the United States Senate; and in the course of the campaign he had spent or bet at least a hundred thousand dollars of his own![11]

Election day came and went. Stevens, along with the rest of the politicians, had to wait a week or more to learn how his gamble had turned out, for it would take that long to gather in and sum up all the returns. One impatient Philadelphian who had bet on Ritner went up to Harrisburg to learn from Stevens "how matters and things were going on." He found the Whig tactician limping along on Front Street and asked him eagerly for information from the different counties. Some people were saying that "the thing was up." Calmly Stevens said he was afraid so; some of the counties had given larger majorities "the other way" than he had

[9] *Pennsylvania House Journal*, 1838–39, vol. 2, part 2, p. 10; *American Advertiser* (Philadelphia), July 31, 1838.

[10] "The Editor of the Sentinel, being a member of the Masonic fraternity, has, by the violence of the abuse heaped upon him, been frequently thrown in local elections upon the side of those with whom he did not agree in general politics. He feels now, however, that high interests are at stake." *Adams Sentinel* (Gettysburg), July 23, 1838.

[11] Alexander H. Hood, "Thaddeus Stevens," in Alexander Harris, ed., *A Biographical History of Lancaster County* (Lancaster, 1872), 580.

calculated at first. If the man would call at Stevens' room early the next morning, more definite news might be available. Just after daybreak the worried Philadelphian climbed the stairs in Wilson's Hotel and found Stevens still in bed. The news was the worst: Ritner had been defeated without a doubt. The disappointed visitor lamented that he had put five hundred dollars on Ritner, all the money he had in the world, but Stevens offered cold comfort. Without bothering to get up he advised the man to go on home, bet that Porter's majority would not be greater than five thousand, and so recoup his loss! He himself, with all he had to lose, remained imperturbable, calm.[12]

But perhaps all was not lost. Their governor had been defeated, but the incoming returns might still give the Whigs a majority in the House of Representatives. Time would tell.

Presently Stevens got out of bed and went to call at the home of Thomas H. Burrowes, secretary of state and chairman of the Ritner party. Early in the afternoon the two made their way to Burrowes' office. There they found, awaiting Burrowes, a sleepless and travel-worn messenger with a sealed package containing the election returns of Philadelphia County. The courier related how he had left the city shortly after midnight on a steam train prepared especially for him and had reached Harrisburg about noon. Why this elaborate haste? He explained that there was to be another set of returns from the county, as the Democrats disputed some of the districts, though only his had been duly authenticated by the county sheriff. He had wanted to be sure that they reached the secretary of state ahead of the false returns. Stevens and Burrowes withdrew to another room to confer.[13]

It was clear that the Whigs would have a majority in the House if they made certain that their members-elect from Philadelphia got the disputed seats. The Democrats must be kept out at all costs! If the Whigs gained control of the House, they could offset some of the damage done by Ritner's defeat, and indeed might even prevent Porter from taking the governor's chair.

[12] Testimony of one Peter Albright, in *Pennsylvania House Journal*, 1838–39, vol. 2, part 2, pp. 205–206.

[13] Testimony of B. F. Hedges (the messenger), in *House Journal*, 1838–39, vol. 2, part 2, p. 143.

Burrowes and Stevens emerged from their consultation with a plan. On the next day, October 15, they took the first step by publishing a notice "to the friends of Joseph Ritner." In this extraordinary pronouncement they asserted that Porter had won through "malpractice and fraud" and that an investigation should be undertaken *"at once."* "But, fellow citizens, until this investigation can be fully made and fairly determined, let us treat the election of the 9th inst. as if we had not been defeated, and in that attitude abide the result."[14] To those who had bet on Ritner this would convey the message that they should refuse to pay their gambling debts, but to its authors it meant far more than that. For the present it would serve to hearten the many Whigs and Antimasons who were acknowledging themselves "licked."

"I never saw Mr. Stevens so determined to go at anything in earnest as he is this investigation," observed William McPherson. "He says he will give Mr. Porter plenty to do *anyhow.*" During the following week Stevens went up and down the land counseling Whig politicians on ways to harass Mr. Porter and the Democrats. "I did state to more than one," he admitted later, "that the proper course to be pursued in the election of a United States Senator would be . . . to agree upon a single Anti-VanBuren candidate"—whose initials would be T.S.—"and give their whole vote to him so that the state should no longer be disgraced by a Loco-Foco Senator in Congress." He also sketched a few bills by which to deprive the incoming governor of his patronage and made plans to adjourn the legislature *sine die* before Porter should be inaugurated, so as to leave him powerless in the gubernatorial chair.[15]

Having determined upon his strategy, Stevens sent out appeals to all the "anti-VanBuren" members of the legislature urging them to appear in Harrisburg several days before the session was to open. "We shall have a turbulent time at the opening of the House," he warned them, "but we must be determined not to give

[14] *American Advertiser* (Philadelphia), October 19, 1838.

[15] W. McPherson to J. B. McPherson, October 14, 1838, in the McPherson Papers; testimony of Stevens and others in *Pennsylvania Senate Journal,* 1838–39, 2:799 ff.

an inch."[16] Responding to his call, dozens of Whigs and Anti-masons crowded into his rooms in Wilson's Hotel one evening late in November to rehearse his program for the organization of the House. He arranged everything with the utmost care—even to the detail of providing his candidate for speaker with a pocket Bible, so that he would be ready to swear in the Whig members-elect, even though the Democrats should get hold of the official Book!

"The [Whig] members from the county of Philadelphia *will* have their seats—peaceably, if possible—but forcibly, if otherwise," the *Chronicle* of Harrisburg told its readers. Loco Focos swore that *they* would have the seats; putative members were labeling desks in the capitol with their names and stealing the keys; and everyone was spoiling for a fight. Harrisburg was filling with strangers during the first few days of December. Always at this time there came a flock seeking loaves and fishes, but these people were different, and there were more of them. On the streets about him Stevens saw what were to his view "rough, ferocious, rude-looking men," swarthy, athletic, and panther-like, whom he knew to be Philadelphia thugs hired by the Democrats.

The fourth of December was an eventful day. When Stevens arrived at the Hall of Representatives, about ten in the morning, he made his way with difficulty through the mob that filled the room. He found his desk surrounded by six or eight of the "stout-est and most ruffianly" of the strong-arm men whom the Democrats had brought up from the city. But he could count upon his own retainers, contractors and laborers from the public works, who were also ready in their places.[17] Also on his side was at least the semblance of legality, and he was prepared to make the most of it.

At the outset the Democrats had one material advantage: according to a long-standing rule, the chief clerk of the previous House was to preside until the new House had elected a speaker,

---

[16] Stevens to John Montelius, October 29, 1838, in *Pennsylvania House Journal*, 1838–39, vol. 2, part 2, p. 188.

[17] *Harrisburg Chronicle*, October 31, 1838; *American Advertiser* (Philadelphia), December 3, 1838; testimony of Stevens in *Pennsylvania Senate Journal*, 1838–39, 2:799 ff.

and the chief clerk was a Democrat. After he had called the meeting to order, Secretary of State Burrowes stepped forward and placed the returns from the several counties, sealed up as he had received them, on the table. Breaking the seal, the clerk proceeded to call the roll by counties. When he came to the county of Philadelphia, a fellow Democrat stopped him, declared that the secretary had not forwarded all the legal returns, and handed him a paper which he claimed bore a correct summation of the vote. So both lists were read.

Stevens now rose and made a few remarks calling for "constitutional" procedure; he explained that until the House was organized the members had no choice but to consider as legal only the returns which the secretary had presented according to the requirements of law. The House could decide later who had the better claim to the contested seats. Keeping the floor, he moved to nominate tellers for electing a speaker, put the question himself, declared the motion carried, nominated tellers, put the vote, took down names, and announced the election of the nominees. In doing this he of course violated the usage of the House, for it was the duty of the clerk and assistant clerk to act as tellers.

Before Stevens had taken his seat, the Democrats began to vote for a speaker of their own. Out of this "orderly disorder" two speakers and two separately organized Houses emerged. The Whigs finished first, and Stevens then moved an adjournment to accommodate, as he said, "certain gentlemen" who seemed "desirous of performing some business" in the hall.[18]

His coup was bold, clever, "legal," but hardly statesmanlike. It was not the only way out nor the best, at least in the opinion of Governor Ritner's brother, who felt that neither group from the Philadelphia district, where fraud was rife on both sides, ought to be allowed to take their seats.[19] To Stevens, however, it was a contest for power and not for justice in the abstract. The experience he gained on this occasion he was to use a quarter of a century later as a leader of Congress when, after Appomattox, he

[18] *Pennsylvania House Journal*, 1838–39, vol. 2, part 2, pp. 114–130; *Senate Journal*, 1838–39, 2:805–806; *Pennsylvania Reporter* (Harrisburg), December 5, 6, 1838; *American Advertiser* (Philadelphia), December 5, 6, 1838.
[19] *Pennsylvania Senate Journal*, 1838–39, 2:968.

had to deal with representatives from the South claiming the right
to sit among their Northern peers. In many respects his strategy
of December 4, 1838, provided the pattern for his *coup d'état*
of December 4, 1865.

On the afternoon of the day when the House organized in two
parts the Senate was to meet and organize. Stevens planned to
attend. Just before three o'clock, the hour set for the meeting
of the Senate, he admitted to his room an excited caller who said
the Democrats were forming a mob and shouting that tomorrow
Thaddeus Stevens would "be no more"—that he would be "in the
bottom of the Susquehanna." He advised Stevens not to go out.
Undeterred, the representative from Adams County appeared in
the Senate chamber promptly at three o'clock, in time to join the
milling crowd and watch from the sidelines.

For a couple of hours he stood there, as the wrangling became
louder and more confused, until finally one of the Democratic
orators began to harangue the crowd in "an excited and exciting
strain." The Democrat appealed to his fellows whether they were
going to sit idly by and see "Burrowes, Stevens, & Co." rob them
of their rights. "The fury of the mob increased," Stevens later
testified, "and the crisis was apparently approaching." At last he
was convinced that his enemies were plotting for his life. Led by
Burrowes and accompanied by several others, he slipped out of
the chamber through a door behind the speaker's chair, crossed
an empty committee room, and eased himself down to the ground
through an open window in the rear of the capitol. It was now
dusk. The fugitives, keeping close to a back fence, scurried toward
town and disappeared in the gathering darkness.

Out the window with Stevens in his self-defenestration and
flight went his chances of remaining a power in Pennsylvania
politics. He left the Democrats in actual possession of the capitol,
and there on the following days the Democratic legislature, the
"Hopkins House," proceeded to carry on its business with every
pretense of regularity, one of its first actions being to discontinue
the building of the Gettysburg railroad. The Whig legislature,
the "Stevens rump," began to hold sessions of its own—in the
parlor of Wilson's Hotel. Which was *the* House of Representa-

tives? That question was left for the Senate, which had a Whig majority, to decide. A committee of Whig Senators visited the "rump" and advised the members that if they would stick together they might yet elect their United States senator and have the benefit of the patronage of the state.[20]

For several days Stevens dared not venture out of his hotel; for the populace of Harrisburg and the local officials sided with the Democrats. While mobs "howled and blasphemed" outside his window or drilled like little armies in the streets, he sent out letters appealing for "volunteers" from the public works. When they trooped into Harrisburg, a battle threatened between them and the local vigilantes. On Ritner's order the keeper of the state arsenal stationed a force of about twenty-five, including several canal men, inside the arsenal building to ward off the attack that was expected. At first the mob indeed threatened a siege but dispersed when the keeper promised not to allow anyone, on either side, to withdraw arms. This compromise disgusted Stevens, and from his headquarters he issued a statement of disapproval: "I should deem it disgraceful to treat with the rebels on any subject or do any act either now or hereafter on their demand." He was defiant, but he kept off the streets.

Even Wilson's Hotel became unsafe. When he passed the door of the barroom, he could hear the roisterers inside cursing him and threatening his life. Presently a "committee of vigilance" called on the hotelkeeper and warned him that "it was unlawful to have the legislature in more than one place," and that if he continued to harbor Stevens they could not be responsible for any damage his hotel property might suffer. So Wilson locked the parlor door against the Whig legislators and induced his unpopular guest to take a bed elsewhere for a time.[21]

Already Governor Ritner had appealed to President Van Buren to send federal troops to restore order, but Van Buren had refused to do so. Ritner then called out several companies of the state militia. "Come one and come all, with buckshot and ball,"

[20] *Harrisburg Chronicle,* December 9, 1838; *Pennsylvania Senate Journal,* 1838–39, 2:817 ff., 875–876, 964; *House Journal,* 1838–39, vol. 2, part 2, p. 185.
[21] *American Advertiser* (Philadelphia), December 7, 8, 10, 12, 1838; *Pennsylvania Senate Journal,* 1838–39, 2:821–822.

mimicked a rhymester—and thenceforth people referred to the events in Harrisburg as the "Buckshot War." Quickly the war attracted national interest, Whigs and Democrats everywhere took their appropriate stands, and United States Senator James Buchanan published a long letter in which he defended the course of his co-partisans at Harrisburg.

The soldiery restored the town to relative peace and quiet, and the members of the rump legislature resumed their sessions in Wilson's Hotel. But as the Senate continued to debate which of the two legislatures to recognize, deserters were, one by one, leaving the Stevens group for the Hopkins House. In vain did Stevens try to hold his bolting Antimasons in line by threatening to have them "broken down" in their respective districts. He was at Governor Ritner's house one day when a wavering member entered. The clubfooted leader greeted him: "Montelius, are you still alive?" "Yes," said Montelius. Stevens went on: "They have not killed me yet, and I will sooner die than give way." Then he muttered something to Ritner about men turning traitors.[22] He was not a man to whine, even when he was nearing his rope's end financially as well as politically. He had spent and bet thousands in the campaign and he was now without funds; but when he asked aid from his banker friend Lewis, he wrote with his usual quip: "I want the within note discounted. I must either borrow that amount or make large sacrifices on iron, which is now so dull of sale as to render it hard to get along. We have some $50,000 [worth of iron] on hand—and likely to keep it. If you can do it, I know you will—If not, why just say there is 'no help for the widow's son.' "[23]

There was some ground for hope in the resolution which the Senate passed when it got around to it—that the Hopkins House was "no House of Representatives legally constituted"—but the Senate did not follow it up by recognizing the Stevens rump. In-

[22] Samuel P. Bates, *Martial Deeds of Pennsylvania* (Philadelphia, 1875), 985; testimony of John Montelius, in *Pennsylvania House Journal*, 1838–39, vol. 2, part 2, p. 186; *American Advertiser* (Philadelphia), December 8, 14, 17, 30, 1838; *Carlisle Volunteer*, December 27, 1838.

[23] Stevens to William D. Lewis, December 9, 1838, in the William D. Lewis Papers, Library of Congress.

stead, they later reversed their decision. On Christmas Day, by the margin of a single vote, they recognized the Democratic legislature which was in actual possession of the representatives' hall. That night the Whig-Antimasonic senator from the district including Adams County died in his bed. No one knew the cause of his death, but rumor had it that he had died of "mortification at the course of the Senate." Mortified almost as deeply, William Mc-Pherson sent the news to his father: "Mob law has prevailed . . . . The vote of 5 men professing to act with us as a political party sanctioned the recognition of the Hopkins House. Now our friends are disgraced—so much so that many of them will go home—Mr. Stevens among that number. The subject is humiliating—our disgrace as a party is acknowledged."[24]

To Stevens the subject was humiliating indeed. After the Buckshot War he rapidly sank to the nadir of his lifetime in politics. He had gambled everything in a desperate attempt to keep himself and his party in power in Pennsylvania, to save his "tapeworm" railroad, to go to Washington as senator—and he had lost. A Democratic governor awaited inauguration and Democrats had control of the House. To this assembly he could not bring himself; he could not take his seat amid the self-satisfied grins of his victorious foes. So, as young McPherson had predicted, he left Harrisburg for home. He told McPherson he would not come back unless he greatly changed his mind. Before he went he issued an open letter to his constituents, justifying his part in the "war" and announcing that he would remain outside the legislature until the people showed their approval of his course.[25]

He arrived in Gettysburg under a cloud—which grew even darker. Troubles, he found, come not singly but in battalions. An unwed girl in the town had recently become a mother, and gossipers pointed to the clubfooted politician as the father of her child. He suspected but could not prove that his enemies were back of the story, for the girl's father had been a friend of his.

[24] *American Advertiser* (Philadelphia), December 15, 1838; *Pennsylvania Telegraph* (Harrisburg), December 25 ("extra"), 26, 1838; W. McPherson to J. B. McPherson, December 25, 1838, in the McPherson Papers.

[25] W. McPherson to J. B. McPherson, January 10, 1839, in the McPherson Papers.

Anyhow, with eager tongues his enemies speeded the tale on its rounds. When Stevens asserted, through the columns of his *Gettysburg Star,* that there existed no state legislature *de jure,* that the so-called House was a usurping body, Loco Focos discovered in the current gossip material for their retort. The *Star* took "the sage position " that Thaddeus Stevens was the "only legal House of Representives," observed the Democratic *York Gazette.* Then followed a satirical journal of this one-man House, with Stevens reporting—to himself—from each of several committees. From one of them, that on "vice and immorality," he reported "an act punishing as a crime . . . the corruption of youthful innocence, and rendering it a pentitentiary offence to steal into a neighbor's family under pretence of friendship and use the opportunities presented by his hospitality . . . for the base purpose of utterly destroying the fair name and happiness of his child and, viper-like, desolating the fireside at which he had been welcomed and warmed."[26]

After a few weeks of such journalistic bickering, in January, 1839, Stevens broke his resolve not to go back to Harrisburg. Indeed, he had no choice, for the Democrats in the legislature had summoned him to appear before a Senate committee investigating "the causes of the disturbance" during the previous month. He would have gone in any event, to take a hand in prosecuting several private suits arising out of damage done by the mob. More important, he hoped that his presence in Harrisburg might enable him to save the Gettysburg railroad from its foes.

"Stevens is here quite funny," William McPherson reported from the capital. "He went into the House today, took his seat, and looked on a while. Such turning around and staring has not been seen here for some time." He did not enter the legislature officially, as a member, for that would have been an admission of its legal existence. He did not think it necessary, anyhow. He told McPherson, the latter wrote, that "from what he could observe yesterday and from what has been said to him by different ones of the Loco Foco party that he could get an appropriation to your [*that is, Stevens' and J. B. McPherson's*] road without going

[26] Quoted in the *Pennsylvania Reporter* (Harrisburg), January 18, 1839.

into the House. He sees where the strings could be pulled." When
the strings failed to work, he had to make the disagreeable decision to resume his place in the legislature after all. Finally he
confessed that, with great reluctance, he had "determined to go
into that den of thieves—the 'Hopkins House.'" But when he
offered to qualify as a member, he found that it was more easily
said than done. In pursuance of a resolution of his old enemy,
McElwee, the House appointed a committee to ascertain whether
he had not forfeited his right to a seat! He refused to appear
before the committee and give them a chance to probe into his
private affairs. "I cannot agree," he said, "to admit the intellectual, moral, or habitual competency of Thomas B. McElwee,
his compeers, coadjutors, and followers to decide on a question
of decency and morals."[27]

From other quarters the evidence against Stevens appeared
rapidly enough. Day after day the members of a special Senate
committee probed into the activities of the "missionary" during
the previous summer, and got "all sorts of testimony." McPherson
complained: "A number of our contractors have turned traitor to
us .... The matter is not so much against the board [of canal
commissioners]—as Mr. Stevens."[28] Soon, to add to the scandal,
the father of the wronged girl in Gettysburg swore out a warrant
for Stevens' arrest on a charge of fornication and bastardy. On
May 24, 1839, Stevens had reached bottom when he wrote to
John B. McPherson, the one man in whom he could confide: "I
have this day been finally excluded from the House, and a new
election [has been] ordered on the 14th June." Explaining that
he was a victim of "persecution" in the morals suit, he went on
to unburden his soul in a long letter, in which he said in part:

I pretend to no prudish sanctity, but the pretence in the case referred to
is so perfectly false, that I shall shew beyond doubt that the girl was

[27] Alexander Harris, *A Review of the Political Conflict in America* ...
Comprising Also a Résumé of the Career of Thaddeus Stevens (New York,
1876), 60–61, 63; W. McPherson to J. B. McPherson, January 23, February 9,
1839, and Stevens to Joseph Wallace, May 4, 1839, in the McPherson Papers.
[28] W. McPherson to J. B. McPherson, January 10, 1839, in the McPherson
Papers.

courted—and worse than merely courted, by a man who turned out to be married at the time—and that too just nine months before the birth of the child. So far from being a seducer, I vow to God I have never yet learned (except by description) the meaning of maidenhead! Nevertheless I wish this cursed matter were ended. But I shall never make advances. I shall carry on the war in the same spirit in which it has been begun, and regret it more for the sake of the weak girl—the instrument of her father's cupidity—than for my own.[29]

Here Stevens, now forty-seven, tacitly admitted that he was a bachelor only in a legal sense: all he denied was that he was guilty as accused. He was "not an immoral man," a person who knew him well said afterward. "In one respect a man of his ardent temperament could scarcely fail to err—that he was the cold-blooded betrayer of female innocence, the heartless libertine, the hoary debauchee which his enemies in times of great political excitement represented him to be, is a most malicious lie." For the source of this particular lie, Stevens was finally able to point an accusing finger so directly at the chief of his political enemies, McElwee, that eventually the charges fell to the ground. The father of the girl did not press the case, and Stevens was never tried.

Outwardly, vexed though he was within, he maintained his usual bold front. After his rejection from the House he published a defiant address to his fellow citizens of Adams County. "I present myself to you as a candidate to fill that vacancy which was created to wound my and your feelings. I do not wait to receive a party nomination from my friends." The people assuaged his, and their, feelings by re-electing him on June 14. The victory was purely symbolic, for two weeks later the House adjourned.[30]

After the adjournment William McPherson composed another of his news reports, this one for his mother: "Mr. Stevens will be home next week to electioneer. His enemies have taken the

[29] Stevens to J. B. McPherson, May 24, 1839, in the Thaddeus Stevens Papers, Library of Congress.
[30] Hood, "Thaddeus Stevens," in Harris, *Biographical History of Lancaster County*, 593; Harris, *A Review of the Political Conflict*, 62. For what is presumably a veiled reference to Stevens' exposure of McElwee, see the *Bedford* [Pennsylvania] *Inquirer*, August 1, 1845.

very course which is about to make him very conspicuous over the Union. He is a most unrighteously persecuted man."[31] Thaddeus Stevens was indeed to be some day "very conspicuous over the Union"—but not so soon.

[31] W. McPherson to Mrs. J. B. McPherson, June 31, 1839, in the McPherson Papers.

V. Ten Years of Exile

S LAVERY and mobocracy rules the country; Prostrate the Monster, cry aloud and spare not."[1] Such was the admonition which, several months after the Buckshot War, Thad Stevens read in a letter from an old party friend. The Monster—the Democratic party—had become truly a frightening two-bodied beast, a combination of the Southern aristocracy of "slavery" with the Loco Foco agrarian "mobocracy" of the North. With one claw upon the capitol in Washington and another upon the state-house in Harrisburg, the beast effectively barred the way to Stevens' advancement in either place. His mission had perforce to become that of a dragon-slayer who should endeavor to "prostrate" the creature by cleaving it into its component halves.

Yet the pursuit of politics was more a humdrum, day-after-day, year-after-year business than dragon-slaying. Every twelfth month local officials to elect, every two years congressmen, every three a governor, every four a president, every six a senator—however much the volume or the pitch might change, here was the steady tempo underlying the career of Stevens. During the decade from 1839 to 1849 this regular activity was to rise and fall and rise again in intensity and interest, but it was to yield little to Stevens in power, place, or fame. Defeat he had known, and disappointment he was to experience over and over again before he was to become "conspicuous" and "figure in the history of the Union."

One of the bitterest disappointments of his life followed the presidential election of 1840. After William Henry Harrison's victory Stevens confidently expected—indeed, he had been promised—a position in the cabinet of the president-elect.[2] This

---

[1] E. F. Pennypacker to Stevens, November 5, 1839, in the Society Collection, Historical Society of Pennsylvania, Philadelphia.

[2] Alexander K. McClure, *Abraham Lincoln and Men of War-Times* (Philadelphia, 1892), 283; Alexander H. Hood, "Thaddeus Stevens," in Alexander

would have been a fitting reward for his services to Harrison and the Whigs, both at the nominating convention and during the campaign.

At the convention, in December, 1839, he had managed by devious means to eliminate one of Harrison's leading rivals, Winfield Scott.[3] So important (or, perhaps, merely so vulnerable) was he in the ensuing campaign that often Democrats attacked his name more viciously than the name of the candidate himself. Their national organ, the Washington *Globe,* repeatedly charged: "The money power is at work in the election wherever it can find such creatures as Thadeus [*sic*] Stevens." Senator James Buchanan, dignified and proper but not averse to hinting at old scandals, reminded Pennsylvanians of the use of the public works "under the control of a gentleman with whom, or whose character, we are all acquainted—I refer to Thaddeus Stevens." When Stevens organized a "Tippecanoe Club" in Gettysburg, he was accused of playing "high priest" and offering the sacrament to local Whigs. Unabashed, he gave his whole attention to the task of spreading light for Harrison in the "dark regions" of Pennsylvania and also in New York.[4]

From November of 1840 to the following March the question of Harrison's cabinet hung in the air. The Whig leaders, Daniel

Harris, ed., *A Biographical History of Lancaster County* (Lancaster, 1872), 582; *Pennsylvania Telegraph* (Harrisburg), January 20, 30, February 3, 6, 1841.

[3] To Francis Granger of New York, Scott had written a letter designed to catch the antislavery vote of that state. Stevens took the letter and dropped it on the floor at the headquarters of the Virginia delegation of Whigs, who previously had held the balance of power in the convention in favor of Scott. Alexander K. McClure, *Our Presidents and How We Make Them* (New York, 1900), 67–68. At the time of the convention Stevens' hotel room was a center at which Whig strategists, among them the enthusiastic young journalist Horace Greeley, gathered to lay their earliest plans for the rip-roaring campaign of 1840. Greeley to Stevens, December 10, 1839, in the Thaddeus Stevens Papers, Library of Congress.

[4] Washington *Globe,* September 24, October 28, 1840; John Bassett Moore, ed., *The Works of James Buchanan, Comprising His Speeches, State Papers, and Private Correspondence* (12 vols., Philadelphia and London, 1908–11), 4:291; Henry R. Mueller, *The Whig Party in Pennsylvania (Columbia University Studies in History, Economics, and Public Law,* no. 230, New York, 1902), 73–74.

Webster and Henry Clay, were expected as a matter of course
to win the most desirable positions—but what of the rest? "No one
will be appointed," predicted the Washington *Globe,* "who is
not a *friend* to Mr. Clay" and "a *friend* to Biddle's Bank." On
the latter point Stevens could qualify, but if the newspaper was
right about the former, he had little chance. Moreover, his efforts
to secure the endorsement of the Pennsylvania legislature were
without success. And so, as one of a record-breaking throng of
job-seekers, he went in person to Washington, where on New
Year's Day of 1841 John Quincy Adams noted that there was
"much said of his claims to notice and distinction from General
Harrison and his friends." "No doubt," observed the *Globe* shortly
before inauguration day, "he has made the worthy incumbents
feel that they are much the dependents of himself and his confederates." But when, a few weeks later, Harrison's appointments
were made known, the prophets were surprised and Stevens himself was shocked. He had to go back, empty-handed, to Gettysburg.[5]

A sense of having been cheated thereafter embittered him—not
so much against Harrison, who in any case died soon after entering the White House, as against Webster, who he felt had not
sincerely urged his appointment, and against Clay, who he was
sure had adamantly opposed it. His resentment against these two
leaders of Whigdom made him more than ever a factionalist, less
and less a true and regular Whig. The wound was certainly not
salved by the fact that, after his return to Gettysburg, he had to
beg favors in the disposal of political jobs from the new postmaster
general, Francis Granger, who had the position in the cabinet
he himself had coveted, and the control of patronage he thought
should have been his own.[6] "You have kept out of sight since the

[5] Washington *Globe,* December 17, 1840; March 3, April 13, 1841; *United
States Gazette* (Philadelphia), January 23, 1841; Charles F. Adams, ed.,
Memoirs of John Quincy Adams (12 vols., Philadelphia, 1874–77), 10:388;
McClure, *Lincoln and Men of War-Times,* 283.

[6] Soon after Granger's appointment Stevens wrote to the postmaster general
from Gettysburg: "There is urgent necessity for the appointment of a Post
Master for this place. The present one is deranged, and the office is managed
by a drunken son." Again: "I would beg leave to suggest whether the continuing of Mr. Sturgeon in office is not calculated to injure us, and cool the

memorable campaign of '38," he now wrote to his fellow "missionary" of two years before. "Perhaps, in these days of treachery,
quietude is the wiser part."[7]

But it was simply not in him to remain quiet for long. He
planned to groom a likely winner for the next election and attach
himself so securely to the candidate that disillusionment could
not come again. The man he selected was the soldier Winfield
Scott—the same man who, as a result of Stevens' stratagem, had
failed before to gain the nomination from the Whigs! In a series
of letters the president-maker outlined to Scott the passive role he
was to play. Scott was willing. "I see many evidences of your power
in many and important quarters," he replied to Stevens, and he
promised that he would "always be found sufficiently docile and
practicable." In the fall of 1841 Stevens began to build the necessary political organization by making himself chairman of a
"Scott State Central Committee." In the first flush of his enthusiasm he was confident that, though the friends of Clay might
"throw cold water on the movement" for a while—"until we whip
them in"—they could not hold out for long.[8]

Issues for the coming campaign he found in slavery and the
tariff. Also, the banking issue was not yet entirely dead; for
although Nicholas Biddle's institution had failed, the Democrats
were hounding Biddle amid the ruins of his Bank. To his defense came Stevens in the Pennsylvania Hall of Representatives,
where, in 1842, he was serving his sixth and final term. The orator
from Adams County, a newspaperman wrote, "made one of the

ardor of our friends, as his father is known to be among the bitterest of our
enemies." Stevens to Granger, April 28, July 12, 1841, in the Papers of Francis
and Gideon Granger, Library of Congress.

[7] Stevens to E. F. Pennypacker, July 13, 1842, in the Society Collection,
Historical Society of Pennsylvania.

[8] Stevens to Scott, October 20, 1841; Scott to Stevens, November 4, 13, 21,
1841, and August 2, 1842, in the Stevens Papers. "I wish you to write a short
biography of yourself," Stevens advised Scott in his letter of October 20, 1841,
"and to have it completed at the earliest possible moment. I will copy the
whole of it and burn your manuscript, unseen by any other eye.... Let me
suggest that a minute, vivid description of the battles and skirmishes should
be given—giving the ardor of battle...placing yourself in the position of
danger you actually assumed." This would have "the greatest charm for the
people."

most powerful efforts ever made by himself or any other gentleman in these halls, during which the galleries . . . , crowded in anticipation of his speech, were as silent as sleep." Equally eloquent was Stevens in pleading for greater protection for American industry. Clay's compromise tariff of 1833 had provided for a progressive lowering of duties until they should reach the low set for 1842. Meanwhile the Panic of '37 had come and a business depression had followed. Prosperity, said Stevens, had been "destroyed by the destruction of the tariff." Related to protectionism, in the sense that it was an attack directly or indirectly upon the South, was the antislavery agitation of the time. This took a new turn when, in 1842, the Supreme Court ruled that states need not aid in enforcing the federal fugitive-slave law. In many of the Northern states friends of the slave now demanded repeal of the enforcement acts, and in Pennsylvania Stevens made himself the voice of such demands. Although he failed to help the runaway blacks, he succeeded perhaps in rallying some of the advocates of "personal liberty" beneath the banner of Scott.[9]

He was not prepared to make the slavery question the sole plank of his platform. On such an unqualified program of opposition to the extension of slavery a Liberty party had already been formed, but he had ignored it in the campaign of 1840. Now, in the spring of 1842, he received a call to join it. From Ohio his old acquaintance Jonathan Blanchard wrote to introduce Salmon P. Chase, a man "of property and extensive connexions" in Cincinnati and a leader of the Liberty party in the West. "Cannot you take ground with us?" begged Chase in a letter to Stevens. "Can you not bring the old Anti-Masonic party of Pennsylvania on to the Liberty Platform?" Stevens hesitated for a few weeks, then replied with a polite refusal. The remembrance of former treachery, he intimated, did tempt him to desert the party of the Whigs: "I am aware how often we have been cheated by the men of other parties—how few of them prove faithful after being elected." Yet he doubted whether a third party could even elect a president; and Winfield Scott was sound on both antislavery

[9] *United States Gazette* (Philadelphia), January 24, February 19, March 10, 1842; *Pennsylvania House Journal*, 1842, 1:341, 1014–1016, 1055.

and the tariff, had a good chance of being elected with the backing of the Whig organization, and, once in office, would surely not "deceive."[10]

In the midst of his Scott-for-President movement, during the summer of 1842, Stevens decided to leave Gettysburg and take up his residence in the city of Lancaster, some sixty miles away. For this decision there were several reasons, but one of them, the fact that Lancaster promised more in the long run for his political career, was sufficient in itself. This greater promise was not apparent at first. The *Lancaster Intelligencer* noted, under the heading "Singular Co-incidences," that Stevens' departure from Adams County was celebrated by a Whig defeat at the polls, and his arrival in Lancaster County was "duly honored" by a Democratic victory in his new home. His fellow Whigs in Lancaster, for their part, disliked the "easy and graceful manner" in which he began at once to flourish "the whip."[11]

Undismayed by the inhospitable reception Lancaster politicians gave him, Stevens remained confident that the next election would force the "Clay men" into line. "They cannot deny that *that* is a test of their power," he wrote Scott. "They of course will be annihilated, everywhere. . . . Our true course seems to be to remain on the turf and await events."[12] Events soon dispelled his optimistic hope of dictating to the Lancaster Whigs. In the local campaign of 1843 they, together with the Antimasons, kept him at a distance. He retaliated with a ticket of his own, not in the hope of winning but of throwing the election to the Democrats. In this, too, he failed.[13] He was powerless now to keep the party from nominating Clay at the national convention of 1844. His well-laid schemes had a way of going wrong, and once more they had gone awry!

Still smarting from past betrayal, he prayed, in 1844, that Clay,

[10] Chase to Stevens, April 8, 1842; Blanchard to Stevens, April 9, 1842; Stevens to Blanchard, May 24, 1842, in the Stevens Papers.

[11] *Lancaster Intelligencer,* October 18, 25, November 1, 29, 1842.

[12] Stevens to Scott, February 15, 1843, in the Stevens Papers.

[13] Mueller, *Whig Party in Pennsylvania,* 89–90; Alexander Harris, *The Political Conflict in America . . . Comprising Also a Résumé of the Career of Thaddeus Stevens* (New York, 1876), 92–93.

the candidate of his own party, would be humbled by defeat. While touring Vermont during the summer before the election he hinted in public speeches that the Whig nominee, opposed as he was by the formidable James K. Polk, would probably lose.[14] Secretly he urged antislavery Whigs in New England to throw their support to James G. Birney, candidate of the Liberty party, his object being to take votes away from Clay.[15] Notwithstanding, after Stevens returned to Lancaster in the fall, he suddenly began to stump in Clay's behalf! "This is indeed rich," a Democratic editor exclaimed. "Thaddeus Stevens—who has abused Henry Clay with all the violence and bitterness which characterize him! —who has, within the last three months, denounced him in the public streets!—who, last fall, declared that he would 'never vote for Clay,' and that nobody but a tadpole would do so!"[16] The explanation of this remarkable about-face was very simple. Needing every possible vote in "doubtful" Pennsylvania, Clay's managers had sent word to Stevens that, should their man win, they would make "atonement" for "past wrong."[17] Defeated as he was in November, Clay did not have an opportunity to prove his word, nor Stevens an opportunity to retrieve what previous "treachery" had taken from him.

Four years must elapse before the next presidential election. Meanwhile Stevens the lawyer had already found it necessary to come to the rescue of Stevens the politician and ironmaster in order to save himself from crushing debt. At the time when he left Gettysburg for Lancaster, in 1842, he was very nearly in danger of being "sold out by the sheriff," so great had been his losses in politics and so small the returns from his Caledonia Iron Works. Yet he refused to take advantage of existing bankruptcy laws and swore he would pay every last farthing that he owed. This was one reason for his removal from the Adams County seat to the more lucrative Lancaster bar. On a snowy

[14] *Vermont Patriot* (Montpelier), July 13, 1844; *Lancaster Intelligencer,* August 6, 1844; *Bedford* (Pennsylvania) *Inquirer,* August 16, 1844.

[15] Harris, *A Review of the Political Conflict,* 503n.

[16] *Lancaster Intelligencer,* October 29, 1844.

[17] Hood, "Thaddeus Stevens," in Harris, *Biographical History of Lancaster County,* 582–583.

day during his first winter in Lancaster a client needed him to plead a case at Columbia, ten miles away. That day Stevens wrote from his home: "I started early this morning, by Sleigh, in hopes to reach you before 10 o'clock A.M. at which time you say the suit is to begin—Between this place and Columbia we broke down, and I have just got back, *on foot,* in time to write this letter. I would come by the cars, but I should reach you too late to be of any service."[18] Old Thad Stevens trudging lamely and reluctantly back through the snowdrifts—that picture perhaps symbolizes his vow to make good his debts.

Persistence and hard work brought their reward and after a few years in Lancaster he stood near the head of the local bar. His earnings increased until they ranged from twelve to fifteen thousand dollars a year. This would be a considerable salary at any time, of course, but it was especially large in a period when day laborers, even if they had the good luck to be steadily employed, could make no more than three or four hundred dollars a year. Yet his income, fabulous though it would have seemed to one of his own employees at Caledonia, was not sufficient to meet his needs. He had to make interest payments on obligations that at one time reached a total of nearly a quarter of a million dollars.[19] To meet these demands he began to turn into cash much of the real and personal property which he had accumulated during his more prosperous years in Gettysburg. In the eighteen-forties he sold, one after another, tracts of woodland, town lots, houses, farms. In 1841 he deeded to the trustees of Pennsylvania College, for $646, a parcel of land in Gettysburg "(being the same whereon the College Edifice and buildings stand)," and later he sold to the college a few additional acres. (Previously the campus had belonged to him!) He also disposed of some of the securities he owned, including a couple of thousand dollars worth of Erie Railroad stock.[20]

[18] Stevens to E. Chapin, March 20, 1843, manuscript in the possession of T. Fred. Woodley, Bangor, Pennsylvania.

[19] Harris, *A Review of the Political Conflict,* 87; obituary notice of Stevens in the *Philadelphia Press,* August 12, 1868.

[20] Records of Deeds, especially vol. R, p. 60, in the Adams County Courthouse, at Gettysburg; Dudley Selden [Stevens' broker] to Stevens, September 26 and November 12, 1845, in the Stevens Papers.

This process of liquidation he was forced to continue even after the business of the nation began to recover from its long slump. Prosperity seemed not to reach into South Mountain to touch the Caledonia Iron Works. No profits were forthcoming to Stevens, and at times he thought of selling out his share in the business. So completely had he left the management to his partner, James D. Paxton, that he knew little or nothing of the true state of affairs. When he finally examined the company's books, he found that, far from making a profit, Paxton had actually run deeply into the red. Stevens refused to declare the business bankrupt. He bought out Paxton for twenty thousand dollars in the spring of 1848 and promised his creditors that he would pay all the obligations of the partnership in addition to his personal debts.[21]

From his preoccupation with making money and paying bills Stevens turned aside in the summer of 1846 long enough to give

[21] Records of Deeds, vol. R, p. 45, in the Adams County Courthouse. On Stevens' determination to pay his debts, see the sketch of Stevens by Jonathan Blanchard in the latter's *Christian Cynosure* (Chicago), April 5, 1883. Contemporary evidence of Stevens' attitude is in a letter he wrote to one of his creditors:

"Having lately undertaken to look into the affairs of J. D. Paxton & Co. at Caledonia Furnace I find you are a creditor to the amount of upwards of $3,000 with a judgment. But you are in a second class of judgments a previous set of judgments having been given where indorsers were concerned. The class before yours is, I regret to say about or over $40,000 forty thousand dollars. Then comes yours and many others of equal date being in all about $70,000 debt. I had hoped when time was given, that this large sum would have been much reduced by this time—but it is not. What I write you for is to say that I am anxious to see you paid. But it is apparent that when the real estate comes to be sold (as it must be next year) it will not pay off the first class of judgments so as to reach yours. Now all the way which I see to pay you, is out of the proceeds of the furnace before it is sold. . . .

"Others in the same class with you have proposed to take pig iron for the amount of their judgment at the rate of $35 per ton at the furnace. It is first rate metal—the price higher than the market price now, but not as high as it was last fall. I do not wish to agree with all who ask thus to be paid untill I hear from you. I write to say if you will take the amount of your judg't in pig iron at that rate I will direct my manager to give you 50 tons this blast and the balance next year while we still have control of the property. Please answer me soon as other creditors are waiting for answers."

This letter, written to Jacob Barritz on August 2, 1848, is in the Pennsylvania State Library at Harrisburg. As it happened, Stevens was not to sell the ironworks.

some attention to the issues of national politics. The war with
Mexico—which had resulted from the annexation of Texas and
President Polk's schemes for further Mexican lands—was in full
swing. It was to be expected that Stevens would object to his
country's waging a war "just to lug new slave states in," as Lowell's
Biglow Papers had it. His opposition was tempered, however, by
the news that came from the front; for his erstwhile protégé Winfield Scott was winning publicity and popularity as a result of his
exploits in Mexico. The general might yet be made president!

So in July of 1846 Stevens called a "Tariff and Scott" meeting
in the Lancaster courthouse. "For some years past," he told the
gathering, "I have withdrawn from politics; resolved that no ordinary occasion should induce me again to enter its stormy arena."
But the present occasion was no ordinary one, what with the
slaveholders' war and the impending destruction of the tariff
(by the Walker bill). Despite the opposition of the "managers" of
the Whig party, this was the time to declare for the nomination
of Scott. There was in all the land no statesman more devoted
than he to the principle of a high protective tariff; none more
firmly set against the blandishments of "our Southern friends—
perhaps I ought to call them our Southern Masters—and their
pale satellites of the North." As for those who impugned the general's heroism on the field of battle—they were mere "silken
knights," "perfumed critics," "smelling-bottle gentry," "lady's
male waiting-maids."[22]

But for all Old Thad's enthusiasm, the revived Scott-for-
President movement soon petered out. As it happened, the
Whigs boasted not one but two heroes of the Mexican War; and
the "managers" of the party preferred the more popular general,
Zachary Taylor, for the nomination in 1848. Finally Stevens him-
self boarded the Taylor bandwagon, after it had begun to roll.[23]

The war with Mexico, though it thwarted his ambitions in
respect to Scott, brought on a crisis that was to offer new possibilities for Stevens' career. Even before the peace the prospective

[22] *Bedford Inquirer,* July 10, 1846.
[23] Stevens spoke at a Fourth of July rally of the Lancaster "friends of Taylor" in 1848. *Lancaster Examiner,* July 5, 1848.

spoils of victory, the territories to be acquired from Mexico, were beginning to cause discord among Democrats as well as among Whigs. There were Northerners in the party of Polk who regretted that the president had pressed their claim to the Oregon country with much less vigor than the claim of Southerners to new lands in the Southwest. "Fifty-four forty or fight!" had been the campaign cry of the Northern Democracy, and later many of them were indeed ready to "fight"—against their party brethren in the South. In Congress their chagrin found expression in the famous resolution of David Wilmot, a Democrat from Pennsylvania, to keep slavery out of any territory won as a result of the war. Renewed time and again in one form or another, the Wilmot Proviso was used as a wedge with which to rend the Democracy farther and farther apart. Here at last was a weapon ready-made with which Stevens might cleave the "Monster" of "slavery and mobocracy" that ruled the land. Accordingly, he determined to run for Congress in 1848.

In running for Congress his first task, not an easy one, was to secure the nomination from the Lancaster Whigs. These were divided into three factions—the largest being the regulars or "Silver Greys"; next, Stevens' own group, mostly Antimasons who, like him, had turned to antislavery, and as self-proclaimed friends of the Negro were dubbed "Woolly Heads"; finally, the "Native Americans," who sought to capitalize upon the antiforeigner sentiment that developed as Catholic Irishmen, driven by the famines of the forties from their Emerald Isle, crowded into the cities of the Eastern seaboard. Stevens faced the problem of detaching the Natives and, if possible, some of the regular Whigs. He induced a friend of his, one of the Silver Greys, to present his name for candidacy, somewhat irregularly, at a Taylor rally in August, 1848. The county convention was only a few days away, delegates had already been chosen, and a majority of them were pledged to Abraham Herr Smith, the nominee of the Silver Greys. At the convention, nevertheless, enough of the delegates violated their instructions to give the nomination, after a last-minute deal with the Natives, to Stevens. Nonplussed leaders of the old guard charged at once that his victory had been "bought."[24]

Nomination to Congress was tantamount to election in the Whiggish Lancaster district, yet Stevens was not satisfied. In a few months the Pennsylvania legislature would elect a new United States senator. With that in mind he extended his electioneering beyond Lancaster County to other parts of the state. After the Whig successes in October and November the Lancaster organization, which now had little choice but to support him for the senatorship, presented his claims. The official organ of the local Whigs announced that Stevens was "deeply and personally interested in the great Pennsylvania question of the contest—the re-establishment of the Tariff of 1842. He labored in the campaign with a zeal and activity which strained the powers of his strong physical constitution, and it is not too much to say, that he contributed to the expenses of the contest more liberally than any other individual in the State."[25] Deeply and personally interested as he was, Stevens the politician spent money freely at the very time that Stevens the ironmaster was promising his creditors to see them paid! However, with little strength outside his own county, he had to be content with going to Washington not as a senator from Pennsylvania but as a mere representative from the Lancaster district. The Democrats of the district gave him a send-off:

The conviction that this county . . . should be represented in Congress by one capable of a more expanded effort of intellect than the drawling out of a sleepy "Aye" or "No," has forced upon the boards one who for

[24] Harris, *A Review of the Political Conflict*, 968; *Lancaster Examiner*, August 9, 1848; *Lancaster Intelligencer*, August 29, 1848.

[25] *Lancaster Examiner*, December 20, 1848. Stevens had indeed "strained the powers" of his physical constitution, to the point where he had to beg off from some of his speaking engagements. Toward the end of the campaign he had written: "My throat is so inflamed this morning that I am advised that it would be dangerous for me to attempt to make a speech. My physician says that it is not a cold but likely to be bronchitis if I do not suspend public speaking. . . . Addressing several meetings last week in the open air in Adams County has greatly aggravated the difficulty." Stevens to W. Townsend, September 25, 1848, manuscript in the possession of T. Fred Woodley, Bangor, Pennsylvania.

years had been banished into political exile, and between whom and
the party . . . there is little genuine affinity. Mr. Stevens has never . . .
belonged to that fraternity of frail politicians. . . . He has frequently
exercised himself in . . . "whipping in" this tractable party. . . . Whilst
that infatuation lasted, Mr. Stevens was an Anti-Mason, but when the
ghost of William Morgan had fulfilled its purposes . . . he turned *Native;*
. . . to whom he is indebted for this triumph over the "established
church" of Whiggery.

We have ascribed the nomination of Mr. Stevens to the homage
awarded to commanding intellect, but . . . yet more potent reasons exist
at the bottom. *He is the sworn foe of the South*—avowedly selected as a
champion able and willing to "worry" the representatives from beyond
Mason and Dixon's line. He goes into Congress the predetermined agitator of sectional jealousies and divisions. . . . His mission is to be one of
Strife, of Division, and of Hatred, and surely there is no one so well
qualified to fulfill it.[26]

[26] *Lancaster Intelligencer,* August 29, 1848.

VI. A Mission of Strife

THERE was no doubt that Thaddeus Stevens had become qualified as an agitator of ill-feeling when, in December, 1849, he joined a Congress hopelessly torn by sectional discord. Yet the role he was to play during his trial period as a congressman, from 1849 to 1853, was so small as to indicate that he had not yet definitely returned from his political "exile." At the outset, it is true, he received some mention for speaker of the House.[1] But after three weeks of balloting the Southern Whigs, rather than see an antislavery Whig as speaker, threw the election to a Southern Democrat, Howell Cobb. Cobb filled the congressional committees with Southerners and "doughfaces," and Stevens had to take a back seat. In the ensuing debates on the Compromise of 1850 he was to take only an insignificant part. And as the sectional crisis passed and the public at large accepted the way of compromise, politicians who lived upon crises were all to be in temporary oblivion—and Stevens was certainly one of this agitator type.

The issue dividing the Thirty-first Congress, in which he was serving his apprenticeship, was the one bequeathed by the Mexican War: how to deal with the territories acquired in the Treaty of Guadalupe-Hidalgo. At one extreme were Southerners like John C. Calhoun and Jefferson Davis who claimed the right to carry the seeds of slavery into the farthest corners of the American domain. At the other extreme were Northerners like Stevens who asserted that Congress ought to exclude slavery from all the unorganized territories of the West. In between were

[1] On the thirty-ninth ballot Stevens received four votes—one of them a tribute to the "savior" of Pennsylvania's schools from Horace Mann, the famous educator, who at this time was a representative from Massachusetts. On subsequent ballots Stevens' support rose as high as twenty-seven votes. *Congressional Globe*, 31 Congress, 1 session (1849–50), 31, 37.

moderates who, with James Buchanan, proposed that the institution be allowed below but not above the latitude 36° 30′ (the "Missouri Compromise line") or who, with Lewis Cass, suggested "squatter sovereignty," that is, giving the settlers themselves the power to decide. The question involved far more than mere spinning of constitutional theory; in its answer lay the future disposition of political power in the United States. As yet the Southerners ruled, but the census returns were telling against their section. With its greater numbers the North, if unified, could legislate tariffs destroying the profits of slavery, or even abolition acts destroying slavery itself. Rather than see these things happen, Davis and Calhoun and others were ready for secession. The terror which they dreaded, a solid antislavery North devoted to protectionism, was precisely the object that Stevens had set himself to achieve.

On February 20, 1850, he spoke out in his maiden speech in the House. Abolitionism he disavowed, conceding that the Constitution gave Congress no power over slavery within the states; yet he condemned the institution for its calamitous effects upon both the morals and the economy of the South. Virginia, in particular, had been reduced to the point where she was "only fit to be the breeder, not the employer of slaves." "Instead of seeking for the best breed of cattle and horses to feed on her hills and valleys, and fertilize the land, the sons of that great state must devote their time to selecting and grooming the most lusty sires and the most fruitful wenches, to supply the slave barracoons of the South!" Yet the rub lay elsewhere though Stevens did not put it exactly that way: "the South has always furnished officers for our armies; Presidents for the Republic; most of the foreign ambassadors; heads of departments; chiefs of bureaus; and sometimes, in her proud humility, has consented that the younger sons of her dilapidated houses should monopolize the places of clerks and messengers to the Government." He warned Southerners and their "doughface" allies that, though they had "more than once frightened the tame North," they would not forever "monopolize" the power and the jobs.[2]

[2] *Ibid.*, 141–142.

It was a vigorous speech, but unoriginal in its conception, and it aroused no considerable stir. True, the antislavery journals of the country gave it a good deal of space, but Washington papers gave it little, so little indeed that one antislavery editor had to write to Stevens for a copy of the text. "I have been expecting you to speak out—as I knew you could and would when the proper time came," wrote the editor; "we shall give you all the space we can."[3] But to others, even some abolitionists, the speech seemed weak and of little account. One of Stevens' hearers wrote to Charles Sumner:

> I spoke to you, perhaps you thought extravagantly, of Mr. Stevens' talents and eloquence. He has made his speech since, and I confess myself greatly disappointed. I expected something else and something better from him. I want to say to you that Thaddeus Stevens has not kept to my apprehension the promise of his earlier life. He has made an abolition speech, he has put its common places well, but not better than it is done by somebody or other every month in the year somewhere in the Union. Even his verbal eloquence is not at all remarkable. I do not retract the opinion formed of him 15 years ago. He deserved it then if he does not now.[4]

On June 20 Stevens made a second address on the same general theme, and it passed with a similar lack of notice, except among Democrats in his district, who were enough aroused to denounce it as "treasonable and revolutionary," another "infamous speech."[5]

Meanwhile Henry Clay had introduced in the Senate his complex of compromises, which he hoped would settle the entire sectional conflict once and for all. What he proposed, in brief, was to admit California as a free state, give Utah and New Mexico territorial governments without forbidding slavery there, prohibit

[3] Morton McMichael to Stevens, February 21, 1850, in the Thaddeus Stevens Papers, Library of Congress. McMichael was editor of the Philadelphia *North American*. Another antislavery paper, the Washington *National Era*, spread the speech over the entire front page of its issue for March 7, 1850. It must be remembered, of course, that at that time the inside pages, rather than the first page, were reserved for the most important news.

[4] William Elder to Sumner, March 4, 1850, in the Charles Sumner MSS., Harvard College Library. Scattered sentences, which do not alter the meaning, have been omitted from this quotation.

[5] *Lancaster Intelligencer*, quoted in the *Lancasterian* (Lancaster), March 20, 1850.

the slave trade (but not slavery) in the District of Columbia, and provide a drastic federal fugitive-slave law. Congress had spent months debating these measures, Seward had given his "higher law" speech, Webster his "Seventh of March" address, and Calhoun his uncompromising valedictory, and still the debate continued. In September, after the fortuitous death of President Taylor, the last of the Clay measures was enacted into law. Calhoun had not survived the summer to repeat his warning that the end of the Union would be the result; but his antithesis, Stevens, was alive to foretell the same gloomy outcome. In the House he said of one of the compromise bills: "It will become the fruitful mother of future rebellion, disunion and civil war, and the final ruin of the Republic." Such was the blindness, such "the timidity, not to say the cowardice, of the North."[6]

During the controversy Stevens had been busy with a politician's chores. Against Pennsylvania's Senator James Cooper, who held the office he himself had desired, he had been carrying on an intrigue for the control of federal patronage in the state. "The only way is to take no notice of him [Cooper]," Stevens advised a job-seeker, "but break down his power by telling the other members of the Senate . . . what he is."[7] Alive to the sources of personal "power," Stevens gave some attention to estimating the effects of the Compromise upon his own fortunes and upon national politics. The outlook was not favorable so far as the Pennsylvania congressional elections in October were concerned. "You are right," he confided to an old henchman, "—the North will yield and the South triumph—Penna. will furnish seven Locos to aid them. I think, no Whigs—."[8]

During his campaign for re-election to Congress in 1850, Stevens continued to "keep alive the flames of discontent and dis-

[6] *Congressional Globe,* 31 Congress, 1 session (1849–50), 1106–1109. The bill in question was that to indemnify the state of Texas for agreeing to a settlement of the boundary dispute in favor of the territory of New Mexico.

[7] Stevens to W. D. Lewis, December 14, 16, 1849, in the William D. Lewis Papers, Library of Congress. Cooper had been a bitter factional foe of Stevens from the latter's early years as an Antimason in Gettysburg. Stevens to W. D. Lewis, March 23, 1851, in the Lewis Papers.

[8] Stevens to E. F. Pennypacker, September 13, 1850, in the Society Collection, Historical Society of Pennsylvania, Philadelphia.

union," but his more cautious followers played down the slavery issue and hailed him as "the peculiar champion of the coal and iron interests." Fearing that he would be "struck" in parts of Lancaster county, some of his adherents, in order to keep him up to the rest of the ticket, resorted to the expedient of "striking" the whole Whig ballot except his name. Even so, though he was sent back to Congress, he ran behind the more conservative Whigs on the local ticket and received considerably fewer votes than in 1848.[9] Thus was he rebuked for his anti-Compromise stand in the House.

As if this were not a sufficiently discouraging sign of the times, he now had other reasons for thinking of calling a temporary halt to his political career. A few days after his re-election to Congress in October, 1850, he confided to his friend J. B. McPherson, of the Bank of Gettysburg:

I have been greatly disappointed at the operation of my iron works this season. Bad as the times are I had expected them to realize at least $5,000, and still think they should have done it—Instead of that I have paid out of my own funds several thousand to keep them going. This, and my foolish absence in Congress have greatly deranged my calculations.

I have come to the determination to use up the stock on hand, and such further amount as is necessary to work the present to advantage, and close operations, sell off all the property real and personal to pay my debts.

This will all be done within the next twelve months—If there should be any deficiency I shall resign my seat in Congress, and devote my time to paying the balance and making a living. This is all intended for your eyes alone.[10]

Stevens did not find it necessary to resign his seat in Congress, though he might as well have done so, for all that he accomplished there during the ensuing winter. A visitor in the House galleries on the rare days when the gentleman from Pennsylvania chanced to be on hand would probably not have noticed the queer person with a wig of abundant reddish hair who through the proceedings muttered and mumbled in an indistinct heckling tone but seldom

[9] *Lancasterian,* October 2, 16, 23, 1850; Philadelphia *Daily News,* October 24, 1850.
[10] Stevens to McPherson, October 13, 1850, in the Stevens Papers.

if ever had anything to say aloud.[11] Usually Stevens was absent
from Congress and busy with his law practice in various parts
of Pennsylvania, while he kept an eye open for possible shifts of
public opinion respecting the Compromise of 1850. What people
thought on that subject would determine the fate of his Woolly
Heads as against the conservative Silver Greys in the Whig party
of the state. In the spring of 1851 he was continuing his attempts
to "break down" James Cooper, the senator of the Silver Greys.
"I believe he is still popular in Phila.," Stevens told an ally, "and
has one or two friends *only* in the 'rural' dists."[12]

As preparations began for the presidential campaign of 1852,
Cooper and his followers favored the re-election of Millard
Fillmore, while Stevens again bethought him of his old protégé
Winfield Scott. A prelude to the nomination was to be the Pennsylvania gubernatorial campaign. If he could put Governor O. F.
Johnston back into the chair, Stevens would have some influence
upon the disposal of the patronage of the state. In Lancaster, as
the summer wore on, the Stevens and anti-Stevens men "began to
show their teeth at each other." His enemies bit first, when they
prevented his going as a delegate to the state convention of the
Whigs. But "Thaddeus had a shrewd and cunning ally in Governor Johnston, and the two together moulded and fashioned the
Convention to suit their own purposes." Johnston was re-
nominated, and a resolution approving the new fugitive-slave
law (a part of the Compromise) was voted down.[13]

Before the October elections an event occurred that was to
widen the rift between those in Pennsylvania who, whether Whig
or Democrat, upheld the Compromise and those who condemned
the fugitive-slave act. In September a group of slaves fleeing from
Maryland took refuge in a friendly farmhouse near Christiana,
about ten miles from Lancaster. When the owners and a United

[11] Stevens "was very imperfectly heard at the Reporters' desk" (December
30, 1850), "made a remark wholly inaudible at the Reporters' desk" (January
21, 1851), kept his voice "so low in tone that it failed to reach the Reporter"
(February 4, 1851), etc. *Congressional Globe*, 31 Congress, 2 session (1850–51),
130, 298.

[12] Stevens to W. D. Lewis, March 23, 1851, in the Lewis Papers.

[13] *Lancaster Intelligencer*, June 17, July 1, August 19, September 9, 1851.

States marshal approached in pursuit, they were met by a volley of shots. One man was killed and another badly wounded. For a time it seemed that the "murder" of the Marylander "by the negroes and white abolitionists of Lancaster county" might provoke a small-scale civil war.[14]

A significant result of the Christiana affair was that it threw conservative Whigs and Democrats together in opposition to the radical Stevens-Johnston group. In the opinion of a Lancaster Democratic editor the "atrocity" was one of "the fruits of the doctrines advocated by Johnston and Stevens." The Lancaster *Examiner and Herald,* conservative Whig, opined: "The parties really responsible for this occurrence are the abolition lecturers and their aiders and abettors *in and out of Congress.*" Senator Cooper's paper, the *Philadelphia News,* laid the tragedy to the "Higher Law" teachings of Stevens and W. H. Seward (who, in the debates on the Compromise, had appealed from the Constitution to the "higher law" of God). Associated as he was with the "riot," Governor Johnston failed of re-election, though Stevens carried Lancaster county for him.[15]

Johnston's defeat, some thought, would affect the Whig presidential nomination by putting Winfield Scott *hors de combat.* Undaunted, Stevens pressed the general's cause. He organized a company to buy one of the Lancaster newspapers and in December issued the first copy of his campaign weekly, the *Independent Whig,* flying at its masthead the name of General Scott.[16]

At about the same time, in December, 1851, Stevens went to Washington to appear in the House on the opening day of the new session. In caucus a majority of the Whig members agreed to resolutions approving the Compromise and urging that all the measures, not excluding the fugitive-slave law, be faithfully carried out. On the floor of the House antislavery Whigs denounced the caucus and asserted they would not be bound by its

[14] W. U. Hensel, *The Christiana Riot and the Treason Trials of 1851* (*Lancaster County Historical Society Papers,* vol. 15, Lancaster, 1911), 30–39.
[15] *Lancaster Intelligencer,* September 16, 23, October 21, 1851; Hensel, *The Christiana Riot,* 51–52.
[16] *Lancaster Intelligencer,* October 28, November 25, December 9, 1851; *Independent Whig* (Lancaster), December 2, 1851.

decisions. "I call the gentleman to order," Old Thad quipped as one of these spoke, "as destroying the harmony of the Whig party."[17] Stevens, who owed the party nothing, did not much care whether its members hung together or not. He did not bother to remain long in Washington but left shortly for Philadelphia, there to participate in proceedings which were still further rending Whigdom in two.

The rivalry between Stevens and Senator Cooper had come to a dramatic head when, late in November, a federal court met on the second floor in Independence Hall to try the participants in the Christiana "riot" on a charge of treason. As counsel for the state of Maryland, Cooper appeared on the side of the prosecution, and Stevens assumed the task of planning the defense. In the opening arguments of the soon-to-be-famous "treason trials" Stevens took a prominent part. After the slave-catching marshal had testified, he brought all eighteen or twenty prisoners into the courtroom and, in his cross-examination, defied the witness to identify the accused. Cleverly he played the prosecution's witnesses against one another by insinuating that one of them had charged the officer with cowardice. He scored heavily again when, offering to prove many instances of alleged kidnapping of free Negroes in southern Pennsylvania, he secured the admission of evidence of that type. Then, strangely, he retired from open participation in the case. Those who waited to hear him make a glorious summing up for the defense were disappointed.[18]

"There were good reasons for the course he pursued," one of his legal assistants cryptically explained afterward.[19] The attorney who took his place, William B. Read, was a prominent Democrat. Now, if the defendants lost, Stevens would escape some of the obloquy. If they won, the trials might become a *cause célèbre* not only for antislavery Whigs but also for Democrats disaffected by the Compromise. As it happened, all the

[17] *Congressional Globe*, 32 Congress, 1 session (1851–52), 6.

[18] *Lancaster Intelligencer*, December 2, 9, 1851; Hensel, *The Christiana Riot*, 74, 77–78; Alexander K. McClure, *Abraham Lincoln and Men of War-Times* (Philadelphia, 1892), 293.

[19] Alexander H. Hood, "Thaddeus Stevens," in Alexander Harris, ed., *A Biographical History of Lancaster County* (Lancaster, 1872), 584–585.

defendants were acquitted, and the fugitive-slave law was thereafter a dead letter in Pennsylvania, though no considerable fusion of anti-Compromisers followed.

When, after a lapse of over a month, the Lancaster representative reappeared in Congress, he received no hearty welcome from most of his peers. "What service did the gentleman from Pennsylvania render this House or the country," demanded one, "while he was away for several weeks of the present session, in defending those who were engaged in a mob which destroyed the lives of our citizens?" Angrily Old Thad refused to reply to the carping congressman: "God forbid that I should descend so low as to answer him!" Repeated absences, during which he pursued his remunerative law practice, later provoked a Whig paper in Lancaster, the *Examiner,* to take up the attack: "Our member is now at Harrisburg arguing cases before the Supreme Court—for which service his clients doubtless fee him well, besides which recompense his country pays him eight dollars per diem, as a member of Congress." On second thought the *Examiner* concluded that "it would perhaps promote the general weal were he paid *sixteen* dollars a day to absent himself altogether from the halls of Congress." Such was the "harmony" among Whigs as the time for the presidential nomination approached.[20]

In June, 1852, a few days before the national Whig convention was to meet, Stevens visited Congress long enough to make a kind of stump speech. He said he had "no remarks to make in relation to the Presidency"; the Whigs did not need to discuss the question, for among them "perfect harmony" prevailed, though he was sorry to see the dissensions of the Democrats! The well-being of the nation, he added, required the highest protection for American industry.[21]

If at their June convention in Baltimore the Whigs had chosen Fillmore as their candidate, Stevens would have been forced at once into complete eclipse. But they nominated Scott, though they adopted a conservative platform pledging fulfillment of the Com-

---

[20] *Congressional Globe,* 32 Congress, 1 session (1851–52), 582; *Lancaster Examiner,* quoted in the *Lancaster Intelligencer,* May 18, 1852.

[21] *Congressional Globe,* 32 Congress, 1 session (1851–52), 1557.

promise. At last, after a dozen years of effort, Old Thad had succeeded in bridling the horse—his man was the Whig nominee! Now he seemed to be in a position to rule Pennsylvania Whigs "as with a rod of iron." Before the end of the summer, however, he learned that his victory was a hollow one. In Lancaster his popularity had waned since the "treason trials," and in August, 1852, a Silver Grey was nominated for Congress by the local Whigs.[22]

The *coup de grace* came in the November elections. With Southern Whigs hostile to Scott and Northern Whigs apathetic, the general made a poor showing against the Democratic candidate, Franklin Pierce. So went the hopes of Stevens. His *Independent Whig* blamed the factionalism of the Silver Greys; they in turn blamed the "abolitionism" of Old Thad. If, as they charged, his ambition had been to "rule or ruin," he had succeeded, for he had achieved one alternative. He had bridled the horse, but the nag was practically dead.

In the ensuing session of Congress Stevens was not only an ineffectual lame duck but, like other erstwhile Whigs, a man without a party. At the end of his term, in March, 1853, he spoke as one about to give up politics. If he had offended any member, he was sorry, he said; he was about to depart from the representatives' hall for good and wished to leave no ill-feeling behind.[23] In truth, though he did not say it, there was little to attract him in national politics so long as Democrats controlled the government and seemed immovable. Their alliance of Western frontiersman and Southern planter, of Southern planter and Eastern artisan and merchant, held firm. They managed to ride out the Compromise, whereas the Whig party had gone to pieces as against a rock.

In Congress and out of it from 1849 to 1853, Stevens had done his bit to bring about this result. As a congressman he had hardly been able to see beyond the borders of his own state. He proposed bills to amend the tariff of 1842 and read petitions for the repeal of the fugitive-slave act; but he offered little or nothing that

[22] *Lancaster Intelligencer*, June 29, November 16, 1852.
[23] *Congressional Globe*, 32 Congress, 2 session (1852–53), 1049.

might have brought Pennsylvania protectionists an alliance with the farmers of the West. In fact, he frankly denied his aid to Western representatives seeking easy laws for the acquisition of unsettled public lands. Why give homesteads out West to the landless poor? "It would be a very unhappy condition in society if that country was to be settled altogether by paupers—by men who had no means." Why yield to the demands of squatters and pre-emptors? They were simply "wrong-doers and trespassers," thoroughly undeserving of federal aid.

Stevens would willingly have granted free land and "internal improvements" to Westerners had he been sure that they would give him a high tariff in return. But there had been no hope of that. Some of his colleagues had thought so, he said. They, he believed, had "voted for all these Western measures, to give away all the wet lands to the States, and all the dry lands to corporations and slave laws to the South, in order to get a tariff, and they got it—*didn't they?*" They did not, of course. He hoped they were satisfied![24] He himself was disillusioned over the prospect of building a new protectionist party out of a sectional swap.

Nor did an anti-Compromise platform fill the need. If he had forgotten, his Silver Grey opponents in Lancaster reminded him how his bitterness against the Compromise had cost him votes in his re-election to Congress in 1850 and had ruined his chances for renomination in 1852. Now, in 1853, the public seemed to be done with the sectional quarrel.

While the Whig factions engaged in journalistic badinage in Lancaster County, each group accusing the other of having "bolted" the party, Stevens was arguing law cases, expanding his ironworks (which shortly before he had thought of giving up), and politically marking time. "Mr. Stevens," asserted the Silver Grey *Examiner*, "claims to have the control of thirty-five hundred votes"—enough to swing Lancaster elections his own way. "Instead of discussing politics in decent style," rejoined Old Thad's *Independent Whig*, his opponents had "re-commenced their vulgar personal attacks on Mr. Stevens, although he [was] no candi-

[24] *Ibid.*, 130, 298, 419, 445; 32 Congress, 1 session (1851–52), 1278.

date for office."[25] He was waiting, watching, keeping an eye
peeled and an ear to the ground. His problem was to discover a
new political cause.

From out of the Northeast—from Maine, the state of Neal Dow
and Prohibition—came suggestions for a platform that was narrow
yet not without appeal. The anti-drink cause now seemed as
opportune as Antimasonry had seemed twenty-five years before.
Himself a puritan and a cold-water man by habit and taste,
Stevens found prohibitionism not only timely in politics but congenial to his soul. In the summer of 1853 he was, indeed, sternly
admonishing a nephew: *"Never* taste intoxicating drink—a little
is folly—much is a crime."[26] Previously, as a member of the Pennsylvania legislature, he had listened to men who called themselves
(with no awareness of paradox) a "Total Abstinence Temperance
Society," and he had proposed to hedge the sale of drink with
legal restrictions.[27] In the fall of 1853 it appeared that the Stevens
faction of Whigs might turn into a Prohibition party. In Lancaster "the great apostle of the Maine Liquor Law in this latitude," a Reverend Pennell Coombe, denounced the Silver Greys
but spared Stevens and the Woolly Heads. The *Independent
Whig* intimated that Whig regulars were "in favor of *slavery,
libertinism,* and *liquor,"* and it attacked one of the conservative
candidates as "an habitual drunkard." Only for a season, however,
was Old Thad a political prohibitionist. He did not succeed in
making a party out of "abstinence," because, for one thing, the
Democrats themselves insisted on being the party of the drys.[28]

But they could not claim to be the party of the nativists, of
the "Americans." Stevens had long before excoriated "raw Irishmen and imported Democrats"; he had claimed, in the tautology
of the political harangue, to be the friend of "native" labor and

[25] *Lancasterian,* August 31, September 21, 1853; *Independent Whig* (Lancaster), August 31, 1853.
[26] Stevens to Thaddeus Stevens, Jr., August 30, 1853, manuscript in the
possession of Mrs. F. P. McKibben, Black Gap, Pennsylvania.
[27] Stevens to the Committee of the Total Abstinence Temperance Society
[of Adams County], September 25, 1841, in the Stevens Papers.
[28] *Lancaster Examiner,* September 7, 1853; *Independent Whig* (Lancaster),
September 20, 1853; *Lancasterian,* September 21, 1853.

of "native" laborers, and he had "gone Native" in order to win his first nomination for Congress. After Scott's ill-starred campaign in 1852 many Whigs had joined the nativistic Secret Order of the Star-Spangled Banner (which was similar to the Ku Klux Klan of the nineteen-twenties), and in the course of a year had converted it into a sizable political organization. Outsiders, rebuffed by the strict secrecy and the refusal of members to answer questions, called them "Know-Nothings," and they soon adopted that name for themselves. After a "council" of the Secret Order had been organized in Lancaster, Stevens "always knew as much outside as most of the insiders did" and from the beginning pulled "at least one wire." The one-time scourge of secret societies eventually took the "holy oath" and was "clandestinely sworn in" as a member of the order, according to the testimony of two men later expelled.[29]

This was early in the fall of 1854, in the midst of a hectic local campaign. Stevens was desperate, for he believed that his future depended upon the outcome. "We must make an efficient effort now," he told a henchman, "or be hereafter proscribed." Still busy as a lawyer, he was not himself running for Congress but had picked a friend, A. E. Roberts, to run as a kind of proxy. No longer was it a matter of capturing the Whig machine, for the party was hopelessly split, and Roberts ran as an "independent Whig."

Old Thad schemed by subtle devices to get for his candidate the support of both old-fashioned Whigs and new-fangled Know-Nothings. He bargained with regular Whigs running for state and local offices. "I think," he said of one of them, "North ought to get his friends to vote for Roberts, as *he* expects our votes." On the eve of the October elections the veteran tactician gave last-minute instructions to a Know-Nothing ally: "I think we will have to look to you to arrange Columbia at this election. I think your poll committee should be appointed *inside*." He got hold of a quantity of regular Whig ballots (in those days each party

[29] *History of the Rise, Progress, and Downfall of Know-Nothingism in Lancaster County*, by Two Expelled Members (Lancaster, 1856), 10–11, 18–19, 24–25.

supplied its own) and used them in such a way as to deceive the "regular" voters. "I send you some tickets," he wrote to his lieutenant at Columbia, on the Susquehanna. "I wish you would change the half of them, by folding, and substituting the Whig state ticket with the county independent ticket and properly distribute them."[30] His attention to tactical details was not in vain. By means of his association with the Know-Nothings he elected Roberts to Congress and gained his revenge upon the Silver Greys.

This faction, with its defeated candidate himself leading the way, now went over to the Democracy in droves. Naturally this pleased the Democrats, yet at the same time they professed alarm. "In exact proportion as the Whig party has been compelled to give way to the insidious and fatal influences of Thaddeus Stevens," said one of their papers, "so has sectionalism advanced . . . and the Democratic party [been] left the only rampart of the Union."[31] Of those Whigs who did not turn Democratic, many became Know-Nothings. The question now presented itself to Stevens, after his successful experiment with "Americanism" in the fall of 1854, whether that sentiment would not provide the basis for a nation-wide party opposed to the Democracy. A negative answer came within a few months, when the Know-Nothings disagreed upon the same issue as had divided Whigs—that is, slavery in the territories—and broke into "North American" and "South American" wings. Know-Nothing votes in Lancaster could at any election send Stevens back to Congress, but, with Democrats in power, there was little he could do or be after he got there.

Meanwhile, far from Lancaster, events were transpiring the news of which could not fail to elicit the attention of Old Thad. In 1854 Congress passed the Kansas-Nebraska Act. This momentous measure repealed the Missouri Compromise and provided for the organization of the territories of Kansas and Nebraska with "popular sovereignty." Stephen A. Douglas, its author,

[30] Stevens to Samuel Evans, October 5, 8, 1854, manuscripts in the Pennsylvania State Library, Harrisburg; Alexander Harris, *A Review of the Political Conflict in America . . . Comprising Also a Résumé of the Career of Thaddeus Stevens* (New York, 1876), 104.

[31] *Dollar Weekly Pennsylvanian* (Philadelphia), September 20, 1856.

assumed that the first would become a slave state and the second a free state, so as to satisfy both North and South. To his amazement, he soon found that he had roused, not quieted, the restless dogs of sectionalism. Overnight free-soilers of all persuasions, Whig, Know-Nothing, and Democratic, took their stand against the act. Out of this "Anti-Nebraska" movement emerged the Republican party, vigorous, aggressive, full of the vim of institutional youth. Organized first in Michigan and Wisconsin, the new party at once scored heavily in elections in many of the Middle Western states.

Here at last, perhaps, was the party that Stevens had been seeking ever since he first entered politics. As a politician he had always been an "anti." By turns he had taken his stand against Masonry, against slavery, against the Compromise of 1850, against intoxicating liquor, against foreigners. These were but the guises of an unceasing and unchanging opposition to the Democratic party. Thus far none of his negative platforms had brought positive results. Perhaps the Anti-Nebraska program would succeed where the others had failed.

VII. A Victorious Defeat

YET when the political stir created by the Republican party first reached Lancaster, Thaddeus Stevens seemed indifferent if not hostile to the new movement. This was a party originating in the West; its membership consisted largely of farmers and its platform demanded homesteads, free soil, and internal improvements at federal expense. In the beginning it promised little for Pennsylvania industrialists, whose primary interest was tariff protection, especially for iron and coal. Its platform was not a satisfactory substitute for the Know-Nothing creed. When the new party found a group of interested followers in Lancaster, however, Stevens as an antislavery leader had no choice but to join and attempt to take the lead. At an "abolition, Know-Nothing, Whig assemblage" in March of 1856 he appeared to be the "controlling spirit" among the local Republicans.[1]

He acquired a special interest in the approaching Republican national convention and the prospective campaign of 1856 when the Democrats of the nation, meeting at Cincinnati on June 2, nominated his old rival and fellow townsman James Buchanan for president. Buchanan was a paragon of availability, the man of all men least likely to alienate voters North or South. If he was to be properly humiliated and if the Republican party was to succeed in its first great test on a national scale, the Republicans must choose a candidate equally safe and just as unlikely to antagonize any large portion of the electorate, at least in the North. So Stevens could not endorse either of the Republican favorites, William H. Seward and John C. Frémont, for both

[1] Alexander Harris, *The Political Conflict in America . . . Comprising Also a Résumé of the Career of Thaddeus Stevens* (New York, 1876), 172; Alexander K. McClure, *Old-Time Notes of Pennsylvania* (2 vols., Philadelphia, 1905), 1:248; *Lancaster Intelligencer*, March 25, 1856; *New York Times*, March 31, 1856.

were suspect in the eyes of Native Americans. He would much
prefer to see John McLean of Ohio run against Buchanan. He
knew McLean well. When a congressman in Washington, he had
boarded with McLean, a justice of the Supreme Court, at the
same bachelor "mess." He had tried his best to induce the Antimasons to nominate him in 1831. The judge, now as then, was
a "conservative"; he was free from any taint of Catholicism; and,
not least, as president he would be a Stevens man. Before the
meeting of the Republicans, Old Thad prevailed upon a number
of conservative-minded politicians to join the Pennsylvania delegation as volunteers. On the June day before the convention
opened, at Music Hall in Philadelphia, he brought his powers of
persuasion to bear upon the delegates from other states as they
arrived.[2]

Early in the proceedings it became apparent that he would fail
to get a conservative candidate and platform. The last plank of
the platform, as reported from the resolutions committee, invited
the "affiliation and cooperation of the men of all parties" but in
veiled language condemned the Know-Nothings by declaring for
"liberty of conscience and equality of rights." To Stevens, with
his knowledge of the strength of Know-Nothingism in Pennsylvania, these seemed like incompatible aims. He rose on the convention floor to say that if Republicans were to unite all parties
opposed to the Democracy, they must omit the offending paragraph. "The cunning enemy will misconstrue that," he warned.
"They will read it as though it were in opposition to the largest
party in Pennsylvania. It will . . . affect dangerously our prospects,
and therefore I trust it may be changed." But changed it was not.

A second defeat for Stevens soon followed. One of the Ohio
delegates, waving a letter he had just received from McLean, got
up to withdraw the judge's name. Over Old Thad's objections
(as at Baltimore in 1831!) it was withdrawn. Amid the confusion
and din that followed, Stevens finally succeeded in getting the
floor. He told the delegates he had but one thing to say. He saw

    [2] Russell Errett, "The Republican Nominating Conventions of 1856 and
1860," in the *Magazine of Western History*, 10 (1889): 261; McClure, *Old-Time
Notes of Pennsylvania*, 1:248; *New York Times*, June 17, 1856.

what the current of the convention was and he did not desire to oppose it, but he would ask them to be careful lest the current sweep away their friends as well as their foes. The name, he might say the only name, that could have saved his state had been stricken off the list. In consequence he feared that Pennsylvania would be lost by a majority of fifty thousand or more. During a recess he induced the Ohio delegate to recall the withdrawal of McLean's candidacy. He then made a strong plea before his own delegation to stand behind McLean. On the first ballot seventy-one of the Pennsylvanians voted for the judge, but on the second ballot most of them deserted to Frémont, and the "Pathfinder" won.[3]

Old Thad left the convention with a heavy heart. Earlier in the year the Native Americans of the North had nominated ex-President Millard Fillmore, and a remnant of the Whigs had seconded that choice. With a safe and inoffensive candidate like McLean, the Republicans could have hoped to draw off most of the Fillmore vote. With Frémont, they seemed to stand little chance of doing so, at least where Stevens lived. "We are troubled with Fillmore ism here," he confessed in August. "The North is a dastard & Slavery I fear will always triumph. The cry of Freemont's Catholicism has done us much [harm] & lost us the Nation. Americanism is the deepest feeling in the Southern part of the State. We will do our best here but will not promise much."[4]

In this situation Old Thad's strategy was to combine the county, state, and national tickets of the parties of Fillmore and Frémont. This was his ambitious "fusion" plan. As a beginning he "whipped in" the *American Citizen,* the Lancaster Know-Nothing press. He then staged a "union" convention at which the Whigs, Native Americans, and Republicans agreed upon a single ticket for the county. Though he himself was not among the candidates, his proxy, Congressman A. E. Roberts, headed the list. So far, so good. But against the further spread of his fusion scheme were

[3] Errett, in the *Magazine of Western History,* 10:259; Elihu B. Washburne, ed., *The Edwards Papers (Chicago Historical Society Collections,* vol. 3, Chicago, 1884), 246–247n.; *New York Times,* June 19, 20, 1856.

[4] Stevens to E. D. Gazzam, August 24, 1856, in the Edward McPherson Papers, Library of Congress.

arrayed most of the Know-Nothing newspapers of the state. Presently, one by one, these capitulated, even the *Daily News* of Philadelphia, where "Fillmore ism" was particularly strong. As the "subserviency" of Native American editors became obvious, the suspicion grew that they had "sold themselves" to Stevens.[5] And so they had! As he related to the chairman of the Republican state committee in September:

I negotiated with the leading American editor at York who was doing much mischief; indeed was keeping 4000 Fillmore men from both the State and electoral ticket. He was to change his course and have $350. I have advanced $50 of it.... As I have already expended $4,000 in securing presses I have resolved to go no further. Now if your friends could send ... $300 it would secure York County—If not it must slide. ... It is mortifying to need money for the public and not have it.

Forthwith the chairman raised the fund so badly needed, and Stevens acknowledged within a week: "I returned last night from a mission through York Adams & Franklin Counties and only this morning got both your letters (including your chk for $300). I have been at York and arranged the business (if it holds)."[6] Old Thad was the sort who believed an honest man to be one who, once bought, would stay bought, and in this instance he had his doubts.

Having prepared the public mind by generous use of his own and the party's funds, he took steps during October to give concrete form to his scheme for fusing the electoral tickets. The plan as he outlined it was this: there would be two tickets, one headed by Fillmore and the other by Frémont, but the twenty-six electors on each ticket would be exactly the same. They would be pledged to cast their ballots for the respective candidates "precisely in proportion to the popular votes cast for each." Ostensibly the purpose of the plan was to "enable every voter to act efficiently against Buchanan without any sacrifice of principle." Actually the aim was to throw to the leader of the two candidates all, and not merely the proportional part, of the combined electoral vote.

[5] *Lancaster Intelligencer,* July 1, August 12, September 2, 9, 1856; *Dollar Weekly Pennsylvanian* (Philadelphia), September 20, 1856.

[6] Stevens to Henry C. Carey, September 24, 30, 1856, in the Edward Carey Gardiner Collection, Historical Society of Pennsylvania, Philadelphia.

The result would be to nullify Fillmore's strength where it was greatest, as in Philadelphia. "Stevens will be able so to overwhelm that vote by his organization in the Wilmot district, in Lancaster, in Allegheny, and other heavy abolition districts, that the electoral vote would go for Fremont and Fremont alone in the event of the defeat of James Buchanan." So Democrats were saying. "Is it possible that this hoary political gambler, with his loaded dice, his marked cards, and his tainted history, can again deceive any portion of the white men of our state?" The nation's leading Know-Nothing paper, the *American Organ* at Washington, and Fillmore, too, objected to the scheme. Nevertheless, Old Thad effected a fusion of the electoral tickets a few weeks before election day.[7]

Meanwhile, he was active on the stump. In its efforts to carry pivotal Pennsylvania for Frémont, the Republican party sent into the state a "gang of abolition emissaries and agitators" from almost every part of the country, but Stevens was the "ablest canvasser" of them all, the *New York Tribune* applauded. He could not say much for his Republican fellow workers. "The State is worse managed in this campaign than I ever knew it," he complained. "York is in the worst condition of any county in the State. Speakers should be poured into the Bradford and Franklin Congressional dist., as it also is not in good keeping."[8]

The issues of the campaign were not entirely clear from the speech-making on either side. Asserting that a Republican victory would mean disunion and the immediate emancipation of the slaves, Democrats appealed to Northern workingmen to consider whether they were "prepared for an inroad of three millions of negroes from the South to compete with them." The tariff question hardly came up for debate. As for Stevens, he made the contest a personal quarrel with his old antagonist, the Democratic nominee. "There is a wrong impression about one of the candi-

[7] *Dollar Weekly Pennsylvanian*, October 11, 18, 25, November 1, 1856; *Philadelphia Daily Times*, October 18, 1856; *American Organ* (Washington), October 22, 1856, quoted in the *Lancaster Intelligencer*, October 28, 1856.

[8] Stevens to Carey, September 30, 1856, in the Gardiner Collection; *New York Tribune*, September 17, 1856; *Dollar Weekly Pennsylvanian*, October 11, 1856.

dates," he said, alluding to Buchanan's silence during most of the campaign. "There is no such person running as James Buchanan. *He is dead of lockjaw.* Nothing remains but a platform and a bloated mass of political putridity." Old Thad also stirred up rural nativism against urban Democracy, which was largely Irish Catholic. At a Lancaster rally he said he relied upon the "yeomanry" of the state to insure a Republican triumph, and he warned his audience that, unless the counties turned out en masse, they would be beaten by the cities. In answer to the assertion of Democrats that Republican success would mean disunion, he declared: "The cry of 'The Union is in danger' is the argument of fools to an audience of idiots!"[9]

After the November elections were over, Stevens found that his oratory and his bribery of Know-Nothing editors had been in vain. Buchanan, though he had only a plurality in his own county, carried Pennsylvania by a narrow majority over the combined vote of Fillmore and Frémont.[10] Yet all was not lost. Reflecting upon the results of the local elections in October, Old Thad could congratulate himself upon the return of his man A. E. Roberts to Congress. Several other districts had also elected Republican congressmen, and in the state legislature Republicans could hope almost to balance the Democrats. Forgetting the pessimism that had haunted him before and during the campaign, Stevens now wrote: "The smoke having somewhat cleared off after our victorious defeat we must look a little further how to promote the cause of freedom." He concluded that one of the best ways to promote the cause was to make a Republican senator out of Simon Cameron.

Cameron, a thin-faced, gray-haired, canny Scot, had been a Democrat and a friend of Jackson, Calhoun, and Buchanan, but that would not now prevent his becoming a friend of Old Thad. Cameron's abilities and his smooth voice and winning manner had brought him far since the day of his birth in Lancaster

[9] *Dollar Weekly Pennsylvanian*, October 18, 1856; *Lancaster Intelligencer*, November 4, 1856.

[10] In Pennsylvania Buchanan's vote was approximately 230,000; the combined vote of his opponents, 229,000. Edward Stanwood, *A History of the Presidency from 1788 to 1897* (2 vols., new ed., New York, 1916), 1:276.

County fifty-odd years before. He began his career as a printer's apprentice and rose to a position of wealth and power as the editor and owner of several newspapers; as a contractor on the Pennsylvania public works; as a banker, insurance broker, and ironmaster; and, in 1845, as senator from Pennsylvania. Then he and Buchanan reached a parting of the ways. In 1855, as a Know-Nothing, he was one of "an unholy conclave of political conspirators" (as a Democratic writer phrased it) who met with Stevens in the back room of a Harrisburg hotel to combine the Native American and Republican state tickets. In 1856 he campaigned as a Republican for Frémont.[11]

After the campaign was over, Old Thad corresponded or conversed with the governor, the secretary of state, several members of the legislature, and "other influential men" in Cameron's behalf. This was his message to one of them:

It would be a great victory if we could send a Republican Senator to the U. S. Senate. If you tender the nomination to S. Cameron I have reason to believe that he can get enough of his old friends to elect him. I opposed him before because I did not think him true to freedom. . . .

He is now a genuine republican as his late acts have shown. It is clear that we can elect no one else, and I submit to you whether it would not be better to elect him than be defeated.

To Cameron himself Stevens wrote of his activities, his intention to see obstinate Republicans and try to make them "magnanimous," and the prospects of success. "It would require four democrats," he reported. "Can they be had?" The requisite number of legislators were "had" at Harrisburg early in 1857.[12] If the fall elections had been a "victorious defeat," this was for Stevens a defeating victory, for in the years to come he was often to rue his action in helping Cameron to become Republican boss of Pennsylvania.

[11] A. H. Meneely, The War Department, 1861: A Study in Mobilization and Administration (Columbia University Studies in History, Economics, and Public Law, no. 300, New York, 1928), 74–82 (comprising a sketch of the earlier career of Cameron); Lancaster Intelligencer, October 2, November 5, 1855; Dollar Weekly Pennsylvanian, October 9, 1855.

[12] Stevens to Cameron, November 30, 1856, in the Simon Cameron Papers, Library of Congress; Stevens to E. D. Gazzam, December 4, 1856, in the McPherson Papers.

For the time being, however, the optimism of Old Thad could
be justified by events, even though catastrophes followed. Soon
after the inauguration of Buchanan the Supreme Court issued its
Dred Scott decision, which, by legalizing slavery in the territories,
seemed to declare unconstitutional the free-soil plank of the Republican platform. Later, to the horror of protectionists, a Democratic Congress lowered a tariff which they considered already too
low. And then came the Panic of '57. Republicans could take this
as proof of the unwisdom of Democratic policies. In any case, the
advent of hard times had always in the past presaged good luck
for the party of the outs. And at this time the party of the ins
was being rent asunder as the followers of Buchanan and the followers of Stephen A. Douglas quarreled over the question of
"Bleeding Kansas." To Stevens the ironmaster the Panic came as
an ill wind, yet it blew favorably upon Stevens the politician. As
he surveyed the political scene, in his own county and state, and
in the nation as a whole, he concluded that the Republicans could
probably gain a majority in the next House of Representatives.
The time was ripe for him to run for Congress again.[13]

To make as broad an appeal as possible, he gained the nomination in the summer of 1858 not as a Republican but as a
"People's" candidate. "Thump-lumping" his way to the rostrum
in Russell's Hall to make an acceptance speech, he declared that
his chief aim in Congress would be to restore the protective tariff
and raise it to higher levels. Lancaster Democrats might sniff:
"Mr. Stevens owns a furnace up in Adams County, and would
fain raise the duties on Iron so high as that he would be able to
make a fortune in a short time off the Farmers, Mechanics, and
Consumers of the country." But the farmers, mechanics, and consumers were all feeling the pinch of depression; to many of them
protectionism, rightly presented, would have the appeal that
nativism had lately had. In his speech Stevens went on to ridicule
both the Dred Scott decision and the "popular sovereignty" doctrine of Douglas. "Out upon the old hypocrite!" Democratic

---

[13] *Colonel Alexander K. McClure's Recollections of Half a Century* (Salem,
Massachusetts, [1902]), 418; McClure, *Old-Time Notes of Pennsylvania,* 1:337–
338.

hecklers were tempted to exclaim. "Now, as ever, he knows but one topic, and that is Niggerism." In conclusion Stevens referred to Buchanan. "If I should be elected," he said, "perhaps I may come in contact with the worthy President, who claims this city as his home, and oppose his measures (although I do not hope to be especially noticed by him for it) and also say something against him; but if saying that he is the *meanest* man that has ever occupied the Presidential chair ... brings his displeasure upon me, *then I shall say it*."[14]

There was real animus behind this denunciation of Buchanan. During September, 1858, the president made a visit to Wheatland, his estate on the outskirts of Lancaster, ostensibly for a short vacation from his Washington cares. Old Thad knew that he was coming to direct the Democratic campaign in person. The local *Times,* a Stevens paper, received the distinguished son of Lancaster with several columns of abuse. In reply the *Lancaster Intelligencer* devoted a whole issue to the scandals in which Stevens had been involved in his earlier career, such as the jobbery of the tapeworm railway and the election frauds of 1838. When he obtained a writ for libel, the editors countered that this was "an attack on the liberty of the press." Joining in the journalistic warfare on the Democratic side, the *Examiner,* formerly the organ of the regular Whigs, contended that Stevens had secured his nomination in 1858 also by fraud.[15]

He pressed the fight against Buchanan not only at home but on a wider front. If his own re-election to Congress was to bring the substance of power, Republicans must be sent to the House from other districts in Pennsylvania and elsewhere throughout the North. And so he went to Chambersburg, called upon Alexander K. McClure, a friend and the attorney for his property interests there, and urged him to run for Congress from that district. McClure refused. Once safely Whig, his district had become Democratic after the Know-Nothing movement had alienated Catholic Whigs. Stevens then went to Gettysburg and ap-

[14] *Lancaster Intelligencer,* August 31, 1858.
[15] *Lancaster Examiner,* September 1, 1858; *Lancaster Intelligencer,* September 7, 21, 28, 1858; *Lancaster Times,* September 22, 1858.

pealed to Edward McPherson, the twenty-seven-year-old son of
John B. McPherson. Young McPherson agreed to run for Congress if McClure would run for the state legislature, so that they
could combine their strength. Such an arrangement was made.[16]
Stevens meanwhile kept in touch with strategists and organizers
like himself in other states. Toward the end of the campaign he
summed up his hopes and fears in a letter to Salmon P. Chase, of
Ohio, who, by way of the Liberty party, had become a Republican:

> Politics in Penna. are hard to manage. Our population, in the heavy
> dists. South & East, are much less inclined to Republicanism than in the
> North and West. The only difficulty in my election is that I am ahead
> of the people in Anti-Slavery. Still I expect to be elected although our
> leading Whig & Repub. paper has gone against me. I fear we shall not
> elect as many Members of Congress as we had hoped, owing to divisions
> growing out of the old American feeling which is very strong in the
> most populous parts of the State—Still I think we shall gain four or five.
> I had hoped that Ohio would have given us an increase. If not I see
> but little prospect of a majority in the next House. Mr. Buchanan is
> very busy in aiding to defeat me. The Gov't's money will do much in a
> population like ours, but still I do not think they can succeed.
>
> I suppose you will agree with me that the President intends to be a
> candidate for reelection—I shall rejoice if he procures the nomination.[17]

A few days later the October election returns came in from
Lancaster. They more than justified the optimism of Stevens
regarding his own prospects: he got nearly three-fourths of the
county's votes. Encouraging to him also were the results in other
places, though in the next House the Republicans would lack
half a dozen of a clear majority. Edward McPherson would be
there. He had carried the Franklin-Adams district by a margin
of some two hundred and fifty votes—just about the number of
voting employees of Old Thad at Caledonia! The new Republican
congressmen from Pennsylvania were hailed in the party press as
"exponents of the vigor of the canvass" that had elected them.
One of them in particular seemed to have the vigor of an ambition

[16] McClure, *Old-Time Notes of Pennsylvania*, 1:337–338.
[17] Stevens to Chase, September 25, 1858, in the Salmon P. Chase MSS., Historical Society of Pennsylvania.

long repressed and now at last released. "Thaddeus Stevens,"
went the report, "comes to his position with a determination to
make himself felt, having been so long out of legislative position
as to be entitled to congratulation as a new man."[18]

[18] *New York Tribune,* October 12, 1858; *Lancaster Intelligencer,* October
19, 1858; *North American* (Philadelphia), quoted in the *Lancaster Examiner,*
October 27, 1858.

VIII. The Gentleman from Pennsylvania

THE "new man" who was re-elected to Congress in 1858 was then sixty-six years old. At an age which for many would have meant approaching dotage he was about to begin his political career in earnest. So important was he to become, as compared with the past, during the oncoming decade of crisis and conflict, that he was to seem indeed a new and different man from the hackney politician who had spent most of the preceding two decades, so to speak, in exile. Yet physically, of course, he was the same person, though time had left its marks. His limp was more noticeable, his figure somewhat more stooped and gaunt, his eyes more sunken and his features sharper, and there was perhaps more truculence in his habitual pout. Mentally, too, in his memories, interests, aspirations, and ways of thought and action, there was every reason to suppose that he was the same Old Thad.

Already—except for the president himself, James Buchanan— he was the most famous citizen of Lancaster, Pennsylvania. Since his arrival there in 1842, Lancaster had about doubled in population and now was a prosperous city of some sixteen thousand. The place had an air of wealth and self-respect. In the public square on top of a hill stood the old courthouse, which once had been the capitol of Pennsylvania and earlier, for a short time during the Revolution, the capitol of all the thirteen states. Downhill from the square ran the two main streets, King and Queen. Well paved they were, well kept, and closely lined with neat rows of red-brick, white-shuttered houses, all spic and span. When, in 1847, William H. Seward had stopped at the leading hostelry, the Swan Inn, and "recalled old recollections" with Stevens, he had been favorably impressed by the town. His chief complaint had been that he could not sleep, for throughout the night he had heard the hours announced—first by the "shrill German house clock" at the Swan Inn, "then repeated by the iron tongue of the town clock," and then reiterated by the town watchman's chant, "one o'clock and all is well." The "aspect of so much wealth" which Seward noted was owing to the rich farming country roundabout for which Lancaster was a mart, and to the factories making rifles, hats, and combs, stoves and steam engines, threshing machines and ploughs, carriages, wagons, and railroad cars.[1] According to a well-informed commentator, however, the industries and farms had to fight against "the paralysing influences of a superfluous professional population" who consumed but did not produce. Lancaster suffered, it was said, from being "literally overrun with professional men—including a horde of smiling, friendly politicians." Among this horde was "one of the most brilliant lawyers in Pennsylvania." Personally, Stevens was "one of the best men living"; politically, he was too much of an extremist. It was his "splendid personal and intellectual qualities" that made him noteworthy.[2]

Some of these personal and intellectual qualities were reflected by the house in which Old Thad lived, as well as by the circumstances under which he had acquired it. At a sheriff's sale not long after his arrival in Lancaster he purchased, for four thousand dollars, a lot with two houses, "the property of one Klein." He did not at once move in, however, for reasons that he explained some ten years later to his friend J. B. McPherson, president of the Bank of Gettysburg, which held a mortgage on the estate. The former owner, Klein, eighty years of age at the time of the sale, had requested that Stevens let him live on the place during the rest of his life. "He and his wife and daughter did occupy the main house ... up to last spring," Stevens wrote to McPherson in the fall of 1853, "when the old man being dead I desired to

[1] Frederick W. Seward, ed., *Seward at Washington as Senator and Secretary of State: A Memoir of His Life with Selections from His Letters, 1846–1861* (New York, 1891), 51; Charles B. Trego, *A Geography of Pennsylvania ... with a Separate Description of Each County* (Philadelphia, 1843), 266–268.

[2] Eli Bowen, *The Pictorial Sketch-Book of Pennsylvania* (8th ed., Philadelphia, 1854), part 2, pp. 48, 59–60.

take possesion. The She Devils now claim to live there during the old woman's life who was 20 years younger than her husband." Rather than evict the "She Devils" himself, Stevens asked Mc-Pherson to send a lawyer to deal with them. His generosity he now rued, saying, "I get often such returns for the kindness I extend to others; and it serves me about right."[3]

The dwelling was unpretentious, one of a row of houses that stretched down South Queen Street away from the public square. It was a double house, with two doors in front, beside one of which was a brass plate reading "Office, Thaddeus Stevens, Attorney at Law." The interior of the living quarters was so plainly furnished as to be almost ugly. A marble-topped table in one corner, several un-upholstered chairs scattered around, a large mirror and a few portraits on the walls (including an oil painting of Stevens, done by Eichholtz in 1856)—such were the bare furnishings of a parlor that could have been made cozy and attractive, looking as it did upon a small garden in the rear. More livable was the library upstairs, adjoining Stevens' bedroom and ministering conveniently to his habit of reading in bed. The shelves were well filled with books—not many novels but dozens of weighty tomes upon politics and history, especially the history of the American Revolution, and most of the well-known classics of Greece and Rome. As in his days at Gettysburg a generation before, Stevens' personal collection served almost as a public library, so freely did he lend his volumes.

When in Lancaster, Stevens spent most of his waking hours in the law office. This consisted of two large rooms furnished with rude and well-worn tables and chairs. The walls were lined with cases containing shelf upon shelf of legal works, among which were many British law reports and journals. To add to his collection, Stevens in 1858 requested a bookdealer to import "the back no.s of the Jurist as far back as 1840." His library bespoke his interest in English law and political institutions, which he greatly admired. Years before, during his first term in the Pennsylvania legislature, he had urged the repeal of an act (passed as an anti-

[3] Stevens to J. B. McPherson, September 23, 1853, in the Thaddeus Stevens Papers, Library of Congress.

British gesture at the time of the War of 1812) which prohibited
the citation of English cases dated later than July 4, 1776. Altogether, Stevens' collection was one of the best in the state;
but not satisfied, he had long agitated for a "law library association" through which Lancaster attorneys might pool some of
their books and keep them in the courthouse for the use of all.[4]

Such an office as Stevens' served as the law school of his time,
and he was one of the most popular of instructors. Sometimes as
many as nine or ten young men were "reading law" with him at
the same time. They became attached to him, it was said, as "children to a father," and indeed a number of his legal acolytes became
loyal henchmen in politics. The nature of his relations with his
apprentices was suggested by the experience of one applicant, to
whose inquiry Old Thad replied: "Have room. Take students.
Terms, $200. Some pay—some don't." When the newcomer ap-
peared, Old Thad tried him with a few jokes, then with a sudden
stern look advised him against taking up law as a career. The
tension lightened after a few moments of suspense, when Old
Thad explained: "You have too honest a face to be a lawyer."[5]

Despite the riches of his library, Stevens the attorney was noted
more for his persuasiveness and grasp of principles than for
profundity or knowledge of details. Usually he left the drudgery
of research and brief-making to students or colleagues, while he
himself shaped the facts to appeal to the minds of jurors or
judge. In the court he spoke from few notes or none, but from
memory, pithily, and to the point. He sneered at those who made
a show of their erudition or dragged out their argument with
long-winded citations. "What are all these books for?" he demanded on one occasion, amid the laughter of those present,
when he entered a courtroom and found that the opposing

[4] Obituary notice of Stevens in the *New York Tribune*, August 18, 1868;
Stevens to T. W. Johnson & Co., March 6, 1858, manuscript in the possession
of T. Fred. Woodley, Bangor, Pennsylvania; Alexander Harris, *A Review of
the Political Conflict in America ... Comprising Also a Résumé of the Career
of Thaddeus Stevens* (New York, 1876), 422n; *Pennsylvania House Journal,*
1833–34, 1:328-330; *Lancaster County Historical Society Papers,* 39 (1935): 3–4.

[5] *Lancaster County Historical Society Papers,* 11 (1907): 37. Among the students who became political followers of Stevens were A. H. Hood, O. J.
Dickey, and Simon Stevens (no relative).

counsel had piled his table high with impressive-looking tomes. Sarcastic, positive, imperious, Old Thad displayed the same demeanor at the bar as on the stump or in the legislative hall. And in both places his clientele was much the same. Among his larger clients were bankers and business men who supported him most resourcefully in politics. On the other hand, his political opponents, too, recognized his legal ability and prestige. It was a tribute to his standing as a member of the Pennsylvania bar when, after the death of the great chief justice John B. Gibson, he was called upon to make the obituary remarks before the state supreme court, even though Gibson had been a Freemason and a Democrat.[6]

The care of his law office and dwelling made it necessary for Stevens to employ a housekeeper, for he had remained and was to remain without a wife. Several years after settling in Lancaster he had chanced to hire "a colored woman, nearly white" to look after the house. Lydia Hamilton Smith was then about thirty-five years old, rather short and slight but well-formed, attractive, intelligent, neat. The widow of a Negro teamster, she brought her two sons with her, one of whom was four years of age, the other twelve. According to one account Stevens employed her, upon the recommendation of a friend, merely as the successor of a number of servants who had worked for him in turn. Another story related that he had already known Mrs. Smith for some time, having first become "intimate with her" in Harrisburg, or perhaps in Gettysburg, her previous home. In any case, many of his neighbors came to look upon her as more than a housekeeper, and some went so far as to speak of her, though never in his presence, as "Mrs. Stevens."[7]

His political enemies were properly horrified. They found in his relationship with Lydia Smith reasons for his antislavery stand in Congress. Whenever he thought of "the black people

---

[6] Harris, *A Review of the Political Conflict,* 87–90.

[7] Charles I. Landis, "A Refutation of the Slanderous Stories against the Name of Thaddeus Stevens Placed before the Public by Thomas Dixon," in *Lancaster County Historical Society Papers,* 28 (1924): 49–52; William M. Hall, *Reminiscences and Sketches, Historical and Biographical* (Harrisburg, 1890), 16–17.

with flat noses and wooly heads on the southern plantations," he had shed "crocodile tears." Why? asked the Democratic *Lancasterian*. "Strange sympathy, and stranger still that its existence within him has . . . been whispered by the tongue of scandal! . . . No other course was to have been expected from this declaimer upon natural rights and the Equality of races, with whom all colors and odors are alike inoffensive."[8]

With Mrs. Smith almost a *materfamilias* in all but name, Stevens had become a kind of *paterfamilias* of the household on South Queen Street. In the place of children of his own were two of his nephews, Thaddeus and Alanson, not yet of age. Before the death of their father, Morrill, in 1856, Old Thad had been a somewhat indulgent uncle to them. On one occasion Morrill, then a country doctor disabled by dropsy, had written: "Dear Brother—I received your letter with one hundred dollars which I could use to advantage to myself and family by which I am much obliged, if I should get to doing business I may possibly repay it if not you may consider it a bit of charity it will not be misapplied. The Boys have yet got their knives [*gifts from their uncle Thaddeus*]. Thad attends school, his teacher calls him a good scholar." After their father died and their appointed guardian had been incapacitated by illness, the boys became, in 1858, wards of their uncle.[9]

In the role of parent Old Thad was less indulgent, more stern. Previously he had taken Thaddeus, Jr., under his care and had sent him to an academy in Pennsylvania, where young Thad seemed not quite the "good scholar" that his earlier teacher had

[8] *Lancasterian* (Lancaster), March 20, 1850.

[9] Morrill Stevens to Stevens, October 5, 1846, in the Stevens Papers; *Estate of Thaddeus Stevens, Deceased: Audit. Notes of Testimony* (Lancaster, Examiner Publishing House, 1893), 41–42. This is a rare and interesting pamphlet, a copy of which is in the library of the Wisconsin State Historical Society at Madison. It contains depositions taken at Lancaster on June 24, 1887, and at Chambersburg on January 5, 1891, in regard to a claim of one Mary J. Clason (who asserted she was the widow of Stevens' nephew Alanson) against Stevens' estate. It also contains reprints of various legal documents, including Stevens' will (this has been mutilated in the copy possessed by the Wisconsin State Historical Society). Scattered throughout the 105 pages is much incidental information about Stevens, his relatives, and life at the Caledonia Iron Works.

called him. From his uncle he received admonitions revealing something of the character of each of the two. "Be first in your class," Stevens told the boy. Later: "I fear . . . you love rum. . . . If so, the sooner you are abandoned the better, as there is no hope for anyone who ever tastes strong drink." And again: "You can study hard enough to regain your standing. . . . I must say that until you have redeemed yourself from disgrace, I have no desire to see you." The other boy, Alanson, went to live at Caledonia furnace, where he was not left idle for long. In January, 1859, Stevens was to make him a clerk at the furnace on a salary of $400 a year, against which all "previous accounts" should be charged and thus "squared."[10]

Old Thad, once a sickly boy, had enjoyed years of vigor and robustness and had outlived the rest of the Stevens clan. His younger brothers, Morrill and Alanson, had died in Vermont; finally, in April, 1858, had come news of the death of the older brother, Joshua, in the West. After Sarah Stevens died, there was an emptiness in the old home at Peacham, which Stevens had been wont to revisit from time to time. Having bought the property for his mother, he was loath to sell it when, in 1854, he was offered twenty-five hundred dollars for the farm with "four cows thrown in." The last letters from her had been full of her "bereavements" and of her concern lest Thaddeus be next. "I was very sorry you could not come home," had at one time been her plaint. "I feel that it would be better for your Helth to come home and Stay this winter, then to go to them Hote Springs." Yet, though his health had finally begun to break, Thaddeus was still alive when at a ripe old age Sarah Stevens went to her "better rest," her last thought doubtless being similar to the one she had once expressed to her son: "Our help is in God, Sickness and dieses [disease] are at His command let us put our trust in Him."[11]

In most of his mother's letters might be traced an uneasy feeling

[10] Stevens to Thaddeus Stevens, Jr., August 30, 1853; October 23, December 4, 1854, manuscripts in the possession of Mrs. F. P. McKibben, Black Gap, Pennsylvania; *Estate of Thaddeus Stevens, Deceased: Audit. Notes of Testimony*, 28–29.

[11] *Philadelphia Press*, April 21, 1858; Robert Gilfillan to Stevens, November 3, 1854, and Sarah Stevens to Stevens, July 20, [——?], in the Stevens Papers.

that Thaddeus had not quite kept to the narrow path: in all of them lurked a note of covert appeal. Almost never did he attend religious service, although he maintained a pew in a Presbyterian church and contributed to such organizations as the Lancaster Bible Society. For that matter, he was little interested in any of the polite forms of social life. His nonattendance at church marked him as an "atheist," and preachers despaired. One of them, the Reverend Jonathan Blanchard, had long ago told him: "I am very anxious that you should become a Christian, for the salvation of your own soul."[12] But the preacher had not yet made him a convert.

Apparently Old Thad's early Calvinist training had left him little more than a residue of fatalist attitudes, and yet he held too dear the memory of his mother to show contempt for her beliefs. Whenever he mentioned her name (or so an acquaintance afterward recalled), "all the harsh lines of his countenance appeared to give place to the tenderness of a child. That one devotion was like an oasis in the desert of his affections." He once dismissed a self-proclaimed "free-thinker" with the remark: "My mother was a soft shell Baptist" and "held the Ten Commandments to be good law and the Sermon on the Mount as orthodox. I am one of her poor disciples; good morning, sir."[13]

Although many who knew Stevens thought he broke the Ten Commandments more often than he observed them, most of them gave him credit for the Christian virtue of charity. Numerous were the stories told to illustrate his generosity—how he kept broken and decrepit old men as pensioners; how he sent poor boys to school; how he ransomed fugitive slaves; how, hobbling on his way to the courthouse one day and meeting a girl who had lost a gold dollar, he handed her another and turned her tears into smiles.[14] The theme these tales adorned, at any rate, was authentic. One of Stevens' clients once appealed to his "reputed generous

[12] Blanchard to Stevens, April 9, 1842, in the Stevens Papers.
[13] Alexander K. McClure, *Abraham Lincoln and Men of War-Times* (Philadelphia, 1892), 287; J. B. Grinnell, *Men and Events of Forty Years* (Boston, 1891), 191.
[14] Obituary of Stevens in the *New York Tribune*, August 18, 1868.

nature," and got quick results thereby.[15] His treatment of the old man ("one Klein") who had owned the house on South Queen Street, of his law students, and of his relatives—all this bespoke his generosity.

Of course, it well beseemed a politician to confer favors, and Stevens mixed his charity with cynicism. In the later judgment of one of his former students, he was easily flattered—"any scamp" could "soft-soap" him—yet he was too shrewd not to know when he had been imposed upon. As he aged, his disillusionment grew, until he came to regard most of mankind as essentially mercenary and fit only to be the tools of those skillful enough to use them.[16] Only a few intimates did he trust. In one of the more bitter moments of his solitude he recorded his feelings thus:

> When you have passed through the romantic period of your existence, and found your warm sympathies and ardent hopes all chilled or blasted; and the milk of human kindness which flows in your breast is in danger of being curdled by the cold ingratitude of those upon whom you have continually bestowed nothing but benefactions, you will learn to appreciate the truth of the remark "that he is a happy man who has one true friend; but he is more truly happy who never has need of a friend."[17]

Some of this bitterness had arisen from the repeated dashing of ardent political hopes. The success of Lancaster's most eminent politician, James Buchanan, was an unhappy contrast to the hitherto blasted career of Old Thad. Since that day in 1827 when the two had taken separate paths, the one to become a Democrat and the other a Whig, Buchanan had advanced from state legislator to congressman, from senator to secretary of state, from first-class ambassador to president of the United States. For many

[15] S. G. Boggs to Stevens, May 28, 1842, in the Stevens Papers. Boggs apparently desired payment for his aunt from Stevens, the trustee of her deceased husband's estate. He wrote to Stevens: "I ... must say, from your reputed generous nature, [I] expected more prompt attention in behalf of the widow." Stevens at once sent the letter on to the Gettysburg Bank with the notation: "Will Mr. McPherson give heed to the within, and make us pay off and he pay the poor widow?"

[16] Alexander H. Hood, "Thaddeus Stevens," in Alexander Harris, ed., *A Biographical History of Lancaster County* (Lancaster, 1872), 589–591.

[17] Undated note in Stevens' handwriting in the Stevens Papers, vol. 16.

LYDIA HAMILTON SMITH (1813–1884)

This photograph, in the possession of the Lancaster County Historical Society, though it was made at some time after the death of Stevens, suggests the comeliness, capability, and good taste of the younger woman whom he knew.

years these two Lancaster lawyers had exchanged scurrilities from the stump but had refused to exchange civilities on the street. They passed each other by without a word or even a nod. Stevens had once taken umbrage, the story went, when, at a reception in the house of Dr. Henry Carpenter (the regular physician of both), Buchanan had failed to notice his outstretched hand. Beneath an ill-concealed personal hostility, nevertheless, there existed a certain professional camaraderie between these two politicians. Thus, when the Whig, Fillmore, was president and Stevens as congressman was thought to have his ear, Buchanan had once politely requested a favor—"I address you and *you* alone . . . without expecting that you will be able, consistently with the duty which you owe to your political friends, to do anything for me"—and Stevens had politely complied by recommending Buchanan's nephew for an appointment to West Point.[18]

Quite different from the Stevens household on South Queen Street was the Buchanan estate on the edge of town. At Wheatland Buchanan, a more handsome and dignified-appearing bachelor than Old Thad, spent his vacations from political office somewhat in the style of a Southern planter. There his charming niece, Harriet Lane, presided as hostess when he politely entertained. On a summer evening the rays of the setting sun would soften the outlines of his Georgian mansion; tree frogs would buzz and clack above lengthening shadows on the spacious lawn; small boys would invade the orchard at the rear of the house and make off with apples not yet ripe. There was about the entire place an air of gentility.

No such country gentleman as Buchanan was Old Thad, and yet at times he, too, displayed a gentleman's tastes. Once, for example, when he sent an order to his tailor, he specified "a light summer coat—black—well made & genteel." Moreover, along with Buchanan and the best of society, he went occasionally to Bedford Springs in the mountains—"par excellence, *the* place for comfort and enjoyment during the hot summer months," and a place

---

[18] Obituary of Stevens in the *New York Tribune*, August 18, 1868; Buchanan to Stevens, July 31, August 10, 1850, in the Stevens Papers.

that at least aspired to be "the most fashionable" of Pennsylvania resorts.[19]

Even Buchanan had no such gentlemanly power as Stevens enjoyed at his Caledonia Iron Works. Here, as owner of more than twelve thousand acres and master of more than two hundred workmen and their families, Stevens was monarch of all he surveyed. His was indeed a position which many a lesser plantation owner of the South might well have envied. He was doubtless as kindly an employer as the most "patriarchal" of slaveholders. Few of his employees left him; when they were hired, he paid the expense of moving in; if they quit, they had to bear the expense of moving out. They were completely dependent upon the iron-master. Houses he provided, with no visible rent. Repairs they made with nails and lumber that he supplied. Food, clothing, and other necessaries they charged against their accounts at the company store; and if they got behind during a slack season, they had a chance to work out their bills in busier times. Even their religious pabulum came largely from revival meetings held upon the furnace grounds.[20] Thus, in the exercise of influence over other lives, there was doubtless compensation for the ironmaster even when his business ran, as it often did, at a loss.

So unprofitable had Caledonia been during much of its history that Stevens often referred to it ironically as his "sinking fund." Between 1848 and 1852 he repeatedly resolved to sell the property. A wave of prosperity, following the gold discoveries of '49 in California, caused him to change his mind. Thereafter he began to add hundreds of acres of timberland, sawmills, and iron-working equipment, instead of reducing his investment in the

[19] Stevens to Messrs. Rohle and Winebrun, May 25, 1846, manuscript in the possession of T. Fred. Woodley; *Bedford Inquirer*, July 16, August 1, 1845.

[20] For a brief history of the Caledonia Iron Works and a sketch of life at the furnace, see [Mira L. Dock], "Thaddeus Stevens as an Iron-Master," in the *Philadelphia Times*, July 14, 1895. In the summer of 1939 Miss Dock, then a keen-minded woman of about eighty-five, elaborated upon her article in conversations with me at her home near Black Gap, Pennsylvania. The chief source of the information she then gave, as well as of the facts in her article, was John Sweeney, Stevens' manager, whom she interviewed in the 1890's and on whose remarks she made careful notes.

works.[21] Temporary prosperity could hardly hide the fact, however, that he operated at a disadvantage against the competition of more modern plants which, in place of charcoal, were now using anthracite. Although his "Pond Bank" ore had the reputation of being unusually rich, it lay in pockets that were difficult to mine, and the nearest "fluxing stone" had to be secured from a distance of several miles. Also, the nearest railroad station was six miles away; Caledonia even by rail was relatively far from the larger markets, and transportation costs were therefore high.

As a whole the charcoal-iron industry was declining in Pennsylvania (though expanding in some of the Western states, where abundant timber could still be found in conjunction with surface deposits of ore). From the year 1715, when the first one was established, the number of charcoal furnaces in Pennsylvania had increased annually until 1847, and every year thereafter one or more had been abandoned for every new one that had been built. This decline had been accompanied by a steady increase in the number of furnaces using raw coal or coke.[22]

With a view, perhaps, to hedging his investment, Stevens began during the 1850's to buy up coal lands, at the same time that he was enlarging his Caledonia works. In May of 1855 he wrote to his friend and banker, Samuel Shock, of Columbia:

As money is about out with you I send you notes to discount amounting to $5000 all at six months but one ($1500) at twelve, which you may either discount or not as suits your interest. This money I intend to leave on deposit, drawing it out in your own small notes as I need it to pay my workmen who are building my rolling mill in Franklin County. I suppose none of it will be needed for a month; and then about $500 at a time as the work progresses. I suppose the 6 mo. notes will be due before most of it is needed; but I desire to have the fund provided so that I may be at liberty to ramble this summer free from care.

In August Stevens wrote to another friend:

[21] In 1852, for example, Stevens bought (for six hundred dollars, at a sale by the Orphans Court) several tracts of woodland aggregating about eleven hundred acres, "with two Saw Mills & several log houses thereon erected," on the headwaters of the Conococheague and lying in both Franklin and Adams Counties. Records of Deeds, vol. S, pp. 650–651, in the Adams County Courthouse, at Gettysburg.

[22] [Henry McAllister, Jr.], *Report of the Secretary of the American Iron and Steel Association* (Philadelphia, 1868), 11–14.

I have just returned home from my summer excursion, and rec'd your letter. . . . I was glad to hear from an old friend, whom I now seldom see. . . .

I (and several others) own the Rape tract. I suppose it (at least a considerable portion of it) is coal. Now sir, can you say what is its value? What can you and I afford to give for it? I could buy the others out I think—write me before it is further explored, as some of them in interest are about to do.

Apparently the outlook darkened soon, for in October Stevens again wrote to Shock: "From a letter which I rec'd from N. York I infer that Thompson and his brother-in-law will fail to pay their notes. Perhaps, like us, they find coal land speculations not profitable."[23]

But worse was to come. Whatever had been his prospects in 1855 of paying off old obligations and replacing them with new, productive debts, all optimism was abruptly ended by the Panic of '57. As prices dropped in 1857 and 1858 the fires went out in more than half of the charcoal furnaces of the state. Stevens managed to keep Caledonia from going out of blast, but sales were slow. In December, 1858, he received a report from Alanson at the furnace that the "Chalfery Forge" had not been running at all "for want of coal," that the "Finery" had made in a week only eight tons of "small Blooms," and that there were "25 tons slabs" lying unsold in Chambersburg. Still the work went on, producing quantities of bar iron, nail rods, wagon tires, plowshares, and other kinds of manufactured iron, as well as unworked blooms. Responsibility for the business had devolved upon Stevens for a decade—ever since, in 1848, he had bought out his partner and become sole owner. He had been reasonably successful as an absentee ironmaster but now, with the depression and with his anticipated duties as a congressman, he found it necessary to hire a full-time manager. In that capacity John Sweeney went to Caledonia on September 20, 1858.[24]

[23] Stevens to Samuel Shock, May 20, October 21, 1855, manuscripts in the possession of T. Fred. Woodley; Stevens to Lewis Coryell, August 10, 1855, in the Coryell Papers, Historical Society of Pennsylvania, Philadelphia.

[24] *Philadelphia Press*, March 18, 1858; Alanson J. Stevens to Stevens, December 12, 1858, in the Stevens Papers; deposition of Sweeney in *Estate of Thaddeus Stevens, Deceased: Audit. Notes of Testimony*, 28–29.

Considering the condition of his own ironworks, Stevens had real and personal reasons for demanding a protective tariff when, after his six-year absence, he re-entered Congress in 1859. He now planned to be no mere transient visitor in Washington as he had been when a congressman before, no longer a boarder at the bachelor "messes." He rented a house behind the capitol at 279 South B Street (almost a duplicate of his own in Lancaster), to be kept by Lydia Smith. Before Congress met, however, an event occurred which made "impending crisis" and "irrepressible conflict" seem like more than merely current catchwords, and which for the time submerged the tariff issue beneath more dramatic aspects of the sectional fight.

The event was John Brown's raid. During the summer of 1859 John Brown had made his preparations right in the Caledonia area. The good people of Chambersburg had been given no reason to suspect the stranger in their midst, the fierce-eyed, soft-spoken man with the long white beard. Nevertheless, after the October raid, they seemed to be touched with a kind of complicity, at least in the minds of those with an excessive imagination and political or sectional animosity. In the opinion of Lancaster Democrats, Stevens—along, indeed, with the whole of his party—was directly or indirectly to blame. "The Republican party is responsible for the recent insurrection and bloodshed at Harper's Ferry," said the *Lancaster Intelligencer*. The editor recalled the "Christina negro riot" of 1851 and challenged Old Thad to tell which side he was on, then and now—the side of the "blacks" or that of the "whites." In such a chiaroscuro were the issues set.

While the old man of Ossawatomie was going calmly to the gallows in December, 1859, congressmen were assembling in the electric atmosphere of Washington. Would the Republicans be able to control the new House? They could claim a plurality but not a majority of the membership, which included 113 Republicans, 93 Democrats, 8 "anti-Lecompton" Democrats (those completely disaffected over the Kansas question), and 23 "Americans" from the South. To elect a speaker would require 119 votes—6 more than the Republicans had. After days of balloting (as ten years before, in 1849) the House remained leaderless and unorganized, with no prospect of an early agreement. The proceedings degenerated into an orgy of speechmaking, in which Northern and Southern extremists struggled for the privilege of denouncing the sectionalism of the other side.

Stevens quickly jumped into the verbal fray. With his sarcasm he tried to scourge or shame the anti-Lecompton Democrats and even the "South Americans" over to the Republican side. Had they anything in common with the party of Buchanan? Could they hope for any of the patronage of the president? What did they fear in a Republican victory? The party had no intention of freeing the slaves but desired only to go ahead and "provide for the wants of the country." In reply to one of the harangues of Old Thad, a Southerner hailed the leader of the "opposing forces" as "the distinguished hero of the Buckshot War." Another war might come, but the "saltatory accomplishments" of Stevens would enable him to leap out of difficulty. He had already, in 1838, given "in an ingenious way a practical illustration of peaceable secession."[25]

As the argument dragged on, some of the more hot-tempered members threatened to use more upon their opponents than mere words. Many came to the sessions with bulging pockets and were prepared to pull out their hidden guns if need be. When a Southern member challenged a Westerner to a duel, the latter named bowie knives as weapons, and the former refused—then Old Thad stepped in to suggest that they use dungforks. On another occasion he rose to renew a point of order. Southerners were taking up the time of the House with their denunciations of the "Union meetings" in the North and of the Republican pamphlet based on a Southerner's attack on slavery, *The Impending Crisis of the South*. Old Thad objected that the House was not competent to entertain any such questions; it must proceed with the election of a speaker or adjourn. Before he had concluded his remarks, Representative Crawford of Georgia got up to reply

[25] *Lancaster Intelligencer*, November 1, 1859; *Lancaster Examiner*, November 23, 1859; *Congressional Globe*, 36 Congress, 1 session (1859–60), 584–586.

and moved menacingly toward Stevens in the area just in front of the speaker's desk. It looked for a few minutes as if there might be a fight, but some of the friends of Crawford finally drew him away. Having stood quietly and calmly in the fact of this interruption, Old Thad now smiled as he turned to the Republican side and said, "That is the way, gentlemen, they *used* to frighten us."[26]

After days of ill-tempered gestures and futile speechmaking, Stevens wrote to a lawyer colleague in Lancaster: "The organization of the House is not yet in sight." As a result of this discouraging prospect life in Washington during the greater part of the winter of 1859–60 was to be extraordinarily dull. At best the city was a trying place to live in, with its streets alternately mud and dust, its vast distances, its unfinished capitol—symbol, perhaps, of a Union not yet complete. But by comparison it had been "heretofore the gay and crowded political metropolis." Now, because of the stalemate in Congress, the metropolis was "sunk in deplorable apathy and stagnation," the usual crowds of visitors were lacking, the hotels quiet, almost deserted. Unable to draw the pay and mileage due them, congressmen freely passed out their I O U's. Washingtonians, instead of greeting each other on the street with "how de do," would ask, "When do you think the House will organize?"

Busier than ever, though, were the gambling halls, or, as they were commonly known, the "gambling hells." The proprietor of one of them, it was said, soon held I O U's from nearly every member of the House. And none of the congressmen was a more devoted gambler than Old Thad. His favorite amusement, after Mrs. Smith had served his supper in their home at the east of the capitol, was to go down Pennsylvania Avenue and spend the evening at Hall and Pemberton's Faro Bank. This was one of a number of such places on the Avenue, all of which were easily recognizable by the heavily curtained windows and the general darkness, except above the door, where the street number ap-

[26] A. G. Riddle, *Benjamin F. Wade* (Cleveland, 1886), 236 and footnote; Washington *Republic*, quoted in the *Lancaster Examiner*, December 14, 1859.

peared "brightly gilt on the transom light," illuminated by the "red glare of the chandelier" in the vestibule within.[27]

As compared with his colleagues, Stevens was not an exceptionally "heavy player," though another congressman recorded that he once won fourteen hundred dollars on a twenty-dollar goldpiece. Money was not the object. One evening he was playing in what he called "hard luck." One of the clerks of the House, always at his elbow, urged him to "put a stack on the ace," which had lost three times in a row. "I will stake my reputation," said the clerk, "that the ace wins." With a doubting glance at his self-appointed adviser, Stevens shoved a stack of blue chips, worth fifty dollars, over to the ace. The ace lost. To the man who had staked his "reputation," Old Thad now said without a smile, "Martin, you owe me a quarter."[28]

After more than two months, in February of 1860, the House finally agreed upon a speaker. The compromise candidate was a Republican, but a moderate one: A. C. M. Pennington of New Jersey. Yet the Republican victory was none the less real, as became apparent when the membership of the committees was known. A Lancaster editor rejoiced: "The complexion of the Committee of Ways and Means, which is most important to Pennsylvania, is entirely satisfactory to the interests in which she is most vitally concerned. The Hon. Thaddeus Stevens will represent them." So also would the chairman, John Sherman of Ohio and four others—all "tariff men." "The policy of protecting American industry will be represented by six members of the committee out of nine, thus *exactly reversing the cast of the last Democratic Congress.*" Stevens at once fulfilled the expectation of his Lancaster constituents by making a speech in which he criticized the previous Congress for its disregard of the American manufacturer. "Take, for instance, iron," he said, as he warmed

[27] Stevens to Thomas E. Franklin, December 11, 1859, manuscript in the library of the Lancaster County Historical Society, Lancaster; *Philadelphia Press,* January 18, 1860; J. B. Ellis, *The Sights and Secrets of the National Capital* (New York, 1869), 404.

[28] James M. Scovel, "Thaddeus Stevens," in *Lippincott's Magazine,* 61 (1898): 549.

up to a discussion of his favorite subject. Business was bad, and
even if "a little spurt of a rise came in the iron market," English
iron would be "taken out of warehouses and thrown upon the
market" to force prices down again.[29]

He presented the case with vigor but added nothing new to
the philosophy of protection. The tariff philosopher was Henry
C. Carey, chairman of the Republican state committee in Pennsylvania, who, during the winter made black by depression and
political confusion, was clarifying the party attitude in public
letters upon "Financial Crises—their Causes and Effects." All
agreed, he wrote, that the great question of the day was "Slavery
and Freedom." Slavery could exist in the South only so long as
that region depended upon a one-crop agricultural economy.
Slavery existed in the North so long as there were depressions, for
depressions made paupers, and paupers were slaves in all but
name. The way to maintain prosperity and diversify the industry
of the whole country—and thus to abolish slavery both North and
South—was to build up home markets and manufactories through
a high protective tariff.[30] Carey's program was the same in principle as Henry Clay's old American System, but it was given a new
antislavery twist. By such reasoning might the "niggerism" of
men like Thaddeus Stevens be reconciled with their protectionism.

Although intrenched in the crucial committee of the House, the
party of iron could not hope for immediate success. The party of
"slavery" still held the Senate and the presidency, not to mention
the Supreme Court. The ruling group was essentially the same as
Stevens had assailed for a generation: Northern mercantile and
banking interests and Southern planting interests devoted with
more than an abstract loyalty to the idea of free trade. During
the session of 1859–60 he had berated "the old women and the
men in petticoats and the misers at the North" who allowed the
South to frighten them into the belief that if they elected a
"northern man with northern principles," the Union would "be

---

[29] *Lancaster Examiner*, February 15, 1860; *Congressional Globe*, 36 Congress,
1 session (1859–60), 1956 ff.
[30] *New York Tribune*, January 27, 1860.

dissolved, and all their industrial and pecuniary interests sacrificed."[31] In the spring of 1860 Republicans turned to the task of
nominating a Northern man with Northern principles who might
win the November campaign.

[31] *Congressional Globe,* 36 Congress, 1 session (1859–60), 584–586.

IX. Peace—or the Party?

THE future looked auspicious for Republicans as they prepared to gather at Chicago in May of 1860 to nominate a man for president. Already the Democrats had met in convention at Charleston and had disbanded after failing to find a mean between Northern and Southern extremes. Their leaders were divided, their organization was splitting in two. The Republican party, on the other hand, frankly sectional in membership and in aims, had no need to reconcile within itself a seemingly irreconcilable North and South. Republicans had reason to rejoice.

And yet Thaddeus Stevens felt little enthusiasm as the day of the convention approached. In April, viewing the party's prospects and his own from Washington, he hesitated even to go to Chicago. He could honestly plead that his health was none too good, and the trip would be a long one—longer, indeed, than any he had ever made before. He could protest that he had cases to argue at the spring term of the supreme court in Harrisburg and might not get back in time. But what moved him more was the knowledge that if he went it would be as a follower and not a leader in the Pennsylvania delegation. Simon Cameron would be in command. As a senator from Pennsylvania Cameron had been able to attract a following throughout the state, while as a representative from Lancaster Stevens had acquired little influence outside his own congressional district. True, Cameron must share his power with Andrew G. Curtin, but between them the "two C's" had things pretty much their own way. Early in 1860 Cameron had agreed to support Curtin as the candidate of the People's party for governor, and Curtin in turn had promised to back Cameron as Pennsylvania's favorite son at the convention in May. To appease Old Thad, Cameron had secured his appointment as one of the delegates at large. At the last minute Stevens decided to attend, but he could have taken little comfort in the prediction of the *Philadelphia Press* that he would "undoubtedly exercise great influence over the deliberations."[1]

On the Chicago-bound train, accompanied by his nephew Thaddeus, Jr., Old Thad discussed the various presidential possibilities with Alexander K. McClure, the new chairman of the Pennsylvania state committee. Stevens believed that William H. Seward of New York, the general favorite and the outstanding leader of the party, would be a poor choice. Seward would "drive off the American vote." The wisest policy, said Stevens, would be to nominate a man thoroughly safe and sound who would disarm the conservative opposition, especially in Pennsylvania, to the radicalism of the Republican platform. Again, as in 1856, he had in mind Judge John McLean. He was willing to grant that McLean, now an old man, would probably not last through a four-year term; but the party could choose as a running mate some vigorous young Republican and McLean would "pull him through."[2]

At Chicago the Pennsylvanians proved to be a factious crew. Most of them, like Stevens, were "decidedly, immovably averse" to the nomination of Seward, but they could not agree on a substitute. A majority stood by Cameron, and even Stevens seemed publicly to support him, but a determined minority held out for McLean. At this juncture the shrewd managers of Abraham Lincoln brought their man forward as a candidate upon whom the divided Pennsylvanians might unite. They finally decided to vote for Cameron on the first ballot, McLean on the second, and Lincoln on the rest. But Stevens, a dissenter to the end, voted for McLean even on the third ballot which nominated the railsplitter from Illinois. Old Thad did not join the claques who now cheered and stamped and whistled in the Wigwam while the

---

[1] Alexander K. McClure, *Abraham Lincoln and Men of War-Times* (Philadelphia, 1892), 395; *Philadelphia Press*, May 4, 1860; Stevens to Thos. E. Franklin, April 25, May 7, 1860, manuscripts in the library of the Lancaster County Historical Society, Lancaster.

[2] *Colonel Alexander K. McClure's Recollections of Half a Century* (Salem, Massachusetts, [1902]), 419; *Lancaster Examiner*, May 16, 1860; *Philadelphia Press*, May 21, 1860.

cannon boomed upon its roof. The only result of the convention he could approve was the tariff plank; this much, at least, the Pennsylvanians had succeeded in putting into the platform.[3]

Back in Washington, Old Thad did not openly criticize the choice of Lincoln or resent the role of Cameron; for if the Republicans were to win the autumn campaign, it was time for all good men to hide their differences and come to the aid of the party. Much was to depend upon Pennsylvania, a doubtful and pivotal state, whose election in October was expected to show how other states would go in November. There the tariff would be a shibboleth to which all might rally. "We will call Pennsylvania to arms in every section of the state," McClure was writing to Cameron, "and make Protection the battle-cry." With this cry Republicans would have good prospects of victory against the divided foe. As the campaign got under way there were three candidates in the field opposed to Lincoln: Douglas, the nominee of the Northern Democrats; Breckinridge, of the Southern Democrats; and Bell, of the Constitutional Union party. But there was danger that none of the four candidates would have a clear majority of the electoral vote. In that case the election would devolve upon the House of Representatives, and there Breckinridge might possibly win. It was well that Stevens and Cameron should stick together.

In the summer of 1860 it began to appear, however, that all was not as it should be between these Republican friends. Stevens was having to fend against Cameron's encroachments upon his own bailiwick. After the Lancaster County convention of the People's party it was said that the "Republicans, *par excellence,*" had been sold out to the "Cameronian, or guerilla, wing of the party." Except for Stevens, all the important candidates on the

---

[3] McClure, *Lincoln and Men of War-Times,* 36; F. B. Carpenter, "How Lincoln Was Nominated," in *Century Magazine,* old series, 24:854–855; *New York Herald,* May 15, 1860; *Lancaster Examiner,* May 16, 1860; *Philadelphia Press,* May 21, 1860; *New York Tribune,* May 28, 1860. At Chicago Stevens apparently followed a very devious course, and his attitude was not well understood even among the members of his own delegation. One of them, an adherent of Cameron, wrote to Cameron "testifying to the fidelity of some of your friends," among whom the writer included Old Thad. Bobbs to Cameron, May 19, 1860, in the Simon Cameron Papers, Library of Congress.

local ticket were out-and-out friends of Cameron. "Mr. Stevens will be re-elected to Congress," ran the report, "but that election is intended by his great rival to finish his political course. Henceforth he is to be laid upon the shelf, and the political destinies of the Old Guard will pass into the hands of his more adroit and unscrupulous adversary. . . . If he is passive under the lash of Gen-Cameron, he is not the same man he was ten years ago. We shall see." The reckoning was to be postponed until after Lincoln's election.[4]

Meanwhile, during September, Old Thad traveled back and forth in Pennsylvania, stumping loyally for the Republican candidate. Upon such speakers as he fell the burden of the campaign, for the candidate himself remained at home, silent as the sphinx. From such canvassers came pronouncements which, uncontradicted, had to be accepted as authorized exegeses of the party platform. Democrats both North and South might well take alarm when they read reports of Stevens' address at the Cooper Union in New York, where during the previous winter Lincoln had spoken in thoroughly noncommittal terms. At Cooper Union Old Thad was introduced as "one of the earliest, ablest, and most uncompromising Republicans" in the land. While he talked a band of "Wide-Awakes," dressed in capes and bearing lighted torches, filed in and took their seats.[5]

There were, said the speaker, two main issues in the campaign. One was, of course, "liberty or slavery"; but more important was the question of protection or free trade. If any of the three candidates of free trade was elected, there would be no prosperity until long and severe suffering had wrought a revolution in public opinion. If Lincoln, the candidate of protection, was elected, a high tariff would follow as soon as the Democratic majority in the Senate was overcome, and a Republican president would be the

[4] McClure to Cameron, June 6, 1860, in the Cameron Papers; *Lancaster Intelligencer*, September 11, 1860.

[5] Frederic Bancroft and William A. Dunning, eds., *The Reminiscences of Carl Schurz* (3 vols., New York, 1908), 3:215; *Philadelphia Press*, September 20, 1860; *Lancaster Intelligencer*, September 25, 1860; *New York Tribune*, September 27, 1860.

forerunner of a Republican Senate. Both the West and the South would remain poor until (with protection) they developed industries of their own. But Southerners could never have "manufactures or commerce" while they were "cursed with slavery": their "domestic institutions" must be changed! In the territories "every inch" of land should belong to "free men." The Dred Scott decision, legalizing slavery therein, was only an *obiter dicta*— which, "being fairly translated," meant "the idle gabble of a judge." Breckinridge was honest in frankly advocating slavery in the territories; but Douglas with his doctrine of popular sovereignty was only a "fraudulent trickster," and his sycophancy to Southerners had been a disgrace. As for the Constitutional Union party, the *"live* men" in it would vote Republican; the "trafficking leaders," metropolitan merchants who feared the loss of sales to the South, were beyond hope and beneath contempt. "Being of no gender, cool, passionless, and mostly busied with mercenary pursuits, they claim to be safe guardians of the Union, for the same reason that eunuchs are entrusted with the harem." Only "a few old women in pantaloons" were afraid of the Southern threat that the election of Lincoln would lead to secession and perhaps to war. On the contrary, "every avenue leading from Virginia to the White House" would be "blocked by the bold chivalry begging for office."[6]

While Stevens and other Pennsylvania Republicans were shouting the battle cry of protectionism, the rivalries among them continued quietly but intensely during October. Not until January, 1861, was the legislature again to elect a United States senator, but the probability that he would be a Republican was already exciting the ambitions of hopefuls of the party. Among these was Old Thad. The two C's, however, were backing a Cameron man for senator. Stevens' problem was to break up the alliance of the two C's. And so Cameron heard from his lieutenant in Lancaster:"Stephens [*sic*] has been successfully baited for the Senate and is now disposed to give you quiet digs by representing you as

[6] Stevens' address at the Cooper Union Institute on September 27 was printed in full in the *New York Tribune*, September 28, 1860.

desiring Curtin's defeat." After the October victory at the polls, which made Curtin governor and assured a Republican legislature, Old Thad was no less determined to wear the senatorial robe. To Edward McPherson, who published newspapers in Gettysburg and elsewhere, he wrote: "I have some aspirations for the U. States Senate—If you could furnish a paragraph in my favor in each of your papers I would esteem it a favor—coming from my old home I should greatly prize it." In return he assured McPherson: "Whatever the request is that you have to make of Lincoln you may count on my aid to the fullest extent." The successes in Pennsylvania made it reasonable to promise federal patronage thus early, and yet it would not do to become overconfident. "We must not get a sleep until after the 6th Nov.," Old Thad warned, "as the democrats are always alive."[7]

On November 6 vigilance got its reward. Yet Lincoln, though he had a large majority in the electoral college, had only some two-fifths of the popular vote. Republican voters were a decided minority in the country as a whole and, furthermore, they were not agreed on what the election of Lincoln meant. To those in the West it meant free homesteads and internal improvements at federal expense. To Pennsylvanians it signified protection for iron and coal. To all, however, it promised an eventual end of Southern power in national politics as a result of the closure of the West to slaveholding colonists and statemakers. It might even lead, as Old Thad had hinted at Cooper Union, to a change in the "domestic institutions" of the South. Even if it failed to go that far, the Republican program would reduce the profits of slavery and threaten the continued existence of the plantation way of life. During the campaign Stevens had called the bluff of Southerners who swore they would secede from the Union if Lincoln won. Now, as soon as they heard the returns, the legislators of South Carolina began to take steps for the withdrawal of their state. In some ways the beginning of secession compli-

[7] McClure, *Lincoln and Men of War-Times*, 395; J. P. Sanderson to Cameron, October 1, 1860, and David Wilmot to Cameron, October 26, 1860, in the Cameron Papers; Stevens to McPherson, October 23, 1860, in the Thaddeus Stevens Papers, Library of Congress.

cated, and in other ways simplified, the problem that Republican politicians recognized as theirs—the problem of unifying the Northern party and consolidating their victory at the polls.

The four months from the election of Lincoln to his inauguration were to seem like an interregnum. In Washington, at the opening of Congress early in December, Old Thad could see at close hand the indecision and helplessness of the national government. The message that President Buchanan sent to Congress denied the right of secession but also denied his constitutional power to prevent it. Indeed, what was there to be done? Three proposals were in the air: the government might simply let the "erring sisters" go in peace, as Greeley suggested; it might crush the "rebellion" by armed force; or it might effect a compromise, as it had done in 1820, in 1833, and again in 1850. The president and many a congressman hoped to find some middle ground acceptable to both North and South. In the Senate John J. Crittenden of Kentucky proposed to settle the sectional quarrel by dividing the territories along the latitude of 36° 30′ and prohibiting the introduction of slavery above but not below that line. If Republicans should agree to this, they would be abandoning the free-soil plank of their platform. And so, while congressmen debated the Crittenden Compromise, Old Thad left the capital in disgust.

He had business in Pennsylvania, for its legislators were soon to assemble and elect a senator, who he hoped would be himself. But the outlook there was no more cheering than in Washington. From Caledonia he dispatched a letter on December 19, while in Charleston people were getting ready to secede on the morrow, to Representative McPherson: "I had expected to be back before this. But a touch of rheumatism made me halt, expecting an adjournment for the holidays. If that is not likely to take place please inform me . . . and I shall then return. If likely to take place soon I will stay till New Years. I do not care to be present while the process of humiliation is going on—Buchanan is a very traitor." The secession of South Carolina made real and urgent the question, heretofore theoretical, of the disposition of the federal property there. Did it belong to the Carolinians or to the United States? When Stevens returned to Congress after Christmas, he demanded that the president inform the House what he had done and what he intended to do about the various government buildings and particularly the fort.[8]

While Stevens had been sulking at Caledonia, other prominent Republicans had been traveling, at the call of Lincoln, to Springfield, Illinois, to confer with the president-elect about policies and personnel. Lincoln advised several that Republicans in Congress must assent to no compromise which, like that of Crittenden, would violate the free-soil plank of the party platform. To Cameron he gave a letter promising him a place in the cabinet. When Cameron got back to Washington, just after New Year's day, 1861, he met Stevens and told him of Lincoln's offer. "Which," thought Old Thad, "is no doubt true." He was chagrined. Granted that he had no chance of being the new senator from Pennsylvania, he would in any case much rather join the incoming administration as secretary of the treasury. "Seward will also go in," he feared; and Seward like Cameron was advocating a compromise with the South! At once he wrote to Salmon P. Chase, governor of Ohio, and, complaining of "too many weak knees" in Congress, requested information about the prospective strength of the cabinet. Meanwhile the badgered president-elect was receiving so many protests against his commitment to Cameron that he was beset by serious doubts. His manager at Chicago had contracted in his name to give Cameron a cabinet place. What was he to do? Finally he wrote and asked Cameron to let him recall the offer he had made at Springfield. Concerning all this Stevens remained in the dark. Confusingly, the newspapers said that Cameron had refused a position, that he had not even been offered one, that he had in fact been offered it and had not turned it down. Chase's reply to the pointed queries of Old Thad, though praising him for his uncompromising stand, evaded his questions and shed no light.[9]

[8] Stevens to McPherson, December 19, 1860, in the Stevens Papers; *Congressional Globe*, 36 Congress, 2 session (1860–61), 219–220.

[9] Lincoln to Cameron, January 3, 1861, in the Cameron Papers; Stevens to Simon Stevens, January 4, 1861, in the Stevens Papers; Stevens to Chase, January 4, 1861, in the Salmon P. Chase MSS., Historical Society of Pennsyl-

On January 10 Stevens was at last able to record: "Genl Cameron has just informed me that he has positively declined. Some of our delegation wish to recommend me. But I have no faith in their sincerity." While a petition began to circulate among the Pennsylvania members of Congress demanding his appointment, he wrote to Simon Stevens (no relative but a former law student of Old Thad's and now a lawyer in New York) asking for "a word of commendation from New York friends." He composed another letter, for him unusually long and legibly written, to Alexander K. McClure, chairman of the Pennsylvania state committee. McClure sent back a discouraging reply. Having lately come from a conference with Lincoln, he could say that, though it was true that Cameron had been rejected, no other Pennsylvanian would be called to the cabinet. (Indeed, Lincoln had told another visitor at Springfield that "Thad Stevens was too old. Cameron or nothing.") Undeterred, Stevens made an appointment to meet McClure in Harrisburg. There McClure found him more interested in reaching the cabinet than he had ever known him to be in any other of his political aspirations. Stevens tried to induce the legislature to recommend him and allowed the rumor to get out that he had the blessing of none other than Cameron himself! If in fact Cameron had approved the candidacy of Old Thad, he soon had good reason to change his mind. On January 13 Lincoln wrote guaranteeing to make no appointment for Pennsylvania without consulting him. The president-elect explained that he had recalled the original offer only to keep the matter from being "complicated with the Penn. senatorial election." That election went to Edgar Cowan, Cameron's man. So vanished Stevens' hopes, like snow upon the desert's dusty face.[10]

vania, Philadelphia; Chase to Stevens, January 9, 1861, in Robert B. Warden, *Private Life and Public Services of Salmon Portland Chase* (New York, 1874), 377; *Philadelphia Press*, January 5, 9, 11, 1861; *New York Times*, January 11, 1861.

[10] Alexander K. McClure, *Old-Time Notes of Pennsylvania* (2 vols., Philadelphia, 1905), 1:452; McClure, *Lincoln and Men of War-Times*, 282–283; Stevens to Simon Stevens, January 10, 1861, in the Stevens Papers; William Larimer to Cameron, January 13, 1861, and Lincoln to Cameron, January 13, 1861, in the Cameron Papers. One of the Pennsylvania state senators, who was

Preoccupied as he was with the pursuit of his own political fortunes, Old Thad had been able to give little attention to the secession crisis. It was worsening fast. The steamer *Star of the West*, sent to provision Fort Sumter, had been fired upon. Mississippi, Florida, and Alabama had followed South Carolina out of the Union; and Georgia, Louisiana, and Texas were getting ready to go. When Old Thad returned to the debates in Congress, he had little to say but now and again heckled the proponents of compromise. The House committee of thirty-three, appointed to formulate a sectional adjustment, was a "committee of incubation" which would hatch no young; the idea of calling a convention of all the states was ridiculous; the Crittenden Compromise was merely a "delicate piece of satire."

At last, on January 29, Stevens rose to speak his mind. He apologized for his poor health and his poor voice. In truth his rheumatism was getting bad, and his hundreds of harangues in the open air had long since strained his vocal chords. But the words he uttered, whatever the quality of the voice which uttered them, were strong. The American people, he said, had legally and constitutionally elected the man of their choice as president of the United States. "The American people dared to disobey the commands of slavery; and this is proclaimed as just cause of secession and civil war. Sir, has it come to this? Cannot the people of the United States choose whom they please President, without stirring up rebellion, and requiring humiliation, concessions, and compromises to appease the insurgents? Sir, I would take no steps to propitiate such a feeling. Rather than show repentance

also the owner of a newspaper in Lancaster, confessed that he was puzzled by the cabinet question. From Harrisburg he wrote to Cameron: "There is a report here that you have recommended Mr. Stevens for the cabinet to Mr. Lincoln, or at least have proposed it to Stevens and his friends here are trying to get the state administration to recommend him, and they wish *me to lead off with a recommendation* of Senators and Members. They all admit he cannot be appointed unless *you agree to it*. I do not wish to go into it, unless he is likely to go in with your approbation.... If there is no hope for Mr. S. getting in & there is a move here for him, why coming from his county self protection would indicate that I should join in it. Of course this is taking for granted that *what appears* about your own position upon the Cabinet is settled." John A. Hiestand to Cameron, January 14, 1861, in the Cameron Papers.

for the election of Mr. Lincoln, with all its consequences, I would see this Government crumble into a thousand atoms." In the light of the election returns the statement that "the American people" had elected Lincoln was true only in a juristic sense. In simple fact, the Republicans of the North had elected him. "The plain question now presented to the North," observed the *Lancaster Intelligencer,* "is, shall the Republican party or the Union break?"[11]

Perhaps the reports of Old Thad's forthright address would reach Springfield, Illinois, and, if so, perhaps the president-elect would reconsider some of his decisions about the cabinet. Again Old Thad sought encouragement from Chase. He began his letter disingenuously, expressing his wish to see it "authoritatively announced" that Chase was to be a cabinet member—Chase, whom Pennsylvania protectionists were denouncing as a free trader, whom people were mentioning as the next secretary of the treasury, which Stevens aspired to be! He continued:

I . . . write to ask your opinion as to the prospects of our maintaining republican principles. I fear that the party will soon cease to exist. Mr. Seward's course has mortified and discouraged me. That coupled with the apostasy of Cameron, who is his echo, seems to indicate that our platform and principles are to be sacrificed to peace. The belief that they are to be two of the Cabinet (Seward certainly) makes all the mercenary (Legions) preach submission. Can we stand up against such a prime minister? Will Lincoln have nerve enough to resist?—Will he have a Cabinet who will resist?

You may possibly view Mr. Seward's cause differently from me—But I confess that with him in the State Department, and with Cameron, to make whatever department he may occupy a den of thieves, I have but little hope that we shall be able to survive the next election. If, when Mr. Lincoln came into power, he should imitate Jackson and act vigorously about coercing obedience, the people will admire and rally again to the republican standard—If he seeks to purchase peace by concessions, and ignoring platforms *a la mode* Seward I shall give up the fight being too old for another seven (or thirty) years war. I wish you could give me some hope of better things—of course, what you say will be strictly confidential.[12]

[11] *Congressional Globe,* 36 Congress, 2 session (1860–61), 231, 621–624; *Lancaster Intelligencer,* February 26, 1861.

[12] Stevens to Chase, February 3, 1861, in the Chase MSS., Historical Society of Pennsylvania.

Politicians like Old Thad could see no future for themselves or for the party should they yield one jot or tittle of their platform, but most of the people they professed to speak for favored conciliating the South. The people who had voted for Douglas or for Bell had expressed a desire for moderation, and certainly no more than a few of those who had cast their ballots for Lincoln or Breckinridge had asked for war if they could not win with peace. In local elections throughout the North during the winter of 1860–61 voters showed their disapproval of the program of violence and force. In Lancaster, at the municipal elections a few weeks after Stevens' speech of January 29, the people chose a Democratic mayor by a large majority.

But Stevens had a chance to regain some of his popularity when, in February, the Morrill bill for raising the tariff came before the House. As he saw it, the tariff was as much a political stratagem as an economic reform. He now recalled that, in response to the battle cry of protectionism, the miners and mechanics of his state had swelled the Republican vote in the recent campaign. He urged that the House pass a much more thoroughly protective measure than the Morrill bill. "You will never pass it at all," he exclaimed impatiently, "and God knows whether next year there will be a Republican party any more than there is a Democratic party." The ultimate revision of the tariff was mild, but it could be welcomed by protectionists as the first fruit of secession and an earnest of better things to come. Yet even if it reconciled Pennsylvanians to the doctrine of coercing seceders, it could hardly be expected to do the same for critics and doubters in other states of the North. The future of the Republican party would depend upon the men and measures to be chosen by the new president.[13]

Late in February Lincoln arrived in Washington after foregoing a stop in Baltimore, where an alleged assassination plot was brewing. At the various stopping places along the route from

[13] *Congressional Globe,* 36 Congress, 2 session (1860–61), 1188–1189; *Lancaster Intelligencer,* February 12, 1861. On public opinion in the nation during the winter of 1860–61, see Mary Scrugham, *The Peaceable Americans of 1860–1861 (Columbia University Studies in History, Economics, and Public Law,* no. 219, New York, 1921), 53–77.

Illinois he had repeated a brief, almost meaningless talk. He had revealed nothing of what he would do or whom he would call upon to help. At his temporary headquarters in Willards Hotel he was at once beset by politicians from all quarters and of all opinions who had favors to beg and advice to give. Among this horde was Old Thad. His old friend Joseph Ritner and his young friend Edward McPherson desired jobs for themselves or for their friends, and he himself had not been quite able to choke off his ambition for a place in the cabinet. Whether he entered it or not, he must keep Cameron out, if his own position in Lancaster County was not to be jeopardized. A Lancaster adherent of Cameron, begging him to use his influence in naming a postmaster for the district, explained: "We want to beat the Stevens faction which is dreadfully opposed to you." Certainly, with Cameron disposing patronage from the cabinet, the Stevens faction would be badly handicapped. But Old Thad received no satisfaction from Lincoln. As inauguration day drew near, the prospect was still obscure.[14]

By March 4, 1861, secession was an accomplished fact, the seceders had formed a Confederacy, and the issue before the nation was no longer how to keep the Union together but how to keep its remnant at peace. The attention of the people was focused upon Fort Sumter. Should the federal government abandon the fort and allow it to fall? Or should the government provision the fort, strengthen it, and encourage it to hold out? The Buchanan administration had made a tenuous arrangement with the Confederacy whereby each side had agreed to refrain from taking an aggressive step, but in the nature of things this delicate balance of the status quo could not last. Rather than evacuate Fort Sumter, Stevens had advised, the federal government should resist force with force. "I have full confidence," he had said, "that the gallant officer in command will successfully defend the stars and stripes, or gloriously descend, with his last soldier, to his gory bed." Thus did the coercionists drape themselves in the flag! Southerners daring to assault the Stars and

---

[14] Joseph Ritner to Stevens, February 27, 1861, in the Stevens Papers; Owen Hoppel to Cameron, February 28, 1861, in the Cameron Papers.

Stripes would perhaps send the Northern people rallying like patriots to the support of the party in power. Outright aggression upon the South, however, would certainly have the opposite effect. "No blood need be shed," Stevens, like a skillful propagandist, had said. "If it should be, on the heads of the malefactors let it rest." Very similar was the verbal strategy of Lincoln in his inaugural address. To the seceders, and particularly to those in Charleston, he said: "In your hands, my dissatisfied fellow-countrymen, and not in mine, is the momentous issue of civil war."[15]

At the inauguration James Buchanan made his last appearance as a public man, immaculate to the tips of his white hair, dignified despite his wry neck; certainly he looked more like a statesman than his bearded, slovenly clothed, ungainly successor to the White House. The ordeal of tergiversation and doubt and hesitancy was over for him, and he was about to go into retirement at Wheatland. In his eclipse there was consolation for one of his fellow lawyers of Lancaster. But the revelation of the membership of Lincoln's cabinet, which shortly came, led Old Thad to question whether the Republican administration would deal any more effectively than had Buchanan's with the traitors of the South. Sure enough, Cameron was to be in the cabinet and, of all places, in the office of secretary of war! Seward, too, was to be in, at the head of the ministry as secretary of state. And Chase, as secretary of the treasury, was to have the position Old Thad had especially desired. In the past there had been times when each of these three had come cup in hand to him. In 1831, at the Antimasonic convention in Baltimore, Seward had deigned to beg his help; in 1842, as an organizer for the Liberty party, Chase had sought him out; in 1857, in the Pennsylvania senatorial election, Cameron had accepted his aid. Lincoln, too, had been beholden to him when, in 1848, casting about for "the undisguised opinion of some experienced and

[15] Stevens presented this argument in the House of Representatives in his speech of January 29, 1861. *Congressional Globe*, 36 Congress, 2 session (1860–61), 621–624.

sagacious Pennsylvania politician," he had written to Lancaster for advice.[16] Certainly there was no justice in events, for none of these was a better man than Old Thad!

[16] Lincoln had desired to know how the election of 1848 was likely to go in Pennsylvania, and Stevens had replied promptly and at length. Lincoln to Stevens, September 3, 1848, in the Stevens Papers; Stevens to Lincoln, September 7, 1848, in A. J. Beveridge, *Abraham Lincoln, 1809–1858* (2 vols., Boston and New York, 1928), 1:462.

X. All's Fair in War
and Politics

A S THE war clouds gathered in the spring of 1861, Thaddeus
Stevens, reading his *New York Tribune*, followed the course
of events from his Lancaster home. On April 12 he read the news
that Fort Sumter had been fired upon. The effect upon Northerners was even greater than he could have hoped for. Immediately,
in towns and cities throughout the North, excited crowds ran
through the streets waving the Stars and Stripes and compelling
hesitant householders and shopkeepers to hang out their red,
white, and blue bunting. For a few days everyone was a patriot,
no one a partisan, and hordes of brave young men were ready to
go down and conquer the rebels as soon as the president gave
the call for volunteers. And when, on April 19, he issued a proclamation declaring a blockade of the Southern ports, popular enthusiasm was still at a high pitch.

But Old Thad was amazed as he soberly read the news. This
was not the way to deal with a domestic insurrection! As he had
already advised from his place in Congress, the thing to do was
to repeal the laws creating ports of entry at Charleston, New
Orleans, and elsewhere in the South. At once he packed up and
went to Washington, to lecture the president on international
law. At the White House he pointed out to Lincoln that by
declaring a blockade he had in effect recognized the Confederacy
as a belligerent and in consequence would have to carry on a
war, not merely suppress a revolt. Their conversation, as Stevens
recalled it, continued in this fashion:

"Well, that is a fact. I see the point now, but I don't know anything
about the law of nations and I thought it was all right."

"As a lawyer, Mr. Lincoln, I should have supposed you would have
seen the difficulty at once."

"Oh, well, I'm a good enough lawyer in a western law court but we don't practice the law of nations up there, and I supposed Seward knew all about it, and I left it to him. But it's done now and can't be helped, so we must get along as well as we can."[1]

Lincoln may have dismissed the policy of blockade as a *fait accompli,* to be made the most of, but his visitor perceived in it a momentous legal truth. Thereafter, whatever the protestations of the federal government, its armies were not simply putting down a large-scale well-organized riot but *legally,* as in fact, were waging war against a separate and independent belligerent. Always before Old Thad had been forced reluctantly to admit that the Constitution forbade interference in the domestic institutions of the slave states. He would abide strictly by the letter of the law. He was still a legalist, but Lincoln's proclamation had altered the facts: the Confederate states no longer came within the purview and protection of the Constitution, for officially, albeit indirectly, the Confederacy had been acknowledged a nation at war. From his law books, from the works of the publicist Vattel, Stevens concluded that "the law of nations is plain . . . *inter arma silent leges.*"[2] Or, in the layman's idiom, in war all's fair.

There was nothing that Old Thad could do about the prosecution of the war until the president should call a special session of Congress. In the meantime Lincoln dealt with the emergency in the light of his own conscience, by presidential decree. When Congress met, on the Fourth of July, Old Thad, the hitherto insignificant gentleman from Pennsylvania, came forward as a "natural leader" of the lower house. Previously, in 1859, he had been unable to secure the election of his fellow Pennsylvanian, Galusha A. Grow, for speaker. Now he again nominated Grow and, with the Southern members absent, saw him easily elected. His own reward was the chairmanship of the most important standing committee of the House—the committee of ways and

---

[1] This account of the conversation was given by Stevens to a newspaper reporter several years later and was published in the *New York Herald* of July 8, 1867.

[2] See Stevens' speech in Congress on January 22, 1862, in the *Congressional Globe,* 37 Congress, 2 session (1861–62), 439–441.

means (which then had comprehensive powers later to be divided among three committees). According to the rules its chairman had special privileges, notably the right to take the floor at any time to introduce or discuss tax, finance, and appropriation bills. Also, according to the custom of the House, he took precedence in speaking on matters other than those pertaining strictly to means and ways. Stevens was quick to make the most of his new opportunities. If he could not sit as a member of the cabinet, he was nevertheless in a position to make himself heard by the president and the country at large.[3]

For the time being he listened to the president. Lincoln had called armies into being, suspended laws, and made commitments to spend the government's funds, and it would take myriads of additional men and millions more in money finally to crush the rebellion. In his message to Congress he asked for approval and support, and Stevens got diligently to work with the necessary bills to come from his committee. Within Congress there was, for the nonce, a fair degree of unanimity, though there was criticism on the outside. Horace Greeley, who a few months before had talked of letting the seceders go in peace, now went to the opposite extreme and through the columns of his *New York Tribune* urged the Union armies "Forward to Richmond!" In response to popular clamor federal troops, Old Thad's nephew among them, went out from Washington as far as Bull Run and then suddenly returned. The *New York Times* (edited by Henry J. Raymond, a friend of Seward's) commented that some in Congress had prayed for just such a military disaster, hoping that it would force the government to free the slaves as a last resort. On the day after the battle, however, congressmen went about their business as calm as if nothing had happened and voted for the Crittenden resolutions, which declared that not abolition but only the preservation of the Union was the government's war aim. Stevens did not vote. A few days later, while preparing

[3] The phrase "natural leader" was applied to Stevens by James G. Blaine in his *Twenty Years of Congress: From Lincoln to Garfield* (2 vols., Norwich, Connecticut, 1884), 1:325. See also the *Congressional Globe*, 37 Congress, 1 session (1861), 5.

a speech on the resolutions, he wrote to Thaddeus, Jr., a major in the army and like his uncle a lawyer: "I suppose you are at home, and hope now you will tend closely to the office, and build up a professional business—I am glad that your corpse [*a slip of the pen that perhaps betrayed the writer's concern for his nephew's life*] had an occasion to show their valor as accidents might have happened and a stampede was possible." When Stevens had completed his speech, the president would know that his congressional honeymoon was over.[4]

On August 2 Old Thad took the floor. He did not like the Crittenden resolutions, he began, because they looked like an apology from Congress for carrying on the war. Those who made the war should tell what was its object. "Our purpose is to subdue the rebels." And the way to do this was to liberate the slaves and use them against their masters. The Constitution no longer applied, but only the laws of war, and the first of these was self-preservation. An objection had been made that the Southern people would never yield if it were to be made a racial conflict, that they would rather suffer themselves to be slaughtered and their farms and plantations to fall to ruin. "If their whole country is to be laid waste, and made a desert, in order to save the Union from destruction, so let it be. I would rather, sir, reduce them to a condition where their whole country is to be repeopled by a band of freemen." There must be no bargaining, no negotiation, no truces until all the rebels should have sued for mercy.[5]

Here was a policy and a tone that the president did not like. The House followed the lead of Stevens, though at a distance, and on August 6, the last day of the special session, passed a partial confiscation act. This provided not for the wholesale emancipation and arming of the enemy's slaves but only for the seizure of such of his property as was being used for "insurrectionary purposes." Lincoln was soon to demonstrate that he would hold the agents of the federal government closely to the terms of this law.

[4] *Congressional Globe*, 37 Congress, 1 session (1861), 72–77, 222–223, 250–251, 267, 307; *New York Times*, July 25, 1861; Stevens to Thaddeus Stevens, Jr., July 30, 1861, in the Thaddeus Stevens Papers, Library of Congress.
[5] *Congressional Globe*, 37 Congress, 1 session (1861), 180–181.

Out in Missouri General John C. Frémont, commander of the Union Army in the West, went beyond the provisions of the act and issued an order freeing all slaves of the enemy within the state whether they were being used for military purposes or not. Lincoln finally had to countermand this order. The dispute between the general and the president was merely the outward sign of a growing divergence of opinion within the Republican party and throughout the North generally. The Missouri emancipator rapidly became a hero in the eyes of those who had hearkened to the words of Old Thad. Lincoln stood firm, however, for he realized the political necessity of conciliating Kentucky and the other slaveholding border states. And if he himself should be in danger of forgetting it, there was the family of the Blairs to keep him reminded.

The Blair family had exerted, and was to continue to exert, no inconsiderable influence upon the course of American politics. Francis P. Blair, Sr., had been a member of Andrew Jackson's "Kitchen Cabinet" and now, having turned Republican, lived on his estate just outside the District of Columbia and had access to President Lincoln's ear. The sons, Frank and Montgomery, not only kept a hand in Missouri and Maryland politics, respectively, but also shared in the making of national policy, the one as chairman of the House committee on military affairs and the other as postmaster general in Lincoln's cabinet. The Blairs, indirectly related to the Frémonts by marriage, had long been most friendly to General Frémont; and it was they who had induced Lincoln to put him in command. Already, however, at the time of Frémont's break with Lincoln, there were signs of a widening rift between the Blairs and Frémont. According to rumor, one reason for the estrangement was the fact that the general, while generous to the point of extravagance with the army patronage, had been granting few contracts for supplies to friends of the Blairs. Indeed, it was said that he had issued his emancipation proclamation in order to cover up the financial irregularities (and the military inefficiencies) in his department. But if the Blairs found Frémont strangely unapproachable after they had put him in office, Simon Stevens, the protégé of Old

Thad, found it possible to get next to the general and secure a lucrative contract for supplying him with guns.[6]

As the summer of 1861 turned to autumn Old Thad in Lancaster had cause for pessimism whether he looked to the West, to the East, or to affairs at home. Toward Missouri congressmen and cabinet members were traveling as sleuths to track down the alleged peculations of Frémont. On the Potomac front the new general of Napoleonic bearing, George B. McClellan, in politics a Democrat, made elaborate preparations but did nothing positive to avenge the defeat at Bull Run, despite the clamors of a populace that knew little of the intricate art of war. In Lancaster the conservative Republicans, encouraged by the example of the Blairs and Cameron, were inaugurating a "Union movement" which threatened to undermine the power of the "Stevens faction." Old Thad managed to put down this movement, but presently found himself strangely powerless even within his own group. He suspected an intrigue against him but did not learn till later that some of his trusted followers had formed a secret clique whose object was to prevent "foreigners"—that is, persons not born or raised in Lancaster County (and Cameron, it should be remembered, was Lancaster born)—from being nominated on the local ticket. And if these troubles were not enough, Old Thad was being harassed again by his rheumatism, which, with his club-foot, almost completely hobbled him. He thought of trying hydrotherapy, and Simon Stevens offered his hospitality so that he might take the treatment in New York, but his Lancaster physician advised that he was much too old to attempt the rigorous water cure. Pained by his disease and "nursing it at home with but little profit," he wrote to Simon, now the contractor for war supplies: "I find you are rising in the military way. I infer

[6] For the place of the Blair family in American history, see William E. Smith, *The Francis Preston Blair Family in Politics* (2 vols., New York, 1933). According to Simon Stevens' own account, the war department in June, 1861, discarded and sold five thousand carabines (which had been bought at $17.50) for $3.50 each. From the buyers, Simon got them on August 1 for $12.50 apiece. He improved them by rifling the bore and enlarging the breech. On August 5 he offered them to Frémont for $22 and on August 6 he delivered them at that price. Simon Stevens to the Editor, July 11, 1862, in the *New York Times*, July 12, 1862.

that your duties lie at some distance from the rebels. It were a pity to hurt those that our Government treat so tenderly."[7]

During October and November, as he waited to go to Washington for the regular session of Congress, the Government continued to treat the rebels much too tenderly, and Frémont much too roughly, to please Old Thad. Cameron joined those who went on "extraordinary missions and commissions" to Missouri. Suddenly, after his return, Greeley's *New York Tribune* came out with an editorial in praise of the secretary of war! "What is gone with Greeley's back bone . . . ? " Old Thad demanded of Simon Stevens. "I see by today's *Tribune* that he has turned sycophant to Cameron. His somersets are worse than [James Gordon] Bennett's [of the *New York Herald*]. He too tempted! Cameron has subsidized the whole press of the country." The "somerset" was especially amazing in view of the fact that Greeley had been known as an archenemy of William H. Seward in the politics of New York state; and for Greeley to laud the supposedly conservative Cameron seemed much like patting the conservative Seward on the back. "I suspect that Seward must have swapped off," concluded Old Thad, "or Greeley would not have thus debased himself." As yet, Stevens had no inkling that it was Cameron, not Greeley, who had on this occasion performed a somerset. "Where are you," he asked Simon Stevens, "that you let the hounds run down your friend Frémont?" On the next day came the news that Lincoln had removed the general from command.[8]

By the time Congress met in December, Cameron had already revealed his conversion to Stevens' cause by the publication of his annual report for the war department. In it he boldly advocated

[7] Stevens to Simon Stevens, September 5, 1861, in the Stevens Papers. At the Lancaster County elections in October the voters gave a "death-blow to the Stevens domination in the Old Guard." The "end of the tether" had been reached in the nomination of the "HOOD ticket," which had led to a "breaking of the 'ring.' " *Lancaster Intelligencer*, October 15, 1861. See also the issues of September 17 and 24. Two years later Stevens told Hood that the latter's influence in the nominations had been "unaccountable" to him until he had recently heard of the plot against "foreigners." Stevens to A. H. Hood, November 2, 1863.

[8] *New York Tribune*, November 5, 6, 1861; Stevens to Simon Stevens, November 5, 1861, in the Stevens Papers.

what Frémont had been overruled for attempting—the confiscation of the enemy's slaves—and he refused Lincoln's request that
he modify the report. On the first day of the session Stevens introduced a bill to abolish slavery and at the same time to make full
reparation to loyal slaveholders who might suffer loss as a result
of "that mode of warfare." At a caucus of Republicans called to
consider this measure he declared that the government could
never win the war without it. He denounced McClellan as an
aspiring dictator, condemned Lincoln as an untrue and unsound
Republican whom the Northwest had foisted upon the party,
and lauded Cameron as the only member of the administration
who evinced "correct notions" about the conduct of the military
campaign. The reports leaking out of the caucus made it plain to
all that the Republican party was divided into two distinct and
antagonistic factions: Conservatives and Radicals. And among the
latter Stevens and Cameron were now brothers in arms![9]

The true philosophy of the Radicals was implicit in a letter
that Old Thad penned to Gerrit Smith, the well-to-do and
eccentric patron of the old abolition movement, to assure him
that he meant to liberate the slaves of loyal as well as of rebel
masters. "I can see no other way to establish a firm Union," he
wrote. "Leave slavery anywhere and it will soon go everywhere in
the South." For a quarter of a century he had fought "slavery,"
which in his mind was synonymous with "Democratic party,"
and at last the war had given Republicans a chance to make
their victory permanent and complete. But with Lincoln in command he could only be pessimistic. "I have no hope," he confided to Smith; "Republicans are cowards, and Democrats will
soon be in power, as pro-slavery as ever."[10]

Old Thad had expected to be back in Lancaster well before
Christmas, to spend the holidays with his nephew Thaddeus,

[9] *New York Times*, December 4, 10, 1861; *New York Herald*, December 10,
1861. Stevens, it was said, "startled the caucus" by stating that McClellan had
gone to Lincoln and threatened to resign unless that part of Cameron's report
was modified which proposed the emancipation and arming of slaves. This
was taken as proof of McClellan's dictatorial power over the administration.
New York Tribune, December 10, 1861; *Lancaster Intelligencer*, December 17,
1861.

[10] Stevens to Smith, December 14, 1861, in the Stevens Papers.

but the necessity of providing ways and means of preserving the Union and the Republican party kept him in Washington. On December 30 he made a speech in favor of a bill repealing the acts that had established certain ports of entry in the South. "Nations do not," he pointed out, "correctly speaking, blockade their own ports." Those of his listeners who had expected him to attack the foreign policy of the administration, however, were surprised. An American warship had taken the Confederate commissioners Mason and Slidell from an English ship on the high seas, and for a time it looked as if the United States would be involved in a foreign as well as a civil war. Stevens thought war with England unlikely but if not, let it come! The people of the North would then gladly turn the slaves loose in the South, and these "enemies of the enemy" would keep him busy while the Union armies overran the British possessions in North America—"and our banner would wave over freemen, and none but republican freemen, from the Gulf of Mexico to the Arctic Ocean, and from the Bay of St. Lawrence to Puget Sound!"[11]

The new year, 1862, opened without a war against England and, it seemed to many, without a war against the South. On January 8, "St. Jackson's Day," a constituent wrote Stevens to contrast the inactivity of General McClellan on the Potomac front with the masterly activity of General Jackson at New Orleans. "As this is a great day in the annals of the nation and as I have nothing else to do," the man wrote, hinting his disappointment of having no government job, "I thought I might as well let you know that I am not quite dead yet, although I soon will be of vexation unless something is done by that crowd of loafers around Washington of which one George McClellan is said to be the chief . . . . Strange that almost everybody except myself can get a pull at the public teat."[12]

But on Jackson Day Old Thad, at least, was not idle. Secretary of the Treasury Chase that evening "gave the usual dinner to the Committees of Finance of the two Houses." Jay Cooke, the

[11] Stevens to Thaddeus Stevens, Jr., December 21, 1861, in the Stevens Papers; *Congressional Globe*, 37 Congress, 2 session (1861–62), 180–181; *New York Times*, December 31, 1861.
[12] A. H. Hood to Stevens, January 8, 1862, in the Stevens Papers.

Philadelphia banker, was also present. The guests talked of ways and means to pay the cost of war, and they talked gloomily, because on New Year's Eve the metropolitan banks had all suspended specie payments, and the coin which the government urgently needed was not to be had. What should be done? On that they disagreed. Chase and Cooke thought Congress should establish a system of national banks which would buy government bonds and, with these as security, issue government-guaranteed banknotes that would serve as money. Only the day before, however, Stevens' committee had approved the suggestion of one of its members that the government itself should print paper money, "legal tenders," to the amount of perhaps half a billion dollars. "The Committee of the House are perfectly *wild* on the subject," Jay Cooke, before leaving Philadelphia, had heard from his brother Henry at the capital. "I learn (but not from Gov C) that he has declared that if Congress persists in such a course, and fails to carry out his policy, bank bill included—he will no longer be responsible for the national finances by remaining in the Treasury." But Chase and Cooke were unable to influence the members of the House committee.

A week later Chase, though he had arrived at an understanding with the banks and boards of trade of New York, Philadelphia, and Boston, still had come to no understanding with Old Thad. The chairman and the members of the ways and means committee were convinced that the secretary's plan would not meet the exigencies of the hour. Stevens confessed to the House that on the subject of finances he and the secretary had wholly different opinions, which they could not "harmonize."[13] Already he was making his power felt, as against that of Chase, who held the position in the cabinet which he coveted as his own just due.

Meanwhile Cameron resigned from the war office and accepted the position of minister to Russia. His enemies said he was evading the exposures of a congressional investigation of war contracts;

[13] H. D. Cooke to Jay Cooke, January 7, 1862, in the Jay Cooke MSS., Historical Society of Pennsylvania, Philadelphia; manuscript diary of S. P. Chase, entries for January 8, 15, 17, 1862, in the Salmon P. Chase Papers, Library of Congress; *Congressional Globe*, 37 Congress, 2 session (1861–62), 380; *New York Times*, January 18, 1862.

his friends said he was registering his protest against Lincoln's rejection of his program for confiscating slaves. On behalf of Cameron and other advocates of a total war against the South, Stevens delivered, on January 22, a challenge to those who with "weak minds" and "weak nerves" were siding with the president.

Prejudice may be shocked, weak minds startled, weak nerves may tremble, but they must bear and adopt it. Those who now furnish the means of war, but who are the natural enemies of slaveholders, must be made our allies. Universal emancipation must be proclaimed to all.... The sympathizers with treason would raise an outcry about the horrors of servile insurrection, and would prate learnedly about the Constitution. Which is the most to be abhorred, a rebellion of slaves fighting for their liberty, or a rebellion of freemen fighting to murder the nation? Which seems to you the most cruel, calling on bondsmen to quell the insurrection, or shooting down the masters to effect the same object? You send forth your sons and brothers to shoot and saber and bayonet the insurgents; but you hesitate to break the bonds of the slave to reach the same end. What puerile inconsistency![14]

Many who heard or read this speech added their amens and expressed their eagerness to take up a holy crusade against the devils of the South. "There is a 'Jeff Davis'—though his proper name is *Devil*," wrote the witty pastor of a Lancaster Methodist church to Old Thad. "You have made more hearts glad than are beating within the bounds of your congressional district," submitted an admirer from upstate New York; "for I doubt not every true patriot throughout the North . . . as he rises from the reading of that speech ejaculates from the 'Holy of Holies' of his heart, 'God bless you, Thaddeus Stevens' amid all the obloquy and insults of the *pro Slavers* & *Devils* you have dared to stand up a man. In the good time coming you will be honored for it." Enthusiastically another correspondent advised: "Let the Ware Department call out a million of men for next spring campaign. . . ." An even more spirited suggestion: "Should Congress fail to pass a law for the emancipation of slaves, should not those of us who believe in the necessity of preserving our country and our liberties, raise an army of one hundred thousand or more men, arm and equip them at our own expense . . . ?"[15]

[14] *Congressional Globe*, 37 Congress, 2 session (1861–62), 439–441.
[15] W. W. Keith to Stevens, February 2, 1862; John Steuart to Stevens,

His daily mail was reassuring to Old Thad. It proved that much of the war fervor aroused by the firing on Fort Sumter was still alive. But the North no longer spoke, as it had seemed to do then, with a single voice. There were Conservative Republicans and moderate Democrats who regretted that Stevens saw fit to use his influential position in the House in such a way as to embarrass the president. There were Democratic pacifists who, it was said, weakened the administration in the face of the enemy, just as Stevens did at the other extreme.[16] As between Radicalism and pacifism, however, the former was much the more firmly intrenched and by far the harder for the president to resist. Not only did he have to deal with Stevens, holding a strategic position in the House; in the Senate sat such powerful antislavery men as Charles Sumner of Massachusetts and Benjamin F. Wade of Ohio, the latter of whom headed a junto of Radicals called the Committee on the Conduct of the War. Within the cabinet itself were two secretaries ready to use the sentiment of Radicalism against the president. One was Chase, who with all his faults was still a Radical. The other was Edwin M. Stanton, the new secretary of war, whose protean personality enabled him to roar with the Radical lions and lie down with the Conservative sheep. Early in 1862 the lines were drawn between the two groups of Republicans, and thereafter their internecine quarrel was to be as bitter as their conflict with the Northern Democrats. Indeed, though bloodless, it was often to be as bitter as the war against the Southern foe.

February 4, 1862; Uriah Bruner to Stevens, February 8, 1862; J. N. Magee to Stevens, April 17, 1862, all in the Stevens Papers.

[16] John W. Forney, then a Conservative Republican, wrote in his "Occasional" column under date of January 25: "The opinions of Mr. Stevens have always been decided—and, while in the political calendar he has generally been gazetted as a radical, no one knows better when expediency becomes the duty of a statesman. He was one of Mr. Lincoln's most efficient supporters in Pennsylvania—he is attached to the Government as chairman of Ways and Means, almost in the capacity of a Cabinet minister, and aids to shape most of the legislation of the country. It is therefore to be regretted that on the occasion of his recent speech in the House, he should have led in an attack upon the Administration of Mr. Lincoln." Old Thad, he felt, was as bad as C. L. Vallandigham of Ohio, leader of the peace Democrats. *Philadelphia Press*, January 27, 1861.

XI. Ways and Means

MR. STEVENS, we are getting old," one of his allies in by-
gone party battles reminded him. "You, a bachelor, in
active public life may not be aware of the fact." And, indeed,
though not strictly a bachelor in the minds of some who knew
the keeper of his house on B Street, the chairman of ways and
means led a public life so active that he had little time to remember that his seventieth birthday, April 4, 1862, was drawing
near. In his strategic position he had power, within limits, to
make or mar the fortunes of many of his fellow countrymen, and
they came to him from all sections of the country—literally from
Wall Street to Dubuque. "I am very desirous of making your
acquaintance and consuming perhaps one hour of your time,"
wrote, for example, an entrepreneur in the new coal-oil industry.
"I think you won't complain that I don't talk fast enough &
confine myself to facts." Idealists black and white besought him
to "abollish Slavery in toto" or requested, in the words of a
Quaker who had seen his difficult hand, "If thee could write so
I could read it I would be very willing to know what thy opinion
is." And, like many a lesser man in public office, he had to give
much of his time to those in search of petty places on the federal
payroll. Besides a politician's chores he had those of a lawyer
and many of those of a business man. The problems of the
Caledonia Iron Works were demanding his attention. For many
years he had been involved in litigation with the owners of the
neighboring Mont Alto furnace. His workmen had cut and
coaled timber on what they claimed as their land, and he had
now to send advice to the attorney who was going to argue his
case at the April term, 1862, of the Franklin County court. He
also had the duties of an uncle toward his fatherless nephews,
Alanson and Thaddeus, Jr., both in the army. "I *heard* that

cousin Thaddeus was dead How is it? Where is Alanson now?"
wrote a third nephew to Old Thad. Ten years earlier Thaddeus
M. Stevens had been a student at Jefferson Medical College in
Philadelphia; now he was getting established as a physician in
Indianapolis. "I hope that you enjoy good health do not overwork
yourself," young Dr. Stevens wrote, with a professional air. "You
know that you are older than you were ten years ago." He ended:
"Please give my respects to your kind Housekeeper Mrs. Smith."[1]

After delivering his emancipation speech of January 22, the
aging and ailing leader of the House got back to work with the
unfinished business of government finance. Toward the end of
January Chase wrote that he was acceding to the House committee's plan for issuing legal tender treasury notes. Earlier, according to Henry Cooke, he had sworn that he would resign rather
than yield! Hardly more enthusiastic than Chase about the plan,
Old Thad presented it in Congress as "a measure of necessity,
not of choice," secured its passage, and set a precedent for later
issues of greenbacks.

This was a victory for him, but Chase was to win out on another
test, the question of a public loan. Having failed to prevent the
issuance of "United States notes," Chase and the Cookes feared
that government bonds, if purchasable by the notes, would be
payable in money of the same kind. Stevens believed that at
least the interest on the bonds ought to be paid merely in "lawful
money" rather than specifically in coin. At the last minute he
managed to insert such a proviso in the bill for "five-twenties"

---

[1] Eli Lewis to Stevens, March 5, 1862; Thos. Whitson to Stevens, March 20,
1862; F. Miles to Stevens, March 21, 1862; Thaddeus M. Stevens to Stevens,
April 4 [?], 1862; Sam Downer to Stevens, March 11, 1864, all in the Thaddeus
Stevens Papers, Library of Congress. Thaddeus Morel (or Morrill), the son
of Joshua Stevens, Jr., was born in Indianapolis in 1830 and died in 1885,
after making a name for himself as the founder of the Indiana state board
of health. J. G. Wilson and John Fiske, eds., *Appleton's Cyclopaedia of
American Biography* (6 vols., New York, 1888–89), 5:678. At the court in
Chambersburg in April, 1862, the case of Hughes *v*. Stevens was decided, after
twenty-five years of litigation, in favor of Old Thad; and later in 1862 the
judgment was affirmed by the state supreme court. Wm. McClellan [Stevens'
attorney] to Stevens, April 23, 1862, in the Stevens Papers; *Pennsylvania State
Reports, Containing Reports of Cases Adjudged in the Supreme Court*,
43:197–206 (Philadelphia, 1870).

(bonds redeemable in five to twenty years) which passed the House early in February. The Cookes, after a "long talk" with John Sherman, chairman of the Senate finance committee, left it to him to kill all "wild" legislation on the part of the House. They were not disappointed. When Stevens saw his bill emerge from the Sherman committee, with a provision for paying interest in gold, he complained that the senators had "so disfigured and deformed it that its very father would not know it." Lancaster bankers and brokers and the people generally had congratulated Old Thad on the original bill, but, as he said, from the "caverns" of the metropolitan banks had come a "doleful sound." The "deformed" bill for selling five-twenties and the bill for issuing legal tenders became law on the same day. "It had turned out as I supposed it would," grimly observed Old Thad a fortnight later as, against his better judgment, he advised the House to let the secretary of the treasury borrow at a high rate of interest in order to buy gold from the "bullion brokers" to pay the interest on the bonds which, even so, were selling at a ruinous discount.[2]

The credit of the government was low, and the problems of Chase and Old Thad therefore complicated, largely because the Army of the Potomac was winning no victories. Although in the Mississippi Valley General Grant was going from one success to another, in Washington General McClellan was finding one excuse after another to delay his advance. His dilatoriness was disgusting the people, some of whom, like those who wrote congratulations to Old Thad on his emancipation speech, were

[2] Chase to Stevens, January 25, 29, 1862, in J. W. Schuckers, *Life and Public Services of Salmon Portland Chase* (New York, 1874), 243–244; Chase to Stevens, June 7, 1862, in E. G. Spaulding, *History of the Legal Tender Paper Money Issued during the Great Rebellion* (Buffalo, 1875), 155–156; H. D. Cooke to Jay Cooke, February 1, 1862, in the Jay Cooke MSS., Historical Society of Pennsylvania, Philadelphia; *Congressional Globe*, 37 Congress, 2 session (1861–62), 687–691, 900, 938–939, 1103; *New York Times*, January 25, 1862; *Philadelphia Press*, February 15, 1862. From Lancaster a constituent wrote to Stevens about his original bill for paying interest on bonds simply in lawful money: "Your friends here, and your political enemies, laud it as a master production, J. K. Reed tells me that the Banks, and brokers here, are all satisfied and well pleased with your course on that subject." John Fondersmith to Stevens, February 24, 1862, in the Stevens Papers.

almost ready to take things into their own hands. Finally even Lincoln's patience reached an end. No longer content with nudging and prodding, the president commanded McClellan to move toward Richmond. McClellan moved a short way and then decided, in March, to take his army to the mouth of the York River and attempt to enter the Confederate capital by its back door.

He was just settling down for a siege of Yorktown when, on April 10, Old Thad rose in the House of Representatives to move the consideration of a Senate bill to abolish slavery in the District of Columbia. Other bills were ahead of it on the calendar of the House. "The Chair will call the Calendar in order," the speaker of the House declared. "And I will move to lay them aside," Old Thad answered, "until I get to the bill I have indicated." So he did. On the next day he shut up the opponents of the bill by repeatedly moving, whenever they proposed amendments, that all debate cease in one minute. He put the measure through without a change, and soon the Negroes of Washington were to be free at last.[3]

Sunday morning, two days later, he went at the invitation of Secretary Stanton to the war office, where he found a roomful of men assembled to talk of affairs military and political. "Bluff Ben" Wade of Ohio, sensitive about nothing, and dyspeptic Senator Fessenden of Maine, sensitive about his illegitimacy, were there with the rest of the Committee on the Conduct of the War. Also present, but looking out of place, was the chairman of the committee on military affairs of the House, Frank Blair. Old Thad spoke up and asserted bluntly, with a bit of profanity for emphasis, that no one in the cabinet—the present company excepted—was fit for his place. While the group glanced slyly at Blair, whose brother Montgomery had thus been hit, the House leader went on, saying that he was "tired of hearing d——d Republican cowards talk about the Constitution; that there *was* no Constitution any longer so far as the prosecution of the war was concerned." Stanton, nervous and shifty-eyed, nodded assent

[3] *Congressional Globe*, 37 Congress, 2 session (1861–62), 1613–1614, 1643–1649.

to every word. The conference broke up with the conferees berating McClellan, who, it seemed, was merely sitting down outside of Yorktown instead of sitting down outside of Washington.[4]

Before the end of April Frank Blair had his chance in Congress to strike back at the Radicals. The committee investigating war contracts was making public the evidence it had gathered in Missouri, and Blair seized the occasion to make an oratorical attack upon the hero of the Radicals, Frémont. Old Thad then rose to ridicule the investigators—"picking up every scrap of scandal, from what an old woman told them in Cincinnati to what old womanish men told them in St. Louis"—and tried to turn suspicion upon Blair by hinting that in the recent parting of the Blairs and Frémont there was something very queer.

If the separation of Frémont and the Blairs was remarkable, declared Representative H. L. Dawes of Massachusetts, the late reunion of Stevens and Cameron was even more so. Dawes sought to explain the healing of this "political feud" by implicating Stevens in the alleged frauds. Cameron had held a banquet, he said, with Stevens and other prominent Republicans as guests, and had there agreed to share the profits from several mysterious "horse contracts." Dawes recalled how Simon Stevens (who was popularly supposed to be a cousin or even a brother of Old Thad) had bought guns discarded by the war department and had resold them to Frémont for nearly double the price he had paid. With one hand, said the critic, the chairman of ways and means aided the plunderers of the treasury while with the other hand he was making a tax bill "to wrench out of the hard earnings of the people money to supply the leaks." The listeners believed that these insinuations were too broad for Old Thad to let pass without a reply.

When he spoke on April 28 as attorney for the defense, there were four defendants, though not all present before the bar of the House: Simon Stevens, Frémont, Cameron, and himself. "I

[4] P. H. Watson [assistant secretary of war] to Stevens, April 12, 1862, in the Stevens Papers; George W. Julian, *Political Recollections, 1840 to 1872* (Chicago, 1883), 212–213. The characterizations of the conferees are not Julian's.

will say," he began, "that Simon Stevens is in no way, even in the most remote degree, any kindred of mine." But he did not mean to cast any reflection upon Simon, whose father he had known when "very young" in Vermont. "He read law with me, and hence I speak of him with more confidence as being a man of unimpeachable character." Old Thad's tone and expression made his hearers laugh as he went on: "If Simon Stevens purchased these arms from the owner at a cheap rate, had them altered, and then sold them back, it was a speculation which may not be very pleasant to look at; but it was a legitimate business transaction, and involves no officer of the government." Neither Frémont nor Cameron should be connected with this "legitimate" deal of Simon's!

Now, sir, a word about a personal matter, which has been given much publicity by the eloquence of the gentleman from Massachusetts. He denounced me with once having been on unfriendly terms with General Cameron, and with not being in social intimacy with him. As I have said already, I have not introduced the name of General Cameron in this debate. It is unpleasant to go into one's biography. It is true, as the gentleman has said, before the appointment of General Cameron to a place in the Cabinet of Mr. Lincoln, I, together with eight or ten others of my colleagues, waited on Mr. Lincoln and protested against his appointment as a member of the Cabinet. We did not think that he was the proper person to go there, nor did we think that he had the capacity. We gave other strong reasons why he should not be appointed. It is true that those reasons did not appear very strong, for the executive power treated them as I expect they deserved to be treated, with silent contempt. General Cameron was appointed a member of Mr. Lincoln's Cabinet. There was no reason why, if he spoke to me, I should not speak to him. He had done me no harm, but he took it into his head that it was offensive for me to go with others to the President to protest against his appointment as a Cabinet officer, as no doubt it was. He cut my acquaintance, and we had no further intercourse until I came here to Congress last July.

In the meantime General Cameron was a Cabinet officer, and I made up my mind, as a Christian, I suppose, to forget what I had said about him, and to judge him by his official conduct. . . . I was somewhat surprised that he took the same view of conducting and handling this war that I did. I know that there was a difference of opinion whether he was right or wrong. I thought that he was right. I thought he was better upon that ground than any other member of the President's

Cabinet. I had ascertained, not through him, but through others, that he had written instructions to General Sherman, in Cincinnati, which had been materially altered before they reached him. He was in favor of employing fugitives from labor or service in the service of the United States. . . . I felt that he was right, and I said here, and I stated everywhere, that I would support him so long as he pursued that course. After I had said that publicly, General Cameron waited on me, and he came, he said, to renew our acquaintance. He said that he saw I was supporting him, and as we had to act together he desired to be on terms of personal intercourse. I replied that I had not the slightest objection. I told him that I would support him so long as he followed out the course which he had started. I told him further, that I would look upon his past record as a blank sheet, and that I would judge him by his official conduct as a Cabinet officer. That is how General Cameron and I came to speak.

A day or two later Old Thad received from Frémont a note of thanks written at his headquarters in western Virginia, where he had been restored to command. Cameron came in person to congratulate Stevens in the House.

But the case was not yet won, and the parliamentarian who had lately forced the antislavery bill on his colleagues was now powerless to win it. Before the House were resolutions censuring Gideon Welles, secretary of the navy, and Cameron, former secretary of war, for alleged mismanagement of their respective departments. The resolution against Welles failed, but the other passed. "Some men who I thought your friends deserted," Stevens explained to Cameron. "The difference between being in office and out of it can be seen in the votes between you & Wells. You will owe him their malice."[5]

As the spring of 1862 turned to summer, McClellan advanced slowly up the peninsula between the York and the James toward Richmond—too slowly for the Radicals, who yet would be loath to give credit for success to a Democratic general. Stanton, while sending him warm messages of encouragement, weakened his army by drawing away part of it for the defense of the capital, which was being threatened from time to time, largely because of

[5] *Congressional Globe,* 37 Congress, 2 session (1861–62), 1752–1753, 1841–1842, 1848–1853; *New York Times,* April 28, 1862; Frémont to Stevens, April 28, 1862, in the Stevens Papers; Stevens to Cameron, May 2, 1862, in the Simon Cameron Papers, Library of Congress.

the inefficiency of Frémont in the Virginia mountains. General Hunter, in command in the Department of the South, gave an order freeing the slaves in three states, and Lincoln countermanded it. General Butler, in command in conquered New Orleans, startled the world by announcing that Southern ladies disrespectful to his soldiers were to be treated as ordinary women of the streets. At the outset of the war he had created a sensation with his ruling that slaves escaping into his lines were "contraband." Far more spectacular, his "woman order" aroused the chivalry of bellicose Britishers and seemed to bring nearer the day of war between England and the United States.

In Washington, as the first regular session under Lincoln drew to a close, the Republican congressmen hastened to write into law the various planks of their platform of 1860. "Free soil" they now made a reality by prohibiting slavery in the territories and in all other areas that came under their jurisdiction. Homesteads they provided to appease the land hunger of the West. Protection they furnished in the form of higher duties (which were supposed to "compensate" for internal excises already laid on almost every taxable thing) to satisfy the profit-seekers of the East. Internal improvements they also arranged, with loans and gifts to the builders of transcontinental railways, but on this plank they found themselves divided as between East and West. The gentleman from Pennsylvania being at the head of ways and means, the Westerners found themselves at a disadvantage in the sectional dispute.

One of the pet schemes of Republicans from Illinois, whose leader was Elihu B. Washburne of Galena, was a project to improve the waterway connecting the Illinois River and Lake Michigan. Now Stevens had a personal reason for disliking Washburne. The latter, one of the investigators tracking down Frémont, had led and continued to lead the opposition to paying the full claim of Simon Stevens, dealer in arms, against the government. When the Illinois canal question came up on June 30, Old Thad quashed it and quelled Washburne by the resourceful use of both his sarcastic eloquence and the technicalities of the parliamentary rule book. On the improvement bill he hung an

amendment to appropriate an additional hundred million dollars
to slackwater the Susquehanna River from its mouth to its source,
and then to construct a canal on to Lake Erie at Buffalo! "I offer
that amendment for the purpose of showing that we are not
selfish," he explained, "that we are willing to take our full share
of the many millions which these internal improvements will
cost." At least his river had water in it—which, during most of
the time, was more than the Illinois members could say of theirs!
They had advocated their canal as a defensive measure against
the British, for it would permit American gunboats to enter the
Great Lakes. "If Great Britain is to wait four years and a half for
this Michigan and Illinois canal to be finished," said Old Thad,
"their heat about these New Orleans women will have cooled off,
and the gunboats may not be wanted after all." He said he had
heard that woman was *causa belli* in the time of Helen of Troy,
but he did not believe "those females" were going to be a cause
of war now. "I think all this is done," he concluded, "as an em-
bellishment to the canals which these gentlemen are so industri-
ously digging through this House."[6] The House laughed, but
Washburne was not to forget.

In the last days of the session of 1861–62 Congress turned to a
project upon which most of the Western men could agree with
Old Thad and rally again beneath his leadership—the passage of
a second and more sweeping confiscation act. But even with
Radicals East and West once more behind him he could not get
all that he wanted in the confiscation bill, drastic though its
clauses proved to be. It redefined treason and defined rebellion as
a crime. It directed the president to seize the lands, money, and
other property of military and civil officers of the Confederacy
or the Confederate states and, after sixty days of public warning,
also the property of others aiding or abetting the crime of rebellion. It freed forever the slaves of those convicted of rebellion
or treason and slaves escaping into the Union lines or coming
into any area controlled by the federal government. It gave the
president alternative ways of dealing with Negroes thus freed or

[6] *Congressional Globe,* 37 Congress, 2 session (1861–62), 2052–2054, 2886,
3033–3034, 3125–3127.

already free: he might colonize "persons of African race" outside the country or he might enroll them as soldiers in the army. Old Thad would have directed, not merely authorized, the president to use Negro troops. In any case, Lincoln sent back the measure with the message that since it amounted to a bill of attainder, he would have to veto it as unconstitutional. Stevens opposed making changes and thus destroying the life and virtue of the bill. Some of the Conservatives supported him because they wanted a bill that Lincoln would veto. And so, at the last minute, Congress simply passed a resolution denying that it was a bill of attainder, and the president signed both the resolution and the bill![7] Thus was enacted most of Old Thad's program for war to the hilt. Now it was up to the executive. But would Lincoln carry out the provisions of the law?

Gloomy was the outlook as congressmen adjourned the next day, July 17, and started home to prepare for their re-election in the fall. Only sweeping Union victories would bring out Republican voters at the polls, but the old story of failure and defeat continued. For his own election, Old Thad had little to fear. Already the county convention had met in Lancaster and had unanimously approved his course in Washington. But he must worry about the fate of others, for unless Pennsylvania and the rest of the states sent back enough Republicans, he could not keep his position of command in the next Congress (that is, the one to meet in December, 1863). With the approaching campaign doubtless in mind, he had presided over a "large and enthusiastic" group of Pennsylvanians meeting in Willard's Hall who formed an organization to give "aid and comfort" to ill and wounded Pennsylvania soldiers.[8] And yet, when election time came, it was to be hard to gather in the votes of grateful boys in blue.

In Lancaster during the summer of 1862 Old Thad found little cheer in the news from Washington. Lincoln was calling for no colored troops, indeed was turning down even those who did apply. "Anxious to see" what Lincoln would do with a "noble

[7] *Ibid.*, 3375–3380; James G. Blaine, *Twenty Years of Congress: From Lincoln to Garfield* (2 vols., Norwich, Conn., 1884), 1:373; *New York Times*, July 17, 18, 1862.
[8] *Lancaster Intelligencer*, June 17, 1862; *New York Times*, June 18, 20, 1862.

regiment" of Negroes on whose behalf Simon Stevens led a committee to the White House, Old Thad was chagrined to learn that Simon and his delegation had "made but little out of the President." "It seems to me we are just as far from the true course as ever," he confided to Simon. "Unless the people speak in their primary assemblies, no good will come, and there seems little chance of that."

From what he saw "in the papers," Old Thad suspected that the president, while ignoring the clause about colored troops, was misreading another provision of the confiscation act. "How unexpectedly the Pres't is applying our appropriation for a purpose never intended by Congress?" he wrote to Chase. "I moved the appropriation of half a million for general colonization purposes, but never thought new and independent colonies were to be planted—I intended it to aid in sending to Hayti Liberia, and other places the liberated Dist. of Columbia Slaves." Lincoln, it appeared, was about to be taken in by a group of unconscionable land speculators with possessions in Chirique, in the Isthmus of Panama, which, according to Old Thad's description, were "so unhealthy as to be wholly uninhabitable." This letter Chase read to Lincoln, who promised to investigate before doing anything definite about land in Chirique. Replying to Stevens, Chase agreed that colonization would not solve the "home problem" and exulted that, at last, McClellan had been reduced to the command of only a part of the Army of the Potomac. "This is late, but well, though not well enough." Certainly, Old Thad believed, the wiser political and military move would be not to send freedmen to unhealthful foreign climes but to send them back into the South, in arms against the oppressors of their race.[9]

At the county nominating convention early in September, in his speech accepting renomination, he explained that the reason the Union armies had made so little progress was that the slaves were not giving the rebels enough trouble. He said that, time and again, he had told Lincoln and his cabinet members to their

[9] Stevens to Simon Stevens, August 10, 1862, in the Stevens Papers; Stevens to Chase, August 25, 1862, in the Salmon P. Chase MSS., Historical Society of Pennsylvania; Chase to Stevens, August 31, 1862, in Robert B. Warden, *Private Life and Public Services of Salmon P. Chase* (New York, 1874), 457.

faces that they were "exercising too much lenity at the request of border statesmen." They should arm the slaves. "It may come to this," they had replied. *"Come to this!"* exclaimed Old Thad to his Lancaster audience, "—when another half million lives shall have been lost, and millions of dollars laid upon you in taxation! I cannot and will not stand this—and if you elect me I shall vote that every man be armed, black and white, who can aid in crushing the rebellion; that every inch of rebel soil be taken and sold to pay the debt of this war."[10]

Still Lincoln seemed not to hear nor to heed. His dismissal of the two antislavery generals Hunter and Butler rankled in the mind of Old Thad, who wrote to Simon Stevens a few days after his Lancaster speech:

> The symptoms give no promise of good. The removal of Hunter and Butler, and the continued refusal to receive Negro soldiers convince me that the Administration are preparing the people to receive an ignominious surrender to the South. It is plain that nothing approaching the present policy will subdue the rebels. Whether we shall find *any body* with sufficient grasp of mind, and sufficient moral courage, to treat this as a radical revolution, and remodel our institutions, I doubt. It would involve the desolation of the South as well as emancipation; and a repeopling of half the Continent. This ought to be done but it startles most men.[11]

Thus would American society be refashioned to please the fancy of a Pennsylvania ironmaster!

A ray of hope appeared after the battle of Antietam on September 17. As Lee's army was moving northward and Pennsylvanians were taking alarm, Stevens had remarked one day that anyone else would have sense enough at least to instruct a toll-keeper not to let Lee's men pass, but God only knew what McClellan would do! At the bridge over Antietam Creek, nevertheless, McClellan proved he had sense enough to turn Lee back. Taking this battle as the victory he was waiting for, Lincoln then issued the preliminary proclamation of emancipation he had decided upon during the summer. This did not free a single slave; indeed, it did not go nearly so far as the confiscation act that Congress had

[10] *Lancaster Intelligencer,* September 9, 1862.
[11] September 5, 1862, in the Stevens Papers.

lately passed; but it did indicate to such men as Stevens that the president had come to appreciate their concern over the approaching elections. At once Old Thad asserted on the hustings that the proclamation embodied "precisely the principles" he had advocated himself. Now he promised, if re-elected, to give his wholehearted support to the "patriotic President."[12]

As a stratagem to aid campaigning congressmen, the proclamation failed. True, when the Pennsylvania returns were announced in the middle of October, one fact emerged: "Thad Stevens goes back to Congress." But from many other sections of the state came tidings of disaster. Especially ominous to Old Thad was the news that Galusha A. Grow, speaker of the current House, had lost out, for to Grow he owed his position as chairman of ways and means. "I was surprised to hear of your defeat," he wrote to his friend McPherson, another victim of the catastrophe. Perhaps something could be salvaged from the political wreckage, for there remained the possibility of gathering in the votes of soldiers absent in the field. "How would the army vote if counted affect the result?" Stevens asked McPherson. "If it would elect you should have it registered and preserved. My opinion is that Congress ought to count them. It would be constitutional—Think of it." For the present, it had to stay in the realm of thought. Bad enough in themselves, the October returns in Pennsylvania also foreboded defeat in November in the rest of the states. "I am getting up slowly," said Old Thad. "Nothing seems to go right. I am almost despairing. Without a new Cabinet, there is no hope. People won't work at the elections who are despairing. I have great fear for New York." The fear was justified; New York (and four other states) followed Pennsylvania in going Democratic. In the next Congress the Republicans, both Radical and Conservative, would hold only a very narrow majority.[13]

In the interim before the existing Congress was to meet for its last session, Stevens, while engaged in arguing law cases before the Lancaster court, mulled over the adverse results at the polls.

[12] Alexander K. McClure, *Abraham Lincoln and Men of War-Times* (Philadelphia, 1892), 283, 392; *Lancaster Intelligencer,* September 23, 30, 1862.

[13] *New York Times,* October 15, 1862; Stevens to Simon Stevens, October 17, 1862, and to Edward McPherson, October 30, 1862, in the Stevens Papers.

He had long felt that a reform of the cabinet, and nothing less, would save the Republican party. Now he was convinced of it. "It would be a great blessing if Seward could be removed," he concluded during November. "It would revive hope, now nearly extinct. But I fear it cannot be done." Even if it could be done, who would take Seward's place? Some had proposed the irascible Senator William Pitt Fessenden (who had once intrigued with Radicals in Stanton's office), but Old Thad questioned the sincerity of Fessenden's devotion to the Radical cause. "He has too much of that vile ingredient called Conservatism, which is worse than secession. He is not so great as at one time I had hoped he would prove." George Bancroft, the historian, might be better than the tainted Senator from Maine. "But no one will succeed."[14] No one—unless perhaps Old Thad himself?

At the beginning of December, 1862, when congressmen again assembled in Washington, the Radicals could rejoice that McClellan was no longer in command; General Burnside had reluctantly taken his place at the head of the Army of the Potomac. Still the military outlook was dark. Many were the hearts growing weary, indeed, wishing for the war to cease. They could not be silenced by the epithet of "Copperhead!" But Congressman Stevens was determined that those in high places in Washington should not take up the pacifist cry. Laying an impeachment trap for Seward, Montgomery Blair, or perhaps the president himself, Old Thad offered a resolution denouncing as guilty of a "high crime" anyone in the executive branch of the government who should propose a negotiated peace. "Provoked" by the late actions of peace Democrats, notably Vallandigham of Ohio, he then introduced a bill indemnifying the president for suspending the writ of *habeas corpus*. "Provoked," the Democratic humorist S. S. ("Sunset") Cox heckled, "probably by the action of the people at the last fall elections."

Whatever the provocation, Old Thad made it plain that the indemnity was a congressional grant. "I hold that Congress is the sovereign power of this nation," he said, "not the President." Here he gave a forewarning of conflicts to come between the

---

[14] Stevens to Simon Stevens, November 17, 1862, in the Stevens Papers.

legislative and executive branches of the government. Again, though he approved the admission of West Virginia as a state, while others were straining logic to make the act appear constitutional, he justified it only "in virtue of the laws of war"—and "these laws," he was frank to say, "are just what we choose to make them." All along, the federal government had been treating the Confederacy as a belligerent power, had been exchanging prisoners, not executing them as traitors, had been granting all the usual belligerent rights. If the Constitution still operated in the South, said Stevens, the president could not have authority to appoint military governors in conquered Tennessee and Louisiana, as he had done![15]

Turning to the business of his ways and means committee, Old Thad determined to achieve repeal of the stipulation that interest on the five-twenty bonds should be paid in coin. He had only just begun the struggle among his committeemen when, in Virginia, there occurred the bloodiest Union defeat since the beginning of the war.

The dispatches from Fredericksburg told others what Burnside already knew, that he was unfit for command. They also convinced the Radicals that the time had come to get rid of Seward, in their opinion even more unfit for office. A group of senators took their grievance to the White House; Seward resigned; and the Radical Chase, thus put in an embarrassing position, did likewise. At the height of the "cabinet crisis," on December 21, Old Thad wrote to Simon Stevens: "All is uncertainty here. It is not known whether the President has accepted either of the resignations." Who would take their places, if Seward and Chase were definitely out? "These things go by a very wild chance." On the same day, however, the secretary of state resumed his office; and two days later the secretary of the treasury did the same; for Lincoln, having the Conservative head and the Radical head both at his mercy, shrewdly refused to let either of them go. Uncertainty ended in disappointment for Old Thad.

And so back to work with the ways and means committee. Its

[15] *Congressional Globe*, 37 Congress, 3 session (1862–63), 22, 50, 240; *New York Times*, December 8, 1862.

members, unwilling to follow their leader, addressed a letter to
Secretary Chase in which they asked him to frame a bill embody-
ing his own ideas in regard to another public loan. To the joy
of Jay Cooke and Company, Stevens was again in defeat. During
the Christmas holidays Henry Cooke wrote from Washington to
his brother Jay in Philadelphia:

Stevens is here, personally looking into financial matters, posting himself up generally, and holding himself "open to conviction"; but he is
doing nothing beyond this, and is not committed to any particular line
of policy. I am sure, from what I learn *reliably*, that he is sick of his
first rash scheme, and that he will be less presumptuous and more
tractable in future. But he is of comparatively little importance, as he
will be governed by, rather than govern, the action of the rest of the
committee, of whom Spaulding, Horton, and Morrill are good financial
men. The final shaping of the legislation of Congress . . . will be made
by the Senate Finance Committee.

So persuasive were the Cookes and so "tractable" was Stevens that,
early in 1863, he became the advocate of their views as against
those both of his committee and of Secretary Chase. The bankers
now desired to replace the outstanding legal tenders with new,
interest-bearing notes. When Stevens, opposing the more infla-
tionary ideas of some of his colleagues, insisted that new money
should not augment but should merely replace old issues, Henry
Cooke confided to his brother: "Now, Jay, we rather like this
plan. . . . It is substantially your plan." In an effort to convince
the other members of the House committee Jay Cooke appeared
before them in person and explained the mysteries of finance in
an allegory of his own. The treasury, he said, was like a great
ocean. Paymasters of the government were like clouds which took
moisture from the ocean and dropped it on the land. The recipi-
ents of government notes would use them to buy bonds, and thus
water would flow back again to the sea. There was, however, the
danger of a sudden downpour unless the treasury were restrained
by having to meet the interest on notes outstanding. Plain greenbacks might go out in such numbers as to cause a disastrous flood.
All this seemed to make sense to Stevens but did not suffice to
waken his colleagues to the possibility of the inflation which Jay
Cooke feared. They enlisted the aid of the secretary, who may

have seen an opportunity to disprove the current rumor that "Jay Cooke was running the Treasury machine for Chase." In the House Stevens fought for the Cooke bill "inch by inch" but eventually lost.[16]

During January and February, 1863, Old Thad kept up the fight against Conservatism, in the cabinet and wherever else it might appear. Helping to revive the intrigue against Seward, he requested the aid of Cameron in getting, "privately and discreetly," the names of prominent Republicans on a petition for the removal of the secretary of state. Publicly he opposed the policies of Seward, who dreaded "servile war," with a bill directing the employment of colored troops. Lincoln had authorized the raising of a few Negro regiments; and in his final proclamation of emancipation, at the opening of the new year, had proposed the use of freed slaves in auxiliary capacities; but that was by no means enough for Old Thad. He insisted that Negroes be put in the front ranks. But he opposed sending unwilling white men there. When the federal conscription bill came before the House, having in mind the Quakers and Mennonites in his constituency, he offered an amendment exempting conscientious objectors from the draft and so making it unnecessary for them to purchase substitutes.[17]

The tragic failure of Burnside had made it seem possible, even likely, that McClellan would be restored to command. Devoting a whole speech to the subject, Old Thad objected on the ground that McClellan had "allowed himself to be made the basis of a Democratic opposition to this administration, and this war." That was candidly said! Or, as he was putting it in letters to Cameron: "He must be broken down or he breaks us down." Slyly imputing cowardice to the general, he told the House how McClellan had

[16] *New York Times*, December 13, 15, 16, 1862; Stevens to Simon Stevens, December 21, 1862, in the Stevens Papers; H. D. Cooke to Jay Cooke, January 3, 7, 8, 24, 26, 1863, in the Cooke MSS.; memoir of Jay Cooke, quoted in Ellis P. Oberholtzer, *Jay Cooke: Financier of the Civil War* (2 vols., Philadelphia, 1907), 1:374–375, 377; *Congressional Globe*, 37 Congress, 3 session (1862–63), 487.

[17] J. W. White to Cameron, January 11, 1862, and Stevens to Cameron, January 12, 1862, in the Cameron Papers; *Congressional Globe*, 37 Congress, 3 session (1862–63), 1260–1263 and appendix, 79–82.

pursued the Confederates before the battle of Antietam: "He started after them with an army of 120,000 men before him, and marched that army at the rapid rate of six miles a day until they stopped and he came up with them." Stevens fortified his argument with letters which Cameron had supplied, particularly a communication from Winfield Scott in which the former general-in-chief accused McClellan of insubordination. When one of his listeners wanted to know where Stevens got the letter, he explained evasively: "It was furnished to the Senate."[18]

At the end of the short session of Lincoln's first Congress, on March 3, 1863, the leader of the House could pause to take stock of his losses and gains. So far as the army was concerned, Mc-Clellan continued to be out of a job, but in the cabinet the Conservatives Blair, Welles, and Seward were still intrenched—despite Old Thad's repeated prayer: "May God renovate our strength, and give strength and energy to the Cabinet!" He could congratulate himself that a bill for the employment of Negro troops had passed, but this could hardly console him for the fact that his proposal to give outright exemption to conscientious objectors had failed to become law. Against his opposition, Congress had adopted Chase's plan for a system of national banks. Once more, however, he had been able to prevent the passage of Washburne's Illinois canal bill, in a way that had made him appear, as so often before, a very tyrant of the House.[19] In Lincoln's second Congress would he still be ruler of the representatives?

[18] *Congressional Globe*, 37 Congress, 3 session (1862–63), 1263; Stevens to Cameron, April 6, 1862, and February 5, 1863, in the Cameron Papers.
[19] *Congressional Globe*, 37 Congress, 3 session (1862–63), 37–38, 811–812, 1419.

XII. Curses Come Home to Roost

IN THE spring of 1863 congressmen dispersed and from their respective districts viewed their private affairs, the course of the war, and their prospects at the meeting of the new Congress in December. With Grow of Pennsylvania out of the picture, it appeared that the next speaker of the House would be a Western man, either Schuyler Colfax of Indiana or Elihu B. Washburne of Galena, Illinois. From his home in Vermont Representative Justin S. Morrill was writing to Colfax to assure him that the speakership would be his. "You need not fear any combination against you," said Morrill. "None is possible, I think, but Lancaster and Galena and that would be unnatural. Personal relations—as they were at the close of the session—would hardly permit the requisite negotiations." Ignorant of this correspondence, the man in Lancaster was going about his legal business, borrowing money not because he needed it but because he could "use it to advantage" in investments, and writing to Secretary Stanton to ask permission for one of his constituents to raise a colored regiment in the district.[1]

During the first week in May came the despatches from Chancellorsville telling of another Union disaster. Fighting Joe Hooker had fought no better than his timorous predecessor Burnside. Some said Hooker had been drunk. Old Thad, after talking to officers who had seen the general on the field, pronounced the story false.[2] However that may have been, the way to Pennsylvania now

[1] Stevens to Mrs. S. Haines, April 9, 13, 1863, and Stevens to Stanton, April 10, 1863, in the Thaddeus Stevens Papers, Library of Congress; Morrill to Colfax, May 5, 1863, in the Justin S. Morrill Papers, Library of Congress.
[2] Stevens to Simon Stevens, May 18, 1863, in the Stevens Papers.

was open to the Army of Northern Virginia, should Lee choose to go in that direction.

Early in June, while along the Mississippi Grant was making what seemed a hopeless siege of Vicksburg, Stevens went to Washington to press the cause of colored soldiers and of the Radical favorite, Frémont. The general had resigned his army command to become president of the Union Pacific Railway Company, Eastern Division (for which Simon Stevens was an attorney), with offices in New York. Old Thad spent a week at the capital, but "owing to accidental circumstances" did not get to see the secretary of war. He did manage to visit the White House. "I learned from the President (who professes still great friendship for Genl Fremont)," he wrote to Simon Stevens, "that he was about to offer the General the command of the Negro army, which he hoped would soon be 100,000 strong. I hope Fremont may accept it, and beat all the white troops in action, and thereby acquire glory."[3] Then might the brave Radicals, with glorious Frémont at their head, ride into power in the presidential election of 1864!

Upon his return to Lancaster Stevens was ready for his summer visit to Caledonia Iron Works. His trips to the furnace offered him a choice between two routes. If he had business in Adams County, he could take the train direct to Gettysburg and then continue by carriage over South Mountain on the Chambersburg turnpike. If in a hurry he could take the train all the way to Shippensburg, by way of Harrisburg; from there he had only five or six miles more to go. By either route he descended upon a "long meadow" enclosed by forested hills, where, along the forking Conococheague and Rocky Mountain creeks, were scattered the stone and wooden buildings of his ironworks. The place was humming with activity when he arrived in June, 1863. The war had boosted the price of iron, and orders were crowding in faster than the furnace and forges and rolling mill could turn the metal out. No longer need he worry about sales, and he told his manager, John Sweeney, to make sure that their old customers were supplied first. No more need he be concerned about the boundary

[3] Stevens to Simon Stevens, June 9, 1863, and Simon Stevens to Stevens, November 28, 1863, in the Stevens Papers.

dispute with the owners of the Mont Alto ironworks to the south, for the Franklin County court and the state supreme court had both settled it in his favor. And at last his thousands of acres of timberland and ore were unencumbered by debt.

But hardly had he arrived at Caledonia when new troubles appeared. A rumor was spreading throughout Pennsylvania and the North that a Confederate army was about to invade the state. "Great Excitement!" was in the newspaper headlines, and in a panic many Pennsylvanians began to demand that McClellan be called back to head the Army of the Potomac or at least the state militia. At Caledonia there was excitement indeed on June 16. From the direction of Mont Alto, down the wagon track cut by the spring haulings of wood and charcoal, a band of gray-clad foragers and scouts was advancing. Sweeney, as soon as he got wind of their approach, advised Old Thad to flee at once. But Old Thad protested that he was no coward. His manager insisted; it would not do to run the risk of being captured and taken prisoner. Hastily the workmen hitched up a team and hurried the old man off to Shippensburg over a byroad.

In a day or two he was back at Caledonia. The raiders, he learned, had proved to be Jenkins' cavalry; they had given warning that they would requisition forty or fifty horses and mules and miscellaneous supplies, and had promised in return to spare the ironworks. Old Thad was far less wrought up over that than over the news the papers were bringing. Cameron, the reports said, was advising Governor Curtin to put McClellan in command of the Pennsylvania troops! Perhaps Cameron, out of hostility to Curtin, merely wished the governor to "disgrace himself"! "But even that would be too dearly accomplished at the expense of your country," Old Thad scribbled in a hasty note to Cameron. "I trust the report is but another of the slanders to which we are too often subjected—If the advice were uttered it was surely ironical."

Defiantly he stayed on at the ironworks, even after it became clear that much more than an excursion of cavalry was on the way up from the direction of Hagerstown. During the previous autumn Jeb Stuart and Wade Hampton with their mounted men had passed the furnace, and from the company store Hampton had politely requested a pair of shoes for his colored boy. Now Lee's whole Army of Northern Virginia was swarming through the mountain passes. On June 22 part of that army was tramping into Chambersburg, only a few miles down the pike from Caledonia, and Old Thad concluded that it was time to leave.

On June 23 a hundred cavalrymen dashed upon the ironworks. The next day General Jubal A. Early came up the pike with his division of Lee's army, placed a guard around the buildings, and pitched camp on the meadow below the fork of the creeks. After waiting a day, while his men gathered all the supplies the army could conveniently take, Early gave an order to set fire to the works. That morning Sweeney went up to the general, as he sat upon his horse outside the office building, and begged him not to carry out the order. Sweeney pleaded that Stevens would be better off if the works had been destroyed ten years before but their destruction now would throw more than two hundred poor people out of jobs. "That is not the way the Yankees do business," Early replied. "They do not go on unless they make money." He had read some of Stevens' speeches in Congress, and he remembered that federal troops had burned the ironworks of John Bell (candidate of the Constitutional Union Party in 1860) in Tennessee. And so the torches went around. When General Lee himself rode up the pike on Traveller, three days later, he was distressed to see the blackened ruins. Early's action was not a part of his grand strategy. He had timed his invasion to coincide with a wave of pacifist agitation in the North which had caused the federal government summarily to arrest the Copperhead leader Vallandigham and to close down a Copperhead organ, the *Chicago Times*. While advising that confederate generals in the West distract the attention of Grant from Vicksburg, Lee had planned to win over the peace lovers of the North by both the victories and the chivalrous deportment of his men in Pennsylvania. At Caledonia his quartermaster informed Sweeney that any families in need could draw upon him for provisions, and Lee's army moved on.[4]

[4] *Lancaster Intelligencer*, June 16, 1863, and Stevens to Cameron, June 19, 1863, in the Simon Cameron Papers, Library of Congress. The account of

Meanwhile, on June 23, Old Thad had arrived in Lancaster. He had left Caledonia, he said, "pretty well surrounded by rebels." "I expect they will borrow from me about forty horses & mules with other articles." In less than a week it began to appear that even Lancaster would not be safe. The Confederates were at York, and the burghers surrendered the town. Fleeing across the Susquehanna into Lancaster County, the state militia-men burned the bridge at Columbia after them. Rumors came to Lancaster from Harrisburg that Ewell's army was shelling the capital. And then, in the first days of July, arrived vague informa-tion about an engagement at Gettysburg. This would at least draw the Confederates back from the Susquehanna, but as the reports from Gettysburg took more definite shape, Lancastrians learned of heavy Union casualties there. Tentatively on the Fourth of July, and conclusively on the fifth, the news brought joy. Now Old Thad could think of affairs at Caledonia again. To inquiries from Simon Stevens, he replied:

My losses have been exaggerated. I have not heard directly from my manager as he has been constantly surrounded by the rebels. According to the most reliable information, my losses are as follows. On Tuesday (week) they took horses, carriages & mules, about $7,000 or $8,000 worth. On the following Friday or Saturday, they burned down a furnace, two forges, and a rolling mill nearly new. The buildings cost me about $65,000. They took a large stock of provisions and some store goods. I suppose my losses to be about $75,000. But as they were now (for the first time) in profitable operation, I suppose the loss might well be called $15,000 more.

The government does not indemnify for such losses.

But all this gives me no concern, although it was just about the sav-

Caledonia before and during the invasion is based upon the following: [Mira L. Dock], "Thaddeus Stevens as an Ironmaster," in the *Philadelphia Times*, July 14, 1895; *Estate of Thaddeus Stevens, Deceased. Audit Notes of Testimony* (Lancaster, 1893), 55 and *passim;* and Jacob Hoke, *The Great In-vasion of 1863; or, General Lee in Pennsylvania* (Dayton, Ohio, 1887), 107, 170–171. Hoke (p. 171n.) publishes a letter written by Early in which the general frankly acknowledged that revenge had been his motive. Other sources on the invasion are memoranda (written shortly after the event by John Sweeney) itemizing "the property taken and destroyed by the rebels" at the ironworks and giving a day-by-day account of "the passing of the rebel forces." Miss Dock has generously given me copies of these interesting documents.

ings of my life—not the earnings. The rest has been lavished in the payment of other people's debts and otherwise. I have, I think, enough left to pay my debts. As to my personal wants nature will soon take care of them.

We must all expect to suffer by this wicked war. I have not felt a moment's trouble for my share of it. If, finally, the government shall be re-established over our whole territory, and not a vestige of Slavery left, I shall deem it a cheap purchase.

I hope to be able with my remaining strength, to sustain myself, until that strength and my temporal events shall cease together.[5]

The next day, July 7, the newspapers carried accounts of the final surrender of Vicksburg, as Old Thad went for a brief visit to the state capital. From Harrisburg militiamen were being sent to hold Gettysburg while General Meade followed after the retreating forces of Lee. Through Harrisburg, across the bridge over the Susquehanna were pouring tourists by the thousand— on horseback, in buggies, wagons, carts, for westbound trains were not yet running—on their way to the rain-soaked and littered battlefields. Old Thad, too, felt like going on a tour. "Tomorrow trains will run to Shippensburg within six miles of my ashes," he noted, with a touch of whimsy. "I think I shall go down to morrow to see their color." People in Harrisburg were jubilant over the Vicksburg news and the retreat of Lee. To Stevens, however, it looked as if the wily Virginian was drawing Meade into a trap and would turn and strike again. Other amateur strategists in the capital disagreed, and he hoped they were right. "Vicksburg news would be glorious," he thought, "if our anxiety about Mead did not expel it."[6]

When he got back from Harrisburg the *Lancaster Intelligencer* was saying: "Curses, like chickens, come home to roost—and Mr. Stevens has had it verified in his own experience." There were kinder voices, however. Simon Stevens had set to work and had

[5] Stevens to Simon Stevens, June 23 and July 6, 1863, in the Stevens Papers.
[6] Stevens to O. J. Dickey, July 7, 1863, manuscript in the library of the Lancaster County Historical Society, Lancaster. At the time of the battle of Gettysburg many of the culverts and cuts and fills and much of the roadbed of Stevens' old "tapeworm" railway were still intact, though no tracks had ever been laid. There was a certain irony in the fact that one of these cuts, just west of the town, became a trap in which the Confederate dead were piled in heaps.

quickly raised a subscription of one hundred thousand dollars
to reimburse Old Thad. He was grateful. "But I hope to be able
to get along without troubling my friends," he replied. "If it
should be necessary (as I suppose it will be), old as I am, I find I
can still earn considerable by my practice. Perhaps I may find it
necessary to resign my seat in Congress and return to the bar." In
any case, he had just sold his lands in Luzerne County for fifty-
five thousand dollars in railroad stock, and this, he was confident,
would turn out to be valuable if the company were "fairly dealt
by." (Eventually the fund which Simon Stevens had collected
went to the support of the Lancaster County poor.) The full
extent of the bad news from Caledonia now arrived. On July 11
Old Thad wrote to Simon:

> I have just received the first communication from my manager since
> the rebs visited him, as he has been cooped up. They were led to where
> our teams were, on Tuesday, by some friend, and took all my horses,
> mules, and harness, even the crippled horses that were running at large.
> They then seized my bacon (about 4,000 lbs.), molasses and other con-
> tents of the store—took about $1,000 worth of corn in the mills, and a
> like quantity of other grain. On Friday, they burned the furnace, saw-
> mill, two forges and a rolling mill. They slept in the office and store-
> room on that night, and burnt them with books[7] and all on Saturday
> morning.
> They even hauled off my bar iron, being as they said convenient for
> shoeing horses and wagons about $4,000 worth. They destroyed all my
> fences. (I had just built a large quantity of post and rail fences, as I
> was cleaning out a farm.) My grass (about 80 tons) they destroyed; and
> broke in the windows of the dwelling houses where the workmen lived.
> They could not have done the job much cleaner. It is rather worse than

[7] The office building at Caledonia was burned, it is believed accidentally,
during the retreat of the Confederate troops. Stevens apparently assumed, or
had been informed, that the books of his firm had been destroyed. There is
evidence, however, that at least some of the records escaped destruction. At
the hearings on the disposition of Stevens' estate, in 1887 and 1891, Sweeney
read excerpts from a Caledonia "Day Book and Ledger" giving dates as
early as 1859. Miss Mira L. Dock informed me in 1939 that she had borrowed
the furnace journals from Sweeney and used them in the preparation of her
article for the *Philadelphia Times* in 1895. With her aid I traced them as
far as the office of the Strite brothers in Chambersburg, the lawyers whose
firm handled the estate of Sweeney. They were unable to explain what had
become of the books.

I expected. All the bellows and bellows houses, and run-out establishments are gone.

They finally expressed great regret that they were not so fortunate as to meet the owner, who seems to be very popular with the chivalry. I know not what the poor families will do. I must provide for their present relief.

Having learned the worst, Old Thad could not decide what to do with his *"late* iron works," as he began to call them. He might rebuild, he might sell, he might rent. A prospective renter, after studying the condition of Caledonia and of the charcoal-iron business in general, came to the conclusion that the terms were too steep—"namely $6,000 a year and be limited to 5,000 cords of wood per annum." So Old Thad considered the construction of a new plant but kept his eyes open for a good buyer.[8]

During the rest of the summer of 1863 he was making up his mind whether to continue in politics, if indeed he had seriously thought of quitting. He invited Henry Winter Davis, the great Maryland Radical, to come to Lancaster for a visit. The two could talk understandingly, though in outward appearance they were quite unlike: the one ancient and gnarled, the other youthful by comparison, handsome, and dashing. Davis was busy with politics at home, busy fighting the Republican faction of Montgomery Blair. He had no time for a visit now. "I trust to meet you in Wash. this winter," he said, "& help you to strengthen the weak knees." He added: "I was outraged by the despicable malice which destroyed your property for an old political grudge. God do so to them and more also—Amen."[9] He was more bitter about it than Old Thad himself!

Before the summer's end Stevens was back in harness as a politician. In the county campaign he began to work with determination, and determination was needed at this hour, for the Copperheads were more than ever arrogant. Out in Ohio they

[8] *Lancaster Intelligencer,* July 7, 1863; Stevens to Simon Stevens, July 10, 11, 1863, and H. P. Knotwell to Stevens, December 3, 1863, in the Stevens Papers.

[9] Henry Winter Davis to Stevens, undated manuscript in the Stevens Papers, vol. 16. Internal evidence places the writing of the letter in August or September, 1863.

had nominated Vallandigham for governor, and their candidate, exiled from the Union by Lincoln, was campaigning from Canada. In a speech at Christiana in September Old Thad asserted that the Democrats of Ohio and the Democrats of Lancaster were more "infamous traitors" than the "rebels at Richmond." He repeated his old assertion that the Confederacy could never be defeated until the slaves were armed, and added a new note: "We must conquer the Southern states, *and hold them as Conquered Provinces.*" His language on the stump was far more vengeful than it had recently been in his private letters, but this was politics! A few weeks before the October election day he wrote to Chase and requested him to grant leaves of absence to employees in the treasury department whose homes were in Lancaster County. "The interest of the nation, you will agree, requires that the ensuing election in this State should be carried for the administration. To do that we shall need every vote we can legally get."[10]

While in Lancaster Stevens' pen was scratching across the page, a Union army hundreds of miles away, near Chickamauga, was finding the rebel yell too fierce and the rebel shot too thick, and was retreating back into Tennessee. When the papers brought reports of Chickamauga, Old Thad must have felt relieved that Thaddeus, Jr., was nearer home with the now relatively quiet Army of the Potomac. Thaddeus' recent letters had been full, not of battles, but of camp conditions, the lack of news, bewilderment among the soldiers, the evils of the draft. "I received Mrs. Smith letter and will answer it soon," he would write. "Enclosed is a letter for Alanson please frank it and send it to him." Alanson, his brother, was with the Army of the Cumberland, in Tennessee.[11]

The story of Alanson Stevens explains the making of many a soldier and reveals the origin of much of the martial spirit. In

[10] *Lancaster Intelligencer,* September 17, 1863; Stevens to Chase, September 21, 1863, in the Salmon P. Chase MSS., Historical Society of Pennsylvania, Philadelphia. The italics in the quotation from Stevens' Christiana speech are in the original as given in the *Intelligencer's* report.

[11] Thaddeus Stevens, Jr., to Stevens, September 2, 1863, and an undated letter in the Stevens Papers, vol. 16.

THE CALEDONIA IRON WORKS

As it appeared about 1895. In the foreground is Rocky Mountain Creek. To the left of the willow tree is the bellows (or power) house. To the right are the run-out wall, the charcoal house above the furnace stack, and the main storehouse. These are only a few of the buildings re-erected after the burning of the works. From a

the spring of 1860 he had gone "to housekeeping" at Caledonia with a certain Mary Primm. Alanson and Mary were not wed, so far as the other families at the furnace knew. A little later Old Thad paid a visit to Caledonia. He was standing along the turnpike with his manager, between the Big House and the office, when he noticed a wisp of smoke rising from one of the dwellings beyond the millrace. He pointed to the smoke and inquired about it; he had thought that particular house unoccupied. As Sweeney recalled the occasion years afterward, he "answered that Alanson had gone to housekeeping there with Mary Primm. Mr. Stevens said it was very bad behavior on the place; that was all that was said on the subject, and Mr. Stevens remarked as we parted, 'Charge him with whatever he gets.' " The next spring, when President Lincoln called for volunteers, Alanson promptly enlisted for the three months. When he returned in the fall, he told one of the workmen at the furnace that he wished he had "got killed" when he was in the three months' service. "For why?" asked the workman. "I would be out of this trouble," he replied. He recruited a company of his own and was soon off to the war again. Finally, at Chickamauga, his prayer was answered. His brother Thaddeus went South to claim the body. "Alanson was shot through the left brest," Thaddeus informed his uncle. "His body is in the hands of the enemy and I do not suppose it can be obtained." Old Thad, for all his severity, had been fond of his nephew 'Lans.[12] More curses had come home.

And still more were apparently to come. The Western Republicans in Congress had not forgotten the treatment they had received at the hands of Old Thad. Just after Chickamauga he received a letter from Edward McPherson, on treasury department stationery, warning him that there was afoot a plot to "dethrone" him in December from the chairmanship of the ways and means committee. "The design grows out, I am satisfied, of jealousy of Penn[a] power and interests," McPherson had written, "&, I think, is based upon the influence the position has given to resist such

---

[12] Depositions of John Sweeney and others then dwelling at Caledonia, taken in 1887 and 1891 and printed in *Estate of Thaddeus Stevens, Deceased. Audit Notes of Testimony,* 29–30, 50, 66, and *passim;* Thaddeus Stevens, Jr., to Stevens, September 28, 1863, in the Stevens Papers.

cherished schemes as the Illinois Canal, & the like. I am afraid, this interest intend, if possible, to organize the House, get the Com^tees, & press through that measure." Here was a challenge Old Thad could hardly refuse, and yet the fall campaign was going so badly in Pennsylvania that he had little heart for taking up the fight. He told McPherson the plot was "very probable, as some of those in interest would do anything to carry their projects. If they succeed, it will greatly relieve me."[13]

He was doing what he could to carry his state and county for the Lincoln administration, but victory looked doubtful when McClellan came publicly to the support of the Democratic candidate running against Governor Curtin. As if the struggle were not difficult enough already, Lincoln allowed his postmaster general, Montgomery Blair, to make a campaign address in Maryland just a few days before the elections to the north. In the slaveholding "Free State" Blair gave his hearers to understand that unionists in the South need not fear that the government was going to deprive them of their slaves. "I have read with more sorrow than surprise the vile speech made by the P. M. Genl. in Md.," Old Thad wearily wrote to Chase.

It is much more infamous than any speech yet made by a Copperhead orator. I know of no rebel sympathizer who has charged such disgusting principles and design on the republican party as this apostate. It has and will do us more harm at the election than all the efforts of the Opposition. If these are the principles of the Administration no earnest Anti-Slavery man will wish it to be sustained. If such men are to be retained in Mr. Lincoln's Cabinet, it is time we were consulting about his successor.

On no subject was Chase more willing to consult at this particular time; already he was planning that Lincoln's successor should be himself. The cabinet was, in fact, taking the form of two committees for the management of the next presidential election. One was that of the Radicals, championed by Chase, and the other was that of the Conservatives, led by Seward and Blair, whose candidate was Lincoln. To Chase Old Thad had made it plain

---

[13] McPherson to Stevens, September 21, 1863, and Stevens to McPherson, September 22, 1863, in the Stevens Papers.

whom he would be fighting against, but he had yet to show whom he would be fighting for.[14]

Despite Montgomery Blair's Maryland speech, the Radicals won their campaign in Pennsylvania on October 13. This inspirited Old Thad for the struggle that was sure to come at the assembling of Congress in December. As early as the first week of November it began to appear, according to the Conservative press, that Montgomery's brother Frank would be the next speaker of the House, for he was expected to have the backing of the president. Moreover, though the Radicals and the Conservatives would be nearly equal in the House, the Radicals were divided as a result of the rivalries of Washburne, Colfax, and Stevens. While Lincoln was getting ready to make his Gettysburg address, Old Thad in Lancaster was casting about for ways to defeat Lincoln's candidate for the speakership and keep himself at the head of ways and means. "What combinations we shall have to make to organize the House right I do not know," he wrote in mid-November to Edward McPherson. "Everything must yield to that." McPherson, having been defeated in 1862 for re-election to Congress, was asking Old Thad to get him the position of chief clerk of the House. This Stevens promised to do for his "old neighbor," if it was politically possible. He invited McPherson to meet with the Pennsylvania delegation in Washington "at the Continental on the 1st prox."[15]

At the beginning of December the West, or a vocal part of it at least, was expressing its discontent with Old Thad. The *Chicago Tribune* attacked him for having "employed dishonest means" against Western interests in the previous Congress. The Radical *Tribune* admitted only that he was "true and stedfast on questions of personal Freedom." "On national measures of

---

[14] Stevens to Chase, October 8, 1863, in the Chase MSS., Historical Society of Pennsylvania; editorial, "The Presidential Question in the Cabinet—The Ball Fairly Opened," in the *New York Herald*, October 20, 1863. In August Chase had noted the information given him that "a majority of the loyal men preferred" him for the nomination in 1864. Manuscript diary, entry for August 30, 1863, in the Salmon P. Chase Papers, Library of Congress.

[15] *New York Herald*, August 28, November 3, 1863; Stevens to McPherson, November 15, 1863, in the Stevens Papers.

finance, revenue, currency, and improvements, his mental vision is bounded by Lancaster County, and the Atlantic Coast." Secretly, meanwhile, in the informal meetings and formal caucuses preceding the organization of the House, Stevens was making the combinations he desired. On the opening day it was Washburne himself who rose to nominate Colfax for speaker, and Colfax was easily elected. In return, as had been predicted, Colfax offered Washburne the chairmanship of ways and means, but Washburne graciously and surprisingly declined in favor of Old Thad. And the latter's friend McPherson was appointed chief clerk.[16] By uniting at the last minute the Radicals had managed to remove the possibility that a Blair would preside over them. This was only a preliminary skirmish between them and the president. The real battle was yet to come.

[16] *New York Herald*, December 7, 9, 1863; *Chicago Tribune*, December 10, 1863; *Congressional Globe*, 38 Congress, 1 session (1863–64), 5–8.

XIII. With Malice toward
Lincoln

WHILE our existence—certainly, at least, our peace in future
& our prosperity as a Nation—depend on the Republican
Party keeping the Control of the Government, we should make
all other questions yield to that consideration." With this advice
from one of his constituents Thaddeus Stevens could agree as he
looked forward, at the beginning of the second Congress under
Lincoln, in December, 1863, to the presidential election in the
following autumn. The president was doing nothing to change
Old Thad's opinion that it was time for Republicans to consult
about his successor.

In his annual message to Congress Lincoln made the report,
welcome to Old Thad, that one hundred thousand Negroes were
already in the army, half of them actually bearing arms. But he
also offered his unwelcome "ten per cent plan" for the reorganization of the Southern states now in federal hands. "We may conquer rebels and hold them in subjection," Old Thad replied to
Lincoln in the House, but it was a "mere mockery" of democratic
principles to say that a "tithe" of the resident inhabitants of a
conquered state could carry on government because they were
"more holy or more loyal than the others." When representatives
sought admission from the reorganized state of Louisiana, the
House leader objected to their being sworn in and had the matter
referred to a special committee on elections. He received letters
from Ben Butler in which the Radical general, delving into his
memories of New Orleans, supplied information to be used
against the putative Louisiana members. Looking to the future,
when the war should end and he should face an influx of hostile
congressmen from the South, Old Thad prevented the endorse-

ment of any definite line of policy toward the territories detached from the Confederacy. The record of Republicans in Congress, he said, should not so "entangle" them that later they might be "estopped from denying the particular condition of those states." He summed up his criticisms of the presidential plan in a speech advocating repeal of the explanatory resolutions attached to the confiscation act of 1862. As a Washington correspondent wrote, he "took decidedly the most ultra ground" yet taken by anybody in the reconstruction debates. One of his followers requested copies of the speech so that he might broadcast them "to stifle the devilish copperhead sentiment."[1] This message, and not that of the president, would enable the Republican party to keep control of the government!

The Radicals were convinced that, in encouraging the early formation of loyal governments in the South, Lincoln aimed to build up a private political machine that would insure his renomination in 1864. Behind most of the activities of Congress during the winter of 1863–64 lay this question of the presidential succession. Secretary Chase, no longer coy about his availability, counted upon Stevens' aid and relished a story that the president had told at a cabinet meeting. On the day of the ceremony dedicating the national cemetery, went the anecdote, someone asked Stevens where Lincoln and Seward were going. "To Gettysburg," replied Old Thad. "But where are Stanton and Chase?" "At home, at work," was the surly answer. "Let the dead bury the

---

[1] *New York Herald*, December 7, 1863; *Congressional Globe*, 38 Congress, 1 session (1863–64), 5–8, 686; Garfield to Mrs. Garfield, December 9, 1863, in Theodore C. Smith, ed., *Life and Letters of James Abram Garfield* (2 vols., New Haven, 1925), 1:365; Butler to Stevens, December 11, 1863, in *Private and Official Correspondence of Benjamin F. Butler during the Period of the Civil War* (5 vols., [Norwood, Mass.], 1917), 3:204; D. W. Patterson to Stevens, January 14, 1864, and J. H. Reigart to Stevens, March 1, 1864, in the Thaddeus Stevens Papers, Library of Congress.

About one of the claimants to a seat in the House from Louisiana, Butler advised Old Thad: "Ask him if in the New Orleans Delta between the 26th of April and the first of May 1862—he did not publish a card, stating in substance, that some persons had slandered him by saying he had gone on board a Yankee Gunboat ... but that his known character for loyalty to the South should forbid the imputation from being believed ...." "If he had claimed repentance I would not have brought up this reminiscence against him." Butler to Stevens, January 31, 1864, in the Stevens Papers.

dead." The critics of Lincoln were mentioning other names, however, besides that of Chase. There was Frémont again. There was General U. S. Grant, who had gone from success at Vicksburg to victory at Chattanooga. There was Ben Butler, who, if no one else would present him, was always ready to mention his own name. To which of these would Old Thad lend his powerful support? Confusion was worse confounded when, in January, 1864, Simon Cameron appeared in Washington with resolutions of the Republicans in the Pennsylvania legislature demanding a Lincoln-Cameron ticket. This surprised the adherents of Chase, for they had included Cameron, as well as Stevens, among their number.[2]

Meanwhile the war dragged on, and though the military picture was brighter than it had been a year before, the end was not in sight. "Lee has fought McClelen Pope Hooker Burnside and Mead and is yet in Virginia at the head of his army Shame Shame that one Genl should be too smart for five." These words, which a Baltimorean addressed to Old Thad, expressed the disgust of millions in the North who thought it time, and long past time, for a change. And so, early in 1864, Lincoln sent for Grant, his one consistently winning general, to give him broad powers of command over all the armies of the Union. In Congress some who thought a good soldier would make a good president proposed a bill to revive the rank of lieutenant general, the highest the nation had ever conferred, for the benefit of Grant. But Old Thad argued that there was no point in all this unless it was to rebuke the president. "Mr. Stevens sides with the Republicans of the Pennsylvania legislature," was the conclusion that newspapermen drew, "in favor of another term for Mr. Lincoln." Just after that, however, Old Thad put through his amendment to the confiscation act, and Frank Blair denounced him and the rest of the Radicals as enemies of the president. Now, the wiseacres

[2] F. B. Carpenter, *The Inner Life of Abraham Lincoln* (New York, 1885), 38; *New York Herald*, January 13 and February 27, 1864. Thomas H. Burrowes, Stevens' ally in the Buckshot War of 1838, was writing to Old Thad: "Gen Cameron, in a letter just received, says 'I hope to be in Washington about the end of next week, and will call on Mr. Stevens at once.'" January 17, 1864, in the Stevens Papers.

believed, feelings within the party were so bitter that Republicans would be able to agree upon neither Chase nor Lincoln, and for the sake of unity would have to choose someone else, probably a military man. And if Old Thad were to declare for such a man, it would presumably be Frémont, not Grant.[3]

While giving thought to the strategy of keeping the Republican party in power, the chairman of ways and means had to turn again and again to a consideration of means to raise money and ways to spend it. On the recommendation of the secretary of the treasury he introduced a bill in January to raise the tax on whiskey from twenty to sixty cents a gallon. Whiskey speculators had stocked up and the price had risen in anticipation of the added tax, or so Fernando Wood, a Democrat from New York, complained. He proposed therefore that those with whiskey on hand should pay forty cents a gallon, the difference between the old excise and the new. At first Old Thad let the Wood amendment pass, but later he voted with those who struck it out. Wood then charged that liquor lobbyists had buttonholed several congressmen and induced them to change their vote. One of the members of the ways and means committee started the story that the chairman himself was "interested" in whiskey and had gone to the telegraph office to send out information when a vote was pending on the tax bill. "Will you be so good," Old Thad demanded of his committeeman, "as to inform me ... on what authority you circulate the slander?"[4]

Another bill which he reported from his committee in January, 1864, provoked a general raising of eyebrows. Critics suspected, when he proposed the reimbursement of the state of Pennsylvania for losses sustained during the late invasion, that he had the ruins of Caledonia in mind. Indeed he was at this time hesitating to rebuild the furnace and forge out of his own pocket. In May the Democrats sank the bill for indemnities by loading it with appropriations for half a dozen other states. Old

[3] John Clark to Stevens, December 11, 1863, in the Stevens Papers; *New York Tribune*, February 5, 1864; *New York Herald*, February 6, 1864.
[4] *Congressional Globe*, 38 Congress, 1 session (1863-64), 215, 218, 271-272, 492; *New York Tribune*, February 16, 17, 18, 1864; Stevens to John A. Kasson, January 25, 1864, in the Stevens Papers.

Thad then decided to sell his property. A few days after the action of the House he wrote to Cameron: "As you sometimes buy good bargains I suggest that you purchase my *late* Iron works." For two pages he went on with his sales talk. "Now sir," he ended his letter to one of the wealthiest men in Pennsylvania, "you may make a fortune if you wish."[5]

Private and public affairs again became mixed in the mind of Old Thad, or so a carper could have believed, as he used his influence in the disposal of patronage. True, he had gained a reputation for "strict attention to the Ladies," as one of them told him, and they could not blame him if in 1864 he was returning their applications for jobs in Washington.[6] And doubtless the man who wrote on behalf of a son named "Thadd" had no cause to complain of indifference, nor the office-seeker who wrote: "Remember me kindly to Mrs. Smith. I desire sending her a box of Catawba wine." But Old Thad stirred up accusations of nepotism when in February the office of provost marshal in Lancaster became vacant. "Yours of the 23d. inst. came to hand *yester-*

[5] *New York Tribune,* January 12, 1864; *Congressional Globe,* 38 Congress, 1 session (1863–64), 2132–2133; Stevens to Cameron, May 10, 1864, in the Simon Cameron Papers, Library of Congress. When the Democrats added appropriations to his bill for indemnifying Pennsylvania, Stevens accepted these in return for Democratic support of his original bill. And when Boutwell, a Radical who sat next to Stevens, protested that this log-rolling was "outrageous," Old Thad shook his fist playfully in Boutwell's face and said: "You rascal, if you had allowed me to have my rights, I should not have been compelled to make a corrupt bargain in order to get them." George S. Boutwell, *Reminiscences of Sixty Years in Public Affairs* (2 vols., New York, 1902), 2:9–10. At the beginning of the year a man in Waynesboro was asking Stevens for a chance to rebuild the furnace and was complaining because he got no reply. W. Hammet to Stevens, January 4, 1864, in the Stevens Papers.

[6] Mrs. Grace Lytle Bennett to Stevens, March 4, 1864, in the Stevens Papers. During the war many jobs in the government offices became available to women workers. In 1864 a scandal came to light in which it appeared that certain officials were taking advantage of working girls new to the strange ways of Washington. At this time Stevens wrote to two of his feminine constituents: "Dear ladies—I went again yesterday to the Treasury Department to see if I could get places for you. But they are investigating certain charges made and making no appointments of Ladies. Indeed at present I would not advise a respectable lady to take a place there." Stevens to the Misses O. Moore and H. Martin, manuscript in the library of the Lancaster County Historical Society, Lancaster.

day," he heard from a disappointed applicant. *"Today* I see by the Lancaster Express, of the 26th, that your nephew is appointed Provost Marshal of our District. You wrote, *'I do not know* whether there will be a change.' I think you did me a great wrong in not giving me an *equal* chance to present my claims." Whatever the cost in votes might prove to be, Stevens, mindful of the fate of Alanson, had now put Thaddeus in a position where his duties were no more dangerous than recruiting soldiers and taking care of the Lancaster house. "Is Mrs. Smith coming home," the new provost marshal inquired of his uncle shortly before Easter, "or shall I send the pig to Washington?"[7]

In Washington Old Thad was hearing also from the Dunkers of Lancaster County, who wanted him to repeal the clause in the conscription act compelling conscientious objectors to pay the government three hundred dollars apiece for exemption. Their spokesman asked him for a letter on the subject but suggested that he dictate it—"as your *chirography would be all latin to them."* In Congress Stevens responded by insisting that the "commutation money," if paid at all, should be used not for purposes of war but for building and maintaining hospitals. He did not consider it right to coerce the conscience of any group on account of its religious belief. "I think the only true sect is the old Hardshell Baptists," he said. "There are those who think otherwise." While he was trying to amend the new draft bill, the Democrats were seeking to kill it entirely, and the House was getting nowhere. "Old Thad is stubborn and meddlesome and quite foolishly mad," thought Representative James A. Garfield, "because he can't lead this House by the nose as has been his custom hitherto."[8]

Certainly he could not lead the House in matters of finance. Those who considered themselves sound on the money question thought him a sort of economic illiterate when, as Grant pro-

[7] N. Ellmaker to Stevens, February 18, 1864; W. L. Bear to Stevens, February 28, 1864; Thaddeus Stevens, Jr., to Stevens, March 6, 1864; M. G. D. Pfeiffer to Stevens, April 25, 1864, all in the Stevens Papers.

[8] *Congressional Globe,* 38 Congress, 1 session (1863–64), 575; Barr Spangler to Stevens, January 6, 1864, in the Stevens Papers; Garfield to B. A. Hinsdale, February 10, 1864, in Smith, *Life and Letters of Garfield,* 1:366.

ceeded stubbornly and at dreadful cost toward Richmond, the evils of paper currency began to appear at their worst. The price of gold rose higher and higher and the value of the greenbacks fell in proportion. Stevens blamed Congress and the treasury department for having refused to heed his warnings and accept his plan. The whole difficulty, he repeatedly said, arose from allowing a certain class of bondholders to have their interest paid in gold, while the other creditors of the government received what was due them in plain "legal currency." Even yet the government could check the speculation in gold by selling its stock of the metal. Gold, he explained, was no longer money in the practical sense of the word. It was a commodity, and its price was going up in the same way as the price of other metals, such as iron, lead, and brass. ("My friends about me say copper too. Well, that is owing more to the amount used in making Copperheads than anything else.") Why should the government put its stock of this valuable commodity into a sinking fund for the later payment of its debts when, with the existing gold premium, it could now exchange a hundred dollars in gold for a hundred and seventy dollars in greenbacks or the same amount in the outstanding bonds themselves? "I leave every school boy who ever dealt in marbles and pennies to answer that question," said Stevens. "It does not require a theoretical financier."

It was a man of iron who thus presented his facts against the theories of the men of gold. During his remarks another member interrupted him: "Does not the gentleman live in an iron region?" Stevens: "Yes." The heckler: "Then that accounts for his having no conscience." Stevens: "That is certainly very smart. I did not believe the gentleman had so much wit, but he has just so much." Evidently the heckler had hit close to home![9]

Stevens gave further evidence that he lived in an iron region in his activities pertaining to tariffs and railroads. In the previous Congress he had opposed the internal improvements requested by Westerners like Washburne and, once more, he burked the Illinois canal bill by referring it to a committee of the whole—which, said a disgruntled member from Illinois, was like "con-

[9] *Congressional Globe*, 38 Congress, 1 session (1863–64), 1145–1147.

signing it to the tomb of the Capulets." He was quite ready, however, to help the Kansas Pacific Railroad, whose president was Frémont and whose attorney was Simon Stevens. Its officials kept regularly in touch with him. He also became the champion of another Western enterprise, the People's Pacific (later the Northern Pacific), whose entrepreneurs were likewise Eastern men. Now it was Washburne's turn to oppose Old Thad's internal improvements bill giving lands generously to the People's Pacific, but Old Thad overcame the opposition of Washburne and the latter's Chicago friends. Before the final passage of the bill a member rose to ask Stevens whether he had taken care that the road should be built of American iron. "It says so in the bill," he replied, amid good-natured laughter. "I go for nothing but American iron, of course."[10]

As an agent of both the railroad and the iron interests of the East, Stevens found himself in the difficult position of serving two masters. For iron men, as sellers of the metal, and railroad men, as buyers, often held conflicting views upon the question of protective tariffs. Thus a letter from a captain of industry in Buffalo came to Stevens bearing the rumor that Congress was about to change the law in relation to the Union Pacific and add legislation "whereby the provision requiring the use of American iron is to be done away with—Another provision is to admit foreign rails *free of duty*—It may be that one Iron Master writing to another might rest here."[11] Soon he introduced a bill for increasing by half the already high duties on protected goods and putting a tax on many which heretofore had been duty-free. Yet he was looking out for the welfare of the railroad-builders, even

[10] *Ibid.*, 1039–1040, 1688–1699, 1794, 2295–2297. McClellan and Grant were listed among the corporators of the People's Pacific company, and Old Thad readily permitted the name of Frémont to be added to the list. "I will suggest to the gentleman," a member interrupted, "that if he intended to insert all the presidential candidates he has omitted the 'rail-splitter.' " "Oh!" replied Old Thad, "This is not a rail-splitting business, it is a railroad line." *Ibid.*, 2612. This, it might be said, was typical of Stevens' raillery in debate. Earlier an entrepreneur of the company had sent Stevens a panel of members suitable for the special railroad committee, a draft of a bill for a land grant, and detailed suggestions about legislative strategy. Josiah Perham to Stevens, December 11, 1863, and May 1, 1864, in the Stevens Papers.

[11] William Wilkeson to Stevens, March 3, 1864, in the Stevens Papers.

if, temporarily, they thought they had cause for alarm. As the president of the St. Croix and Lake Superior Railroad Company wrote to him from New York:

There are some here that contend that the late resolution of both houses raising the duties 50 percent includes goods in bond etc. You will recollect the conversation I had with your honour last tuesday morning in which you assured me that it did not include goods in store etc.

Having (as I informed you) purchaised 1300 tons of Rail Road iron for our Road I acted & relied upon what you then said on the subject. If there should be any doubt on the subject the high position which you hold, more especially on this subject gives your opinions a controlling influence—The duties on most all the goods in store here have been paid therefore the government will not gain much by construing the law to include goods in store.[12]

With such a champion as Stevens, Northern industrialists were steadily intrenching themselves in the favor of a generous government while its armies fought the Southern enemy on the battlefields. And he was interesting himself in policies and politics which, by keeping Republican politicians and their allies in power, would assure to them not only the benefits of war but ultimately the fruits of peace.

In April, 1864, it was not yet clear to the public (nor, apparently, to themselves) to which of the possible presidential nominees Old Thad and the Radicals would finally throw their support. The *New York Tribune* was still arguing that Chase, Frémont, Butler, or Grant would make as good a president as Lincoln, and without violating the tradition of a single term. In reply Frank Blair made a speech in the House in which he thoroughly denounced Frémont and Chase. The secretary of the treasury, he charged, was a swindler who had conspired with Jay Cooke to rob the people in the sale of the five-twenty bonds and had used part of the proceeds to advance his candidacy. The Radicals took this as an attack emanating from the White House, and Old Thad responded to the diatribe, "the distilled virus of the Copperhead," with a move to show that neither Blair nor the

---

[12] D. A. Baldwin to Stevens, May 2, 1864, in the Stevens Papers. See also the *New York Tribune*, April 18, 1864; the *New York Herald*, April 26, 1864; and the *Congressional Globe*, 38 Congress, 1 session (1863–64), 1702.

president was in a position to throw stones. Blair, as a major general in the army, had no constitutional right to sit in Congress, but Lincoln had allowed him to surrender his commission temporarily, with the understanding that he could have it back upon demand. Stevens brought in a resolution calling upon the president to explain precisely how Blair could be a civil and a military officeholder simultaneously.[13] This was the beginning of the end for the Blairs.

In May the Radicals prepared another counter-attack upon the president and his Conservative friends. Earlier Stevens' brilliant protégé Henry Winter Davis had brought forth a reconstruction bill which required a majority (and not just a tenth, as in Lincoln's plan) of the white citizens of a conquered state to constitute a new government, and which further specified that this majority must amend their constitution so as to prohibit slavery. Old Thad desired a stronger bill. He would have it deal with the "so-called states," the "territories" of the South, and provide for the reversion to the federal government of lands therein belonging to rebels who owned a hundred acres or more. A little later, objecting that the president was "controlled by the Blairs," a Republican editor in Lancaster wrote to Old Thad: "I think you and the radical men in and out of Congress should make some demonstration which will force Mr. Lincoln up to some *higher* point & then go to Baltimore and put it in the platform." Before the meeting of the national convention in June, the Radicals were busy with just this kind of project. The result was the Wade-Davis bill.[14]

The Radicals were divided. Horace Greeley, as the fanatical

[13] *New York Tribune*, February 27, April 24, 25, 1864; *New York Herald*, April 24, 1864; *Congressional Globe*, 38 Congress, 1 session (1863–64), 1854, 2041–2043.

[14] *New York Herald*, April 30, 1864; *New York Tribune*, May 3, 1864; J. A. Hiestand to Stevens, May 29, 1864, in the Stevens Papers. Stevens' reconstruction proposals provoked Lincoln's attorney-general to write, on May 1, 1864, " 'Uncle Thad:' Stevens always full of whims and oddities. He is, at once careless and ignorant of the constitution. He thinks it only a bar of Juniata Iron—that may be forged into any shape, and cut into any pieces, to suit the fancy of any Pa. blacksmith." Howard K. Beale, ed., *The Diary of Edward Bates, 1859–1866 (Annual Report of the American Historical Association,* 1930, Washington, 1933), 362. Bates either could not understand

diarist Adam Gurowski wrote, was "highly incensed against Thad Stevens for his bad leadership of the House." But Stevens, said Gurowski, was "an immovable rock battered by hurricanes" as compared with the "uncourageous inconsistencies" of Greeley. At least Old Thad remained immovable in Washington when, at the end of May, a handful of Radicals went to Cleveland to nominate Frémont for president. He was a "true patriot" (which to Gurowski meant an anti-Lincoln man) but would side with Lincoln because he had instructions from Pennsylvania to do so. "Therefore the current cannot be stayed." In truth there was no one but Lincoln with whom the Republicans could now hope to win the election. Grant was continuing to fight it out on his own stubborn line against Lee, but the victory so devoutly wished for was not forthcoming, and many people were beginning to suspect that Grant was a clumsy butcher of men and not the hero they had thought him. Chase had long since been repudiated by the legislature of his own state. Butler had developed no real following. And Frémont, though still popular among the Germans in the West, could attract few voters in the East except among the lunatic fringe of the party. Just after the Cleveland meeting of the Frémonters, Old Thad appealed to Carl Schurz, whom he had met in Lancaster in the campaign of 1860 and who now as then was the outstanding leader of the Western Germans. He urged him to come to the aid of Lincoln and help the Republicans unite themselves in the face of the foe. The opposing candidate, it appeared, was to be none other than the formidable McClellan, whose popularity was rising as the unpopularity of the war increased.[15]

The question of the vice presidency was still to be settled. Though he did not say so openly, Lincoln seemed privately to prefer a man with a wider following than the incumbent, Hannibal Hamlin of Maine. It would be good politics to make the

or could not appreciate Old Thad's thoroughly consistent logic that made the Constitution inapplicable to the seceded areas.

[15] Adam Gurowski, Dairy, 1863–1864–1865 (Washington, 1866), 240, 246 (entries for May 31 and June 5, 1864); Frederic Bancroft and William A. Dunning, eds., The Reminiscences of Carl Schurz (3 vols., New York, 1908), 3:101.

Republicans a "Union" party by selecting some prominent man who was both a Southerner and a Democrat, or so Lincoln probably thought. In a conversation with Stevens and Cameron shortly before the convention assembled, Lincoln asked why Andrew Johnson would not be a good person to nominate for vice president. Formerly a Democrat, Johnson was now military governor of conquered Tennessee, his home state. His nomination would perhaps attract Northern Democrats and Southern unionists to the Republican party. Old Thad could not see it. He said Johnson was a "damned scoundrel" and a "rank demagogue."[16]

At Baltimore on June 6 the Pennsylvania delegation met in caucus and decided upon the renomination of both Lincoln and Hamlin, with the understanding that if Hamlin should be "set aside" Cameron would take his place. If the Pennsylvanians were to get the ticket they desired, they must prevent the seating of delegates from the seceded states of the South, who would of course be handpicked administration men. They must also keep out the Blair delegates from Missouri, whence came two delegations claiming seats. Next morning Old Thad managed to prevent the admission of the Blair men but not of the "Southern" delegates, insist though he did that the areas in secession were not states but "territories." In the evening he attempted to adjourn the convention in order to have time to head off the Johnson movement. Not until "Parson" Brownlow, a colorful editor from Tennessee, had finished his speech nominating Johnson was Old Thad able to get an adjournment for "refreshing sleep." The night was no doubt a sleepless one for him, and the roll call the following morning showed that the delay had done him no good. "Can't you find a candidate for Vice President in the United States," said the exasperated Stevens to his friend McClure, "without going down to one of those rebel provinces to pick one up?" One of the Pennsylvania delegation later reported to the rejected Hamlin: "Cameron was your friend after himself, but Old Thad, who did not want to be Vice President, was really for you." At Baltimore, the papers said, Stevens had been "beaten at every point."[17]

[16] C. E. Hamlin, *Life and Times of Hannibal Hamlin* (Boston, 1898), 472.
[17] *New York Herald*, June 5, 6, 8, 9, 1864; *New York Tribune*, June 8, 1864;

Before the end of the campaign he was to have his revenge on the Blairs. Responding to his earlier resolution inquiring into Major General Frank Blair's status as a congressman, the House now declared that Frank had no legal right to a place among the representatives. And then, in July, 1864, came the final passage of the Wade-Davis bill. It did not go far enough for Old Thad, and when one member voted aye under protest, he spoke up: "I ought to say that I refused to vote, under protest."[18] Nevertheless, here was an answer to Montgomery Blair's assertions that loyal slaveholders in the South need not dread the loss of their slaves.

The work of the session was over and on the night of July 8 Old Thad arrived in Lancaster, to be welcomed with a serenade by the brass band of the local Union League. To the crowd he apologized for having been unable to repeal the clause in the conscription act requiring conscientious objectors to buy exemption from the draft. But there was one consolation, he said. Copperheads would now have to go to war or furnish substitutes! His audience clapped and cheered.

Two days later he read the news that Lincoln had disposed of the Wade-Davis bill by a pocket veto and a declaration that, while he could not hold for nought the reorganization of Arkansas and Louisiana under his ten per cent plan, he would gladly accept any other states that might choose to return to the Union under the plan of Davis and Wade. Old Thad was exasperated:

What an infamous proclamation! The Prest. is determined to have the electoral votes of the seceded States at least of Tenn. Ark. Lou. & Flor. Perhaps also of S. Car. The idea of pocketing a bill and then issuing a proclamation as to how far he will conform to it, is matched only by signing a bill and then sending in a veto [*which was more or less what Lincoln had done with the second confiscation act*]—How little of the rights of war and the law of nations our Prest. knows! But what are we to do? Condemn privately and applaud publicly!—The Conscription Act weighs heavily on our people's judgt. as expected.

Another thing that was to "weigh heavily" on the minds of Pennsylvanians was the Confederate raid upon Chambersburg

New York Times, June 8, 1864; Alexander K. McClure, *Abraham Lincoln and Men of War-Times* (Philadelphia, 1892), 281–282; J. W. Forney to Hamlin, June 20, 1864, in Hamlin, *Life and Times,* 491.

[18] *Congressional Globe,* 38 Congress, 1 session (1863–64), 2043, 3389.

at the end of July. General McCausland demanded a ransom for the town, and when the burghers refused he directed his men to set the place on fire. Meanwhile Wade and Davis were less willing than Stevens to "applaud publicly" and they issued in the *New York Tribune* a manifesto rebuking Lincoln. Stevens gave vent to his condemnation privately; he visited the president in the White House and had a very plain talk with him one hot afternoon in August. Cameron was also present. Said Stevens: "In order that we may be able in our State to go to work with a good will I want you to make us one promise, that you will reorganize your cabinet and leave Montgomery Blair out of it." The discussion ran on for more than two hours, Lincoln pacing the floor, before he finally got around to an outright refusal. He desired to be re-elected, yes, but not on terms that would make him a mere puppet, he said. After his return to Lancaster Old Thad let it be publicly known that he could no longer give his assistance to the president. "If the Republican party desires to succeed," he was heard to say, "they must get Lincoln off the track and nominate a new man."[19]

In other parts of the country Radical leaders were coming to the same conclusion. Most of them were unwilling to accept Frémont, however, for to do so would be to split the Republican vote and throw the election to McClellan and the Democrats. Frémont and Lincoln must both withdraw in favor of a stronger candidate. Frémont was willing, but Lincoln was not. The policy of conspiring Radicals accordingly became one of disaffecting quietly as many men as possible from Lincoln until the opportune time appeared for coming out for a "new man"—perhaps Ben Butler. The friends of Butler kept in touch with Old Thad, who, campaigning for his own re-election to Congress, was keynoting the Radical platform of peace only on the basis of the integrity of the Union plus the abolition of slavery. That would mean, of course, no early peace at all. "Those who advise negotiations for peace on the simple basis of the integrity of the Union," he declared,

[19] *Lancaster Intelligencer,* July 14 and August 18, 1864; Stevens to Edward McPherson, July 10, 1864, in the Stevens papers; J. K. Herbert to Butler, August 11, 1864, in *Butler Correspondence,* 5:35–36; Carl Sandburg, *Abraham Lincoln: The War Years* (4 vols., New York, 1939), 3:206.

"thereby advise the re-enslavement of a people, and offend all good beings among men and angels."[20] Thus did he draw the line between the Radicals on the one hand, and both Lincoln and McClellan on the other.

August had been the darkest month of the war, but in September the skies began to brighten, at least for Lincoln. In their platform the Democrats had branded the Republican conduct of the war a failure. Now came a refutation in the reports from Sherman in Atlanta, Farragut in Mobile, and Sheridan in the Shenandoah Valley. Nevertheless, on September 22 Old Thad intimated that he might accept Butler as the Radical candidate by inviting him to address a rally in Lancaster. "Our people have great admiration for you," he wrote to Butler. But on the same day Lincoln was consummating an arrangement whereby to conciliate the Radical antagonism toward himself. At once he made public the resignation of Montgomery Blair from his cabinet, and at the same time Frémont announced his withdrawal from the presidential race. The Blairs were at last in utter defeat!

Now Stevens began to canvass for the president. For though he retained his intense personal bitterness toward Lincoln, he hated McClellan even more. On the stump he had only praise for the "pilot at the helm" who had risen above "the influence of Border State seductions and Republican cowardice," and who at least by implication had agreed that there was to be no peace with slavery. "Let us forget that he ever erred," Old Thad told the voters, "and support him with redoubled energy." A few days before the state elections in October he summed up the prospects in a letter to Justin S. Morrill of Vermont:

I was glad to hear that you are still alive. You are over your troubles but we are just in the midst of ours. On the 5th we had the largest meeting that I ever saw assembled as a county meeting. I think we shall carry this county.

I have strong hopes of the State though it is fiercely contested. I expect that we shall gain at least four members of Congress; possibly we may lose one but I think not. Blair's removal does us much good—Sheridan's speeches are effective.

[20] Herbert to Butler, August 11, 1864, in *Butler Correspondence*, 5:35–36; *Lancaster Intelligencer*, September 15, 1864.

It is strange that you do not see that Lancaster is in the direct route to W C [*Washington City*], so as to enable you to "drop in." Remember me to my young nephew . . . & the rest of the family.

The results from "Sheridan's speeches" along the Shenandoah more than justified Old Thad's optimism in both the October and November elections.[21]

During the last session of the second Congress under Lincoln, from December, 1864, to March, 1865, Old Thad and the Radicals strove to hold the president to the pledge which they thought implicit in his dismissal of Montgomery Blair. Earlier they had committed him to an antislavery policy, of course, in the confiscation acts which he had echoed, though faintly, in his proclamations of emancipation. But it was one thing to announce the policy and quite another to see it carried out. And so, early in January, 1865, while Lincoln was meeting with Confederate peace commissioners not far from beleaguered Richmond, Stevens pressed upon Congress a constitutional amendment abolishing slavery and insisted that the war should never end so long as there was a single slave left. Forgetting for the nonce his claim that the Confederacy was a belligerent power, he made a fierce verbal onslaught upon its president Jefferson Davis as a traitor.

A Democrat replied that Thaddeus Stevens was just as guilty as Davis or any other Southerner of bringing on the war. This provoked Old Thad to an *apologia pro vita sua* in which he asserted that he had read and believed in the Declaration of Independence from his earliest youth, that he had fixed its principles firmly in

[21] *Lancaster Intelligencer,* September 15 and October 13, 1864; McClure, *Lincoln and Men of War-Times,* 126; Stevens to Butler, September 22, 1864, in *Butler Correspondence,* 5:151; Stevens to J. S. Morrill, October 7, 1864, Justin S. Morrill Papers, Library of Congress. In return for the support of Stevens, Lincoln gave ready heed to the Lancastrian's recommendations for government jobs. On October 15, 1864, Old Thad wrote to the President: "I beg leave to recommend to your favorable notice the Rev. Mr. Bishop. He is both an excellent physician and preacher of the Gospel—the state of his health does not permit him to attend regularly to his clerical duties although he is now much improved. He may be very useful in hospital if employed in either of his professions." On the back of the sheet Lincoln wrote on October 17: "Surgeon General please say in writing whether there is, & when, a vacant Hospital Chaplaincy." Manuscript in the Hayes Memorial Library, Fremont, Ohio.

mind by perusing the classics and the Bible, and that as a consequence he had devoted his career to attacking social inequalities
wherever he found them. "I will be satisfied if my epitaph shall
be written thus: 'Here lies one who never rose to any eminence,
and who only courted the low accomplishment to have it said that
he had striven to ameliorate the condition of the poor, the lonely,
the downtrodden of every race and language and color.' "[22] Such
an inscription on his headstone would well have rationalized a
life of political aspiration and defeat. To the passer-by who had
the curiosity to look beyond the words, however, it would have
appeared that Old Thad Stevens had spent more of his living
hours in ameliorating the condition of bankers, railroad entrepreneurs, and ironmasters than in succoring the miscellaneous
downtrodden, lonely, and poor.

Early in 1865 he saw a slim chance at last to realize one of the
hoary ambitions of his career. A vacancy was soon to be made in
the cabinet. Fessenden, formerly chairman of the Senate finance
committee, had succeeded Chase in the treasury department and
now Fessenden was about to resign. Stevens, as the experienced
chairman of the House committee corresponding to Fessenden's,
seemed logically to be next in line for the position of secretary of
the treasury. Expressing their faith and confidence in his financial
abilities, the Pennsylvania Republicans in the House asked permission to present his name to the president. If his strictures on
the money changers had pleased the manufacturers of his own
state, however, they had offended powerful economic interests
elsewhere. His latest gaucherie, in the eyes of "sound money"
people, was a bill to prohibit any United State note from being
"received for a smaller sum" than was specified on its face.
"Simply impossible!" exclaimed James G. Blaine in Congress.
Charles Francis Adams, Jr., wrote from Boston to his father that
"your old friend, Thad Stevens," after he had fixed the currency,
was going to "regulate by law the rising of the sun." The *New
York World* sneered at the proposal to "legislate fair weather in
finance." Old Thad was a realist who knew that the price of gold

[22] *Congressional Globe*, 38 Congress, 2 session (1864–65), 124–126, 265–266;
S. S. Cox, *Three Decades of Federal Legislation* (Providence, 1885), 336.

moved up and down, not immutably as the tides, but in accordance with the specific actions of government officials and men of business. He was willing to admit that his particular bill might not be practicable. "But," he insisted, "there ought to be some law which shall prevent gambling in gold."[23] As a result of his insistence he stood no real chance of appointment as secretary of the treasury, even had Lincoln been ready to make such a concession to the Radicals. The office eventually went to Hugh McCulloch, a conservative on both financial and political matters, whom Old Thad was later to attack on many occasions.

If the president would not appoint one of the Radicals to his cabinet, neither would they admit his Southern representatives to their Congress. Stevens preferred not even to call the men from Arkansas and Louisiana "claimants to seats," for no one should be so foolish as to suppose that they had any kind of substantial claim! While muttering that Congress would rather have Ben Butler than Lincoln as president, he continued to push his anti-Lincoln or at least un-Lincolnian legislation. On January 31, 1865, the proposed thirteenth amendment came to a vote in the House. Stevens had set the hour at three o'clock, but Representative J. M. Ashley, in charge of the resolution, allowed the Democrats to speak until half past three. A group of angry Republicans gathered around Ashley's seat, Old Thad among them. His eyes blazing, he shook his finger at Ashley and read him a lecture for giving way, while Ashley's face, according to a witness, looked "as red as a fresh cut of beef." Though a few minutes behind schedule, the resolution passed easily enough.[24]

As the last session of Congress under Lincoln ended, Stevens was still pretty much the wirepuller behind the Republicans in the House, even if he was not quite the puppeteer he had seemed from 1861 to 1863. But the president was as far as ever from being his puppet. On March 4 Lincoln in his second inaugural

[23] *Congressional Globe,* 38 Congress, 2 session (1864–65), 5–6, 117–119; C. F. Adams, Jr., to C. F. Adams, December 11, 1864, in Worthington C. Ford, ed., *A Cycle of Adams Letters* (2 vols., Boston, 1920), 2:232; J. K. Moorhead and others to Stevens, January 9, 1865, in the Stevens Papers; *New York World,* February 25, 1865.

[24] *Congressional Globe,* 38 Congress, 2 session (1864–65), 733–734; *New York Herald,* February 2, 1865.

spoke of dealing with malice toward none and with charity for all when, as he prayed, the war should speedily come to an end. Stevens had recently been saying the war would never end without the "desolation of the South" and without giving the Southerners "just retribution for their hellish rebellion." After their armies should be finally crushed, he expected to see at least a year or two of guerilla warfare. While condemning the Southern people as a whole, however, he was capable of dealing leniently with them as individuals. When Lincoln pardoned a captured Confederate officer and gave him into the custody of John W. Forney, Old Thad would stop Forney now and then and ask him: "How is your Democratic friend General Pryor? I hope you are both well." One day he received a request from Forney to sign a petition to Lincoln for the pardon of another secessionist. Forney teased him about being inconsistent when he signed. "Oh, you need not be riled about it," he answered. "I saw you were going heavily into the pardon business, and I thought I would take a hand in it myself." His vindictiveness was not so much personal as political. Politically his chief antagonist was still the president.

Late in March of 1865, as the position of Lee in Richmond was becoming more and more hopeless, he called at the White House to warn Lincoln against making too hasty and too easy a peace. Lincoln looked at his clubfooted visitor a while in silence. "Stevens," he finally said, "this is a pretty big hog we are trying to catch, and to hold when we do catch him."[25] But perhaps they were not trying to catch the same hog. It remained to be seen for whom the war was being won as, in April, Lee took his soldiers out of Richmond and Grant followed, toward Appomattox.

[25] John W. Forney, *Anecdotes of Public Men* (2 vols., New York, 1873–81), 1:38; William H. Crook, *Through Five Administrations* (New York, 1910), 28–29.

XIV. Beginning the Last Battle

THE war was over. Lincoln was dead. "The universal feeling among radical men here," wrote one of them in Washington on the day he died, "is that his death is a godsend." Now they could use the assassination to justify beyond all argument their demand for a Carthaginian peace. And they were confident that they had an ally in the White House when Andrew Johnson was inaugurated, for he had at one time acted with them as a member of the Committee on the Conduct of the War. Before the dead body of Lincoln was cold they met in conclave to plan a "reconstruction" of the cabinet, with Ben Butler as the new secretary of state, and the next day they called upon Johnson to give him their advice. In their Radicalism, at least, he seemed to concur. *"Treason,"* he told them, "is a crime; and *crime* must be punished."[1]

Thaddeus Stevens, traveling about in Pennsylvania on the business of a lawyer, paused amidst the public mourning to send directions to Republican politicians in Lancaster. For Johnson's benefit, they were to draw up resolutions on government policy which should be "firm and broad." A week after Lincoln's death, on the morning of April 22, he was in Lancaster when the funeral train passed through on its way to Philadelphia. He was not in the crowd at the railroad station, where James Buchanan sat quietly in his carriage, but stood alone on a rock near by and lifted his hat as the black-draped cars went past through the cut beneath him.[2] What were his thoughts? Perhaps of the martyred

[1] Journal of George W. Julian, entries for April 15, 16, 1865, in the *Indiana Magazine of History*, vol. 11, no. 4 (December, 1915), 334–336; *New York World*, April 29, 1865.
[2] Stevens to O. J. Dickey, April 18, 1865, in the Thaddeus Stevens Papers, Library of Congress; Carl Sandburg, *Abraham Lincoln: The War Years* (4 vols., New York, 1939), 4:394.

Lincoln. Perhaps of the mass meeting to be held in Harrisburg in a few days for the purpose of sending a delegation of Republicans to call upon the new president.

Stevens was among the Pennsylvania delegates who called at the White House at noon on May 3, to see what sort of a president Andrew Johnson was going to make. Simon Cameron, chairman of the group of visitors, told their host that the people of Pennsylvania did not exactly demand the blood of the leading rebels but did demand that they be punished. Only the day before, the president had issued a proclamation offering a reward of a hundred thousand dollars for the arrest of Jefferson Davis and twenty-five thousand for the arrest of Clement C. Clay (once a senator from Alabama) as abettors of the assassination of Lincoln. Now he replied to Cameron that he would, indeed, mete out punishment to the leaders of the rebellion, but with the "deluded and conscripted masses" he would deal mercifully. These remarks were in line with what Johnson had said earlier in his career. As a congressman in the pre-war years he had boasted of his origins as a tailor and had paid off the snubs and sneers of Jefferson Davis by flailing him as an upstart member of a "bastard, scrub aristocracy." In Nashville in 1864 he had declared that at the end of the war the great plantations of the South "must be seized and divided into small farms and sold to honest industrious men." Knowing Johnson's record, Old Thad might have nodded in agreement as he listened in the reception room on this May day, but he had known the record, too, when he opposed Johnson as a candidate for vice president. The issues were not so simple. And Johnson now was saying, as Lincoln had been saying shortly before his death, that it was folly to speak of the seceded states as having gone out of the Union or having committed "suicide."[3] Stevens left the White House with his head full of doubts.

From Washington he went to Philadelphia, in pursuit of the legal affairs of his old friend and client, Samuel Shock, head of the Columbia Bank and Bridge Company. At the St. Lawrence Hotel, on May 10, he picked up the paper to find his doubts about the president confirmed. Here was a report that Johnson was

[3] *New York World,* April 24, May 5, 1865; *New York Times,* May 4, 1865.

giving his blessing to the Pierpont government of Virginia, which had been leading a shadowy existence in Alexandria during the war. Even Lincoln would have required the support of a tenth of the people of the state. Johnson was going to be worse!

In this emergency who was there that Old Thad could take counsel with? Four years earlier, when it had been Lincoln's prospective policies that he was worrying about, he had written again and again to Salmon P. Chase. In 1865 Chase was at least theoretically out of politics as chief justice of the Supreme Court. But there was Charles Sumner of Massachusetts, the antislavery leader of the Senate as Stevens was of the House. Sumner, even more pompous and self-righteous and pretentiously scholarly than Chase, had his peculiarities. He was set on giving the Negroes the right to vote at once, and he held to a strange theory that the states of the former Confederacy had in the act of secession committed *"felo de se."* Yet he possessed power and could be depended upon to oppose the new president with his wonted stubbornness. To him Old Thad wrote from Philadelphia: "I see the President is precipitating things, Virginia is recognized! I fear before Congress meets he will have so be-deviled matters as to render them incurable."[4]

While Sumner caucused with other Radicals in Washington, Old Thad went back to Lancaster and on to Caledonia. There his ironworks, at least partially rebuilt, were again in operation. They could scarcely continue to be as profitable as they had been, now that the wartime demand for iron was past, and the outlook would be still worse if Southerners should be readmitted to Congress and should join with Northern Democrats to repeal the wartime tariffs. Old Thad sat down, on May 16, and penned a letter to President Johnson. He made it sound as conciliatory as he could. The recognition of Pierpont as governor of Virginia, he patiently wrote, was rather difficult to understand. "Reconstruction is a very delicate question. The last Congress (and I expect the present) looked upon it as a question for the Legislative

---

[4] Stevens to [Samuel] Shock, May 4, 1865, manuscript in the Pennsylvania State Library, Harrisburg; Stevens to Sumner, May 10, 1865, in the Charles Sumner MSS., Harvard College Library.

power exclusively. While I think we shall agree with you almost unanimously as to the main objects you have in view, I fear we may differ as to the manner of effecting them." Old Thad ended by suggesting the "propriety" of suspending further reconstruction until Congress met.[5]

Before the end of the month, however, came the news that Johnson was taking another step along his independent way. With one proclamation he set up a mode of reconstruction for North Carolina, and with another he bestowed amnesty upon all but the leaders and wealthiest men of the former Confederacy, though they too, he announced, could apply personally to him for pardon. To Old Thad conciliation no longer seemed possible between the Radicals and the president. "Could we collect bold men enough," he wrote to ask Sumner, "to lay the foundation of a party to take the helm of this government, and keep it off the rocks?" While he fretted and fumed in the South Mountain, the president went ahead during June with a reconstruction plan for Mississippi, while accepting the "ten per cent" governments of Louisiana and Arkansas and the government formed under his own military governorship in Tennessee. Again Stevens wrote to Sumner and begged him to "get up a movement" in Massachusetts while he did the same in his own state. "If something is not done the President will be crowned king before Congress meets," he warned. "How absurd his interfering with the internal regulations of the States, and yet consider them as 'States in the Union'?" One might believe in the state-suicide theory of Sumner or the conquered-province theory of Stevens, but it was plain to both that Johnson had no theory at all.[6]

With the wand of presidential power Johnson was touching new states to life and sending their former leaders, shriven by his pardon, back to govern them when, in July, Old Thad returned to Philadelphia in pursuit of his legal affairs. Again he addressed a letter to the president. He had not found one leading Republican, he said, who approved the presidential policy. Pardons would

[5] Stevens to Johnson, May 16, 1865, in the Andrew Johnson Papers, Library of Congress.
[6] Stevens to Sumner, June 3 and 14, 1865, in the Sumner MSS.

embarrass Congress when the time came to make the enemy pay
the cost of the war. "Can you not hold your hand and wait the
action of Congress," he appealed to Johnson, "and in the meantime govern them by Military rulers?" Back in Lancaster, soon
after the hanging in Washington of Mrs. Surratt and several other
alleged accomplices of John Wilkes Booth, Old Thad received a
visitor who had come to him on behalf of Clement C. Clay, now
in prison on the same charge. Stevens assured his caller that
neither Clay nor Jefferson Davis could ever be tried for treason,
for the United States by its action in the war had recognized the
belligerent character of the Confederate states. He scorned the
idea that either of the men could have had anything to do with
the assassination of Lincoln, and he unhesitatingly offered his
services as an attorney for Clay, though he asked that the arrangement be kept secret for the time being. Johnson had put a price
on the heads of a few outstanding men of the Confederacy but
was pardoning the others at a rapid rate; Stevens, by contrast,
would spare the few in order that Congress might treat the rest
as denizens of conquered provinces! "You will perceive then, my
dear Madam," wrote Stevens' visitor to Mrs. Clay in Alabama,
"that connected with the proposed trial of your husband, there
are profound questions of statesmanship and party."[7]

His letters to Johnson availing nothing, Old Thad took a train
for Washington toward the close of July. He dropped in at the
office of the secretary of the navy to see Gideon Welles, he of the
long white beard and suspicious eye. Only business, not politics
nor congeniality, could bring these two together. "Thad Stevens
called on me on business," Welles noted in his diary, "and took
occasion to express ultra views, and had a sarcastic hit or two but
without much sting."[8] Old Thad could not be too cheerful about
the situation as he viewed it in Washington. After his return to
Caledonia, he painted a rather dismal picture in another missive
to Sumner:

[7] Stevens to Johnson, July 6, 1865, in the Johnson Papers; R. J. Haldeman
to Mrs. C. C. Clay, July 24, 1865, in the *Lancaster County Historical Society
Papers*, 17 (1913), 162–163.

[8] *Diary of Gideon Welles, Secretary of the Navy under Lincoln and Johnson*
(3 vols., Boston and New York, 1911), 2:325–326.

I was called away from Washington before I had an opportunity to talk with the President on reconstruction as I intended. In other things he seemed nearly right—But I presume I could have done no good—John has the reins—Stanton and Chase desire to be the architects, and fear Congress—Stanton has started Virginia. How ridiculous. But perhaps a very low farce was thought necessary amidst so many bloody tragedies. I have written very plainly to the President urging delay—But I fear he will pursue his wrong course—With illegal courts, and usurping "reconstruction," I know not where you and I shall be. While we can hardly approve of all the acts of the govt. we must try to keep out of the ranks of the opposition—The danger is that so much success will reconcile the people to almost any thing.[9]

On August 17 a Republican state convention met at Harrisburg and offered Old Thad a sounding board. First, however, he had to outmaneuver Cameron in order to get a Stevens man elected as chairman of the state committee. The resolutions of the convention reflected his strategy of laying down the law to Johnson while keeping out of "the ranks of the opposition." They endorsed Johnson, protection, the Monroe Doctrine, and confiscation, but said nothing about giving Negroes the right to vote. This omission surprised the Radical editor Greeley, and Old Thad might have read in the *Tribune* a few days later that he ought to have made the resolutions stronger. But Sumner's next letter, though the senator was a fanatic on Negro suffrage, praised the confiscation plank as "excellent." "Such a voice from Pennsylvania," he had written, "has salvation in it." From Lancaster Old Thad replied, toward the end of August:

I am glad you are laboring to arrest the President's fatal policy—I wish the prospect of success were better—I have twice written him urging him to delay his hand until Congress meets—Of course he pays no attention to it—Our editors are generally cowards and sycophants—I would make a speech as you suggest if a fair occasion offered—Our views "reconstruction & confiscation" were embodied in our resolutions at Harrisburg, amidst much chaff—Negro Suffrage was passed over as heavy & premature—get the rebel states into a territorial condition, & it can be easily dealt with.

That I think should be our great aim—Then Congress can manage it—We need a good committee on elections—I fear Dawes—can he be brought right—to exclude all rebel state members until final reorganization of *all*. I wish you would sound him, & let me know, as it may be proper to "reconstruct" that committee.

[9] Stevens to Sumner, August 17, 1865, in the Sumner MSS.

Old Thad had good reason to fear Dawes, who in Massachusetts was now publicly commending the president's policy, who in Congress in 1862 had arraigned Stevens, Simon Stevens, Frémont, and Cameron as partners in graft! The presence of Dawes at the head of the committee on elections was the only hitch in the plan he was maturing. With the proper sort of a committee, with the so-called states of Johnson's definitely established as "territories," the Radicals should be able to keep their enemies out of Congress.[10]

Carrying out Sumner's suggestion, Old Thad prepared a speech intended to convert the public to his theory of the status of the South. When he spoke out, on September 6, his words went not only to his hearers in the courthouse square in Lancaster; they were to echo and re-echo throughout the land.

The armies of the Confederate states having been conquered and subdued, and their territory possessed by the United States, it becomes necessary to establish Governments therein, which shall be republican in form and principles.... It is desirable that such a course should be pursued as to exclude from those Governments every vestige of human bondage; and render the same forever impossible in this nation; and to take care that no principles of self-destruction shall be incorporated therein. In effecting this it is to be hoped that no provision of the Constitution will be infringed, and no principle of the law of nations disregarded. Especially must we take care, in rebuking this unjust and treasonable war, that the authorities of the Union shall indulge in no acts of usurpation which may tend to impair the stability and permanency of the nation. Within these limitations we hold it to be the duty of the Government to inflict condign punishment on the rebel belligerents, and so weaken their hands that they can never again endanger the Union; and so reform their municipal institutions as to make them republican in spirit as well as in name.

We especially insist that the property of the chief rebels should be seized and appropriated to the payment of the national debt, caused by the unjust and wicked war which they instigated.

How can such punishments be inflicted and such forfeitures produced without doing violence to established principles? Two positions have been suggested. *First*—To treat those States as never having been out of the Union.... *Second*—To accept the position in which they placed

[10] Alexander K. McClure, *Old-Time Notes of Pennsylvania* (2 vols., Philadelphia, 1905), 2:186–190; *New York Tribune*, August 18, 19, 1865; Sumner to Stevens, August 20, 1865, in the Stevens Papers; Stevens to Sumner, August 26, 1865, in the Sumner MSS.

themselves as severed from the union, an independent government *de facto,* and an alien enemy to be dealt with according to the laws of war . . . .

In reconstruction . . . no reform can be effected in the Southern States if they have never left the Union. But reformation *must* be effected; the foundation of their institutions, both political, municipal, and social, *must* be broken up and *relaid,* or all our blood and treasure have been spent in vain. This can only be done by treating and holding them as a conquered people. Then all things which we can desire to do, follow with logical and legitimate authority . . . . Whether those who have fought our battles should be allowed to vote, or only those of a paler hue, I leave to be discussed in the future, when Congress can take legitimate cognizance of it.

There are some 6,000,000 of freemen in the South. The number of acres of land is 465,000,000. Of this those who own above 200 acres each, number about 70,000 persons, holding in the aggregate (together with the States) about 394,000,000 acres, leaving for all the others below 200 each, about 71,000,000 of acres. By thus forfeiting the estates of the leading Rebels, the Government would have 394,000,000 of acres beside their town property, and yet nine-tenths of the people would remain untouched. Divide this land into convenient farms. Give, if you please, forty acres to each adult male freedman. Suppose there are 1,000,000 of them. That would require 40,000,000 of acres, which deducted from 394,000,000 leaves 354,000,000 of acres for sale. Divide it into suitable farms and sell it to the highest bidders. I think it, including town property, would average at least $10 per acre. That would produce $3,540,000,000.

Let that be applied as follows, to wit: 1. Invest $300,000,000 in six per cent government bonds, and add the interest semi-annually to the pensions of those who have become entitled by this villainous war. 2. Appropriate $200,000,000 to pay the damage done to loyal men, North and South, by the Rebellion. 3. Pay the residue, being $3,040,000,000, toward the payment of the National Debt. . . .

If the South is ever to be made a safe Republic, let her lands be cultivated by the toil of the owners, or the free labor of intelligent citizens. This must be done even though it drive her nobility into exile. . . .

It is far easier and more beneficial to exile 70,000 proud, bloated, and defiant Rebels than to expatriate 4,000,000 of laborers, native to the soil and loyal to the Government. This latter scheme [*"colonization" of emancipated slaves*] was a favorite plan of the Blairs, with which they had for a while inoculated our late sainted President. But a single experiment made him discard it and its advisers. Since I have mentioned the Blairs, I may say a word more of these persistent apologists of the South. . . . They are a family of considerable power, some merit, of admirable audacity and execrable selfishness. With impetuous alacrity they seize the White House, and hold possession of it, as in the late administration, until shaken off by the overpowering force of public indignation. Their pernicious counsel had well nigh defeated the re-election of Abraham Lincoln; and if it should prevail with the present Administration, pure and patriotic as President Johnson is admitted to be, it will render him the most unpopular Executive—save one [*Buchanan, of course*]—that ever occupied the Presidential chair. But there is no fear of that. He will soon say, as Mr. Lincoln said, "Your time has come!"

Is this great conquest to be in vain? That will depend upon ... the next Congress. To Congress alone belongs the power of Reconstruction, of giving law to the vanquished. ... Under "Restoration" every Rebel State will send Rebels to Congress, and they, with their allies in the North, will control Congress, and will occupy the White House. ...

Young men, this duty devolves on you. Would to God, if only for that, I were still in the prime of life, that I might aid you to fight through this last, greatest battle of freedom!

Like a state's attorney expounding the law and arraigning a prisoner, Old Thad had prepared his brief cleverly for his jury, the public. The popular idea was that the war had been "rebellion" and "treason" (and indeed the second confiscation act had recognized these crimes), but his own conception was that the war had been a conflict between two separate belligerent powers. In the beginning of his address to the jury he had interwoven his and the popular beliefs by speaking of the "treasonable war" and the "rebel belligerents," and then had gone on to show that real victory for the Northern people was possible only if they accepted his concept of the nature of the war. The verdict was not to come until later. For the present what were the people, or at least the molders of public opinion, saying? The cries of outrage from Democratic editors in Lancaster and throughout the nation could not have surprised Old Thad, but two of the leading Republican editors of the country, Forney of the *Philadelphia Press* and the *Washington Chronicle* and Greeley of the *New York Tribune,* also professed to be shocked. Though giving full publicity to the entire speech, Greeley attacked it on the editorial page. "He seems not to care for the enfranchisement of the blacks," the editor said of Stevens. "And we protest against any warfare on Southern property ... because the wealthier class of Southerners, being more enlightened and humane than the ignorant and vulgar, are

A LETTER TO SUMNER

Showing why Stevens' handwriting was "all Greek" to many of his correspondents. For a translation of part of this, see page 211.

less inimicable to the blacks." And further, Greeley insisted, the confiscation plan simply would not work out as its author claimed it would. All of this was, perhaps, only a rationalization of the sympathy which Northern men of property were beginning to feel for their fellow "wealthier classes" of the South.[11]

But Old Thad knew that, as for the Southern blacks themselves, they could hardly be expected to rise above serfdom unless they were given land, solid land. Surely "forty acres" would do more for the Negro than an illusory right to vote. He knew in a general way of the emancipation of the Russian serfs, beginning on the very eve of the American Civil War, under Czar Alexander II. Even in dark, reactionary Russia the government had seen the need of sealing freedom with some provision for real estate. Interested in finding precisely how things were done there, Old Thad inquired of Sumner, who had the reputation of being a most well-read and learned man: "Where can I find *in English* a correct history of the condition of the Russian serfs, and the terms of their liberation—I know not where to look for it."[12] Unfortunately for the American serfs, Stevens in the years to come was to befriend them more for the benefit of the Republican party than for their own sake. As for their former masters, he knew that a "warfare on Southern property" was the order of the day if Pennsylvania iron men and manufacturers were to keep the advantages they had gained during the war.

At Lancaster Stevens had not assailed the president personally but had laid the blame for his wrongdoing upon the Blairs. At Gettysburg a month later he pointed his remarks directly at Johnson, who, he said, was using the patronage and the pardoning power in such a way as to "build up a throne." Indeed, he was issuing pardons so rapidly, said humorous Old Thad, that human endurance could not stand the strain and so a machine had been invented to turn them out at the rate of three hundred a day.

[11] *New York Tribune,* September 12, 1865; *Lancaster Intelligencer,* September 20, 1865. The Lancaster speech was printed in full in the *Tribune* of September 11.
[12] Stevens to Sumner, October 7, 1865, in the Sumner MSS. "Is there any hope that Congress will overrule the Prest?" Stevens had added. "I fear we are ruined, for I have little faith in Congress."

"I was lately in Philadelphia, and heard of a case (a sample of many others) which stirred my blood, cold as it is." Under the confiscation laws government agents had seized more than one hundred thousand dollars' worth of city securities belonging to a "rich rebel," and then Johnson had issued a pardon restoring these to their "rebel owner." Such a story was well calculated to stir the blood of the residents of Adams and Franklin counties who had suffered property damage in Confederate invasions and raids. *"The President is too much of a plebeian,"* smirked the professed egalitarian, "to indulge in such absolute ideas."[13] In Lancaster again, he wrote to Sumner near the end of October:

> I have just returned & got yours. Our State convention was nearly all right when it was explained to them—So have I found everybody when properly informed except office holders, I am sure our Members of Congress would all be right if we had no villanous newspapers. How far they may intimidate them I know not—
> Seward & others are making great efforts to sustain Johnston—
> I am trying to get up a Soldier's convention to denounce his policy—How it will succeed I know not but should find no trouble if I had a little more time—the patronage is hard to fight against—I wish N York might be lost but fear it will not.[14]

While Stevens was going to and fro in Pennsylvania and arousing the people against the president, the latter was receiving politicians from the South who reported that they had held conventions; had revised their state constitutions so as to repudiate their public debt, denounce secession, and abolish slavery; had elected legislatures; were ratifying the Thirteenth Amendment; and were electing senators and representatives for the December meeting of Congress. The Southern legislators were also dealing, in their fashion, with the tremendous social problem presented by the sudden freeing of millions of slaves. In October they began to re-enact the old slave codes in a modified form. These could be called, and sometimes in fact were, an effort to re-establish slavery in disguise. At any rate the Radicals could cry that President Johnson was conspiring with unreconstructed rebels to undo the victory which the North had so dearly won! The possibilities,

[13] *Lancaster Intelligencer,* October 11, 1865, quoting the *Gettysburg Star,* October 5, 1865.
[14] Stevens to Sumner, October 25, 1865, in the Sumner MSS.

from this point of view, were brought to the attention of Stevens by Henry Winter Davis, the Maryland Radical, in a letter dripping with sarcasm of the kind Old Thad himself might well have authored.[15]

By taking the extremest position of all the Radicals the old man in Lancaster had made himself the focal point of Radicalism, to whom eventually turned even the arch-conspirator of those who had plotted to remake the cabinet immediately upon Lincoln's death. From Ben Butler in Lowell, Massachusetts, he received a letter dated November 15 which began: "I should be glad to see you if possible upon matters presented by the present political crisis." "I expect to be in Washington about the middle of next week," Old Thad wrote in reply. "I should be glad to see you at my rooms 279 S. B. Street Capitol Hill."

On his arrival in Washington the plain red-brick house behind the capitol became the headquarters of men plotting to undo the work of the man in the imposing white edifice a little over a mile away. The visitor from Lowell was a character to match the picturesqueness of his host. Thad Stevens was tall but bent, bewigged, sharp-featured, his lower lip outthrust, his eyes aglow. In conversation there was no disputing his hollow, unmusical voice. Ben Butler was tall but paunchy, his long hair fringing a bald dome, his eyelids drooping above a drooping moustache and half hiding a pair of unmatched eyes. But his looks belied a spirit very much alive, and over some of his associates and even his superiors he had seemed to exert an almost hypnotic influence, as over General Grant. To Stevens he came equipped with the draft of a bill to give civil rights to the Negroes of the South. This, he

[15] "The enclosed extract has just been sent to me from N. O. to illustrate the freedom *you* and Pr. Johnson are giving the negroes and the Yankees down South. Perhaps you feel interest enough in this matter to appreciate it though the President may not. '*Brevis via per exemplis*' is the true maxim: & knowing how slow you are to learn to read the black letter law of the South I send you this to help your education. Wishing you much health & happiness & great moderation of tone in using such offensive matter." H. Winter Davis to Stevens, manuscript in the Stevens Papers. Davis did not date the letter. It must have been written before the end of 1865, because he died at the close of the year. Internal evidence indicates that it was written in October or November, 1865.

was convinced, was the way to "commence the fight" against "Southern injustice to the negro" and to hold "the weak-kneed brethren of the Republican party" in line. Old Thad disagreed. "It seems to me," he had written to Butler from Lancaster, "that we must put the rebel states under territorial governments at once, or they will work into Congress one by one through Executive influence." What about Dawes, from Butler's own state of Massachusetts? Could Butler put him "on the right trail?"[16] Apparently Butler could not, nor could Sumner or any of the other New England Radicals.

The first move of the Radicals, according to Stevens' plan, would be to shut and bar the doors of Congress to representatives from the South. Through his friend Edward McPherson, whom he had made chief clerk of the House in 1863, Old Thad was able to prevent the names of the Southerners from being entered on the roll. He had to confess, though, that if their credentials should be referred to the standing committee on elections, whose chairman was Dawes, he and the Radicals would be "gone." He planned therefore to pass a resolution at the outset declaring that there were no "states" in the South to be represented, and then to secure the appointment of a special committee which would deal with the question of the admission of the Southern members, and which would take charge of the whole business of devising a program for the "reconstruction" of the South. But suppose the Senate should admit the senators elected by Johnson's state legislatures? Suppose Johnson should veto the scheme? Old Thad and the Radicals who consulted with him thought of everything. To bind the Senate and the House together, they decided to make their special committee a *joint* one and to provide that neither branch of Congress should admit members from a state which the other refused to recognize. To avoid the possibility of a veto, they

[16] Butler to Stevens, November 15, 1865, in *Private and Official Correspondence of Benjamin F. Butler during the Period of the Civil War* (5 vols., [Norwood, Massachusetts], 1917), 5:678; Stevens to Butler, November 18, 1865, in the Benjamin F. Butler Papers, Library of Congress; Butler to Stevens, November 20, 1865, in the Stevens Papers. For a pen portrait of Old Thad by a fellow Radical, see Frederic Bancroft and William A. Dunning, eds., *The Reminiscences of Carl Schurz* (3 vols., New York, 1908), 3:214.

would accomplish all of this by means of a *concurrent* resolution, which differed technically from a joint resolution in taking effect without the approval of the president.

"The whole question as to the action of Congress, then," observed the *New York Herald*, "is, does Andrew Johnson represent the views and policies of the Republican members, or is Thaddeus Stevens, with his radical, extreme ideas, the true exponent of the party?" Old Thad, making no secret of his strategy, boasted that he had a majority of the Republicans behind him. Friends of the president doubted this claim. They pointed out that Johnson had an enormous power of patronage, and that most of the office-holders were appointees of Lincoln's. He had saved his ammunition and kept his powder dry. When Stevens was finally accorded an interview at the White House on November 29, the stubborn president, well armed as he was with the patronage, quite naturally rejected this opportunity to avoid a fight by means of a last-minute conversion to Old Thad's views. Every member of Congress was deeply interested in the appointments in his own district. Could Old Thad hold the patronage-conscious congressmen in line? The test would come in a caucus to be held on the night of December 2.[17]

At the caucus "Thad Stevens made the important motions," as was observed by one of those present, Rutherford B. Hayes. There were disagreements over the memberships of the standing committees. Henry J. Raymond, editor of the *New York Times* and a friend of Seward, wanted the chairmanship of ways and means. But when this committee was divided into three parts, Old Thad became the head of the most important, that on appropriations. He stormed and threatened to break up the caucus if the members did not adopt his reconstruction program. And they did so. In the words of a newsman, they "made a formal surrender of the Republican party to the guidance of Thad Stevens."[18]

[17] *New York Times*, November 14, 21, 28, 30, 1865; *New York World*, November 25, 1865; *New York Herald*, November 27, 30, 1865.
[18] C. R. Williams, ed., *Rutherford B. Hayes Diary and Letters* (5 vols., [Columbus, Ohio], 1922–26), 3:7; *New York Herald*, December 3, 4, 5, 1865; *New York Times*, December 3, 4, 1865.

When on the next day one of the representatives from Louisiana had an interview with Old Thad, he became convinced that he had no chance of being admitted to Congress and made up his mind to turn around and go home. But President Johnson was not so ready to give up. After the caucus Secretary Welles called at the White House and suggested that in the proceedings "there was something bad." Johnson agreed but assured Welles that the Radicals "would be knocked in the head at the start." One of the Southern applicants would be Maynard of Tennessee, he explained, who as a loyal unionist had been a member of the House during the war. The present Congress would hardly dare to turn Maynard out, and his acceptance would be the entering wedge for others from the South. Nevertheless, Welles feared that the intrigue, led as it was by Stevens, "an opponent of states rights," had already gone too far to be stopped.[19]

When at last Congress assembled on December 4, 1865, the stage was well set for the dramatic and momentous events that were to follow. On Capitol Hill the air was as balmy as on a May day. Inside the scene was resplendent. The chief clerk, while helping spin the plot, had seen to the redecoration of the Hall of Representatives, where it was to be played. On the main floor "a new Brussels carpet of a tasteful pattern and in cheerful colors" had been laid, and the diplomats' and ladies' galleries had also been "handsomely refurnished." Soon after the doors were opened on the springlike December morning, a "brilliant and fashionable" crowd thronged the corridors and galleries. At their desks on the floor of the House the actors were prepared for the parts assigned them. On one side sat the leader of the Democrats, James Brooks, a wily and well-experienced politician from New York. On the other sat "Thad Stevens, grim looking, cool, with a ready wit, perfect courage and the sort of independence which long experience, assured position and seventy years of age gives an able man."

McPherson began to call the roll. When he passed over Maynard's name, Maynard rose and, shaking his credentials in his hand, demanded recognition from the clerk. McPherson refused

[19] *New York Herald*, December 4, 1865; *Diary of Gideon Welles*, 2:387.

to recognize him and offered to state his reasons but Stevens spoke up: "It is not necessary. We know all." When Brooks attempted to protest, Stevens rose to a point of order and (as in the Pennsylvania legislature on December 4, 1838) announced that nothing except the election of a speaker might be discussed until the House should have been organized. "Why, this is not parliamentary propriety, if it is even decency," expostulated Brooks. When Maynard appealed to Stevens to grant the floor to him, Old Thad replied: "I cannot yield to any gentleman who does not belong to this body—who is an outsider." To the repeated appeals of Brooks and Maynard Old Thad responded with remarks which, "jerked out with the peculiar acerbity of the great radical," created a laugh at their expense while he dismissed them with "a Podsnappian wave of the hand." Finally they gave up. After the election of officers he was ready for "springing the drop." Introducing the resolution for a joint committee of fifteen on reconstruction, he staved off motions to adjourn, stifled debate, and, under a suspension of the rules, saw the measure pass by a vote of 139 to 35. He then moved that the House adjourn, the motion was carried, and "the old war horse leaned back squarely and gloriously triumphant."[20]

By this *coup d'état* Stevens had completely overturned Johnson's well-laid plans. "The new members, and others weak in their understanding," wrote Welles in his diary, "were taken off their legs as was designed, before they were aware of it." In his message to Congress on the day after the organization the president, far from announcing the "restoration" of the Union, had to take a negative and defensive tone. The theory that the states could be extinguished, he declared, would be fatal to the Constitution itself. Logical though it was, the message could not give the Southerners in Washington the seats in Congress which Johnson had promised them. One by one they began to return to the South, amid the rejoicing of the Radicals. "The way in which you have opened Congress & thrown down the gauntlet to the President's policy has pleased our radical friends hereabouts so

[20] *New York Times*, November 25, December 5, 1865; *New York Herald*, December 5, 1865; Hayes, *Diary and Letters*, 3:8; *Congressional Globe*, 39, Congress, 1 session (1865–66), 3–4.

thoroughly that we are all hearty, merry, and tumultuous with gratitude!" So Old Thad heard from Theodore Tilton, poet, editor of the *Independent,* and friend of Henry Ward Beecher. "I wish I knew you personally," Tilton had added. "If you ever come to New York will you make my home your stopping place?"[21]

When, about a week after the organization of the House, the Senate returned the resolution for a joint committee, it had been altered in an important respect. The senators, while concurring in the House resolution, had done so only after amending it so as to omit the stipulation that neither chamber should act independently in admitting members. Those who expected a fight in the House over this amendment were disappointed when Stevens blandly moved to concur. On the following day, however, the House declared by a large majority that, so far as it was concerned, the resolution had been adopted with the understanding that none of the rejected members should be admitted to either chamber until the joint committee should report. In the interim all papers bearing on the question were to be referred to the committee without debate. The membership of the committee was not exactly what the Radicals desired. The chairman for the House was Stevens, of course, but the chairman for the Senate and hence the titular head of the whole committee was William Pitt Fessenden of Maine, whom Old Thad earlier had denounced for having too much of "that vile ingredient," Conservatism. Sumner had been "very anxious" for the headship, according to Fessenden, but, "committed to the most ultra views" as he was, had failed to get the support "even of his friends." "If Sumner and Stevens and a few other such men do not embroil us with the President," Fessenden was confident, "matters can be satisfactorily arranged."[22]

[21] *Diary of Gideon Welles,* 2:392; Tilton to Stevens, December 6, 1865, in the Stevens Papers.

[22] *New York Tribune,* December 6, 7, 14, 16, 1865; Boutwell to Butler, December 9, 1865, in the Butler Papers; Francis Fessenden, *Life and Public Services of William Pitt Fessenden* (2 vols., Boston, 1907), 2:20. The official record of the organization and work of the committee is reprinted in Benjamin B. Kendrick, *The Journal of the Joint Committee of Fifteen on Reconstruction* (Columbia University Studies in History, Economics and Public Law, vol. 62, New York, 1914).

The kind of arrangement that would have been satisfactory to Fessenden and Johnson would have defeated the whole purpose of Old Thad. To him it would have meant losing the Civil War. Troops and camps and cannon fire had been but one aspect of a larger struggle for power, and politicians were to continue with the weapons of politics long after soldiers had dropped their guns. Two years after Appomattox Old Thad was still to be saying that there existed only a *"quasi* peace."

XV. "To Secure Perpetual Ascendancy"

FOUR years of warfare between the Union and the Confederacy had obscured the fact that the sectional controversy was not two-sided but triangular, not between the South and the North alone but between the South, the Northeast, and the Northwest. Before 1861 the Democratic party, essentially an alliance of Southern and Western politicians, had for most of a generation held the balance of power against the East. Then the firing on Fort Sumter had united most Northerners on both sides of the Alleghenies behind the Republican party and the flag. Even patriotism, however, had not sufficed to prevent Copperheads in the states north of the Ohio from plotting, as they grew weary of the war, to secede and establish a confederacy of their own or perhaps join that to the south of them. In the first months of peace, if President Johnson had been allowed his way, Westerners and Southerners would have recombined to rule the nation, and they would have found allies in the East. They might do so even yet, if Johnson got his way! This was the situation that Thaddeus Stevens faced after his congressional *coup d'état* of December 4, 1865.

He was not only the embodiment of Pennsylvania capitalism himself but also a go-between for others of that ilk, one whose function it was to convert the votes of the many into the policies of the few. To his house on B street now came letters and personal agents from Eastern ironmasters and railroad entrepreneurs eager to maintain and extend their wartime gains. There was Josiah Perham, lobbyist for the Northern Pacific. There was Tom Scott, vice president of the Pennsylvania Railroad, to whom, at Bedford Springs during the summer, Old Thad had explained "some mat-

ters connected with the Union Pacific R. R.—Eastern division
known as the Kansas Route." Scott was now writing to Old Thad:
"Since that time a number of your friends in Penn^a have become
interested in the enterprise and will make it a success—I can manage the matter satisfactorily to you and I respectfully ask that no
adverse action be taken or permitted at least until I can see you
and explain fully." There was the owner of the Reading Iron
Works, alarmed lest the greenbacks be called in and the price of
iron fall, who was reminding Stevens that "it is a fallacy that we
have too much money in circulation." And there was the proprietor of Barrée Forge in Huntingdon County, who had read the
Lancaster speech and "approved of it highly," and who agreed
that "the major part of the Southern rebels should *undergo Pur-
gation.*" "Now, as to a *tariff for protection,*" he wrote. "It appears
that the domestic manufacturers, East and West, look to our
Penn^a delegation for help."[1] Plainly, in the minds of those closest
to the subject, there was a very real connection between Radicalism and railroads and iron.

At the Radical headquarters behind the capitol it was not all
work and no play for Old Thad. Though he seldom went out
in Washington society, he often mixed business and pleasure at
his home as he entertained a few senators and representatives at
cards. Lydia Smith would bustle about, setting up the table for
the players, adjusting the lamps, bringing in refreshments, and
attending to other details in wifely fashion. Not so brash as to
inquire into the domestic affairs of their host, the guests nevertheless assumed that his regard for the mulatto woman was not entirely platonic. One of them, a frequent visitor during the winter
of 1865–66, believed that "the influence of this colored mistress
was largely the cause of Stevens' bitter animosity to Southern
whites." And that was a belief widespread among men who little
understood the politics of iron and railroads. When not at the
card table Old Thad, as in his younger days, spent his few moments of leisure with his books, especially those on Roman history

[1] T. A. Scott to Stevens, November 30, 1865; Josiah Perham to Stevens,
December 2, 1865; S. Miles Green to Stevens, December 20, 1865; Stevens to
O. J. Dickey, December 23, 1865; John McManus to Stevens, January 2, 1866,
in the Thaddeus Stevens Papers, Library of Congress.

and English parliamentary law. Having promised him a copy of Darwin's *On the Origin of Species,* Joseph Henry, the pioneer secretary of the Smithsonian Institution, sent him the volume a week or so after the organization of Congress and with it a note assuring him that he might keep it as long as he liked. A little later he received from the publishers a complimentary copy of Greeley's *The American Conflict,* a Radical history of the war. He thanked them and praised the "mechanical execution" and the "literary merit" of their "elegant volume," but he was so biased as to be a poor critic and a worse prophet when he wrote: "The great industry and impartiality of Mr. Greeley will make this the text of all future histories of the Great Rebellion."[2] In his reading, as perhaps also in his gambling, he was learning about the struggle for existence and the survival of the fittest as he prepared to fight his party's battles against the president.

He was composing a speech with which to launch the attack. On a piece of scratch paper he hastily calculated the effect of the emancipation of the slaves upon the Republican party. In the Constitution only three-fifths of the unfree population were to have been counted in apportioning representatives to the Southern states; but suppose, now that the slaves were freemen, their whole number should be counted? Old Thad's arithmetic showed that the Democrats would have a clear majority in Congress whenever Southern representatives should be allowed to enter that body. "They will at the very first election take possession of the White House and the halls of Congress," he scrawled in the manuscript of his speech. "I need not depict the ruin that would follow." "As there are no symptoms that the people of these provinces will be prepared to participate in constitutional government for some years, I know of no arrangement so proper for them as territorial governments. There they can learn the principles of freedom and eat the fruit of foul rebellion." They must not be permitted to share in the national government until the Constitution should have been so amended as "to secure perpetual ascendancy to the party of the Union." And an appropriate amendment

[2] *Reminiscences of Senator William M. Stewart of Nevada* (New York, 1908),

would be one that would change the basis of representation to the number of people in a state who were actually entitled to vote. This, according to Stevens' estimate, would reduce the prospective Southern membership in Congress from a dangerous eighty-three to a safe forty-six.[3]

After the events of December 4 congressmen did not question who their master was. "The only blemish in his puritanical, severe appearance is a brown wig," wrote Rutherford B. Hayes, new to the House, to his wife. "He is witty, cool, full of and fond of 'sarcasms,' and thoroughly informed and accurate. He has a knack of saying things which turn the laugh on his opponent. When he rises everyone expects something worth hearing, and he has the attention of all. You remember his speech on confiscation. He is radical throughout, except, I am told, he don't believe in hanging. He is leader." At his desk, as another observer described him, he would sit restlessly, awkwardly, his back bent forward, his knees protruding in opposite directions, his hands pottering about, his face downcast and sad. When he got up to speak he would begin abstractedly, as if talking to himself, while the House tittered in anticipation, and here and there a page made bold to mimic him. Then, rising erect, he would lift his long right arm with a wide sweep, contract his beetling brows, and with a sudden straight thrust of his long yellow finger he would send forth a series of verbal explosions in his loudest and harshest tones. In such a manner on December 18, 1865, the day the Thirteenth Amendment was proclaimed as ratified, he gave the House his argument on the means of maintaining the Republican party in power. "It is time that Congress should assert its authority," thundered the reader of classical history, "and assume something of the dignity of a Roman senate."[4] Then, perhaps, the leader of the House

205; Joseph Henry to Stevens, December 13, 1865, and Stevens to O. D. Case & Co., [January, 1866], in the Stevens Papers.

[3] Undated manuscript in Stevens' handwriting, in the Stevens Papers, vol. 16.

[4] Hayes to Mrs. Hayes, December 7, 1865, in C. R. Williams, ed., *Rutherford B. Hayes Diary and Letters* (5 vols., [Columbus, Ohio], 1922–26), 3:9–10; J. W. Binckley, "The Leader of the House," in *Galaxy*, 1 (1866): 494–496; *Congressional Globe*, 39 Congress, 1 session (1865–66), 72–75.

would become veritably a tribune of the people, the equal if not the superior of the consul in the White House!

At the beginning of 1866, with the untimely death of Henry Winter Davis, he was left alone as the most extreme of Radicals. He started the new year by calling on the president along with two others of the joint committee on reconstruction, one of them his former foe Washburne, of Illinois. At the White House they asked Johnson to take no action in regard to the South so long as the subject remained under consideration by their group, and Johnson replied that for the present it was not his intention to do more than he had already done. Later Old Thad and some of his Radical friends also visited the residence of the chief justice; Chase, though to others he had professed to be "shocked" by Stevens' recent utterances, still was a good enough Radical to advise the congressmen how to avoid trouble with the Supreme Court. Now that he had suspended the checks of the tripartite system of government, at least for the time, Stevens turned to the problem of getting public opinion on his side. In his daily mail he was receiving the praises of carpetbaggers and scalawags in the South, but the Northern newspapers that he saw, Republican as well as Democratic, were many of them hostile. While one Pennsylvania editor was "hammering away" at him, he did not "perceive any counter article" in the other Republican papers of his state. "Had you not better give them a hint?" he suggested to one of his henchmen in Lancaster. "The contest will soon be a real one here."[5]

He took the offensive and once more displayed his generalship

[5] *New York Herald*, January 2, 1866; Benjamin B. Kendrick, *The Journal of the Joint Committee of Fifteen on Reconstruction* (*Columbia University Studies in History, Economics, and Public Law*, vol. 62, New York, 1914), 40–41; Stevens to O. J. Dickey, January 5, 1866, in the Stevens Papers. To A. K. McClure, editor of the *Chambersburg Repository*, Old Thad had sent his thanks for "the grand argument in favor of the right policy" and had added: "You ought to speak from Philadelphia in a daily of 100,000 circulation. Why cannot you get up such a paper?" Stevens to McClure, December 16, 1865, facsimile in Alexander K. McClure, *Abraham Lincoln and Men of War-Times* (Philadelphia, 1892), 291. Some years later McClure was in fact to become the publisher of the *Philadelphia Times*, and at his suggestion Miss Mira L. Dock was to write her article on Caledonia furnace, published in the *Times* of July 14, 1895.

as a parliamentarian when a bill granting Negro suffrage in the District of Columbia came to the attention of the House. In caucus, despite his protests, the Republicans adopted an amendment to limit the vote to those, whether black or white, who could pass a certain educational test. Angrily he muttered something about toadying to the president and swore that, when the bill came up in the House, he would vote with the Democrats. He happened to be on cordial terms with the Democratic congressional chieftain, Fernando Wood, though Wood as mayor of New York had been a secessionist and later a Copperhead. "I don't care who votes in Washington City," he privately told Wood on the floor of the House, "but I want to force these skulks on our side to a test of principle. So, whatever becomes of this bill, you may have all the party advantages and I'll know who's on our side, eh?" Wood agreed. His Democrats, thinking the Conservative Republicans would refuse to accept Negro suffrage pure and simple, voted with the Radicals to defeat the amendment for an educational test. And the Conservatives, gagged by the previous question, then had no choice but to vote with the Radicals and, to the consternation of the Democrats, help to pass the unamended bill![6]

Meanwhile, almost every morning between ten o'clock and noon, Old Thad was meeting with the members of the joint committee to gather evidence on conditions in the South, particularly evidence showing that Yankees and Negroes were not safe down there, and to get approval for the constitutional amendment that he had proposed early in January, by which representatives should be apportioned among the states according to the number of "their respective legal voters." At the end of the month he determined to force this resolution, which the committee had finally adopted with changes and additions, through the House. Hitherto he had publicly kept up the fiction that Johnson and the Radicals were in substantial agreement; now he openly declared war upon the president. After moving the previous question he had an hour in which to close the debate. A few minutes of this time he parceled out to some of his Radical friends, and the rest of the time

[6] *New York Herald*, January 11, 14, 19, 21, 22, 1866; Binckley, "The Leader of the House," in *Galaxy*, 1:499; *Colonel Alexander K. McClure's Recollections of Half a Century* (Salem, Massachusetts, [1902]), 422.

he had to himself; no one was permitted to reply. The speech
was unusually sarcastic and bitter, even for him. Johnson, he said,
was guilty of usurpations greater than those that had cost Charles I
his head. As the speaker's voice grew hoarse, the members left
their desks and crowded around him, while the audience in the
galleries bent forward to catch every word. Every time he mentioned Johnson, "that man at the other end of the avenue," and
Henry J. Raymond, House leader of the Conservatives, "his little
friend from New York," the crowd laughed anew. When he had
finished, his resolution passed the House by a vote of 120 to 46.[7]

But in the Senate it was to make little headway. Sumner, of all
people, spent four solid hours condemning it before his peers.
Unlike Stevens, Sumner was an ideologue and a doctrinaire to
whom outright Negro suffrage was the *sine qua non* of any plan
for reconstructing the South. He seemed not to care that a constitutional amendment giving the vote to blacks would offend many
Northern Republicans, most of whose own states had not yet seen
fit to allow Negroes to appear at the polls. But Old Thad cared.
His state was one which since 1838 had retained the qualifying
word "white" in its election laws.

He soon had his chance to strike back at the Sumner clique.
Early in February the Senate bill for enlarging the work of the
Freedmen's Bureau came before the House. The purpose of the
Bureau, organized a year before, was ostensibly to care for the
Negroes whose way of life the abolition of slavery had uprooted,
but the Bureau also served other ends. Its officials were lining up
the prospective colored voters and keeping Stevens informed of
the most suitable Southern white men to give testimony before his
reconstruction committee. He had asked a further favor of one of
its officials—to give free transportation to some of his black servants who had gone to Georgia. But O. O. Howard, the honest

[7] Kendrick, *Journal of the Joint Committee*, 43–60; *Congressional Globe*,
39 Congress, 1 session (1865–66), 535–538 and appendix, 65; *New York Times*,
January 25, February 1, 1866; *New York Herald*, January 26, February 1, 2,
1866. From Samuel Shock, his friend, constituent, banker, and client, Old Thad
received congratulations on his speech of January 31: "Your friends are
delighted with the dressing you gave the drunken tailor and his lick spittle
2 cent Raymond." Shock to Stevens, February 2, 1866, in the Stevens Papers.

and capable head of the Bureau, had attended personally to the matter and had replied that he could transport the servants only if they could be "found as *loyal Refugees.*" Now, in the House, Old Thad was determined either to defeat the Senate's Freedmen's Bureau bill, or to change it to fit his private views. Remembering that the emperor of Russia, when he had liberated the serfs, had compelled their masters to sell them land at a nominal price, he brought forth an amendment which would give each adult male freedman a homestead of forty acres. It received only thirty-seven votes. "That wrathful voice had lost its mastery," said the *New York Herald,* "that severe satire its power, and that extended forefinger its omnipotence."[8]

Back Stevens went to the joint committee, whose members were discussing a bill for the admission of Tennessee, the home state of the president but, so far as the Radicals were concerned, not one of the United States. "The unmistakable design of Thad Stevens and his associates was to take the government into their own hands," Johnson told Welles, and Welles told his diary, "and to get rid of him by declaring Tennessee out of the Union. A sort of French Directory was to be established by these spirits in Congress, the Constitution was to be remodelled by them, etc." As a matter of fact, a majority of the committeemen were quite willing to end the embarrassment of having a stateless president —until, on February 19, they heard of Johnson's veto of the Freedmen's Bureau bill. Next morning, shortly after ten o'clock, Old Thad told the committee he had changed his mind about Tennessee. In the afternoon he put through the House a pointed resolution to the effect that no state should be entitled to representation

[8] *New York Herald,* February 8, 1866; *Congressional Globe,* 39 Congress, 1 session (1865–66), 655, 658; O. O. Howard to Stevens, December 18, 1865, and I. W. Sharp ["Cap't and Ass't Sup't—Freedmen—Dinwiddie Co., Va."] to Stevens, February 9, 1866, in the Stevens Papers. A New York correspondent warned Old Thad that, while Sumner's plan for Negro suffrage would lead *"possibly to the horrors of a civil war,"* his own program of confiscation would be equally dangerous. "By all that you hold dear in the world I beseech you sacrifice confiscation to the good of the nation. . . . The southern landlords have lost the value of their slaves—a considerable sum—they have lost the investments they made in the war. . . ." John Binney to Stevens, February 6, 1866, in the Stevens Papers.

until Congress should specifically declare it to be so entitled. In the evening Welles expressed to his diary his disgust at this "exhibition of the enlightened legislation of the House."[9]

The second day following was Washington's Birthday. From a mass meeting at Grover's Theater a crowd of Johnson's adherents paraded to the White House, where they were greeted by the president from the north portico. He could not forego an extemporaneous harangue against the "irresponsible central directory" that had usurped the powers of government. "I fought traitors and treason in the South," he declared, as he warmed up to his subject. "Now, when I turn around and at the other end of the line find men—I care not by what name you call them—who still stand opposed to the restoration of the Union of these States, I am free to say to you that I am still in the field." Voices in the audience called for "three of these names at the other end." "You ask me who they are? I say, Thaddeus Stevens, of Pennsylvania, is one; I say Mr. Sumner, of the Senate, is another; and Wendell Phillips is another." Voices: "Give it to Forney!" Johnson: "I do not waste my ammunition on dead ducks." Next afternoon at three o'clock Old Thad thump-lumped into the Senate chamber, made directly for Sumner, took a seat beside him, and began an animated conversation with him about the president's remarks.[10]

The Radical leaders of the House and Senate, lately estranged, were thus reunited, but there was no longer the slightest possibility of a reconciliation between the Radicals and the president. The time had come to drop all pretence and to form a congressional party frankly opposed to the Johnson group. At a caucus on the evening after the day of Stevens' and Sumner's tête-à-tête the House Radicals took steps to raise a campaign fund for the fall elections. "All will soon be forced," observed the Herald, "to

[9] Diary of Gideon Welles, Secretary of the Navy under Lincoln and Johnson (3 vols., Boston and New York, 1911), 2:432, 436; Kendrick, Journal of the Joint Committee, 63–72; New York Herald, February 22, 1866.

[10] New York Times, February 23, 24, 1866. "His enemies charge him with letting down his dignity by that speech," said Johnson's attorney general in defense of the president. "What a burlesque it is for such men as Wade and Stevens to whine about dignity." Howard K. Beale, ed., The Diary of Edward Bates, 1859–1866 (Annual Report of the American Historical Association, 1930, Washington, 1933), 538.

choose between the alternatives—accept President Johnson or Thaddeus Stevens as their leader. There will soon be no medium ground upon which they can stand." This was precisely the strategy of Old Thad: to narrow the middle ground.

Some of his friends advised caution, fearing that he might drive Johnson into the arms of the opposition and so reinforce the strength of the Democrats. But others counseled him to be bold. "For God's sake see to it that we do not go before the people next October with a lie on our lips," was the advice coming to him from a Philadelphian. "The people are all right and will turn from any sugar coated pill in disgust. Let them have the dose in the raw." With this Old Thad agreed as he heard from his district politicians (who were assuring him that they could get a *"Stevens man,"* one independent of both Cameron and Curtin, as the next Republican candidate for governor). To one of his retainers in Lancaster he wrote: "As the convention is near I drop a line—I think it well to entirely omit the name of the President. Then indorse Congress and the rebuke will be better than a resolution of censure. Radical resolutions alone will save us. We shall lose doe-faces at any rate—We must gain correct men."

Stevens might have smiled at the naïveté of Southerners who, apparently unaware of the exigencies of Pennsylvania politics, sent him their protests against his Radical pronouncements and undertakings. "Now, Thad," he was hearing from a Virginian, who oversimplified the issues, "I had no hand in the burning of your foundry.... Which feeling is strongest & uppermost in your Abraham's bosom, *love* of the *negro,* or *hatred* of the *white man* of the South?"[11] The Virginian might better have asked Old Thad which was greater, his love of power or his hatred of the man who stood in his way.

[11] *New York Herald,* February 26, 1866; Stevens to O. J. Dickey, January 18, February 24, 1866; L. Kauffman to Stevens, January 30, 1866; C. H. T. Collis to Stevens, February 21, 1866; Thompson Powell to Stevens, February 22, 1866; D. H. Patterson to Stevens, February 24, 1866, in the Stevens Papers. After a visit to Harrisburg Thomas H. Burrowes wrote to Old Thad: "Most of the Union members of the Legislature speak out on the right side; still more of them than I like to see, talk of the folly of driving Johnson into the arms of the enemy & of the possibility of getting him back." Burrowes to Stevens, February 28, 1866, in the Stevens Papers.

Altogether, despite his rapprochement with Sumner, Old Thad was finding it hard during March to hold his congressional party in one piece. Loath to face the issue he was forcing upon them, congressmen were discovering all kinds of excuses for leaves of absence. And Baldwin, of the joint committee, told Welles that Stevens was losing his influence with its members. "I have no doubt that Baldwin and others so believe when away from Stevens and perhaps when with him," Welles thought, "but without intending it or even being fully aware of the extent to which it is carried, they are subjected, controlled, and directed by him." Two others of the committee, Senators Fessenden and Grimes, though "intense on the negro," abhorred both Sumner and Old Thad. Grimes gave Welles to believe that Sumner was "cold-blooded, selfish, and dangerous" and that Stevens was "a debauchee in morals and politics."

An editorial in the *Herald* compared the one to Don Quixote, the other to Sancho Panza. Sumner was the mad knight, the Negro race his Dulcinea; Stevens was the shrewd and practical squire, trudging along for the fun and frolic, the loaves and the fishes. Indeed, their views and their personalities were so different that it was difficult for them to work together. "I know Mr. Sumner believes in no 'policy' short of absolute justice to all," Old Thad read in a letter from one of his correspondents, "and I am as firm as he but I believe in taking and holding on to each and every straw that will build up the power of the North or give us only what is due." Sumner, the writer argued, should accept Stevens' "representation amendment" and give up his insistence upon his own "complete enfranchisement amendment." Old Thad forwarded the letter to Sumner with his endorsement: "As this is a sensible and good man and his reasoning inanswerable I send it to plead its own cause, hoping that if we are to be slain it will not be by our friends."

Publicly he maintained the appearance of friendship with the senator. One evening in March the two dined together with General Meade. Both insisted in the course of the dinner conversation that a Northerner could not go South in safety; Meade replied that their Southern correspondents were prejudiced. When Forney's *Washington Chronicle* published a letter from Cassius M. Clay, Kentuckian and minister to Russia, which denounced Stevens and Sumner, Old Thad wrote to Forney: "I do not often notice denunciations of Stevens. But I desire to say in this case the course of Mr. Clay is perfectly natural. In the winter of 1860–61 before Mr. Lincoln's inauguration Mr. Clay called on me and spent considerable time trying to convince me that it was best to allow the South to secede without resistance . . . . As Sumner and Stevens never contemplate disunion, it is not strange that Genl. Clay should denounce their course."[12]

Besides the difficulty with Sumner there were other stresses and strains within the congressional party that Old Thad had to overcome. The tariff issue was one divisive force. Westerners were holding public meetings to demand a general reduction of duties, now that their wartime justification was past, and the Western members of Congress, both Republican and Democratic, were forced to pay heed to this clamor. At this juncture there was on the tongues of wiseacres in Washington a "curious explanation" of the "negro agitation" on the part of Pennsylvania and New England Radicals. These men, it was said, discussed the freedmen, confiscation, Negro suffrage, constitutional amendments, and so forth in a kind of filibustering spirit: to stave off any action to revise the tariff.[13] Another grievance of the Westerners was the old one of internal improvements. Outraged by the failure of Congress to take advantage of the use of the Canadian canals offered in a new reciprocity treaty, an editor of the *Chicago Tribune* wrote to Stevens' friend Justin S. Morrill, now chairman of ways and means:

Throwing at us the husk of a Protection Tariff on breadstuffs will not do. What we want and are determined to have is access to the markets

[12] *New York Herald*, March 14, 1866; Chas. W. Wardwell to Stevens, March 3, 1866, and Stevens to Sumner, [March, 1866], in the Charles Sumner MSS., Harvard College Library; Stevens to J. W. Forney, [March, 1866], in the Stevens Papers; *Diary of Gideon Welles*, 2:441, 447–448; *Diary of Edward Bates*, 554. Old Thad had no use for Sumner's theory of state suicide. "There never was an hour," he was later to say (July 6, 1866), "when the eleven States were not in full and active life—no suicide; no suspended animation." *Congressional Globe*, 39 Congress, 1 session (1865–66), 3626–3637.

[13] *New York Herald*, February 2, 1866.

of the world. It is evident that the Committee had no conception of the feeling which exists here on this subject. I tell you now in sober earnest what will be the result of the smothering policy. The South cannot be kept out of Congress forever. When the south does come back the south & west will join hands & rule this country. Despairing of any hope of justice from the East we shall form alliances to secure justice for ourselves.[14]

Here was a challenge to Old Thad!

Still another issue dividing Republicans was the perennial money question, and this one cut across the lines between Easterners and Westerners. The bankers and bondholders of New York and elsewhere and the creditor classes generally were demanding that the wartime greenbacks be retired and the country return to "specie payments." Debt-burdened farmers of the West joined with manufacturers of the East, who had both debts to pay and inventories of unsold goods on hand, to oppose the fall in prices which they were well aware a "contraction of the currency" would cause. Whatever the attitude of Johnson himself, his secretary of the treasury Hugh McCulloch (like his secretary of the navy Welles) was a "hard money" man. "What the Secretary of the Treasury and Mr. Morrill may mean by introducing the bill the latter has just brought into your House I cannot imagine," Old Thad had read in January in a letter from his old banker and friend William D. Lewis, of Philadelphia. "Surely neither of them can be so ignorant as to suppose that . . . sweating as we are under a load of taxation . . . a return to specie payments can be brought about by a few legislative 'Whereases' and 'Be it enacteds.' "

At the invitation of Morrill, Old Thad had dined with him and McCulloch but could not prevent at least the beginning of a movement toward the resumption of specie payments. "Do you see how perniciously these Treasury threats of contracting the Currency are operating on the national industry?" Lewis had then written to remind Old Thad. About the middle of March Morrill brought the McCulloch bill into the House. Stevens succeeded in attaching amendments that would prevent the secretary from

[14] Horace White ["Tribune Office, Chicago"] to Morrill, February 15, 1866, manuscript in the library of Cornell University.

withdrawing more than ten million dollars of United States notes in the next six months or more than four million a month thereafter. "Contraction at this rate," complained the sound-money interests, "may fairly be considered no contraction at all."[15]

In the spring of 1861, when Cassius M. Clay had been futilely urging nonresistance upon Old Thad, the way to hold together Republicans with divergent economic interests had been to take a bold stand against the secessionists of the South. In the spring of 1866 the stratagem was war upon the president.

After Johnson had given his Washington's Birthday speech there were, to the surprise of many observers, signs that the "olive branch" was being passed back and forth between the capitol and the White House. Indeed, it was even said that Johnson was making appointments in Lancaster in accordance with the wishes of Old Thad. The latter, meanwhile, had hit upon an ingenious plan for the admission of Tennessee without any sacrifice of his principles, "facetiously so-called." In the joint committee he presented a resolution the preamble of which denied that Tennessee was already a state and affirmed the exclusive powers of Congress in matters of reconstruction, and the body of which restored Tennessee to her place among the states. This was a measure that Johnson could not sign without confessing that he was in the wrong!

On March 10 Old Thad took the floor to speak to Congress on the Tennessee question and to disabuse those who had the notion that he and Johnson were about to make their peace. "I must apologize to the House for the tameness of the remarks I am about to make," he began in his mumbling, ironical way. Then he launched upon another tirade against the president. He read from a year-old issue of a Democratic newspaper describing Johnson's drunkenness at the inauguration with Lincoln, and insin-

[15] W. D. Lewis to Stevens, January 10, February 8, 1866, and Carey to Stevens, February 22, 1866, in the Stevens Papers; Stevens to Morrill, January 29, 1866, and McCulloch to Morrill, January 31, 1866, in the Justin S. Morrill Papers, Library of Congress; *New York Times*, March 16, 22, 24, 1866. "Manufacturers understand that if the currency remains as redundant as it is they will be able to sell their goods on hand at a profit...they do not see that to resist contraction now is only to postpone the evil day, and to incur the risk of a crisis hereafter." *Harper's Weekly*, 10:210 (April 7, 1866).

uated that on Washington's Birthday he again had been drunk. This was a charge which Old Thad, puritanical at least in respect to smoking and drinking, could safely make. "This wretched old man," noted Welles, however, "displayed ... those bad traits of dissimulation, insincerity, falsehood, scandal-loving, and defamation that have characterized his long life."[16]

Johnson replied at the end of March with the second of his vetoes, killing the bill that Congress had passed to give "civil rights" to the Negroes of the South. At once Stevens joined in a project for purging the Senate of a few of its Conservatives, so that the two houses together might have the two-thirds majority necessary for overriding the presidential negative. On the afternoon of April 5, when senators and representatives went to their places to consider the repassing of the civil rights bill, they found that some thoughtful person had been there before them and had left copies of the latest number of *Harper's Weekly* on several of the desks. They opened the magazine to chortle over the featured article, a sketch of Old Thad. "Of a pleasant humor and personal kindliness," was the theme, "he is no more fitted for the task of reconstruction than a jovial blacksmith to repair a watch." For the subject himself, however, the article was scarcely a laughing matter, for the sound-money author appealed to Republicans to repudiate a leader whose monetary policies would cost them votes in the fall elections. The opposition, it was argued, could attribute the high cost of living to the failure to contract the currency and could claim that if the Southern members had been present in their places in Congress, the contraction bill would have passed without Stevens' amendments. Fortunately for Old Thad, the Republican senators, financially orthodox and financially heterodox, voted together to pass the civil rights bill over Johnson's veto on the evening of the following day.[17]

That same evening General and Mrs. Ulysses S. Grant were giving a reception at their Washington home. Grant, the conquer-

[16] Kendrick, *Journal of the Joint Committee,* 72–81; *New York Herald,* March 4, 5, 11, 12, 13, 1866; *Congressional Globe,* 39 Congress, 1 session (1865–66), 1307–1310; *Diary of Gideon Welles,* 2:451–452.

[17] *New York Times,* 1866: March 28, 29; April 3, 4, 5, 6, 7; May 29; *Harper's Weekly,* 10:210 (April 7, 1866).

ing hero, was fast becoming the most popular man in the United States. His popularity and his position at the head of the army would make him an invaluable ally for either Johnson or the Radicals, especially if they should reach an impasse where guns again took the place of words. And so Stevens and a group of his friends called at the Grants with high hopes of winning the general to the Radical side. When he stepped inside the drawing-room door with his cane and his unmatched boots, Old Thad paused for only a moment, but long enough to give away his surprise. There, among the guests, was Andrew Johnson himself! Who would have thought that the president would have had nerve enough to appear in public so soon after the Senate's rebuke? And there, chatting with some of his ladies, stood Montgomery Blair! And, as if these two were not enough, there was also that shriveled mite of a man, vice president of the late Confederacy, Alexander H. Stephens! Quickly Old Thad recovered his poker face, and the evening passed off quite smoothly. As Hayes afterward described the occasion to his wife: "The President stood between General and Mrs. Grant. Vice-President (Rebel) Stephens stood near. Montgomery Blair, etc., etc. Old Thad shook hands cordially with Andy. Andy presented him to Mrs. Grant. It was the happiest gathering I have seen. Andy looked and behaved very well indeed."[18]

Hayes saw in the Grant reception an augury of better times, but Ben Butler, after the House had repassed the civil rights bill on April 9, was convinced that a collision was about to take place between Congress and the president which, since Johnson was no coward, would probably result in renewed civil war. "Whether Grant will go with him is a question as he is a moral coward and may stand by what will seem to be the forms of Government and as a soldier may think himself bound to obey orders." A constituent was warning Old Thad to look out for assassins in the pay of the president.

In such an atmosphere the joint committee continued its hitherto fruitless labors during April and heard the testimony

[18] E. Ramsay Richardson, *Little Aleck: A Life of Alexander H. Stephens* (Indianapolis, 1932), 286–287; Hayes to Mrs. Hayes, April 8, 1866, in *Hayes Diary and Letters*, 3:22.

of Alexander H. Stephens and Robert E. Lee. Jefferson Davis and Clement C. Clay were still imprisoned at Fortress Monroe. Clay's friend who had visited Old Thad in Lancaster had eventually got from him a letter to the president requesting Clay's release. Again, in January, he had called on Old Thad in Washington, but, finding his host "brooding over the violent speech" he was then composing, had hesitated to ask Stevens to pay a visit to Clay's wife. On April 18 Old Thad told a *New York Times* reporter that the government ought to confiscate his property and let Clay go. At about the same time President Johnson, satisfied that the prisoner was innocent of any part in Lincoln's assassination, released him on parole. Misunderstanding Stevens' motives in this business, the *Herald* suggested that, when their leader had shown such magnanimity, the "small fry" among his followers ought to realize that the day of Radicalism was past.

Magnanimous Old Thad could be, and was, in his private affairs. "Your $10 came to hand," a penniless preacher was writing to him from York. "Thanks. God bless you. When will you give yourself heart and soul? The Lord hastens the day." And in reply to a protest from James Buchanan, long dead to the political world, he promptly and politely sent his apologies for having inadvertently accused the former president of extravagance in furnishing the White House. Meanwhile, ever conscious of the approaching elections, generous Old Thad tried to induce the government to send three copies of Forney's *Chronicle* daily to every one of the American consular and diplomatic agents abroad. Though he failed in his effort to reward Forney with the tidy sum this would have brought him, the editor showed his gratitude by beginning to puff Stevens as the "Great Commoner" of the country.[19]

On April 27 the Great Commoner brought up in the House

[19] Stevens to [R. J.] Haldeman, January 8, 1866, in the Andrew Johnson Papers, Library of Congress; Butler to J. W. Shaffer, April 10, 1866, in the Benjamin F. Butler Papers, Library of Congress; G. M. Slaysman to Stevens, April 19, 1866, and Stevens to Buchanan, April 24, 1866, in the Stevens Papers; R. J. Haldeman to Mrs. C. C. Clay, February 3, 1866, in Ada Sterling, ed., *A Belle of the 'Fifties: Memoirs of Mrs. Clay of Alabama* (New York, 1904), 357; *Diary of Gideon Welles*, 2:486–487; *New York Times,* April 17, 18, 19, 20, 1866.

his bill for granting public lands to the Northern Pacific company. An Indiana representative protested against giving to a private corporation lands aggregating more than the entire area of Indiana. An Illinois member added his demurrer: "Men engaged in the iron interest are anxious, of course, to make railroad iron." "This road is to be built of American iron, cost what it may." Undismayed, Old Thad passed out booklets describing the company and its prospects in glittering terms. Then, with his tongue in his cheek, he praised those with a broad mind and a large view that could take in the whole of the nation. "I know," he said, "that some western people think there can be no western railroad unless it starts from Chicago. That is a narrow view. I do not expect this road to start from Lancaster or to pass through Lancaster." Speaking from the "national" point of view, he went on to tell his dubious hearers how the company planned to bring laborers from the north of Europe, pay them in land, and colonize them along the right of way—"men who will always be on the side of freedom, who will always be ready to aid us, in any rebellious outbreaks." "God grant that we may soon fill up that country with such a population that, with the people of the great North, may be a counterpoise to the rebellious South, whose representatives when they come here will never permit us to do anything which may interfere with their projects." In a few days he got a refutation in a letter from Henry C. Carey, the economist and philosopher of protectionism. What the country needed to tie itself together, Carey wrote, was not another Pacific road but "facility of communication between the North West and South East—the South West and North East. Let us have that and Northern men will go South and govern the Southern States."[20]

Whatever the best means might be, railroad and iron men were determined that the North must somehow consolidate its victory over the South. In the joint committee, however, Republicans had been unable to agree upon a constitutional amendment that would do the trick. Finally a compromise plan had come to them from the outside. Robert Dale Owen, son of the famous English

[20] *Congressional Globe*, 39 Congress, 1 session (1865–66), 2239–2246; Carey to Stevens, April 30, 1866, in the Stevens Papers.

socialist, had suggested to Stevens that until July 4, 1876, the leaders of the former Confederacy be ineligible for Congress; that meanwhile the representation of the Southern states be based on white population only; and that after that date the Negroes be given the right to vote. This, Owen explained, would give the Southerners forty-two members in the House, whereas representation on the basis of total population, white and colored, would give them sixty-six. "Surely," he said to Old Thad, "you can manage that number." "Perhaps," Stevens replied. "But you forget the Senate. The eleven insurrectionary states would be entitled to their twenty-two senators, suffrage or no suffrage." Sumner, unwilling to compromise on his principle of immediate Negro suffrage, had already refused to hear of Owen's plan. Without enthusiasm, Stevens finally consented to offer it to his committee.

On Saturday, April 28, the committee issued its report. Three sections had been added to the amendment, but the one promising Negro suffrage in the future had been deleted. On Sunday morning Owen called at Stevens' house to demand an explanation. "Don't imagine that I sanction the shilly-shally, bungling thing that I shall have to report to the House tomorrow," said Old Thad (according to Owen, who doubtless edited out the profanity). Then he related how the committee had at first adopted Owen's original scheme, how Fessenden had been absent and in bed with varioloid, how out of courtesy he had consented to await Fessenden's recovery, how in the meantime the plan had got bruited about and cowardly Republican congressmen had resolved that they could approve no amendment that had a "nigger in the woodpile." "Damn the varioloid!" exclaimed Old Thad as he finished his story. "It changed the whole policy of the country!"[21]

On Monday, the day Fessenden returned to the Senate after his touch of the smallpox, Stevens presented the proposed Fourteenth Amendment in the House. "I see the Rep't of the Recons.

<hr/>

[21] Robert Dale Owen, "Political Results from the Varioloid," in the *Atlantic Monthly*, 35 (1875): 661–666. The general accuracy of Owen's account is attested by contemporary sources: *New York Times*, April 23, 24, 25, 26, 1866; *New York Herald*, April 25, 29, May 1, 1866; Kendrick, *Journal of the Joint Committee*, 81–120.

Com^{ee}," he heard a little later from Wendell Phillips, the abolitionist orator. "It is a fatal & total surrender." From a Virginian, too, he received criticism, but of a very different kind. "While we of Genl. Lee's followers were passing the *Iron Works* known as *yours* ... and seeing them in flames, I thought it wrong to destroy so much valuable property," read the missive of the man who had signed himself "Your Southern Friend." "But since the War and having seen *so* many of your *vile measures* ... I only wish you had been in your works and had been subjected to a little fire yourself." The members of the House, whose opinions ranged between these two extremes, were not taking readily to the proposal of Old Thad's. A week after he introduced it he took the floor to speak. Referring sarcastically to Sumner, he told how his original resolution in January had been "slaughtered by a puerile and pedantic criticism" and "the united forces of self-righteous Republicans and unrighteous Copperheads." The more conservative of the Republicans now threatened to eliminate the third section, which postponed the eligibility of Confederate leaders for Congress until 1876. Once more, as in the case of the bill for Negro Suffrage in the District of Columbia, he managed a combination of Radicals and Democrats to prevent a change. On May 10 he made his closing appeal. "Give us the third section or give us nothing," he demanded. "Do not balk us with the pretense of an amendment which throws the Union into the hands of the enemy before it becomes consolidated." "Gentlemen tell us it is too strong .... It is too lenient for my hard heart. Not only to 1870, but to 18070, every rebel who shed the blood of loyal men should be prevented from exercising any power in this Government." The House adopted the resolution on the same day, and it went to the Senate.[22]

In the hour of his triumph tidings of trouble were borne to Old Thad from the vicinity of Caledonia. He had borrowed heavily in order to rebuild the ironworks. Now his manager and

[22] Wendell Phillips to Stevens, April 30, 1866, and "Your Southern Friend" to Stevens, May 1, 1866, in the Stevens Papers; J. W. Grimes to Mrs. Grimes, May 8, 1866, in William Salter, *The Life of James W. Grimes* (New York, 1876), 292; *Congressional Globe*, 39 Congress, 1 session (1865–66), 2459–2460, 2544; *New York Times*, May 11, 12, 14, 1866.

his contractor for the rebuilding were frantically in search of funds with which to pay off the debt. "I am sorry indeed," the contractor wrote, "to say our credit is strained." In that part of Pennsylvania there was simply not money enough to go around. The theory of Chase, when as secretary of the treasury he had founded the national banking system in 1863, had been that in due time the new national banknotes would take the place of both the state banknotes and the greenbacks. In 1866, however, it appeared that the authorities of the system were discriminating against certain parts of the country, particularly the South and West but also some of the rural regions of the East. On July 1, 1866, a tax of 10 per cent was to mature on the note issue of all state banks; their currency was being taxed out of existence. If the business men in and about Hagerstown, Shippensburg, and Chambersburg were to be relieved of their distress, something must be done at once. Either the state banks must have an extension of time to redeem their outstanding issues, or they must be entirely exempted from the prohibitory tax, or they must be allowed to join the national system and issue national banknotes. So the contractor wrote to Old Thad. He responded with a "virulent attack" upon Secretary of the Treasury McCulloch in the House. Later, unable to get help for himself and his business friends from the banking authorities, he demanded more and more greenbacks. "In my judgment," he said, "this whole national banking system was a mistake. I thought so at the time it was adopted, and I think so still. I think every dollar of paper circulation ought to be issued by the Government of the United States."[23]

Not so remote as it might seem from the iron and money

[23] *New York Herald*, May 27, 1866; *New York Times*, July 9, 1866; *Congressional Globe*, 39 Congress, 1 session (1865–66), 4135. R. A. Ahl, a man in the contracting and banking business at Newville, Pennsylvania, appealed to Stevens in a letter which well reveals the pressure for easy money that was being put upon him:

"I am sorry indeed to say our credit is strained. We have failed to obtain discount in all our Banks, except the Farmers and Mechanics Bank of Shippensburg has thus far kept us afloat, but owing to the issue of that bank now being sent home ties their hands completely: This bank being

problems was the case of Jefferson Davis, held at Fortress Monroe under indictment for his alleged crimes. About the middle of May his attorney visited Washington and called on Old Thad. Stevens said he had seen the evidence on which the administration was relying to connect Davis and Clay with Lincoln's assassination, and he pronounced it insufficient, their guilt incredible. However, willing though he was to serve as counsel for Davis, he did not desire his release. One day he went to the White House, where Mrs. Davis happened to be calling in her husband's behalf, and in her presence expostulated with the president. She was afterward to recall "a lop-sided man who stood on one leg by preference" and "threatened the President in such a manner as would have been thought inadmissable to one of the servants." When he had gone, Johnson turned to her and said he was glad she had had a chance to see his difficulties in regard to setting her husband free. What Stevens really desired was to have Davis brought to trial on a charge of treason, to defend him and win

conducted under State Charter. We are getting no accommodation from the old Hagerstown Bank. I do hope & pray that you will see the Committee on Banks and have them to report a bill favorable to the extention of the time of redeeming their issue at least one year, and within that time give those few banks who are conducted under the State Charter the privilege to come in under the National System; and in the event of them doing so have a clause inserted in the bill to exhonerate them from the payment of the ten per cent tax maturing July 1st 1866. If this extention and privilege is granted by Congress we apprehend no fears of being accommodated to the extent of the business demands. We certainly are laboring under disadvantages for want of the National banking System at Shippensburg, Chambersburg & Hagerstown. I hope you will see some way to secure us another bank at Chambersburg....

"I write you knowing that you see the importance of the People being accommodated, as we must have circulation. We held a meeting to day. A. G. Miller the cashier of the Shippensburg Bank was here, & begged us to write you on the subject. He has to accommodate many business men in Chambersburg....

"We hope you will see the importance of seeing the committee on Banks at once. We have not circulation at this time to supply the wants of business men. We will do as you directed in your letter to Mr. Sweeney unless we can by some means get the funds at home. We have given him $700 when here which will enable him to meet the pressing demands for a few days. I expect to be in Washington in a few days, but in the meantime be sure to make the points as suggested." Ahl to Stevens, May 5, 1866, in the Stevens Papers.

his acquittal, and thereby prove that as president of the Confederacy he had been no mere rioter or rebel but the leader of a
belligerent subsequently defeated in war.[24] Kept indefinitely in
prison or simply turned loose (as he was eventually to be), Jefferson Davis would serve as a sort of scapegoat for all the sins of the
South. There must be no scapegoat, however, if Old Thad was
to be unrestrained in dealing with the former Confederate states
as conquered provinces and making the victory of Northern
capitalists complete.

Already the capitalists were quarreling, as they had on the
money issue, over the spoils of Republican success, and even the
railroad builders could not agree among themselves. It was up
to Stevens, as their broker, to satisfy as many as possible and still
keep peace among them. In June he introduced a bill to make a
grant of land along a new line for the Eastern Division of the
Union Pacific. He did not want the measure sent to the special
committee on the Pacific railroad, he said, for fear they would
kill it. On behalf of both the "Kansas Pacific" and the Northern
Pacific he was also trying to extend the time limit within which
they had to finish construction in order to qualify for their land
grants. The entrepreneurs of the Northern Pacific and those of the
St. Croix and Lake Superior, meanwhile, were unable to agree
upon a bill for aiding both. "I wish you were here and had time
to investigate that North Western view of it," an official of the
latter road wrote to Stevens from New York. "All my best and
sound friends such as S. J. Tilden Wm B. Ogden &c say I am
sound on it but the Northern Pacific people can't see it & I am
afraid that they won't see anything. Now take care of Mr. P."
Mr. P—Josiah Perham, of the Northern Pacific—insisted upon his
own scheme. "I do really believe," he wrote to Old Thad, "that
with an interview with you of half an hour, to have you suggest
such alterations and additions as you think best, that the Bill
can be put through at this session." The St. Croix and Lake
Superior man told a couple of railroad lobbyists that he would

[24] Robert McElroy, *Jefferson Davis: The Unreal and the Real* (2 vols., New
York, 1937), 2:560–561, 563. (McElroy quotes from the memoirs of Mrs. Davis.)

"become a director and help them out if they desired—provided that they would take care of Mr. P." But the man expressed to Old Thad the fear that they were "very slow & timid" and hardly had "stamina enough for that concern." In the House Stevens did his best to carry out the wishes of the "timid" railroad lobby.[25]

In mid-June the proposed Fourteenth Amendment came back from the Senate with alterations that Old Thad could not approve. When he got to his feet to close the debate, having been ill in bed for several days, he spoke feebly and without his usual fire. "I do not pretend to be satisfied with it," he said of the resolution. "And yet I am anxious for its speedy adoption, for I dread delay." In this remark Conservatives and Democrats detected irony, for they believed that his real aim was to postpone the restoration of the Southern states as long as possible, or at least until after the presidential election of 1868. The resolution passed, to be sent out for ratification. Meanwhile, the joint committee had made its wordy report, whose theme was that the rebels were as yet unreconstructed, had taken their defeat in war with no good grace. Old Thad hurried it to the government printing office to have a thousand copies made.[26] With this as a cam-

[25] A. W. Moore to Stevens, June 20, 1866, and Josiah Perham to Stevens, July 19, 1866, in the Stevens Papers; *Congressional Globe*, 39 Congress, 1 session (1865–66), 2376, 3420–3424, 3399.

[26] *New York Times*, June 9, 14, 1866; *Congressional Globe*, 39 Congress, 1 session (1865–66), 3148. In its final form the Fourteenth Amendment dealt with four subjects. The first section defined citizenship as a national rather than a state matter, and made Negroes citizens; the second reduced the representation of the Southern states to a basis of the voting population only; the third excluded Confederate leaders from office indefinitely (but permitted Congress by two-thirds vote to remove the disability); and the fourth upheld the validity of the federal debt and repudiated the Confederate debt. The first section concluded with the significant clause: "Nor shall any state deprive any person of life, liberty, or property, without due process of law," etc. John A. Bingham deliberately put in these cryptic words, which corporation lawyers were later to recite with telling effect, for the protection of corporate "persons" from the police powers of the states. See Charles and Mary Beard, *The Rise of American Civilization* (2 vols., New York, 1927), 2:112–114. The record does not show whether Stevens was aware of this ulterior purpose, but does indicate that he had no motivating part in the inclusion of the clause. See Kendrick, *Journal of the Joint Committee*, 81–100 and *passim*. His distinctive contribution was the second section, the ulterior

paign document and the Fourteenth Amendment as their platform, the Radicals were preparing to go before the people and
secure their vindication as against the president.

purpose of which, however, was much the same as that of the first. Bingham's
words were intended to protect men of business against hostile legislation by
the states: Stevens' were to protect them against such legislation by the
federal government.

XVI. The People's Voice

THE fall elections were uppermost in the minds of politicians, Radical and Conservative alike, in the summer of 1866. As for Thaddeus Stevens, never in all his forty-odd years of canvassing, not even in 1838 or in 1860, had he sought the people's verdict with a more determined heart. Upon the returns would depend, of course, the success of his Radical program of reconstruction, the maintenance of tariffs for his iron-making associates, the confirmation of gifts of land to his railroad-building friends, and the continuance of his own power as leader of the House. But still another prize was at stake. If the people of Pennsylvania should elect a "Stevens man" as governor, and if the people of his own and other states should endorse him by sending Radicals back to Congress, Old Thad might be in a position to claim at last what had escaped him so many times before—a place in the Senate where he might be first among his Republican peers. "The love of power," a commentator was saying, "is the master passion of his soul." It seemed to this observer, however, that in the Senate his influence would be checked by the greater dignity and smaller membership of that body and its limitations upon the use of such parliamentary devices as the previous question, which in the lower chamber he was wont to employ with devastating effect.[1] The writer was forgetting the higher honor, the greater control of patronage, and the other solid advantages of being in the Senate. No matter. It was one of Old Thad's ambitions to be a senator from Pennsylvania before he died!

While busy with legislative affairs in Washington during the spring, Stevens had found time to keep up a correspondence with politicians in various parts of his state. From them was to arise the

[1] J. W. Binckley, "The Leader of the House," in *Galaxy*, 1:494–496 (June, 1866).

semblance of a popular demand for sending him to the Senate when the time should come—that is, in January, 1867. In July of 1866 he received from his good friend Samuel Shock, of Columbia, a letter bearing a number of signatures and requesting him to be a candidate. He was asked to reply with a letter giving his consent but also announcing his candidacy for renomination as a congressman, "so that," as Shock advised, "your enemies may not raise a clamor that you do not desire to go to the House." "If you consent I think it will have the effect to stop the manouvres of some folks who have been busy for some time past promising the vote of Lancaster City to A. G. Curtin S. Cameron & others." Indeed, the political gossips in Lancaster were hinting that the talk of Stevens for senator was "only a dodge" by which he hoped to get control of the six state representatives from Lancaster County. "These wiseacres do not seem to know," said the local *Intelligencer,* "how Old Thad proposes to dispose of these six votes." To set these rumors at rest, he complied with Shock's request and had his letter and Shock's published together.[2]

Thinking of the exigencies of the congressional and senatorial campaigns, he made up his mind to prevent an adjournment of Congress for the summer. Secure in his own district as he was, he had nothing to fear from remaining in the capital and much to gain by it, but other Radicals faced a dilemma. If they went home, Johnson might take advantage of their absence to effect wholesale dismissals of officeholders sympathetic to the Radical cause; if they remained in Washington, the Conservatives could carry the fight without opposition into their respective districts. "Some are in favor of not adjourning at all," Senator Fessenden wrote to his family in July, "but I see nothing to be gained by staying, and the majority of the Senators agree with me. Mr. Stevens is determined to stay as long as possible, and his position in the House enables him to obstruct and delay us. Members are terribly afraid of their constituents and the officeholders are frightened out of their wits." The weather, if nothing else, was

[2] Stevens to Samuel Evans, July 6, 1866, and to Evans and Kauffman, July 13, 1866, manuscripts in the Pennsylvania State Library, Harrisburg; Samuel Shock to Stevens, July 11, 1866, in the Thaddeus Stevens Papers, Library of Congress; *Lancaster Intelligencer,* July 11, 25, 1866.

against Old Thad. As the heat in Washington mounted to over a hundred degrees, members of Congress began to leave one by one for their shady yards at home. "Whence comes this unseemly haste," he demanded in caucus, "to desert our post and abandon our friends to the tender mercies of our enemies?" The members who remained were refractory. They agreed to admit Tennessee to the Union despite Johnson's message repudiating Stevens' "whereases" which asserted that Congress alone could reconstruct a state. They ignored his insistence that they should not even consider adjournment until they had passed a law compelling the Southern states to start all over again and form new constitutions with suffrage for all, white and black. He wagged his "famous index finger" in vain. On July 28 they adjourned.[3]

If Radicals feared the patronage, Stevens and the rest of them in Pennsylvania could at least count upon the greater part of the soldier vote. In June a convention of the "boys in blue," meeting in Pittsburgh, had given a noisy demonstration of their devotion to the Radical cause. One of those present had sent Old Thad an account: "At every mention of your name cheer upon cheers follows and this morning when a Lancaster delegate claimed honor for old Lancaster as the home of Thaddeus Stevens the entire Convention rose to its feet and cheered lustily." "The politicians here are uneasy and feel that the five hundred soldiers of Penna. now in council in their midst have more power than any convention that ever assembled in the State." Politicians everywhere, according to the *New York Times*, recognized that one of the controlling forces in the politics of the country for many years to come would be "the great army of volunteer soldiers," who were "voters almost to a man."[4]

In the July caucuses Stevens had desired to make the issue against the president frankly his misuse of the patronage. Immediately after the adjournment a much more appealing issue

[3] Fessenden to his family, July 8, 1866, in Francis Fessenden, *Life and Public Services of William Pitt Fessenden* (2 vols., Boston, 1907), 2:117; *New York Herald*, July 12, 15, 17, 21, 1866; *New York Times*, July 14, 16, 17, 18, 1866.
[4] S. Brisbin to Stevens, June 15, 1866, in the Stevens Papers; *New York Times*, August 22, 1866.

was offered, as if made to order, in news reports from the South. Headlines in the Northern papers told of a "great riot, anarchy, and blood-shed" in New Orleans. Earlier in the year there had been violence in Memphis, and an investigating committee appointed by the Radicals in Congress had gone there to look into the so-called "negro riot." From Memphis E. B. Washburne, now united in Radicalism with Old Thad, had reported to Stevens that "the negroes had nothing to do with it but to be butchered" and that the existing state governments in the South gave no promise of safety to Negroes and "loyal" white men (that is, Republicans). "Instead of rebels being reconstructed as Union men," Washburne had written, "I find some of the late Union men reconstructed as very good rebels." Now the New Orleans affair seemed to confirm the conclusions which Radicals had drawn from the events in Memphis. In New Orleans a group of white men and Negroes had attempted to hold a Republican rally (at the instigation of Stevens and other Radicals in Congress) and a general mêlée had ensued. Conservative journalists charged that Stevens and his associates had deliberately created a violence-provoking situation in order to gain by the publicity which they could give to the result.[5]

While stories of Southern atrocities filled the Radical papers, certain politicians in Pennsylvania were jockeying for positions in the coming senatorial race. Among the contenders, besides Old Thad, were Cameron and Curtin, Forney, McClure, and Galusha A. Grow, former speaker of the House. "What is the prospect?" Charles A. Dana of the *New York Tribune* asked Cameron in August. "Grow told me the other day that while you were the strongest candidate, Forney would probably succeed in defeating your election though he could not get elected him-

[5] Washburne to Stevens, May 24, 1866, in the Stevens Papers; *New York Times*, July 31, December 15, 1866. The following was a satirical advertisement printed in Conservative papers: "Wanted—Southern riots to help the radicals.... In order to humbug the voters at the coming elections, a number of riots are desired at various prominent points in the South.... If twenty or thirty negroes, martyrs of liberty, can be killed at each of these places, so much the better for the radical cause. For further particulars, terms of compensation, etc., apply to Old Thad Stevens, or any other member of the reconstruction committee." *New York Herald*, August 14, 1866.

self. Others inform me that Stevens has the best look after all, and will carry off the prize against every competitor." From Republicans in Lancaster Old Thad was securing a renomination to the House and a recommendation for the Senate, but he inadvertently damaged his chances a bit in his acceptance speech. Eager to use every possible issue against the president, the Radicals were coquetting with the Irish-American society of Fenians, whose plots against Canada Johnson was conscientiously striving to forestall. In his talk to the Lancaster Republicans, however, Old Thad revived the old Native American prejudices against the Irish. "We have not yet done justice to the oppressed race. We have not gone as far as the Emperor of Russia," he declared. "We are influenced too much by those persons from foreign lands who, while in search of freedom, deny that blessed boon to them who are their equals."[6]

Meanwhile in Philadelphia the friends of Johnson, Republican and Democratic, unionist and ex-Confederate, were holding a grand convention of the president's party. When the South Carolina and Massachusetts delegations entered the convention hall with their arms linked, Radical propagandists had something new to seize upon. They damned the adherents of Johnson as traitors and contemptuously dubbed this the "arm in arm" convention. The congressional party had scheduled a gathering of its own, to meet in Philadelphia in September. Though Governor Curtin personally invited him to attend, Old Thad went back from Lancaster to Bedford Springs, the "fashionable resort" where he had summered occasionally for the past twenty years, and where he was now recuperating from the illness that had put him to bed in June.

To Bedford Springs came reports which troubled the convalescent. One was the item in the *Gettysburg Star* (a newspaper he himself had founded and had owned for many years) to the effect that the Lancaster County convention had endorsed him for the Senate "with the understanding that Curtin came in second." To the editor of the *Star* he wrote pointedly that this

[6] Dana to Cameron, August 9, 1866, in the Simon Cameron Papers, Library of Congress; *Lancaster Intelligencer*, August 22, 1866.

article was an attempt to "deceive" the readers, that he was himself the first and only choice of Lancaster for the senatorship. Then came a letter from Samuel Shock relaying the newspaper story that the Republicans of Rochester, New York, were sending Frederick Douglass, a well-known mulatto abolitionist and former slave, as one of their delegates to the September convention in Philadelphia. "Our friends here are unanimous in the belief that this is unfortunate," Shock had written, "& I write at the suggestion of several to you to suggest that you will use your influence with Mr. Douglas to induce him to remain at home or decline the appointment. If he goes it will certainly injure our cause & we may lose some Congressmen in the doubtful districts." And another thing: "The concluding part of your speech to the county convention is complained of, when you remark about the foreign vote. Some of our people say that not a foreigner in the County will vote for you."[7]

President Johnson, with General Grant in his entourage, went on a "swing around the circle" to electioneer in the West. To Radical heckling claques in Cleveland, St. Louis, Indianapolis, and elsewhere who demanded that traitors be hung, he was replying: "Why not hang Thad Stevens?" In Philadelphia, meanwhile, Radical leaders from various parts of the country were gathering en masse. Just as Old Thad's friends had feared, the presence of Douglass among the Radicals gave the Conservatives some good material for their propaganda. "Black and white convention"; "the Quaker city full of miscegens"; "Fred Douglass the lion of the city"; "first grand national convention of negro

[7] A. G. Curtin to Stevens, August 23, 1866, and Samuel Shock ["Columbia Nat. Bank"] to Stevens, August 27, 1866, in the Stevens Papers. Old Thad was sensitive on the senatorial question. The nature of his protest to the editor of the Gettysburg Star may be inferred from the editor's reply: "There has been no disposition on our part to 'deceive' the readers of the Star by publishing 'articles like the enclosed.' I read the proceedings of the Convention and understood them to mean, that you were the first and only choice of the Lancaster Co. for the U. S. Senate. You say there was no 'preference expressed for Curtin.' I do not say so either and would refer you again to the paragraph. I say—'with the UNDERSTANDING that Curtin came in second.'...Your charge of 'DECEPTION' don't apply....N. B. Unjust charges don't make friends." J. S. McIlheny to Stevens, August 28, 1866, in the Stevens Papers.

worshippers, free lovers, spiritualists, fourierites, women's rights men, negro equality men"; "negro insurrection to be incited"— such were the headlines with which the *New York Herald* reported the assembling of the Radicals. When the delegates marched up the steps of the Union League house to begin their sessions, Frederick Douglass approached leaning on the arm of Theodore Tilton. Douglass, moreover, was among the speakers in the hall. In a dispatch to the *New York Times* Tilton reported that he created "quite a sensation," but admitted that many of those present thought this "blending of colors" to be "inartistic as well as inexpedient" at the time.[8]

Remaining at Bedford Springs, Old Thad was not among those who listened to Douglass, but he gave his reply to the critics when, on September 4, he addressed a mass meeting in Bedford square. He had already telegraphed his speech to the *New York Tribune;* as he read it by lamplight he was addressing the nation at large and not only the crowd in the darkness around him. He reduced the alarm of Conservatives to a *reductio ad absurdum:* "We shall hear repeated, ten thousand times, the cry of 'negro equality!' The radicals would thrust the negro into your parlors, your bedrooms, and the bosom of your wives and daughters. They would even make your reluctant daughters marry black men." He recalled the Pennsylvania constitutional convention of 1837–38, which had disfranchised Negroes, and said that the insertion of the word "white" in the clause on the suffrage had caused him to refuse to sign the amended constitution. He now urged Pennsylvanians to strike out the offending word. "I care not what you may say of negro equality—I care not what you may say of radicalism, these are my principles, and with the help of God I shall die with them." Meanwhile the Pennsylvania Conservatives were not idle but were holding their own mass meetings and elaborate parades. At one of these, in Carlisle, one of the banners in the procession bore the words, "Thad Stevens' Idea of Reconstruction," and behind it a black-faced man and a white woman were strolling arm in arm.[9]

[8] *New York Herald,* September 3, 4, 7, 1866; *New York Times,* September 5, 1866.

[9] *New York Herald,* August 27, October 7, 1866; *New York Times,* Septem-

Publicly Old Thad could not admit it but privately he regarded the presence of Douglass among the Radicals as indiscreet,
to say the least. When put to the pragmatic test, he was more
disturbed by the concrete question of partisan expediency than
by the abstract question of human rights. Two days after his
Bedford speech he wrote to that man of practical business and
politics, William D. Kelley: "A good many people here are disturbed by the practical exhibition of social equality in the arm-in-
arm performance of Douglass and Tilton. It does not become
radicals like us to particularly object. But it was certainly unfortunate at this time. The old prejudice, now revived, will lose
us some votes. Why it was done I cannot see except as a foolish
bravado. The Massachusetts and S. Carolina was disgusting
enough. This I fear will neutralize it."[10]

As the day of the decision approached, Stevens had with him
most of the former soldiers, the powerful Radical press, and all
the clichés of patriotism. On his side was most of the sound and
fury. But Johnson still had his cogent, though silent, argument:
instead of making wholesale changes of officeholders during the
summer he had "kept his powder dry" and now dangled the
patronage before those who might be tempted to yield to Radical
threats. His tactics infuriated the Radicals. In September a friend
informed Old Thad: "I learned that it is not intended to make
the appointments for Pennsylvania until after the October
election so that the votes of the bought may be secured first. I
also learned that the same office is offered to half a dozen or more
hungry expectants. I had supposed that one office should buy
only one traitor, but by this plan, one office may buy several."
This informant hoped that, when the appointments of the "renegades" later came before the Senate for confirmation, Stevens
would be able somehow to bring about their rejection. Soon
Pennsylvania Radicals began to fear, however, that the president
would not send his nominations to the Senate at all. Nor would
impeachment bring him to terms, for if congressmen attempted it,
"he would have them arrested." In answer to the pleas of his

ber 9, 11, 1866; *New York Tribune,* September 10, 1866; *Lancaster Intelligencer,* October 3, 1866.
[10] Stevens to Kelley, September 6, 1866, in the Stevens Papers.

disappointed friends Stevens set about drafting a bill to punish the president and restrict his powers of patronage. "If the pending elections should go right so that Congress will no longer be cowards," he wrote to Senator Fessenden in Maine, "will they not repair and revenge the present shameful and corrupt abuse of the patronage? How will something in this shape do?" He enclosed a copy of his draft: the germ of the subsequent, and fateful, tenure of office act.[11]

Before election day Old Thad returned to Lancaster long enough to say a few words to his constituents:

I come not to make a speech, but for the want of one. When I left Washington I was somewhat worn by labors and disease, and I was directed by my physician neither to think, to speak, nor to read until the next session of Congress, or I should not regain my strength. I have followed the first injunction most religiously, for I believe I have not let an idea pass through my mind to trouble me since Congress adjourned. The second one—not to speak—I was seduced from keeping; and I made a speech at Bedford,—the only one I have made. The one—not to read—I have followed almost literally. It is true, I have amused myself with a little light, frivolous reading. For instance, there was a serial account from day to day of a very remarkable circus that traveled through the country, from Washington to Chicago and St. Louis, and from Louisville back to Washington. I read that with some interest . . . I expected great wit from the celebrated character of its clowns. . . . I shall not describe to you how sometimes they cut outside the circle, and entered into street broils with common blackguards; how they fought at Cleveland and Indianapolis. But, coming round, they told you, or one of them did, that he had been everything but one. He had been a tailor—I think he did not say drunken tailor. He had been a con-

[11] Samuel Shock to Stevens, September 3, 1866, in the Stevens Papers. The hasty draft which Old Thad sent to Fessenden, and the substance of which he was later to present in Congress, read: "Sec. 1. No person who has been nominated by the President for office and to which nomination the Senate refused its advice and consent shall hold any office under the United States untill the expiration of four years from his such rejection Provided that the Senate may at any time remove said disability by a vote of two thirds of the members present. Sec. 2. Whenever any person is nominated by the President for any office which requires the advice and consent of the Senate and the same office had been filled by another person previously to such appointment; the person thus appointed shall not enter upon the duties of his office until confirmed by the Senate; Whenever such nomination shall not be confirmed by the Senate his predecessor shall retain the office. This section shall take effect from and after the 4th of March 1866—" Stevens to Fessenden, October 1, 1866, manuscript in the library of Dartmouth College.

stable. He had been city alderman. He had been in the legislature. God help that legislature! He had been in Congress; and now he was President. He had been everything but one,—he had never been a hang-man, and he asked leave to hang Thad Stevens.[12]

When the returns of the Pennsylvania elections on October 10 had been counted, they seemed to give a verdict in favor of the Radicals. Even such strongly Conservative metropolitan news-papers as the *Herald* and the *Times* now stated emphatically that, with the October returns forecasting the November results, the people were speaking out clearly in favor of the Radicals in Con-gress and their policy toward the South. "The question may have been more or less modified in particular localities, as in that repre-sented by Mr. Thaddeus Stevens," observed the *Times,* "but as a rule this has been its shape—the President, or Congress? And the answer leaves room neither for equivocation nor doubt. It is over-whelmingly against the President."[13] To a more careful observer, however, the nature of the popular mandate, if there was such a thing, would have seemed less clear. Did those who cast their ballots for the Radical candidates really know what they were voting for? Congressional propaganda had simply won out over presidential patronage.

To Old Thad the returns meant that he ought to have at least an outside chance of winning the senatorial election in the Pennsylvania legislature in January. He sent his congratulations to Governor-elect John W. Geary and received Geary's congratu-lations on his own re-election to Congress in reply.

Back again in Bedford Springs, he found the vast rambling hotel almost empty of guests. There was no one left for him to play euchre or whist with. But the small boys who peddled flowers and maple-sugar candies were still on hand. One day several of them were running races around the fountain. After each race the winner would trot up to the old gentleman sunning himself on the porch steps near by and leaning on his cane. And the old man would bestow the prize—a silver quarter. Then he would handicap the winners and start the boys off again, so that

[12] Edward B. Callender, *Thaddeus Stevens, Commoner* (Boston, 1882), 158–161.
[13] *New York Herald,* October 11, 1866; *New York Times,* October 11, 1866.

each might receive a coin. His doctor had told him that he might enjoy the mineral waters and the mountain air but no heavy reading indoors. Still, he might try more of the "light, frivolous" matter about Johnson in the newspapers, and he had his mail to read and answer. There was a grateful letter from the Kansas Pacific people, asking the "Father of the Pacific RR^d Act" to telegraph them whether he would like to go on a free junket out to Fort Riley, Kansas. There was a fulsome letter from an Adams County German to whom he had given a home for life. "In the very Hon. Mr. Stevens, are concealed all the qualifications that can constitute a noble Gentleman—a good man, and a father. I have experienced him. Oh! that I were in person before him, the Hon. sir, I would press that kind hand of him, into my hand, out of excessive affection—like a son."

Of greater moment were the letters from self-appointed political advisers. In the new state legislature, among others committed to Old Thad, would be F. S. Stambaugh, one of the state representatives from Franklin County, whom he had put in office with the votes of his ironworkers at Caledonia. Soon he began to suspect Stambaugh's loyalty, however, when McClure's *Chambersburg Repository* hinted that Stevens was not serious about the senatorship but preferred to remain in the House. Stambaugh's protestations from Chambersburg hardly reassured Old Thad. From Samuel Shock in Columbia he received warning that other legislators pledged to him were "not reliable" but were "fishy." Simon Cameron, as president of the North Central Railroad, had alienated one of them by giving a relative a job in the company. "I am convinced that if our 6 [Lancaster] representatives will be loyal to you," Shock had ended his letter, "you can be elected. When will you be home?" From Lancaster another henchman wrote to warn Old Thad that "some steps ought to be taken to meet the idea that *you are not in earnest about the U. S. Senate.*"[14] But Stevens hesitated to take any step which might

[14] William M. Hall, *Reminiscences and Sketches, Historical and Biographical* (Harrisburg, 1890), 32–33; Herman J. Gross to Stevens, October 12, 1866; Geary to Stevens, October 13, 16, 1866; Stambaugh to Stevens, October 19, 1866; J. J. Cochran to Stevens, October 22, 23, 1866; Shock to Stevens, October 25, 1866; W. J. Palmer to Stevens, October 25, 1866, all in the Stevens Papers.

make it appear that the senatorship, if he should get it, was else than the unsought gift of the people through their representatives in Harrisburg.

His trip back to Lancaster weakened him again, but the news from the capital roused him into life. Despite the widespread Radical successes at the polls, President Johnson was showing no disposition to yield to the people's voice. Shortly after the middle of November Old Thad took a train for Washington, though he was so feeble that he could not sit up and a bed had to be made for him on the floor of the coach. Only a handful of congressmen were on hand when he arrived, among them Senator Sumner, who, no longer a bachelor, was making the rounds of the house-furnishing stores. Old Thad went back to the residence on B Street kept by Lydia Smith. Newspaper reporters who called at the "Robesperian chamber on Capitol Hill" found him on some days freely predicting an immediate impeachment of the president, on other days professing that he was too weak to talk on political topics.

At the end of November the indefatigable diarist Welles recorded his view of the situation: "The threat of impeachment is less loud for the last few days. . . . If Thad Stevens can get his caucus machinery at work he will grind out the refractory and make the timid guilty participants. . . . The Pres. is passive, leaning on Seward and Stanton, who are his weakness." Seward was a "weakness" because his unpopularity with Democrats in New York and elsewhere prevented their fusion with Conservative Republicans, so long as Johnson retained him as secretary of state, on a scale that would result in a truly effective president's party. Stanton, still secretary of war, was an even more fatal weakness, for he was in conspiracy with the Radicals against his chief. In the privacy of his office, Stanton was dictating to George S. Boutwell, one of the members of the joint committee on reconstruction, the draft of a bill to take control of the army from the president and give it to Congress. The measure would prohibit the president from assigning the general of the armies (Grant) to duty anywhere except in Washington without the Senate's consent. Boutwell took the draft around to Old Thad, who readily agreed to include it in the next army appropriation bill. At the same time, with the approval of Stanton, Stevens was getting ready a measure by which to deprive the president of his powers of patronage as well as his military powers. Johnson had waited until the absence of Congress during the summer to make his removals and appointments. Now Old Thad would have the Senate review all removals and appointments as soon as it assembled, reject those made for "political reasons," disqualify rejected appointees from holding office for three years, and give their places back to the previous incumbents! Both Radicals and partisans of the president looked to the first caucus, on December 1, to foreshadow the course of subsequent events in the House. Here Old Thad rebuked those Republicans who had assured their constituents that the Fourteenth Amendment, and that alone, would be the condition of the restoration of the Southern states. He was not yet through with them! If the president was weakened by the character of his advisers, the Radicals—fortunately for him, as was later to be seen—were weakened by divisions among themselves. Outwardly they appeared harmonious enough at their gala banquet on December 3, though while Old Thad was responding to the toast "to the Congress of the United States," there was a drunken altercation at one of the tables.[15]

More important to Old Thad during December than the antics of congressmen were the actions of Pennsylvania politicians in regard to the coming senatorial race. A hopeful sign appeared when Forney announced publicly, in the middle of December, that he was retiring from the contest and giving his support to the Radical leader of the national House. During the Christmas holidays Stevens made a trip to Chambersburg (still scarred from the raid of the Confederates in 1864, when it had been burned to the ground) to see McClure and induce him to follow Forney's example. In a hotel room there McClure found Old Thad lying on the bed, seriously ill, perhaps dying. This man, now nearly

[15] Alexander H. Hood, "Thaddeus Stevens," in Alexander Harris, ed., *A Biographical History of Lancaster County* (Lancaster, 1872), 587; *Diary of Gideon Welles, Secretary of the Navy under Lincoln and Johnson* (3 vols., Boston and New York, 1911), 2:626–627; George S. Boutwell, *Reminiscences of Sixty Years in Public Affairs* (2 vols., New York, 1902), 2:108; *New York*

seventy-five, could not possibly expect to last through a six-year term in the Senate! Nevertheless he begged McClure to help elect him. He explained that he did not desire aid as against Curtin, McClure's friend, but that he had good reason to believe that Curtin could not win. If a deadlock should arise, he wished himself to be made the compromise candidate. McClure parried this request by reminding Old Thad that he was already the "Great Commoner," the leader of the whole people, by virtue of his position in the House. His place was unique. To leave it for the Senate would be to give up the fullest powers, the highest honors, that the country could bestow. These blandishments did not dissuade Old Thad. The Radicals of the nation, as Forney's *Press* and Greeley's *Tribune* were saying, were cheering him on.[16]

Before the end of December Stevens was back in Washington, while in Harrisburg his friends were girding themselves for the battle in the Pennsylvania House. It would meet to organize on the day after New Year's. Like the state Senate, it was overwhelmingly Republican, but the Republicans were divided among several factions. The group that managed to get control of the legislature would be able to nominate its man for United States senator, and nomination would mean election. As members of the House prepared for the opening day, the leading candidate for speaker was a Curtin man, Matthew S. Quay. Wondering whether to vote for him, one of the Stevens men telegraphed to Washington for advice. "Is there any choice between a Cameron and a Curtin candidate?" In Stevens' opinion there was indeed a difference, for Curtin at this time appeared to be the stronger of the two C's. He must be checked, if the deadlock which Stevens de-

Times, November 8, 15, 26, 29, 30; December 3, 4, 6, 10, 1866; *New York Herald*, December 1, 2, 3, 6, 1866.

[16] Alexander K. McClure, *Old-Time Notes of Pennsylvania* (2 vols., Philadelphia, 1905), 2:206–208; *New York Times*, December 14, 1866; *New York Tribune*, January 2, 1867; *Philadelphia Press*, January 3, 1867. Cameron was writing suavely to Old Thad's close friend McPherson: "On returning home last night, I found a letter from a mutual friend stating that you had to him spoken kindly of me in connection with the coming Senatorial election." But McPherson, apparently, was urging his acquaintances in Pennsylvania to "stick" to Old Thad. Cameron to McPherson, December 16, 1866, and S. E. Duffield to McPherson, January 2, 1867, in the Edward McPherson Papers, Library of Congress.

sired was to ensue: the two C's must be made to nullify each
other's strength. "If they could be kept 'neck and neck' until their
ardent friends become exasperated at each other," another Stevens man was counseling his chief, "the electors may, from the
one or the other, unite with your friends." So, on December 31,
Old Thad wired a terse reply to his backers at Harrisburg: "Defeat
Quay." And Quay lost. But his defeat, instead of bringing the two
C's "neck and neck," put Cameron far ahead. Old Thad had succeeded only too well![17]

Curtin's "staunchest friends" now conceded that Cameron had
beaten them, and their "hope and wish" (so Ben Butler heard
from Harrisburg) was to make some arrangement whereby Stevens would "head off" Cameron. Some newspapers affirmed and
others denied that Curtin was retiring in favor of Old Thad.
Stevens was meanwhile confronted by contradictory advice. On
the one hand he was informed that the failure to elect Quay had
been "morally the utter rout of Curtin" and that the Curtin men
intended to transfer their votes to him only to "cover" Curtin's
sure defeat. On the other hand he was told to disregard this story
as a trick of the Cameron men to get him out of the way. Governor-
elect Geary, he heard, was promising patronage to Cameron's
friends. From several advisers he received warnings that the situation in Harrisburg was desperate, that bribery was rife ("Oh!
Shame where is thy blush when men can be bought as so many
oxen or asses"), that some of the representatives pledged to him
were openly repudiating their vows. He took time out from his
work on the reconstruction bill, which ostensibly was busying him
in Washington, to write a sharp note to one of the renegades,
Representative Stambaugh, from Chambersburg:

Allow me to remind you that before you were nominated you called
me aside to assure me that if nominated and elected you should support
me throughout for U. States Senator; and that after your nomination
and before your election you repeated the same more than once.
You also pledged yourself repeatedly to Mr. Sweeney my manager that

[17] R. W. Shenk to Stevens, December 29, 1866; J. R. Sypher to Stevens,
Shenk and Billingsfelt to Stevens, and Stevens to Shenk and Sypher, December 31, 1866, telegrams in the Stevens Papers. According to McClure, Cameron
had "adroitly" brought Stevens and the Lancaster delegation into the fight
against Quay. *Old-Time Notes of Pennsylvania*, 1:462.

if elected you would give me your full support—Then the votes at Caledonia were needed to save you—I remind you of these things not with any hope that they will change your vote or your nature, but to hope that it may change your opposition to a little more modesty.

In the *Philadelphia Press* Forney was combating the arguments that Stevens was too old, or that he could not be spared from the House. The people, he said, would much prefer "the Great Commoner, Stevens, to the skilful political manipulator, Cameron"; and therefore it had a "strange look" that "the politicians should be rejoicing over what they predict as his certain defeat."[18]

From his allies in the legislature Old Thad was receiving appeals to come on to Harrisburg. Only his presence could save the day! He was reluctant, still desiring to have the senatorial honor conferred upon him as a gift of the people, in appearance at least. He replied in a public letter that he had determined not to "canvass" for any office, but in a postscript he added darkly: "Since writing the above certain facts have come to my knowledge which may impel me to reconsider my determination." Finally, on January 7, 1867, accompanied by Forney, he left his business in Congress and took a train for Harrisburg. Now, said the *Press,* members of the legislature could see for themselves the falsity of the argument that he was too old.

> *Too old, you say? Is mental power*
> *The test of fitness for the post?*
> *See Stevens, at this very hour,*
> *The giant leader of our host!*
>
> *Some men are old at thirty-five;*
> *Some shriveled souls were never young;*
> *Stevens, if any man alive,*
> *Has power of heart, and brain, and tongue....*
>
> *O, send him to the Senate now,*
> *And let the nation hear his voice!*
> *The light upon his kind'ling brow*
> *Shall make humanity rejoice!*

[18] Edward Reilly to Stevens, December 31, 1866; L. Kauffman to Stevens, January 4, 1867; D. McConaughy to Stevens, January 4, 1867; H. M. Watts

When Old Thad saw Stambaugh in Harrisburg (as Forney afterward related), he stomped up to his "betrayer" and whispered:
"You must be a bastard! I knew your father, and he was a gentleman and an honest man!" Quickly he called his Lancaster delegation together and denounced them also with similar frankness.
Then he asked Curtin to join him in going directly "to the
people," but Curtin refused to do so. He went ahead nevertheless
and appealed to the public with an announcement that, "to promote the purity of elections," he would himself refuse a nomination from the "hidden intrigues" of a "secret caucus." This was
the outcry of a beaten man. In the subsequent balloting among
the Republicans in their caucus, Cameron received forty-six votes,
Curtin twenty-three, and Stevens only seven.[19]

In Washington President Johnson and his friends were doubtless enjoying the humiliation of the proud leader of the hostile
House, who just before his departure had issued a new blast
against the president. "Stevens has higher culture, more genius,
learning, and education than Cameron," now reflected Johnson's
ally Welles, who had no use for either of the two, "but less party
tact and sagacity." Though Cameron might be corrupt, Welles
thought, Stevens was "infinitely worse." Old Thad did not think
so. But there was nothing he could do about it now, except to rue
his decision to go to Harrisburg at all after his mistaken order
to defeat Quay had made the fight all but hopeless. The whole
affair was the crowning disappointment of his life. And yet, when
he reappeared at his desk in Congress, he seemed to be bearing
up well, "with his usual philosophy."[20] A gambler in politics as
well as at cards, he would be a good loser—or at least appear to be.

to Stevens, January 4, 1867; Stevens to Stambaugh, January 6, 1867, in the
Stevens Papers; John Cassels to Butler, January 5, 1867, in the Benjamin F.
Butler Papers, Library of Congress; *Philadelphia Press,* January 4, 5, 1867.
    [19] Stevens to Representatives and Senators of Lancaster County, January 10,
1867, in the Stevens Papers; *Philadelphia Press,* January 6, 7, 8, 9, 10, 11,
1867; *New York Times,* January 8, 1867; *Lancaster Intelligencer,* January 16,
1867. The story of Stevens' meeting with Stambaugh (whom Forney did not
mention by name) is told in John W. Forney, *Anecdotes of Public Men*
(2 vols., New York, 1873–81), 2:181.
    [20] *Diary of Gideon Welles,* 3:16, 21; *New York Times,* January 14, 1867.

XVII. What of the Conquered Provinces?

AT LAST, as was shown by the congressional elections of 1866, public opinion in the North had caught up with Thaddeus Stevens. Normally the new Congress, fresh from the Radical people, would not have met until the first Monday in December, but already the Radicals in the existing Congress had set an earlier date, the next March 4. Until then, during the first two months of 1867, it was to be Old Thad's purpose to prevent his Conservative colleagues from ushering in the ten excluded states too quickly and on too easy terms. His task was lightened by the seeming intransigence of Andrew Johnson and the legislators in the Southern states. These men, on the advice of the president, were refusing to ratify the Fourteenth Amendment. Even if they had been willing to accept it, of course, Stevens would not yet have been ready to admit their senators and representatives to his "circus," but perhaps he could not have overborne his more impatient fellow members. As it was, he and others of his kind could tell the Northern people that the rebels were clearly unreconstructed, unrepentant, unshriven of their war guilt. And many congressmen otherwise independent would be driven by public opinion into his grasp.

Only the Supreme Court would remain an obstacle to Radical legislation, since the Radicals could override Johnson's vetoes at will. And the Supreme Court, in three close decisions in January of 1867, declared unconstitutional some of the wartime powers assumed by Congress and delegated by it to the president. The court might go on to pass similarly upon the whole of Radical legislation for the South; and though it could not of course enforce its judicial veto, it might bring about a revulsion of public opinion from the Radicals. Old Thad condemned its recent judgments as "infamous," almost as bad as the historic Dred Scott decision. He and his Radical friends talked of impeaching the justices of the Conservative majority, of requiring a unanimous opinion to invalidate an act of Congress, of taking away entirely the appellate jurisdiction of the court.[1] This kind of talk was to prove sufficient to put a temporary quietus upon the Conservative judges.

One day near the middle of January, while congressmen were discussing such matters as the impeachment of judges and presidents, a thin, wizened, sallow-faced, cigar-chewing man walked down the main aisle of the Hall of Representatives and sat down beside Old Thad for a cozy and friendly chat. Visitors and members alike gaped in surprise. What were Johnson's secretary of state and the Radical leader of the House chatting so amiably about? The mystery deepened during the week as Seward made several drives to the red-brick house on Capitol Hill and Old Thad went to dine and spend the evening at Seward's. To cynical Gideon Welles, however, it was no mystery at all. He did not accept Seward's explanation that he was consulting the chairman of the appropriations committee about the purchase of the Bay of Samaná in the West Indies, for he was sure that there was no object, naval or commercial, in getting Samaná. His impression was that Seward was trying to place himself on good terms with Stevens and other Radicals and to create a sensation that would distract attention from the war between Congress and the president. Nor did Welles hesitate to read the mind of Old Thad. "He has no professed respect for Seward but feels complimented that the Secretary of State should come into the House of Representatives and sit down and court the 'great Commoner.' It is an observance that gratifies his self esteem, a homage that soothes his arrogance." Though Seward won Stevens' support for his imperial enterprise, he failed, if indeed he had intended, to bring about a peace.[2]

Old Thad went right ahead with his bill to disfranchise the

[1] *Congressional Globe,* 39 Congress, 2 session (1866–67), 250–252.
[2] *New York Times,* January 17, 1867; *Diary of Gideon Welles, Secretary*

leading white men and enfranchise all the adult male Negroes of the South. The debate upon the measure indicated that the Radicals could not agree among themselves any more than with the Conservatives or the Democrats. At the end of January a majority sent it to the joint committee on reconstruction, which had not been meeting lately because Old Thad preferred the informal sessions at his home. Now he turned to the task of punishing Johnson for having dismissed from office some of the "best men" in his district during the recent campaign. He told the House that Johnson, by his use of the patronage, was destroying the very party that had elected him, and that this alone was a high crime and misdemeanor sufficient for impeachment. But the House rejected the punitive proposals which Old Thad had suggested to Fessenden in October and proposed to Congress in December.

A few days later the Radicals' cause was further weakened when a story in the *Cincinnati Commercial* concerning the impeachment resolution introduced by Congressman J. M. Ashley of Ohio was reprinted in the Eastern papers. The author of the article claimed that Stevens and Butler had both had something to do with the resolution, and that one of its main objects was to give Butler an opportunity to get at General Grant. In the lobbies Old Thad categorically denied the story in so far as it referred to him. Grant, he insisted, was not only his political but also his personal friend. As if to prove that this was so, Generals Sheridan and Grant, when they visited the House, sat down "sandwiched in" between another Radical and Old Thad. He had a use for Grant, as became apparent the next day, when he reported the new reconstruction bill that he had wrung from the joint committee.[3]

of the Navy under Lincoln and Johnson (3 vols., Boston and New York, 1911), 2:643, 3:26–27; Frederick W. Seward, *Seward at Washington as Senator and Secretary of State: A Memoir of His Life with Selections from His Letters, 1861–1872* (New York, 1891), 344.

[3] *New York Times*, 1867: January 28, 29; February 2, 3, 4, 5, 6; *Congressional Globe*, 39 Congress, 2 session (1866–67), 536–537, 941, 944; Benjamin B. Kendrick, *The Journal of the Joint Committee of Fifteen on Reconstruction* (*Columbia University Studies in History, Economics, and Public Law*, vol. 62, New York, 1914), 122–129.

This measure was far more drastic than his earlier one for disfranchising Southern whites and enfranchising Southern blacks. First, it set aside the "pretended" state governments that Johnson had sponsored. Then it divided the territory they embraced into five military districts, over each of which it set a commandant, whose duty would be simply to preserve order in his respective area. These commandants, it was stipulated, should be appointed by and receive orders from the general of the armies— that is, Grant. Two implications of the plan are noteworthy: Johnson would have no direct connection with it, and the Southerners would have no program at all by which to re-establish states! On February 7 Old Thad made a speech on the bill:

For two years the loyal people of those ten States have endured all the horrors of the worst anarchy of any country. Persecution, exile, and murder have been the order of the day within all these Territories so far as the loyal men were concerned, whether white or black, and more especially if they happened to be black. We have seen the best men, those who stood by the flag of the Union, driven from their homes and compelled to live on the cold charity of a cold North. We have seen their loyal men flitting about everywhere, through your cities, around your doors, melancholy, depressed, haggard, like the ghosts of the unburied dead on this side of the river Styx, and yet we have borne it with exemplary patience. We have been enjoying our "ease in our inns"; and while we were praising the rebel South and asking in piteous terms for mercy for that people, we have been deaf to the groans, the agony, the dying groans which have been borne to us by every Southern breeze from dying and murdered victims.

Enough time had been wasted in idle talk about reconstruction, Old Thad said in conclusion. "Tomorrow, God willing, I will demand the vote." Previously the usual course of action had been for the Radicals to secure the adoption of a bill in caucus and then to force the Conservatives to support it in the House by refusing them a chance to explain to their constituents an adverse vote. On the morrow, however, Representative N. P. Banks made an "unexpected and dramatic heading off of Overseer Thad." The previous question was not sustained. Debate remained open.

John A. Bingham and James G. Blaine then proposed modifications of Old Thad's "military police bill," and after nearly a week a combined Bingham-Blaine amendment was brought into the House. To some the suggested change seemed slight enough, but to Stevens it meant destroying the very purpose of his bill. Bingham and Blaine desired to add a section that would provide an eventual end to military rule and a program for the reconstruction of bona fide states. All the Southerners would have to do would be to grant universal suffrage, that is, to the blacks and to practically all the whites, loyal and rebel alike. This amendment, protested Stevens on February 13, would be a step toward "universal amnesty and universal Andy-Johnsonism." "It lets in a vast number of rebels and shuts out nobody." The Republicans advocating such clemency were "hugging and caressing" those whose hands were red and whose garments were dripping "with the blood of our and their murdered kindred." (Here Old Thad was setting an example that Blaine and others, waving the bloody shirt, were to follow long after he was dead.) He again demanded the previous question, this time he was sustained, the amendment was beaten, and his own bill passed. When the vote was announced from the speaker's desk, he exulted: "I wish to enquire, Mr. Speaker, if it is in order for me now to say that we indorse the language of good old Laertes that Heaven rules as yet and there are gods above?"[4]

In driving his bill through the House the old man had shown astonishing energy, but the effort exhausted him and for a day or two he was too unwell to leave his home. The capitol was not so many rods distant, but he would have had to make his way through February rain and sleet and snow. Meanwhile cheering news came to him from one of his associates in the Pennsylvania legislature. They had obtained the charter he desired for a railroad running within a few miles of Caledonia. "I think the bill quite liberal," his informant had written, "indeed so much so that we can almost go where we wish. D. V. Ahl will doubtless see you ere this reaches you and will ask you whether we need any supplements or anything further.... It is a great pleasure for me to do anything that may directly or indirectly interest or serve

⁴ *Congressional Globe*, 39 Congress, 2 session (1866–67), 1075–1076, 1167, 1213–1215; *Diary of Gideon Welles*, 3:40–41; diary of John Hay, entry for

you." While the inclement weather kept Old Thad from the House sessions, except for brief periods at a time, the Senate was considering his military-police bill and devising substitutes for it.[5]

About three o'clock one stormy Sunday morning there was a knocking at his door, and he awakened to receive an angry and excited caller, none other than Charles Sumner. Sumner had just come from the Senate chamber, where the senators were holding what was going to be an all-night session. At about midnight Senator John Sherman, brother of the general, had introduced a substitute for Stevens' House bill. Sherman's measure provided that the appointment of commanders over the military districts of the South should be given not to General Grant but to the president. Another section was no less than the Bingham-Blaine amendment in thin disguise. The furious Sumner told Old Thad he must contrive some means of defeating the Sherman bill in the House. During Sunday Stevens made his plans.[6]

On Monday morning, February 18, he began to put them into effect. He advised leading Democrats on the floor of the House to filibuster and so prevent concurrence in the Senate bill. Time was short; only two weeks remained of the session and of the thirty-ninth Congress. He promised the Democrats that in the next Congress he would give them something better! Later in the day, taking the floor to speak against concurrence, he said he had simply proposed a "police regulation" of the South because of the "anarchy and oppression" existing down there. Reconstruction itself should be left for the future, at least until after the rebels should have been made to pay the cost of the war.

As far as I can ascertain, more than $2,000,000,000 of property belonging to the United States, confiscated not as rebel but as enemy's property, has been given back to enrich traitors. Our friends whose houses have been laid in ashes, whose farms have been robbed, whose cattle have been taken from them, are to suffer poverty and persecution, while

February 8, 1867, in William R. Thayer, *Life and Letters of John Hay* (2 vols., Boston, 1915), 1:264.
[5] L. Kauffman to Stevens, February 14, 1867, in the Thaddeus Stevens Papers, Library of Congress; *New York Times*, February 12, 13, 14, 15, 1867.
[6] *Congressional Globe*, 39 Congress, 2 session (1866–67), 1459–1469; *New*

Wade Hampton and his black horse cavalry are to revel in their wealth and traitors along the Mississippi Valley are to enjoy their manors. Sir, God helping me and I live, there shall be a question propounded to this House and to this nation whether a portion of the debt shall not be paid by the confiscated property of the rebels.

In the evening Old Thad was seen lobbying again with the Democrats; some of them he allowed to have the floor; and before the next day was over he forced the House into nonconcurrence with the Sherman bill. The Senate replied by insisting upon its own measure and refusing a committee of conference. Again Old Thad hobnobbed and voted with the Democrats in an effort to keep the House from yielding. In conversation he was heard to say that he would rather pass no bill for restoration at all than this one, and anyhow he did not wish to see the South back in the Union until after the presidential election of 1868. Finally, after the Sherman bill had been given a slightly more Radical tinge, he gave up the struggle and let it go through—thinking, perhaps, he could undo it in the next Congress.[7]

The session was about over. Stevens had found little time for new economic legislation on behalf of Northern industrialists, but the continued absence of Southern members and the House's engrossment with the reconstruction question had at least prevented the repeal of any of the wartime and postwar gains. Once he did speak out again for the issuance of more paper money for the benefit of business men. A hundred million dollars of interest-bearing treasury notes were about to fall due. He asked that they be paid with new greenbacks. To the cries of "inflation!" he replied that he could not understand "why gentlemen should call this 'inflating the currency.'" On March 2, when the reconstruction bill came back to the House with a veto, he saw it pass again amid applause. On the same evening, the last of the session, the galleries were crowded with spectators who had braved a nasty sleet and snow storm to hear him make a formal denunciation of the story that he had been interested in impeach-

York Times, February 18, 1867; James M. Scovel, "Thaddeus Stevens," in Lippincott's Magazine, 61 (1898): 548–549.
    [7] Congressional Globe, 39 Congress, 2 session (1866–67), 1315–1340; Diary of Gideon Welles, 3:47; New York Times, February 19, 20, 1867.

ing Grant.[8] On the morrow the new, more Radical Congress would begin its meetings and then, mayhap, he would be able to get some really Radical things done!

He was not to have his way in the Fortieth Congress, however. Early in March the new House rejected the more extreme reconstruction bill which he brought up and turned to the task of providing machinery to set in motion the program the previous Congress had finally agreed upon. During most of the month illness and the continued severity of the winter weather kept him from the capitol. Weeks earlier he had composed a speech on his favorite topic, confiscation, and it was already set up in type at the office of the *Washington Chronicle*. At last, on March 19, he felt well enough to resume his place in the House and make a try at delivering the speech. He started it, but could not go on; and Edward McPherson, still the chief clerk, smoothly read it for him while he sat weakly down, his lips bloodless, pale.[9] In the condition he was in he could not prevent the passage of what was to become the second reconstruction act, directing how new constitutions were to be formed so as to admit the ten states under the terms of the first act.

Even if he had died at this time, his reputation as a parliamentary leader was secure. On the basis of his performances in February, 1867, and those of the previous winter, people were comparing him with the greatest masters of men in the history of the Senate and the House. His scorn and his pointed finger had been more effective even than those of John Randolph of Roanoke, his manipulation of legislators as masterful as that of Stephen A. Douglas and even Henry Clay.

But it was only in parliamentary tactics that he could claim supremacy. He was not a master of political strategy in the larger sense. His worsting at the hands of Simon Cameron at Harrisburg in January had been proof of that. His power rested, in the final analysis, upon the control of a majority of votes in the ninth con-

[8] *Congressional Globe*, 39 Congress, 2 session (1866–67), 1423, 1729–1733, 1771–1772, 1969–1976; *New York Times*, March 3, 4, 1867.
[9] *Congressional Globe*, 40 Congress, 1 session (1867), 203–208; *New York Times*, March 7, 8, 9, 19, 20, 1867.

gressional district of Pennsylvania, and even in that ultimate locus
of his strength he was beginning to lose his hold.

With Cameron he had managed since January to come to some
kind of an "understanding" in regard to federal appointments
to be made in that district, but apparently he and Cameron
interpreted it differently. When it seemed that two Cameron men
were to be given jobs in Lancaster, Old Thad, on the day after
his attempted confiscation speech, sent a curt note to Cameron
in which he said he trusted that in the Senate these appointments
would be "rejected as soon as convenient." Then he thought the
matter over for a few hours and decided to send an apology.
"The note which I indiscreetly addressed you today," he now
wrote, "contained unfair, and offensive suggestions which I have
no way of repairing but by expressing my regret. After what had
taken place between us I ought to have been ashamed (as I am)
for what I wrote." If he expected the appointments to be merely
temporary and a matter of form, he was gradually disabused of
the thought. Suspecting the worst, he turned to Seward, who
alone of the cabinet might have reason to help him out. He
asked Seward "to suggest to the Pres^t (early) to settle an ugly
trouble in my Dist." by appointing a couple of Stevens men, but
he did not explain why he should expect the president to do
such a favor for such a foe. He also appealed to several of the
senators during the first weeks of April. Plaintively the master
of the House finally wrote again to Cameron: "Do not allow me
to be kept in anxiety—it don't become old age. You may need
repose also a few years hence." The plea was in vain. When the
Senate had confirmed the Lancaster appointees, Old Thad found
that only one of them was his own choice. Everyone soon knew
that the patronage quarrel had led to "considerable feeling"
between the two Pennsylvanians.[10]

During the rest of April the sick old man spent his active hours
studying up on the whole mass of reconstruction legislation,
passed and proposed, and attending to the routine affairs of the

[10] Stevens to Cameron, March 20, 1867 (two letters), and April 18, 1867, in
the Simon Cameron Papers, Library of Congress; Stevens to Seward, April 8,
1867, in the Andrew Johnson Papers, Library of Congress; New York Times,
April 19, 24, 1867.

committee on appropriations. Some of the Republican congressmen and newspapers had begun to promise the Southerners that
if they elected "loyal" men under the reconstruction acts, their
senators and representatives would be welcomed in Congress.
Angrily Old Thad issued a denial. "Much is to be done by the
people and Congress before any Representative or Senator or
States can be recognized. Who authorized any orators to say
there would be no confiscation?" Much remained to be done, but
Stevens had not the health to do it. His physicians advised him
not to attempt the trip to Lancaster on the first of May. Spring
was late, and the Washington weather was still bad. But on the
cheerless May Day he nevertheless undertook the journey, in the
special railroad car that had brought Seward from Auburn on
the day before.[11]

[11] Stevens to Edward McPherson, April 12, 1867, and Stevens to "Mr.
Editor," April 27, 1867, in the Stevens Papers; Diary of Gideon Welles, 3:87;
New York Times, April 13, May 2, 1867.

XVIII. Intimations of Immortality

WHEN Thad Stevens shall die, his virtues will be better appreciated and his name will be more highly honored than now," prophesied Henry Ward Beecher, the nation's most famous minister of the gospel, from his Brooklyn pulpit one Sunday morning in the spring of 1867. "For he is one of those men who are very inconvenient when alive, and very valuable when dead."

The admirers of Old Thad were preparing to close the books and make an inventory of his career, and they could hardly blink the fact that there were many "inconvenient" items in it. Edward McPherson had appointed himself the Boswell of Stevens, and so had Edward Reilly, a railroad lobbyist whom the leader of the House had benefited from time to time. When Reilly heard of McPherson's project he abandoned his own and contented himself with suggesting a biographical theme. He told McPherson that "justice" to their mutual friend required that one part of his life "should be particularly dwelt upon by his biographer"— that part revealing his business honesty in his refusals to take advantage of the bankruptcy laws to escape his debts. "I am solicitous that the public should know him as we who are intimate with him know him," said Reilly, "not only as the greatest, but the *purest* of American statesmen." With similar solicitude Theodore Tilton, the friend of Beecher, was asking Old Thad to pen a statement on Negro suffrage for his prominent religious weekly. "If you publish such a letter in *The Independent*," Tilton advised, "it will confirm the opinion of a great many elderly ladies that you are a good, old-fashioned and devout Presbyterian deacon." Once Stevens had replied to the charge that he was an atheist with a letter saying he had always been "a firm believer in the Bible" and also a believer in the existence of a Hell, for the "especial benefit" of his slanderers, but otherwise he had done little to contradict the various stories that his friends feared were tarnishing the splendor of his name.[1]

At home in Lancaster in May of 1867 he seemed unconcerned about his future fame as he looked forward to resting up for the next winter's session of Congress. At first he did not think a special session would be needed during the summer, unless the judiciary committee, which had been investigating Andrew Johnson's public and private affairs, should be ready to report articles of impeachment against the president. As the weeks passed he noticed in the Republican papers a rising tide of criticism of his confiscation ideas, and so he arranged with McPherson to publish a catechism and his replies in McPherson's *Gettysburg Star and Herald,* which would then be taken up by the Associated Press. "Short as your letter is," Old Thad wrote to McPherson in response to the queries he had himself prepared, "I fear I cannot answer it without violating an injunction of my medical adviser, not to become excited." Who said Congress could not seize the property of the rebels? "A *quasi* peace exists between the late belligerents, the terms of which are dictated wholly by Congress, which is under the control of the Republican party." Many innocent Pennsylvanians, Stevens reminded his Gettysburg readers, had suffered from rebel invasions and raids. He insisted that the war was not yet over and never would be over until, in accordance with the well-established law of nations, the vanquished had been made to pay its cost. What he was reading in the papers soon caused him to become even more excited. To the reconstruction acts Johnson's attorney general was giving an interpretation that would make them less harsh than the Radicals had intended. And so in June Stevens began to agitate for a July meeting of

<hr/>

[1] Stevens to J. T. Keagy, January 23, 1867, in William M. Hall, *Reminiscences and Sketches, Historical and Biographical* (Harrisburg, 1890), 18; Reilly to McPherson, April 5, 1867, and Tilton to Stevens, April 23, 1867, in the Thaddeus Stevens Papers, Library of Congress. The quotation from Beecher's sermon is from a newspaper clipping dated April 14, 1867, in the Stevens Papers.

Congress and assumed the responsibility of writing to all the doubtful members and telling them to be on hand on the first of the month.[2]

Day after day, while he tried to hoard his little energy for the congressional struggle in July, politicians from near and far were crowding into the parlor on South Queen Street. On behalf of some of the office-seekers he applied to Secretary Stanton, the Radical marplot in the cabinet, for jobs. The patronage quarrel with Senator Cameron and the late senatorial election itself were bitter subjects that Old Thad could not forget. When a Delaware County politician inquired whether, as a Mr. Barton said, he had instructed his friends to vote for Cameron the previous January, he replied that he had not, since he did not "claim to control any votes outside of Lancaster County." Originally, he explained, Delaware and several other counties had declared for either him or Curtin. "When I reached Harrisburg (where I was reluctantly persuaded to go very foolishly) I found that Mr. Barton was *convinced* that the good of the State required Genl. Cameron's election and never doubted of his [Barton's] treachery. Indeed, whatever might be the reasons I found most of the Anti-Cameron men either openly or secretly converted.... All I mean to say is that in stead of sixteen votes ... a full discussion of the merits of the candidates convinced at least sixty of the superiority of Genl. Cameron." "This," concluded sarcastic Old Thad, "is rather a defence of Mr. Barton, who could not be expected to resist arguments which had convinced, and *changed* so many others." He cautioned against an "extended publication" of this letter, for, as he said, he did not desire to reopen the question.[3] He was having enough trouble with some of his more importunate visitors. One of them, who introduced himself as a "Southern editor," greatly annoyed him by following his servant up the stairs to his room without first giving him a chance to scrutinize the calling card.

[2] *New York Times*, 1867: May 25, 26, 28; June 13, 16, 19; *Washington Chronicle*, May 26, 1867.

[3] Stevens to Stanton, June 11, 1867, in the Edwin M. Stanton Papers, Library of Congress; Stevens to Joseph Shortridge, June 25, 1867, in the Stevens Papers.

A reporter from the *New York Herald,* who appeared on the last of June, was more welcome. This man had been struck by an interesting contrast of public personalities on his approach to Stevens' house. As he afterward wrote:

The city of Lancaster numbers among its eighteen or twenty thousand inhabitants two citizens who have figured somewhat prominently in the public affairs of the country—James Buchanan and Old Thad Stevens; and the relative positions these two celebrities occupy at home affords a fair illustration of the political condition of the country and of the tone of popular sentiment at the present time. The one, who has been President of the United States and properly represents the rank copperhead democracy as it existed before the Southern rebellion, lives in close retirement, and receives no more notice or thought from his neighbors than does the humblest resident of the city. The other, who would not object to being President of the United States, and is the representative of aggressive radicalism born of the rebellion, is the center of attraction to all the country around, as well as to persons from other States, and has his goings and comings, his sayings and his doings duly chronicled and gossiped over, day after day. The one is the embodiment of the dead past; the other of the living present. Your correspondent, who reached this place a few days ago, was impressed with these thoughts by the following conversation, held by him with a citizen of Lancaster soon after his arrival:

"Ex-President Buchanan lives near this place, does he not?," inquired your correspondent. "Well, yes. He lives 'bout a mile and a half out," was the reply. "Is he at home at the present?" "I don't know whether he is at home or not. I suppose he is." "You do not appear to know a great deal concerning so distinguished a fellow citizen." "Distinguished! Well, we know that such a man as old Poppy Buchanan lives away out yonder, but that's about all we do know." "Well, you know Mr. Stevens, I suppose?" "Mr. Stevens—who's Mr. Stevens?" "Oh, Thad Stevens the member of Congress, to be sure." "Oh, you mean Old Thad!" cried the Lancastrian, brightening up with sudden intelligence. "Well, I guess I do. Everybody knows him." "You seem to think more here of Old Thad, as you call him, than you do of the ex-President." "More of him? Well, I should say we do. We're democrats, here, in the city; but then we know Poppy Buchanan's played out and don't amount to anything. But as to Old Thad, while we mayn't like his politics, we know he's alive."

Very much alive Old Thad was indeed, at least politically, as the wheel of fortune continued to turn after having made a complete revolution since that day forty years before when Stevens and

Buchanan had disagreed upon the merits of Andrew Jackson as a prospective president. But Old Thad was not yet satisfied.

What, the *Herald* reporter asked him, would he do in the extra session of Congress that was about to begin? If he had his way, he answered, he would declare null and void every action of the president in the administration of the reconstruction acts, and he would forbid the military commanders in the South to obey any order emanating from the White House. Congress had given them their orders; the whole affair was none of the president's business, nor the Supreme Court's. Did Old Thad still believe in confiscation? Only a "mild confiscation," he said. As the rebels were his fellow countrymen, he would not take their lives or even "beggar or oppress" them. But he could expect to do little about it right away, for there were too many "philanthropists" like Greeley and Gerrit Smith throwing around a lot of "dishwater" to the effect that the North had been just as much responsible for the war as the South.

What about impeachment? The judiciary committee's investigation of Johnson's private life, said Old Thad, was "fussy, unnecessary, and absurd"; for the best grounds for impeachment were a matter of public record: Johnson's defiance of the laws of the United States. Even if the committee should report in favor of it, an impeachment resolution could not be carried, for Johnson's successor would be the president of the Senate, Ben Wade, whose election to that position had aroused the jealousy of the friends of his chief competitor, Fessenden. "Every little tricky politician who wants this man for a postmaster or that man for a constable, and does not think Ben Wade will give him what he wants, will oppose it." Would Stevens favor it? Yes, as a means of reuniting the party in Pennsylvania. "The Republican portion of our Legislature has been so openly, notoriously, and shamefully corrupt," he explained, "that all the honest people in the State are disheartened and disgusted." In January a prominent politician, whom he did not hesitate to mention by name, had "had his men with their handfuls of greenbacks" at work in Harrisburg. "This corruption will certainly beat us here next election, unless we draw out the Republican strength by getting up a furor and excitement on impeachment."

What about the presidential nomination in 1868? Well, Stevens could not say much for the leading Republican contenders. He thought Grant a great soldier but, he prophetically suggested, a success as a general might be a failure as a president. Chase he regarded as a negative quantity, not at all popular. Butler was a humbug. "At first," said Stevens, "I had looked upon him as a man with whom it would be dangerous to measure swords in debate. But I soon found that he had gained a reputation under false pretenses." Old Ben Wade (who in the West was ridiculing confiscation as "damned foolery") had played himself out. "In fact," concluded Stevens' interviewer, "it is very probable that Old Thad believes in the inmost recesses of his heart that if, in the course of human events, the country should look to Lancaster for its next President, and should find him in a two and a half story red brick house on South Queen street, the country would by no means do a foolish thing, and would be very likely to find 'Barkis willing.' "[4]

In Washington during the opening days of July Stevens endeavored to rectify the damage he thought Congress had done in allowing Johnson to appoint and advise the military commanders in the South, and he forced through the House a bill making the commanders independent of the president by prohibiting their removal without the consent of the Senate. On July 8 he found, spread over a whole page of the *New York Herald,* an account of the interview he had given in Lancaster. He had been rather hard on some of his Radical colleagues, and the discretionless reporter had omitted nothing! At his earliest opportunity Old Thad took the floor in the House to make an explanation. Of his interviewer he said: "The only fault I have to find with him is that, without submitting the manuscript to me, he has disclosed what he says was my conversation with regard to my associates on this floor. All the rest of the article, including the criticisms upon myself, I care nothing about, and do not

[4] *New York Herald,* July 8, 1867.

object to their accuracy, although I am charged with entertaining certain foolish political aspirations." The *Herald* in its following issues agreed that it might better have left out the remarks of Stevens about his fellow Radicals, for everyone knew what he thought of them anyway!

The editors of the *Herald* continued to advertise him as a potential candidate in 1868 and, though admitting he was an "old nag" for the presidential sweepstakes, predicted that he would make a strong run against Chase for the prize of the Radical nomination. "Indeed," they said, "Old Thad Stevens will be found a very dangerous competitor, and it will take all the power and influence of the national banks to distance him." His violent Radicalism did not frighten the editors, for they scoffed at the idea that he was motivated by his "apparent vindictiveness" toward the South or by an "avaricious longing" to make good his losses in the invasion of 1863. "His ambition," they pointed out, "induces him to run to extremes in his confiscation programme; but we believe it to be prompted more by his desire to retain the position of the leader of the extremists than by any settled determination to push it to the bitter end." As July wore on, the leader of the extremists in the House loudly demanded an impeachment and denounced the conservatism of the Senate that had meanwhile emasculated his latest reconstruction bill.[5]

With the presidential race in the offing, Old Thad was not quite ready to die, and yet he prepared for the worst. On July 13 he signed the last will and testament that he had drawn up in his own hand. First, he had provided for the payment of one thousand dollars to the town of Peacham for the support of the "Juvenile Library Association" ("if the same still be in existence") which he had formed as a student at the Caledonia County Academy. Second: "I give and bequeath to the trustees or title-holders of

[5] *Congressional Globe*, 40 Congress, 1 session (1867), 560, 566, 588, 637–638; *New York Herald*, July 10, 11, 16, 1867. Welles thought Stevens had prepared the questions and answers ahead of time for his *Herald* interviewer. "Almost all which this vicious old man does is premeditated, dramatic, and for effect." *Diary of Gideon Welles, Secretary of the Navy under Lincoln and Johnson* (3 vols., Boston and New York, 1911), 3:130–131.

the grave yard in which my mother and brother Alanson are buried in the town of Peacham, Vermont, $500 to be put at interest perpetually, and the interest to be paid annually to the sexton, on condition that he keep the graves in good order, and plant roses and other cheerful flowers at each of the four corners of said graves every Spring." Next, after small legacies to Thaddeus M. Stevens and a son of Simon Stevens: "I give to Mrs. Lydia Smith, my housekeeper, $500 a year during her natural life, to be paid semi-annually, or at her option she may receive $5,000 . . . . Mrs. Smith has some furniture of her own used in common with mine, some bought with her money, as well as other which it would be difficult to distinguish. Now she must be trusted on honor to take such as she claims without further proof." To his nephew Thaddeus, Jr., Old Thad bequeathed the rest of his estate, one fourth of it to be conveyed to him at the end of five years, the second fourth after another five years, and the rest after five more, provided he was able to prove that he had abstained from all intoxicating drinks during those periods of time.

Otherwise, if the remainder of the estate should amount to fifty thousand dollars, it should be used "to erect, establish and endow a house of refuge for the relief of the homeless and indigent orphans" in Lancaster. (In later years rum-loving young Thad was to tell his friends that he did not wish to deprive the poor orphans of this gift!) The house of refuge was to be an unusual one in some respects:

The orphans who cannot be bound out may remain in the institution until the age of fifteen years, and longer if infirm, at the discretion of the trustees. They shall all be carefully educated in the various branches of an English education, and in all industrious trades and pursuits. No preference shall be shown on account of race or color in the admission or treatment. Neither poor Germans, Irish, nor Mohammedans nor any other on account of their race or religion, or their parents, must be excluded. All the inmates shall be educated in the same classes without regard to color. They shall be fed at the same table.

This reference to the mess hall was a nice detail, as was that to the Irish, and Old Thad may have compressed his thin lips with inward satisfaction as he propounded this monumental answer to those who might sneer at his earlier career in nativistic politics, or impute to him narrowly partisan motives for his advocacy of Negro rights.[6]

A week or so after he drew up his will, his friend McPherson at the clerk's desk in the House read Johnson's message vetoing the supplementary reconstruction bill which he had introduced and Congress had passed after making changes that he did not like. Quickly both chambers repassed it over the veto, amid cries for impeaching the obstinate president. Old Thad got to his feet and said there was no use to talk of impeachment, for there were "unseen agencies" at work that would prevent its success. Some supposed that he was referring to the plottings among the Radicals for the succession to the presidency. Others fancied—"absurdly," said the *Herald*—that he had the Masonic lodge in mind.

Absurd though it might have appeared, he was in fact thinking of reviving the old Antimasonic agitation at this late date. Earlier in the summer President Johnson had gone to Boston to dedicate a new Masonic temple there. Immediately, from one of the clerks of the House, Stevens had requested a list of the names of "all the Free-Masons who are members of either branch of Congress." If it should turn out that most of the Radicals were non-Masons, the president might well be doomed. The man to whom Stevens' request was referred, himself a member of the order, replied that over a dozen senators and perhaps a hundred representatives were Masons, but he knew the names of only a few. These he listed ("in the hope, however, that the information is not to be used to their prejudice"). On his list was the name of Cameron, a fact which might be useful enough, but also the names of Colfax, Ashley, Butler, and other prominent Radicals.[7] Congress therefore could not properly be divided as between members and nonmembers of the lodge. It was a pity, perhaps, that Old Thad

[6] Stevens' will was printed in full, following its admission to probate after his death, in the *New York Tribune*, August 19, 1868. The attitude of Thaddeus Stevens, Jr., toward this legacy is mentioned in a letter from Junius B. Kauffman to Mira L. Dock, June 13, 1895, manuscript in the possession of Miss Dock, Black Gap, Pennsylvania.

[7] *New York Herald*, July 20, 22, 1867; Stevens to McPherson, June 26, 1867, and B. B. French to Stevens, July 6, 1867, in the Stevens Papers.

could not climax his career with the same kind of Antimasonic flourish as that with which he had begun it!

At the beginning of August, the half-hearted work of the special session done, unsatisfied Old Thad returned to Lancaster on Cameron's North Central Railroad. "We got home safe and comfortable with very little fatigue," he wrote to McPherson, "thanks to Mr. Cameron Prest. R.R." On the day of his arrival he sent a letter of condolence to Simon Stevens, whose father had recently died. Despite its formal phrasing and its Shakespearean and classical allusions, there was in the missive a warmth and mellowness of feeling that few would have expected from the cold and caustic old man:

I suppose you have returned from your sad errand. The burial of a beloved parent is a deep grief to his offspring, but more so to the beloved companion of his life. It is but little consolation to know that she must soon follow. But Nature mitigates our grief by teaching how little enjoyment there is when age or disease has withered our mental or physical faculties.

Since I returned I have been getting rather worse. I am unfit for business. What the result of this disease may be, I am doubtful. Nor does it give me much concern. I remember that we are admonished that there is a time when we must no longer attempt to hurl the discus or bend the bow of Ulysses. That day has come with me. I confess that I should regret to depart without seeing this government placed on a basis of perfect freedom. It is still far from that. But it will be consigned to abler & wiser men to finish. I rejoice that "Heaven rules as yet, and there are Gods above."

Remember me to your wife & boy.

While his disease kept Old Thad at home, Pennsylvania College, of whose board of trustees he was still a member, was celebrating the laying of the cornerstone of its new preparatory building in Gettysburg. Earlier the principal of the college had appealed to him for a contribution of, say, five hundred or a thousand dollars. "If it seems too *small*," the principal had written, "we shall most gladly receive a larger donation, and in that event we shall deem it a duty to name the building 'Stevens Hall.'" And "Stevens Hall" it was now to be, as the Honorable M. Russell Thayer, of Philadelphia, gave the dedicatory address.[8] "I am

[8] C. J. Ehrehart to Stevens, August 24, 1866; Stevens to McPherson, August 3,

much gratified at the commencement proceedings," Old Thad
afterward wrote to McPherson. "I have not seen it but learn that
Thayer was very complimentary and fine."

But the political outlook was less gratifying. "What may turn
up next session is hard to say," he continued in his letter to Mc-
Pherson. "The conservatives are a base set; Trumbull, Fessenden,
Sherman, Wilson will ruin us—We must establish the doctrine of
National jurisdiction over all the States in State matters of the
Franchise, or we shall finally be ruined—We must thus bridle
Penna. Ohio Ind et cetera, or the South, *being in,* we shall drift
into democracy." The Northern states as well as the Southern,
that is to say, must be compelled to give the vote to Negroes as
an ultimate means of saving the Republican party! At this
moment, August 16, Old Thad was full of concern because of the
president's bold defiance of the Radicals. Only a few days before,
Johnson had suspended their ally Stanton as secretary of war and
had put General Grant temporarily in his place. A week later
Johnson ordered the removal of General Sheridan, their favorite
among the district commanders in the South. Hastily Stevens
published an exchange of correspondence with Samuel Shock,
in which he made it plain that in the last session of Congress
he had fostered a bill to prevent just such removals but the Senate
had struck it out. At the end of August he wrote again to Mc-
Pherson: "If you have a copy of Thayer's remarks I wish you
would send me. Is there any danger of the election? It seems a
pity either to lose or win amid such blindness. What a Senate!!"[9]

As the fall elections of 1867 appeared in the offing, public
opinion seemed to be veering away from the Radicals and back to
the president. His forthright assumption of control over the reconstruction machinery and his appointment of Grant, the
popular hero, as secretary of war *ad interim* won many Northerners, tiring of congressional excesses, again to his side. And Old
Thad, confined to his sickbed during most of September, could

1867; Stevens to Simon Stevens, August 3, 1867, all in the Stevens Papers;
New York Times, July 19, 1867.

[9] Stevens to McPherson, August 16, 27, 1867, in the Stevens Papers; *New
York Times,* August 28, 1867; *New York Herald,* August 28, 29, 1867.

THE IMPEACHMENT MANAGERS

Back row: James F. Wilson, George S. Boutwell, and John A. Logan. *Front row:* Benjamin F. Butler, Thaddeus Stevens, Thomas Williams, and John A. Bingham. Photograph by Matthew B. Brady, 1868. Courtesy of the Signal Corps, United States Army.

no longer go out stumping and rousing the countryside to Radicalism. One afternoon a preacher took the train out from Philadelphia to call on the invalid. Years earlier Stevens had heard the man preach in Harrisburg and had lingered after the service to say a few encouraging words. In gratitude the preacher now desired to kneel by his bedside and pray for his soul. But Old Thad was sleeping, and Lydia Smith would not let the visitor go upstairs. Once, however, the old man mustered enough energy to take at least an oblique part in the Pennsylvania campaign. For the benefit of a Republican politician, who had complained that the Democrats were circulating a defamatory article from an Alabama newspaper, he achieved this much of a reply:

I rec'd your letter of the 8 containing a printed libel from the Union Springs Times. In the course of my life I have rec'd a very large number of such attacks—Perhaps no man in the State has received more slanders or been charged with more vices or more great crimes than I have. It has been my fortune for forty years to be the bitter object of attack by violent partisans. I have seldom noticed them—never to contradict them unless they affected my moral character aside from politics or was required by the interests of others. You tell me that this charge may influence your next election—Hence I notice it—

I have already denied a part of it on application from a distant State— The rude doctrines ascribed me by the fellow who wrote them I pass over, with a general denial of their accuracy—

As to the domestic history I have only to say that the whole is totally without foundation except so far as follows. From the time I began business (40 odd years ago) I have kept house through the agency of hired servants having no female relatives. Those servants were of various colors; some white, some black and others of all intermediate colors. My only inquiry was into their honesty and capacity. They have resided with me for various periods from one month to fifteen years. Generally more than one at a time—Indeed I believe always so. I believe I can say that no child was ever raised or, so far as I know, begotten under my roof. Sometimes husband and wife have worked the one for me and the other for another, generally at the same time, cohabiting together on Saturday nights. But I believe none of them became pregnant during the time.

This is a larger disclosure than I believe I have ever made before of my private affairs, and have done it now only out of what you think required by public affairs.

These calumnies and worse have been perennially published against me, by fellows living within sight of my door—I know of no one who has believed one of them, or scarcely pretended to believe them. Having no ambition for office; no aspirations for fame, I have not found it pleasant to turn aside to encounter the offensive odor of diseased dog secretions—

This letter, the recipient may have noticed, was far from being a complete disavowal of all the charges current against the writer of it; but at least the questioning politician could now tell his constituents that the Radical leader had fathered no mulatto children! After putting down his pen Old Thad suffered another relapse, and a fortnight later the rumor reached Washington that he was dead. But shortly before election day he was well enough again to go out for a ride.[10]

The local elections of 1867 in the October states, so greatly had the fickle public changed since the previous autumn, amounted to an overwhelming endorsement of Johnson. "What bad news, sad news tonight," Jay Cooke wrote from Ohio to his brother in Philadelphia. "Pennsylvania and Ohio gone Democratic and the sad lessons of the war all forgotten." But Henry Cooke could not agree that the news was entirely sad and bad. He replied to Jay that the "ultra infidelic radicals" like Stevens had been "dragging the Republican party into all sorts of isms and extremes." Out in Kansas Ben Wade had been "uttering agrarian doctrines" and "trying to array labor against capital"; up in Massachusetts Ben Butler had been urging "wholesale repudiation" of the national debt; in Pennsylvania Thad Stevens had been "joining hands with the traitor Vallandigham and advocating the idea of a flood of irredeemable paper money sufficient in volume to drown the whole country." The defeat at the polls, thought Henry Cooke, would purify the party of these isms and extremes.[11]

In the opinion of Conservatives like Cooke, some of the political Radicals were also becoming economic radicals! The "Ohio idea" of printing more greenbacks had aided the Democrats in the

[10] Alfred Cookman to Stevens, September 4, 1867, and Stevens to [W. B. Mellius], September 14, 1867, in the Stevens Papers; *New York Herald*, August 31, 1867; *New York Times*, September 25, October 5, 1867.

[11] Jay Cooke to Henry Cooke, October 9, 1867, and Henry Cooke to Jay Cooke, October 12, 1867, in Ellis P. Oberholtzer, *Jay Cooke: Financier of the Civil War* (2 vols., Philadelphia, [1907]), 2:27–28.

elections, and by espousing that idea anew Old Thad might steal some of their agrarian thunder, but his motives were not merely those of a demagogue. To his own Pennsylvania industrialists (however it might appear to Pennsylvania bankers such as the Cookes) the issuance of government currency would seem as enlightened a piece of statesmanship as it did to the debt-ridden farmers of the West.

Immediately after the October elections Stevens determined to have his say on this and other national questions, but how was he to attract public attention to his remarks? "I can think of no way so effective as an odd one," he said in a note to a professor at Pennsylvania College, "and no odd way so handy just now as the ancient way of dialogue as used by Socrates and his Compeers." The professor and other "interlocutors" were to quiz him and he was to reply (which of course was just the reverse of the method used by Socrates) in a series of letters to be given to the newspapers.

In one of these he argued the inevitability of Negro suffrage throughout the United States and went so far as to suggest the conquest of Cuba for the purpose of giving freedom to the Negroes there! Greeley and other editors hinted that senility must be affecting his mind. In his next letter he began, to the friend whom he had primed: "I shall not hesitate to answer the questions which you have proposed to me according to my poor ability, although I know that I thereby incur the risk of sharp and frivolous criticism by able New York editors, whose age is scarcely more than eighty years, and who will probably discover in my answer evidence of old age and of decaying mental powers." He proceeded to explode the alleged mysteries of money. "Money! What is money?" "Money is just what the law makes it." As to the public debt—he said he had originally meant it to be paid in money as defined by law, but the New York money changers ("Jew and Gentile mingling in sweet communion to discover some cunning invention to make in a day what it would take weeks for honest men to earn") had persuaded the Senate and the secretary of the treasury otherwise. Now that the war was over, he thought the government should eventually return to specie payments, but not by paying off the bonds in gold and so "breaking the bones of every manufacturer, mechanic, and agriculturist" in the country for the benefit of bankers and bondholders domestic and foreign. Now the national banks were holding bonds against which they had issued banknotes; the thing to do was simply to replace both the bonds and the banknotes with greenbacks. If, instead, the government were to pay the bonds in gold, it would have to pay ten or twelve million dollars more than the value of the paper money it had borrowed in the first place. "But tender consciences have compelled the nation to pay this sum in addition to the legal debt because Mr. Jay Cooke and the *Tribune* had pledged their word that it should be paid."

This line of argument, opined the *Herald*, was thoroughly "statesmanlike" as compared with the "narrow-minded and ruinous" theories of Greeley, the Cookes, and the Radical adherents of the former secretary of the treasury, Chase. It would make a better platform for Stevens as a prospective presidential or vice-presidential nominee than would his other ideas of confiscation and Negro suffrage.[12]

Early in November Old Thad felt strong enough to plan on being present at the opening of Congress later in the month. Always before Congressman Stevens had done all his own writing and other secretarial work, but now he was hiring a private secretary, a man "crippled but smart," to accompany him to Washington and live with him there. Before leaving Lancaster he dictated a codicil to his will giving a thousand dollars toward the building of a Baptist church in the city. "I do this out of respect for the memory of my mother," he explained in the codicil, "to whom I owe what little of prosperity I have had, and which, small as it is, I desire emphatically to acknowledge." (Significantly, he made no mention of his father.) Another thousand dollars he gave to Pennsylvania College for the maintenance of Stevens Hall. Before his departure he also left a note for Isaac, one of the two sons of Lydia Smith, now young men: "Sir: Take notice that before Tuesday night next you have all your things away from

[12] Stevens to M. G. D. Pfeiffer, October 14, 18, 24, 1867, in the Stevens Papers; *New York Herald*, October 15, 31, November 8, 9, 1867.

my house and that you do not yourself enter my House during my absence to sleep or for any other purpose, under the penalty of being considered a Housebreaker." Evidently the daily practice of racial equality had its vexations even for egalitarian Old Thad! On the next Wednesday morning, November 13, he caught an early train for Washington—so early that his Lancaster physician, who reached the station at nine o'clock with a package of medicines, found the patient already gone.[13]

In Washington on Thursday callers crowded into the house on B street to greet Stevens as one arisen from the dead. He felt so well that they had to dissuade him from taking his cane and walking over to the capitol. Exhausted by the crowd, he was worse on the next day, and the rest of the week spent most of his time in bed. At intervals he would brighten up and utter sentences with something of his old vigor and emphasis, but soon he would fall back into a kind of torpor. When able to do so he worked on two measures he hoped to introduce in the House: one providing for universal manhood suffrage (as a fifteenth amendment to the Constitution) and the other suspending impeached officials until after their trial. But he could not promise that he would have strength enough to press either of these matters with adequate force. His poor health gave the critics of his monetary doctrines an excuse for asking Speaker Colfax to replace him with a more able man at the head of the committee on appropriations. Advocates of easy money insisted that he stand his ground and reminded him of the "terrible convulsions, disasters & bank-

[13] Stevens to Isaac Smith, November 9, 1867, copy in the Edward McPherson Papers, Library of Congress; Stevens to McPherson, November 10, 1867, in the Stevens Papers; *New York Tribune*, August 19, 1868. "I could repeat the injunction to save yourself from every labor you can avoid," wrote the physician as he sent the medicines to Stevens, "and place the burthen where you can, upon younger and stronger shoulders." These were the directions for the use of the remedies:

"The iron or tonic mixture in the vial to be continued three times a day as before.

"If the stomach should become disturbed with weakness of appetite &c, the iron mixture may be omitted—and the vegetable tonic used—contained in the packages—one of which to be infused with half a pint of boiling water, poured off after standing a few hours—and a tablespoonful to be taken every 4 hours until better—when the iron mixture may be resumed.

ruptcies" likely to follow if specie payments should be resumed at an early date.

On November 20, after holding a private conference with impeachment men at his home, he announced his intention of being present, regardless of consequences, at the opening of Congress on the next day. After he had made the short trip to the capitol in a closed carriage, he was too weak to sit up while the members were assembling and lay on a sofa in his committee room. To those who offered to help him to his seat, he said: "I can go alone; I am not so dead as some of my newspaper friends have reported me." And when Senator Sumner appeared in the House to greet him, the "Old Commoner" rose to his feet and remained bravely standing during the conversation.[14] But he could not hide for long the effects of his rheumatism and jaundice and dropsy, symptoms of his failing legs and liver and heart. Had he been a younger and stronger man, the history of the United States during the crucial months following might have been quite different from what it was actually to be. And today the name of Thaddeus Stevens would be better known and more highly honored, or more vehemently cursed, than it is.

"If the action of the liver should be suspended, as indicated by the grey or ash coloured stools, a *blue pill* may be taken at bedtime and repeated next morning or evening as may be necessary.

"If the effusion into the pericardium, or the dropsical affection of the heart, should increase—as you will know by the usual oppression, as experienced before—take one of the *'Diuretic Pills'* at bedtime, and repeat every 6 to 8 hours if necessary until relieved. Take as much *nourishing* food as your stomach will comfortably receive and digest—with as much of the punch wine, brandy, whiskey or beer as may be necessary and agreeable." Henry Carpenter to Stevens, November 17, 1867, in the Stevens Papers.

[14] W. H. Winder to Stevens, November 20, 1867, in the Stevens Papers; *New York Herald*, November 15, 16, 22, 1867; *New York Times*, November 15, 19, 20, 21, 22, 1867.

XIX. Prime Minister against President

IF Andrew Johnson were to be removed from office not for any high crime but for his politics, he and his successors in the White House (should the removal become a precedent) would no longer be independent executives but, in the manner of English kings, would reign, not rule. Whatever the constitutional forms, the United States would in fact have abandoned its government of checks and balances for a parliamentary system comparable to that of England. Real leadership would then have gravitated to the responsible head of Congress, to the man who could control a majority in the House of Representatives as the prime minister controlled his majority in the House of Commons.

Indeed, at the assembling of Congress in November, 1867, when impeachment was still only a matter of talk, Thaddeus Stevens already seemed a kind of premier to many of his countrymen as well as to foreigners not conversant with the mysteries of American constitutional law. A professor in the University of Edinburgh spoke of him as "the venerable President of the chamber of representatives," and an African potentate, desiring to place his kingdom "under the protection of the American Govt.," thought him the logical person to address. The *New York Herald*, a not unfriendly critic, called him the "American Robespierre" and pointed out that he had assumed executive powers as ruling spirit of his "Directory," the joint committee of fifteen on reconstruction. Although he disavowed any "foolish political aspirations" for the presidency itself, although his September illness had seemed to disqualify him for the Republican nomination anyhow, he could nevertheless become through an impeachment of Johnson the prime minister of the United States in fact if not

295

in name, and as such he could be as much as or more than a president so long as the breath of life remained in him.

On December 7, the day the vote was to be taken on Representative Ashley's impeachment resolution, he went to the capitol in a closed carriage; two men carried him up the steps in a chair, and from his committee room he totteringly made his way with the aid of the benches and his cane to his seat. He arrived there just in time to cast the last vote in favor of the resolution. His vote was not enough. For the time being, impeachment was lost.[1]

But Old Thad remained the head of his directory, though it was henceforth a committee of the House alone. As the committee began its work a delegation of Negro and white politicians, up from the South, called at its headquarters on B street. Stevens explained to them how impeachment in English law, a punishment for criminal offense, differed from impeachment in American law, a means of preventing political wrongdoing. Ignorance of this distinction, he said, had accounted for the failure of the recent project to remove the president. Turning to the colored delegates, he told them he was about to introduce a bill to give them a special and separate representation in Congress, the Negroes in each state to elect their own congressmen at large. He promised them further that confiscation would yet have its day, asked them about the wealthy planters and large estates in their respective neighborhoods, and disposed of the opponents of confiscation as tender-hearted fellows whose tenderness was really a softening of the brain. As his amused hearers started to go, one assured him that the colored folk of the South prayed daily that he be restored to health and strength, and he graciously replied that he trusted the efficacy of their prayers more than those of a good many white people in the North.

A day or two later he evinced his confidence that he would stay alive for a while by sending Simon Stevens a check for ninety dollars with which to buy clothes for him in New York. Freshly clad, he and Lydia Smith could look forward to a festive Christ-

[1] Sultan Abdullah ["King of Johanna, Comorro Islands"] to Stevens, December 6, 1867, in the Thaddeus Stevens Papers, Library of Congress; *New York Herald*, August 29, December 7, 1867; *New York Times*, December 7, 1867; April 25, 1868; *Congressional Globe*, 40 Congress, 2 session (1867–68), 68.

mas after the news they received from Caledonia. "We are going to butcher tomorrow so you can inform Mrs. Smith that she may look for her hogs soon," Old Thad heard from his nephew at the ironworks. "We are going to kill eight and I think Mr. Sweeney proposes to send you two. He has a turkey for you also." In the mountains freezing weather and two feet of snow had not shut the furnace down: the men maintained two fires in the wheelhouse to keep the hammer wheel free of ice. They had made thirty-one tons of iron during the first week in December, and if they could do as well during the last week in the month they would have a total of six hundred tons for the year.

In Washington, before the adjournment for the holidays, the head of the national directory met defeat in the House on his proposal for congressmen at large for the Southern Negroes, though the rest of his reconstruction bill passed, including a section providing in effect that only a majority of loyal men and not a majority of all the registered voters would be required to ratify new state constitutions in the conquered provinces.[2]

After that Old Thad forgot about the American territories temporarily and began to think of the Russian territory of Alaska, which the czar was eager to sell to the United States. Several months had passed since the arrival of Baron Stoeckl from Russia, the negotiation with Seward for the sale, and the signing and ratification of a treaty. But there still remained a hitch in the deal: it involved payment of more than seven million dollars, the appropriation of which was not yet forthcoming from the House.

Many Americans feared that the czar was trying to palm off a worthless expanse of rocks and ice, but this was not the real reason why congressmen were slow to vote money for the purchase. They delayed because men in key positions had become interested in a notorious "Perkins claim" against the Russian government. The executors of one B. W. Perkins, a dealer in arms, asserted that the czar owed them for military supplies, and they demanded

[2] Thaddeus Stevens, Jr., to Stevens, December 16, 1867, and Simon Stevens to Stevens, December 18, 1867, in the Stevens Papers; *New York Times*, December 11, 18, 1867; *New York Herald*, December 14, 19, 1867; *Congressional Globe*, 40 Congress, 2 session (1867–68), 153–154, 265–266.

that Congress pay them and deduct the amount of their claim
from the price of Alaska. In June they had enlisted the aid of the
chairman of the crucial committee on appropriations, who earlier
had promised both Seward and Stoeckl to get the purchase money
for them at the next session of Congress. At the July session nothing had been done.

Now, in December, trying to persuade Stevens to give up the
Perkins claim, Seward sent him a notice from a man who professed to have a letter of attorney revoking "all other powers and
agencies of all kinds in this business." In a fortnight Old Thad
heard from Simon Stevens, who with the aid of the chairman of
appropriations was still urging his now rather stale claim for
carbines sold to the army early in the war, who was organizing
a "Tehuantepec Railway Company" with himself as president,
and who somehow had a hand in the Perkins affair:

In the Russian matter, I find Baron Stoeckl very, very anxious. So much
so that he has asked one or two friends in Washington whether or not
Congress is really delaying his appr. on acc. of the Perkin's claim. When
he asked me that question last Monday I told him I could not tell
about it. . . . The Baron said he should try and see you and see if the P.
claim could not be settled outside of Congress.

After Christmas, at last persuaded, Old Thad began to dictate
to his secretary a speech in favor of an Alaska appropriation bill,
and the relieved Russian minister reported to St. Petersburg: "I
am counting on the influence of Stevens, who at first supported
that [Perkins] affair but who now is working earnestly on our
side."[3]

When Congress reassembled after the holidays, Seward again
visited him in the House to remind him of Alaska, but Old Thad
let the Russian matter go while he devoted himself to the ever-
urgent task of keeping the Republican party everlastingly on
top. Early in January, 1868, he explained in public letters his
attitude on the question of the suffrage. The vote had been

[3] A. G. Riddle to Seward, December 7, 1867; Seward to Stevens, December 9,
1867; Simon Stevens to Stevens, December 18, 19, 1867, in the Stevens Papers;
New York Times, December 29, 1867. One of the Perkins group had written
to Old Thad: "The man of all men whom I thought was most likely to
speak bold upon a question of clear right, was Thaddeus Stevens—For this
reason the papers are sent you—" J. B. Stewart to Stevens, June 16, 1867, in

granted to Negroes in the first reconstruction act, but a fifteenth amendment would be necessary to confirm this right and extend it to the Negroes of the North. "Universal suffrage is an inalienable right," Stevens now said (having traveled a long way since his controversy with Sumner on this issue two years before). "True, I deemed the hastening of that franchise as very essential to the welfare of the nation, because without it I believe the government will pass into the hands of the loco focos"—or, as he cunningly corrected the words before publication, "into the hands of the rebels and their friends."

During the rest of the month, in the few hours of the day when he had energy enough to work, he kept busy with his reconstruction committee. On January 13 the Senate refused to concur in Johnson's suspension of Stanton from the war office, on the next day Grant resigned as secretary of war *ad interim,* and before long a quarrel developed which made it plain that there was no love lost between Grant and the president. Speaking offhand, Old Thad declared that Grant was now definitely "in the church" of the Radicals and proposed to his committee that they give the whole control over the reconstruction commanders to the general of the army. Planning thus to dispose of the president as an effective check upon his directory, Stevens next contrived a method of getting the Supreme Court out of the way. His scheme was not new but it was thoroughgoing: he would by law deprive the court of appellate jurisdiction over all cases arising from the administration of the reconstruction acts, and for good measure he would forbid that these cases be "reviewed in any other tribunal in any manner whatever."[4]

the Stevens Papers. The quotation of Stoeckl's letter is my translation of the French (*Je compte sur l'influence de Stevens qui le premier a souleve cette affaire, mais qui maintenant travaille assidûment en notre faveur.*) which is quoted from the Russian archives in F. A. Golder, "The Purchase of Alaska," in the *American Historical Review,* 25 (1920), 421.

[4] Stevens to F. A. Conklin, January 6, 1868, in the Stevens Papers; *New York Times,* January 8, 10, 13, 24, February 6, 1868; *Congressional Globe,* 40 Congress, 2 session (1867–68), 663. The question at issue between Grant and Johnson was whether, as the president insisted, Grant had promised to hold the war office until the constitutionality of the tenure of office act could be tested in the courts. On the merits of the controversy see William B. Hesseltine, *U. S. Grant: Politician* (New York, 1935), 107n.

Early in February, after seeing Grant and Johnson call each other a liar in their published correspondence, Old Thad concluded that the time had come to revive the agitation for an impeachment of the president. On February 10 he had the House refer to his reconstruction committee the evidence that the judiciary committee had laboriously and fruitlessly gathered. "Thaddeus Stevens' eyes are sharper in his old age than those of the Chairman of the Judiciary Committee," commented the *New York Times*, "and if he can't find some startling offence hidden away somewhere between the covers of thirteen hundred octavo pages it will be very strange indeed." Hardly had he glanced through the pages when he decided to test the attitude of his committeemen, but they voted six to three against introducing another resolution to impeach. This, muttered Old Thad, was only another sample of the cowardice of Republicans.[5]

They held him back, the cowards, and there was left so little time to finish his life's work by unseating the president and assuming his powers! He did not need the reminder which Jonathan Blanchard, his old acquaintance of the days before the Buckshot War, now sent: "You are five years beyond the allotted time of man." Blanchard begged him to give his soul to Christ before it was too late. "At present, in every part of the United States," the preacher had written, "people believe that your personal life has been *one prolonged sin;* that your lips are defiled with blasphemy! Your hands with gambling!! And your body with women!!!"

What did Old Thad think of these righteous exclamations? Here was an appeal to him in the name of his "mother's God" either to deny or to denounce his sins. He did neither. Was he obliquely proud of them? Time and again in the past he had sneered at his political enemies as eunuchs, lady's male waiting-maids, old women in pantaloons, effeminate men. Expressions such as these had been a recurrent theme in his career. Was there some quirk of his personality, related somehow to his deep and abiding affection for his mother, that made him glad to be damned

[5] *New York Times*, February 10, 12, 13, 14, 17, 19, 21, 1868.

for the vices of a manly man? Was there within him a certain longing for self-assurance, a longing unknown to his conscious self, which in his waking hours translated itself into the gnawings of ambition? These are questions that only a psychoanalyst with the magic of a spiritualistic medium could answer.

"The good you have done the Country (and none has done more if so much) is no offset for vices such as I have named above," Blanchard had added, as a moralist, not as a social scientist. "What makes bad government is *bad sinful men.*" About the time Old Thad received Blanchard's letter, he was overcome by another of his heart attacks and had to telegraph to his Lancaster physician for more of the powders which previously had exerted a "good effect." Unless something happened to hurry events, he might be dead and gone before his chance came to impeach the president.[6]

Something did happen in just a few days. On February 21 Johnson peremptorily dismissed Stanton and named a dependable follower to take his place at the head of the war department. Old Thad received confirmation of this news in a hasty note that J. W. Forney, secretary of the Senate, sent him from the Senate chamber:

The President removed Stanton and appointed Lorenzo Thomas, but gives no reasons, except that he does so under power vested in him by the Constitution. Senate is still in session, but will adjourn before passing needed resolution of disapproval. Stanton has sent a letter to the President denying report in Evening paper that he had been ousted, and that Thomas was issuing orders; that he would hold on in defiance of threat, (unless evicted by force) until the Senate had pronounced upon the conduct of the President.

These tidings had an instantaneous effect upon the members of the reconstruction committee. When they met in Stevens' rooms the next morning, while Stanton barricaded himself in the war office in a ludicrous battle with the newly appointed secretary, a

[6] Blanchard to Stevens, February 15, 1868, and Henry Carpenter to Stevens, February 17, 1868, in the Stevens Papers. Blanchard wrote to request a legacy of "any sum from five cents to fifty thousand" for the erection of the main building of Wheaton College in Illinois as a "breakwater against Secret Societies and all like abominations."

majority agreed that Johnson had plainly violated the tenure of office act and that they could therefore no longer refuse to take action against him.

At two o'clock on the same day, Washington's Birthday, Old Thad entered the Hall of Representatives amid a buzz of excitement. In the midst of a sudden expectant silence he rose in his place and, declaring that the dismissal of Stanton was in itself a high crime and misdemeanor sufficient for impeachment, presented his committee's report. A wordy debate followed, but two days later the leader of the House terminated the discussion with his own remarks. His voice failed him before he had finished the first sentence, and the clerk had to read the manuscript of his speech. This was a "purely political proceeding," he pointed out —it was not like an impeachment in English law. No one could be sure which of the parties was right in the controversy between Johnson and Grant. Perhaps neither told the truth. However that might be, the president had conspired to violate a law of Congress and therefore was in the wrong. After the reading of this indictment, the impeachment resolution passed by an overwhelming vote. On the next day, arm in arm with John A. Bingham, Old Thad trudged to the other end of the capitol. Pale, emaciated, deathlike, but with a voice surprisingly vigorous and a manner stern and lofty as usual, he made the formal announcement to the Senate of the action taken by the House. His message did not detail the charges against the president but merely promised the senators that the House in due time would exhibit particular articles of impeachment and "make good the same."[7]

At a caucus on February 29 the Republicans selected seven managers to prepare a case and conduct the trial on the part of the House. Old Thad, of course, was one of the seven, though not their titular head. In a few days the managers reported and the House adopted ten confused, repetitious, and verbose articles. Their purpose was not so much to make a clear-cut legal case as to produce a combination of charges upon which the Republican senators could agree. Unsatisfied, Stevens later secured the adop-

[7] Forney to Stevens, February 21, 1868, in the Stevens Papers; *New York Times,* February 23, 25, 26, 1868; *Congressional Globe,* 40 Congress, 2 session (1867–68), 1336, 1399–1402.

tion of an eleventh or "omnibus" article which appeared to make confusion worse confounded but which, in fact, cleverly linked Johnson's many "usurpations" to the gravamen, the seemingly provable accusation of violation of the tenure of office act.[8]

"I congratulate you," Old Thad now read in a letter from a Lancaster henchman, "on having got the dogs fairly on the track of the greatest rascal in Christendom." If only the driver of the Radical hounds would have the strength to keep them on the scent! A reporter who called one day at the committee room of the impeachers noted the contrast between his physical condition and that of some of the rest. At one end of a long table Old Thad sat cautiously munching a soda cracker as he waited for his servants to come and bear him to the carriage that would take him home at noon. At the other end of the table sat Ben Butler and another of the impeachment managers zestfully digging their penknives into an enormous cheese. "Boys," said Old Thad, dryly and hesitatingly, to the two young men who arrived to carry him off in his chair, "I wonder how I'll get to the House when you two die." On another day he heard again from his nephew at Caledonia, where, in March, the hammer wheel had finally frozen, the men had discovered new and richer deposits of ore, and there was at last a good prospect of a railroad's being built near by. Nevermore was Old Thad to see the rocks and rills and wooded hills of the South Mountain, where in his younger days he had enjoyed galloping about on horseback. "It is to be hoped that the president will be at last deposed," Thaddeus, Jr., was saying. "I hope your health will allow you to take part in the trial." At the meetings of the managers during March the sick old man, long a teetotaler, kept himself stimulated with dosages of brandy or strong wine.[9]

[8] *New York Times*, March 1, 2, 3, 1868; *Congressional Globe*, 40 Congress, 2 session (1867–68), 1612–1613. There was considerable rivalry among the Radical leaders wishing to head the impeachment committee. Old Thad was considered too aged and too unwell for the job. "The partisan spirit of the prosecution will really weaken it ... especially after Butler's trick of last night in causing tickets to be circulated for manager with STEVENS' name first and his next, so as to give him virtually the chairmanship of the board." *New York Times*, March 4, 1868.

[9] A. H. Hood to Stevens, February 25, 1868, and Thaddeus Stevens, Jr., to

When not among the impeachers, he worked with his reconstruction committee on a project to make impeachment a success.
He had decided, shortly after the Democratic victories in the
local elections of 1867, that he must completely revise his reconstruction program if the Republicans were to win the presidential
and congressional elections of 1868. For one thing, he had come
to the "sincere conclusion" that universal suffrage was one of the
inalienable rights which the founding fathers had referred to in
the Declaration of Independence and which only the slave power
had kept out of the Constitution itself. Early in March, however,
he learned from an ally in the Pennsylvania legislature that the
movement to strike the word "white" from the suffrage laws of
that state had ended in peremptory defeat, and this was but a
symptom of the temper in other Northern states. In the second
place, he had come to the equally sincere conclusion that the
conquered provinces must be hurriedly reconstructed and readmitted to the Union, in time for Southern Republicans black
and white to vote in the elections of 1868. And now, with the
impeachment trial impending, the need for a safe and sure
two-thirds majority in the Senate, so as to convict the president,
gave him another reason for wanting to get the Southern states
and their senators back at an early date. In the House on March
10 he accordingly reported a bill from his committee to recognize
and readmit the state of Alabama.

One afternoon a few days later the rumor was borne to the
White House that this effort had been Old Thad's last, that the
Radical leader was finally and irrevocably dead. Suspecting, perhaps, that it was too good to be true, Johnson said Stevens was
like Vesuvius, which became quiescent at times only to burst forth
again with more lava and flames. Just so, Old Thad came to
himself before long, but he could not generate enough heat and
steam to force his Alabama bill through the House. Two days
after its defeat the trial began, with Ben Butler, chairman of the
impeachers, making the opening address to the senatorial jury.[10]

Stevens, March 8, 1868, in the Stevens Papers; *New York Tribune*, August 14,
1868; George W. Julian, *Political Recollections 1840 to 1872* (Chicago, 1884),
313–314.
    [10] A. C. Reinoehr to Stevens, March 3, 1868, in the Stevens Papers; manu-

SCENE AT STEVENS' DEATHBED

About the bedside are Dr. N. Young, Thaddeus Stevens, Jr., the colored Sisters of Charity Loretta and Genevieve, Simon Stevens, and Lydia Smith. From *Harper's Weekly*, August 22, 1868.

Ben Butler was assuming Old Thad's role of chief impeacher, though during April, as the trial went on, the flames of the Radical Vesuvius reappeared from time to time. The party disciplinarian looked like his former self now and then as he "terrified" and "dragooned" those senators who otherwise would have been bold enough to think of acquitting the president. "Point me out one who dares to do it," he challenged, "and you show me one who dares to be regarded as infamous by posterity." He and the rest of the "whippers-in" sent Radical members of the House around to call on doubtful senators from their respective states and warn the senators of the direful consequences of party disloyalty. The impeachers also stirred up a swarm of letters and telegrams to make it appear that they had the sanction of popular will. In arousing the public they had the support of powerful journalists like Greeley. Planning to be absent from his office for a few days in April, Greeley wrote Old Thad that he was "anxious that the *Tribune* should keep up a steady fire on the impeachment question until the issue is decided. If, therefore, any fact or suggestion should occur to you meantime that seems calculated to aid us in the work, I will trouble you to have it telegraphed at our expense to the *Tribune*." With the Radical press behind him, Stevens might soon be able to dictate to senators as he had long done to members of the House. "It must shame and mortify some of the independent minds in the Senate," reflected Gideon Welles, "to be held in subjection and compelled to receive the excoriations and threatenings of this wicked and bad man."[11]

If Stevens had behind him the force of Northern hatred left

script diary of Colonel W. G. Moore (Johnson's secretary), entry for March 14, 1868, in the Andrew Johnson Papers, Library of Congress; *Congressional Globe*, 40 Congress, 2 session (1867–68), 1790, 1818, 2216. Stevens had once prepared articles of impeachment against President Lincoln (which charged that Lincoln "did erect North Carolina and other conquered territories into States ... giving them Governments of his own creation, and appointing over them rulers unknown to the laws of the United States"), according to the *New York Times*, March 4, 1868. "The rumors of Thad Steven's death, which usually follow with dramatic effect any extraordinary effort in Congress on the part of that long-lived gentleman, have been frequent since his long attendance at the Impeachment trial Friday last." *Ibid.*, March 17, 1868.
[11] J. B. Ellis, *The Sights and Secrets of the National Capital* (New York,

over from the war, the president had on his side the weight of
legality and shrewd and able counsel. Johnson's attorneys were
making the most of a loophole that the Radicals had unwittingly
left in the tenure of office act. As the ambiguous law was worded,
it did not clearly prevent Johnson from removing Lincoln's appointees, and Stanton had been one of the hold-overs from the
Lincoln cabinet. "Stanton was appointed Secretary of War by
Lincoln in 1862 and continued to hold office under Johnson,"
Old Thad argued, preparing his own brief against the president,
"which by all usage is considered a reappointment." At last, on
April 27, he had his turn among the lawyers in Congress avid to
be heard before the nation's most exalted bar. Shortly after noon,
standing weakly before the bench at which Chief Justice Chase
presided, he began to read from a sheaf of printed slips. In a few
minutes he asked permission to sit down and continue; after half
an hour his voice became inaudible and he handed his script to
Ben Butler, who read the remaining two-thirds of the address.
When it was over, James A. Garfield, one of the listeners, was
moved to remark that the impeachers had been "wading knee
deep in words, words, words," and not the least prolix among
them had been Stevens, "reeling in the shadow of death, struggling
to read what could not be heard twenty feet off."[12]

Meanwhile, as the trial dragged on, Old Thad's friends were
lining up the Negro voters in the South, while he drafted new
bills for recognizing Alabama and the other excluded states (which
had been finally reorganized on the basis of Negro suffrage and
which, except for Alabama, had ratified the Fourteenth Amendment). From various points in the South organizers of the new
colored citizens were assuring their congressional chief that he

1869), 147; *Diary of Gideon Welles, Secretary of the Navy under Lincoln and
Johnson* (3 vols., Boston and New York, 1911), 3:301, 340, 354; Alexander
Harris, *A Review of the Political Conflict in America ... Comprising Also a
Résumé of the Career of Thaddeus Stevens* (New York, 1876), 498; *New York
Times,* March 4, 7, 1868; Greeley to Stevens, April 20, 1868, in the Stevens
Papers.

[12] *Congressional Globe,* 40 Congress, 2 session (1867–68), supplement, 320–
324; *New York Times,* April 28, 1868; *Philadelphia Press,* May 2, 1868; Garfield to J. H. Rhodes, April 28, 1868, in Theodore C. Smith, ed., *Life and
Letters of James Abram Garfield* (2 vols., New Haven, 1925), 1:424.

could depend upon loyal "Stevens men" being sent to Congress. "The colored people here," the chairman of the Republican committee of Florida informed him, "have been led to look upon you with the highest respect and the most unshaken confidence." In explanation of this the politician added: "The colored preachers are *the great power* in controlling and uniting the colored vote." As boss of the nation, after the conviction of Johnson, Old Thad would have at his back a strong political machine in the South. Already, however, the unrepentant Southern whites were countering with secret organizations of their own. On the same day that Stevens received a letter from Peacham telling him "even the Copperhead town of Danville" claimed the honor of being his home, he received another from New Orleans: "Thou hast sown the wind, thou shalt reap the whirlwind in the *moon's* last quarter. Thy end is nigh. The last warning." It was signed "K. K. K."[13]

As the time approached for the impeachment court to give a decision, it became obvious that, though the president was defended by able counsel, legal considerations would not determine his fate. The brief for the defendant might confirm Democrats in their belief in his innocence, but there were only a dozen of them in the Senate. If all the Republicans or if all of them except six should hew to the party line, the impeachers would have the two-thirds majority that they needed to convict. If seven of the Republicans should bolt, however, impeachment would be indubitably lost. And there were more than seven Republican Conservatives in the Senate.

To forestall a verdict of not guilty, Old Thad asked the House early in May to admit the reconstructed states at once, so that

[13] F. A. Dockray to Stevens, March 18, 1868; Jacob Blanchard to Stevens, April 2, 1868; K. K. K. to Stevens, April 3, 1868, in the Stevens Papers. "Our academy is in a prosperous condition," Jacob Blanchard informed Stevens. "The library which you patronized so liberally is in good condition and generally read." To some extent Lydia Smith (as well as carpetbag politicians) was a go-between for Stevens and the colored race. A colored soldier desiring back pay had once written to him: "I was informed by my mother who is now in Washington City that having seen your good Lady on my behalf you would foward my interest in a plain matter affact manner." J. H. Quarles to Stevens, July 2, 1866, in the Stevens Papers.

their senators could vote. First he presented an enabling bill for Arkansas and secured its passage under the previous question. Then he brought in a similar bill dealing with five other states in one batch. The Democratic leader objected because black men were allowed to vote in those states. "Now I advise the gentleman to become dramatized," said Old Thad in his closing speech on May 14, "to become the hero of a second play like that of Rip Van Winkle which is now so well played by that admirable actor Mr. Jefferson." The gentleman must have been asleep for several years and must fail to realize that in the interim, through warfare and bloodshed, God had made the country free. "And I trust the Almighty ruler of nations will never again permit this land to be made slave; or in other words that He will never permit the Democratic party again to gain the ascendancy." Once more the previous question and the passage of the bill. But the Senate hesitated to pack the jury in the midst of the trial, and not till several weeks later, over Johnson's veto, were the enabling bills to become law.[14]

Old Thad induced the managers to have the Senate vote first on his eleventh article, for he thought it the strongest, the one that would most favorably test the Radical case. On the appointed day, May 16, 1868, he took his seat in the Senate well before the time the court was to meet. While waiting he talked quietly with Senator Sumner. After the roll call on the article began, he sat "with one unvarying look of contempt." All went well until the name of Fessenden was called. He said, "Not guilty." So, one by one, did six others among the Republicans on the jury. After the court had adjourned, his servants carried Old Thad out of the Senate chamber and, riding high above the heads of the crowd in the corridor, he appeared pale, silent, grim. But, as if to indicate that he was not yet done, he summoned his physical resources before reaching the committee room and insisted on being put down to walk, on his own.[15]

[14] *Congressional Globe*, 40 Congress, 2 session (1867–68), 2399–2464.

[15] *New York Tribune*, May 18, 1868. Between the time of Stevens' address to the jury and the first vote there were rumors of various attempted settlements between Johnson and the Radicals. In one of these, the notorious "Alta Vela affair," it was made to appear that a number of Radicals had

"Treason is triumphant. Scoundrelism is in the ascendant." "I fear we must all become rascals in self defense." Such were the reactions of Old Thad's Lancaster friends to the decision of the impeachment court. To them even more reprehensible than the "seven traitors" was Chief Justice Chase, whose private ambitions a successful impeachment would not advance, and who was doing his best to restrain the proceedings and give them the semblance of legality, judiciousness, and fair play. Get Johnson out—legally if possible, otherwise if not! Keep Congress in session until March 4, 1869, so as to prevent Johnson from using the patronage to defeat the Republican candidates in the next election. Let the Senate vote on one article a month until the new senators from the South could be given their seats. "I shall try," Old Thad replied to his importunate counselors. He had considered all the suggested measures but doubted whether "a majority of our friends" could be "brought to it." "Money is irresistibly powerful," he explained, implying that one or more of the recalcitrant senators had been bribed.[16]

He set to work at once to prepare another set of articles, one of which alleged bribery as a high crime and misdemeanor of the president. The managers examined one James Wooley, who had recently withdrawn twenty thousand dollars from a Washington bank and could not explain, to their satisfaction, how he had spent the money. Stanton himself, who all along had used his position to aid the impeachers, was urging Stevens on, but age and illness slowed the old man down. "I have been confined to bed ever since I saw you," he said in a note to Stanton on May 20. "This accounts for my having made no movement. I hope to be up today." Those who expected him soon to report on new

signed a paper giving an implied promise that they would spare Johnson if he would send a warship to the island of Alta Vela to protect the claims of a group of land speculators. Among the signatures was that of Stevens, but he explained in the House that he had put his name to the document without even reading it and "had no idea it was to be taken to the President." *Congressional Globe*, 40 Congress, 2 session (1867–68), 2366; *New York Times*, May 2, 1868.

[16] Samuel Shock to Stevens, May 14, 18, 1868; J. R. Sypher to Stevens, May 15, 1868; A. H. Hood to Stevens, May 16, 1868; Stevens to Samuel Shock, May 18, 1868, all in the Stevens Papers.

charges were disappointed. He had something he called an article
of impeachment, but associates to whom he read the manuscript
said it was only an incoherent jumble of words. On May 25 the
managers voted not to introduce any additional charge, all of
them except Butler and Stevens having concluded that impeachment was a thing of the past.[17]

On the next day, too ill to leave his bedroom, Old Thad learned
that the Senate had adjourned *sine die* as an impeachment court
after acquitting Johnson on the second and third counts. As soon
as he recovered he began again to go through the motions of
renewing the trial. Gideon Welles doubted whether the "malig-
nant and vicious old man" would actually make the attempt. "But
he likes notoriety and power, and his threat exhibits both to his
satisfaction." He was in earnest, however, and was making ar-
rangements by which to carve Texas into three states and thus
produce six new senators to offset the seven traitors. And then on
July 7 his fellow representatives put an end to all thoughts of
another impeachment by voting down his revised articles.[18] Thereafter the bitterness of defeat, final and irreparable, filled the
house at No. 279 B Street, Capitol Hill—the house that might
have become the No. 10 Downing Street of the United States.

[17] Stevens to Stanton, May 20, 1868, in the Stevens Papers; *New York Times*,
May 19, 20, 24, 25, 26, 1868; *Philadelphia Press*, May 20, 1868; *New York
Tribune*, May 23, 27, 1868. Old Thad was refusing at this time to receive
visitors at his home. C. L. Robinson to Stevens, May 29, 1868, in the Stevens
Papers.

[18] *New York Times*, May 27, June 23, 1868; *New York Tribune*, June 23,
29, 1868; *Diary of Gideon Welles*, 3:391; *Congressional Globe*, 40 Congress, 2
session (1867–68), 3786–3791.

XX. Emancipation

AS Washington warmed up with the advent of the summer of
1868, the seventy-sixth for Old Thad Stevens, the Republicans
in the capitol forgot about their late project to impeach the man
at the other end of Pennsylvania Avenue. In any case, Johnson's
term was to expire soon, even if not soon enough. His enemies,
patient perforce, now interested themselves in the campaign to
put Grant in Johnson's place the following March 4. One among
them, however, could not join in the campaign with a whole
heart. Old Thad damned Grant and Colfax with faint praise and
outspokenly condemned the "tame and cowardly" platform that
they were running upon. To him the Democratic ticket was a
still greater evil—Horatio Seymour, a peace Democrat as wartime
governor of New York, and Frank Blair, worst of the hated Blair
clan—but at least the Democrats had shown the good sense to put
an easy-money plank in their platform. Old Thad could find
little enthusiasm in his soul for Grant so long as the Republicans
refused to abandon their insistence upon a currency sound enough
to suit the great bankers and bondholders.[1]

As congressmen began to electioneer from their places in the
House, word came to them from Lancaster that James Buchanan
had quietly died, as he had quietly lived during the past seven
years, at Wheatland. Old Thad did not begrudge him his repose.
Not long before he had told a Democratic acquaintance that
those who had "fawned on Mr. Buchanan in the day of his power"
and had since deserted him were base and contemptible men.
And yet, when the House was composing a resolution appropriate to the occasion of a former president's demise, he felt that as a
good Radical he must make a public show of undying enmity
toward his erstwhile doughface foe. He cynically suggested an

[1] Samuel Shock to Stevens, June 17, 1868, and Stevens to Charles S. Spencer,
June 24, 1868, in the Thaddeus Stevens Papers, Library of Congress.

amendment to strike from the cautious eulogy reported in the
House the words "ability and patriotic motives."[2] Such was
politics!

No good word must be said for leading Democrats, dead or
alive, so long as their appealing platform with its greenback
plank was threatening to give the White House back to the party
of rebellion. "I have doubts about the election of Genl Grant, if
the Whiskey Ring is not exploded," Samuel Shock was advising
Old Thad from his place of business in Columbia. "I am sorry
to say, that the acquittal of Johnson has left us in a bad predica-
ment, & negro suffrage is injuring us with the people." In truth,
however, it would not do for Old Thad to explode the Whiskey
Ring, lest the explosion should open up other scandals, in which
he himself was involved. Agents of the Union Pacific Railroad,
fearful that Congress might regulate freight and passenger rates
or take other action harmful to the best interests of the company,
were lavishly passing out their stocks and bonds to congressmen
who could do them the most good. As chairman of the committee
on appropriations, Stevens was still doing favors for the Union
Pacific and other railway enterprises, and he was not averse to
accepting in return favors from the railroad men which amounted
to a *quid pro quo.* On June 24 a lobbyist for the Union Pacific in
Washington left a note for him:

> In reply to yours of the 19 Inst—I will state that in the event Congress
> shall provide for the Extension of the road of the Union Pacific R Way
> Co. to the Pacific, and shall grant the necessary *aid* in land and Bonds,
> therefore, I will give you Government *or first mortgage bonds* of the
> said Company, for the twenty nine (29000) thousand dollars of full paid
> stock held by you in said Rway Co. which is an acceptance of your
> proposition.[3]

[2] *Congressional Globe,* 40 Congress, 2 session (1867–68), 2810–2811; W. B.
Reed to Edward McPherson, January 13, 1869, in the Stevens Papers.

[3] Samuel Shock to Stevens, June 6, 1868, and John D. Perry to Stevens, June
24, 1868, in the Stevens Papers. A year earlier Old Thad had asked the treas-
urer of the Union Pacific what he could do to help the company out. W. J.
Palmer to Stevens, June 26, 1867, in the Stevens Papers. He was also doing
favors for an official of the Pennsylvania Railroad, who was interested in the
Eastern Division of the Union Pacific. Tom Scott had written to him: "I am
delighted with the contents of your letter of May 12th & glad to know that
the Government has finally concluded to do justice to those people. Will see

Only his timely death and the principle of *nil nisi bonum* were to keep Stevens' name unbesmirched when the railroad bribes, along with the activities of the Whiskey Ring, should eventually be exposed.

And there was that other dubious undertaking in which Old Thad had his hand—the Alaska project. In May, 1868, the appropriation bill that Baron Stoeckl so much desired had been reported in the House, but to it was attached a preamble implying that the House shared the treaty-making power with the Senate. Senator Sumner, chairman of the foreign relations committee and a stickler for form, would very likely object to the impudence of the lower chamber. And so Baron Stoeckl, worried again, sent his American agent, R. J. Walker, to Stevens' residence. When Walker got there he found that Old Thad was upstairs, indisposed, and so the visitor penciled a note for him: "If the Senate insists, I think the House will not recede, and the appropriation will be lost. I am in the parlor downstairs—Can I see you for a moment?" The upshot of this interview was that the Senate agreed to accept the appropriation on the House's terms. In the House Old Thad, his voice clearer and louder than it had been for months, made several talks in favor of the purchase during the first two weeks of July. It would mortify the Republican party to refuse the appropriation, he said, for in a manner of speaking the czar was himself a Republican, a friend of freedom, as he had amply proved by his emancipation of the serfs. Whether moved by this argument of Old Thad's or impelled by the more substantial persuasions of Stoeckl and Walker, the congressmen finally voted to buy Alaska.[4] Had the public known of the activities of Walker and Stoeckl, the Republicans would have had something else to worry about in the elections of 1868.

They had troubles enough as it was. With the nation's business languishing after the wartime boom, their sound-money platform was being eyed coldly by people along Main Street and on the

you next week." Thomas A. Scott to Stevens, May 13, 1868, in the Stevens Papers.

[4] R. J. Walker to Stevens, undated note in pencil in the Stevens Papers, vol. 16; *New York Times*, July 3, 15, 1868; *Congressional Globe*, 40 Congress, 2 session (1867–68), 3660–3661, 4045, 4136.

farm, as coldly as Stevens' ideas of Negro suffrage. In this emergency the discussion of a funding bill before the House, on July 17, gave Old Thad an opportunity to reiterate his demand that the five-twenty bonds ought to be payable in money—that is, in greenbacks—and not in gold coin. If it was the intention of the Republican party to stand by the money-changers, he challenged, then he and the Republicans had at last come to a parting of the ways. "If I knew that any party in this country would go for paying in coin that which is payable in money," he said, "I would vote for the other side, Frank Blair and all." After hearing this startling outburst, a Democrat spoke up: "The Democratic doors are open, and we will take the gentleman in." But soon Old Thad received warnings from some of his constituents that in Lancaster his words had created "some stir" and "a good deal of discussion" and "quite an excitement." Nettled by these reactions, he arose in the House to make an explanation, but confessed he was "too feeble" to "undertake to explain the whole of the matter" and failed to make an explicit retraction of his offending remarks. To the hypercritical editor of the *Evening Express* in Lancaster he wrote: "I trust that my good friends will reconsider their censorious opinions and agree with what their representative held from the start.... I have never adopted a political principle which the party do not now hold. Excuse this vanity into which I have been goaded."[5] That Old Thad should have thought he had the party with him was not only vanity; it was also a delusion.

Washington was always a hot place in the summer, but the heat during July, 1868, as Old Thad lashed out at his tormenters, was ten degrees higher than the usual average. On the hottest afternoons he would lie on his bed, coatless and without a vest, his bald head tied up in a red handkerchief and his feet in a pair of plain and well-worn slippers. To visitors who dropped in he would apologize for his dishabille and explain that he was seek-

[5] *Congressional Globe*, 40 Congress, 2 session (1867–68), 4177–4178, 4335; letters to Stevens from Samuel Shock, July 21, 1868, J. Piersol, July 23, 1868, O. J. Dickey, July 24, 1868, and O. P. Swisher, July 24, 1868, and Stevens to the "Editor Evening Express," July 28, 1868, and to the "Editor Examiner," July 28, 1868, all in the Stevens Papers.

ing a renewal of his strength. He faced the dismal prospect cheer-
fully enough as he dictated a letter to his old crony and one-time
fellow congressman John Law, an Indiana Democrat:

> I am whittled down to a very narrow *pinte* at one end. If that should
> not be entirely shaved off before the next session of Congress I hope you
> will come here and give us a couple of weeks. I shall be glad to give
> you a room & a bed. We could easily assemble Brodhead & Meehan [for
> a game of euchre] at any time. Don't forget to live yourself if I should
> die. A little of the old stock will be needed, whoever has the helm.

And then Old Thad added a sentence that showed how little the
horrified preachers had succeeded in making him worry over the
fate of his soul. He was confident of going up to whatever heaven
might exist. "P. S. If you should come up after me, just knock &
enquire & I will have it opened." During his last two sickly years
he had played cards but little; perhaps he and John Law could
resume their euchre in heaven! A few days after he had composed
this letter, Congress adjourned for the rest of the summer, as the
heat wave was temporarily broken by rain that fell in torrents
and made the city as dreary as only Washington could be.[6]

After the close of Congress the agents of Baron Stoeckl began
quietly to distribute "gifts" as tokens of the czar's appreciation to
those congressmen who had made possible the sale of Alaska.
Most of this money (taken from the fund appropriated for the
purchase) was to go to those who had at first obstructed the deal
by espousing the Perkins claim. Of all this the public knew
nothing, though there were whispered rumors in the capital. The
president himself was not to learn of it until more than a month
afterward (Stevens being then in the grave) when he took a ride
out of Washington one Sunday afternoon with his secretary of
state, Seward, and they stopped for "refreshment" in a shady grove.
Johnson, later penciling a memorandum of the conversation,
noted with evident satisfaction "that the 'incoruptable' Thad-
deous Stevens received as his 'sop' the moderate sum of $10,000."
A few weeks later, at an after-dinner game of whist, Seward told
the story to other friends. One of those present recalled Seward as
saying, after listing the chief bribes: "One thousand more were to

[6] Stevens to John Law, July 21, 1868, in the Stevens Papers; *New York Times*,
July 28, 1868.

have been given to poor Thad. Stevens, but no one would undertake to give that to him, so I undertook it myself. The poor fellow
died, and I have it now." In December, 1868, Congress began an
investigation, but, as in the case of the subsequent Union Pacific
scandal, respect for the dead operated to protect the name of
Stevens—if, indeed, he had been guilty of agreeing to accept a
bribe. That any of the money actually reached his hands is unlikely, for after the first of August he was gravely ill.[7]

An attack of diarrhea left him extremely weak, but on August
6 he was able to sit up again and, according to a news bulletin,
take "charge of his ordinary business." That night he slept
soundly and on the next day he was reported as "entirely recovered." There was a letter for him from John Law, out in
Indiana, containing a long discussion of the money question and
concluding with the heartening words: *"You are right,* and nine-
tenths of our people, without distinction of party, are with you."
"Nothing would afford me more pleasure than to accept your
kind invitation to come on to Washington and partake of your
hospitality—and a game of 'euchre' with the Professor and Brod-
head, to whom remember me."[8] But there was to be no more
euchre, on this earth, for Old Thad.

His last days provided an opportunity for a little of the retro-
spection in which he seldom had indulged when he was whole.
One day a reporter from the *New York Tribune* called to ask for
some information about his early life and history, and at the word
"history" Old Thad cast up a suspicious glance. "You newspaper
men are always wanting to get at a man's history," he said. "As
I said to a young girl who came to see me some time ago to collect
materials for a biography of me, I have no history. My life-long
regret is that I have lived so long and uselessly." He was reminded
that he was the leader of the House. "I lead them, yes," he replied,
"but they never follow me or do as I want them until public
opinion has sided with me." To another caller, Alexander K.

---

[7] William A. Dunning, "Paying for Alaska," in the *Political Science Quarterly,* 27 (1912): 385–386; diary of Bigelow, entry for September 23, 1868, in
John Bigelow, *Retrospections of an Active Life* (5 vols., New York, 1909–13),
4:217.

[8] John Law to Stevens, August 1, 1868, in the Stevens Papers.

McClure, he confessed that his life had been a hopeless failure—
except, on second thought, for his part in saving the free schools
of Pennsylvania.[9]

These were the feelings of the man who had exerted more
influence upon American legislation, during the decade of conflict, than any other person in the United States! True, sometimes
Congress had not followed the leader; true, his words, as when
he demanded confiscation of Southern estates, had not always been
literally transcribed into law. But of the many forces that contributed to the course followed by the government his brain and
will were by no means the least. War taxes, tariffs, greenbacks,
transcontinental railroads, "forty acres and a mule," the Thirteenth, Fourteenth, and Fifteenth Amendments, the reconstruction acts, the impeachment proceedings—these things and many
more were largely his handiwork. A failure? He had grounds for
reproaching himself thus only if he contrasted his actual attain-
ments with the goals his ambition had set.

Faithful to the last, Lydia Smith watched over Old Thad
during his final illness. On August 8 she scrawled a note to
Thaddeus, Jr.: "Your uncel has bin quite low I had almost given
up but he is better he has diarhear which would sit hard on him
he was so weak I will write to you every day and lett you know
how he is." Helping Lydia to care for the patient were several
colored nuns, for whom, it was said, Old Thad "entertained a
deep affection" and who in turn nursed him with the "tenderest
solicitude." This was no more than a fitting return for the aid he
had given them in securing a government appropriation for their
Providence Hospital, located only a few blocks from his residence.[10]

On August 11 a number of personal and political friends visited
the house on B street to inquire about the patient's health. Late
in the afternoon, after they had gone, Old Thad felt like talking.
Around his bed were his nephew Thaddeus, Simon Stevens, Lydia,

[9] Alexander K. McClure, *Abraham Lincoln and Men of War-Times* (Philadelphia, 1892), 287; *New York Tribune*, August 14, 1868.

[10] Lydia Smith to Thaddeus Stevens, Jr., manuscript in the possession of
T. Fred. Woodley, Bangor, Pennsylvania; *New York Times*, August 5, 7, 8,
1868.

the Sisters of Charity, and his colored body-servant, Lewis West. The August weather was steamy again. Lydia and the nuns took turns fanning Old Thad and feeding him pieces of ice. He turned to Simon and spoke of public affairs. Seward had done a big thing in the purchase of Alaska, the biggest thing in his career. There was a silence. Simon remarked that he had seen General Rosecrans, and the general had spoken highly of Alanson Stevens, who fell at Chickamauga. "He was a brave boy," said Old Thad. Evening came and he dozed off. Occasionally he would awaken and offer a comment on the politics of the time. "Simon," he said, "the great questions of the day are reconstruction, the finances, and the railway system of this country." He dozed off again. Then: "I believe Grant will be elected, and he will carry out the reconstruction laws." Later he had a word for each of those at his bedside, and finally one for his nephew Thaddeus: "We'll have a nice trip home; I'll visit the foundry with you, perhaps." And then the old man wanly smiled a smile of disbelief. There were so many things yet to do, and he would not live to see them done! He fell asleep.

In the evening his Washington physician, Dr. N. Young, came and stayed long enough to caution the household against disturbing the patient or allowing him to fatigue himself with talking. Two colored clergymen called. When Stevens was asked whether they should be admitted to his room, he answered, "Certainly, certainly"—his last intelligible words. They went in. He turned on his side and reached out his hand to them. They sang a few hymns and prayed, then went out. At about nine o'clock Dr. Young returned. He told the patient he was dying. Old Thad only nodded. An hour later Loretta and Genevieve, two of the colored Sisters of Charity, entered the sickroom and prayed. One of them held the old man's wasted hand. Two or three times they put small pieces of ice into his mouth. After a while the entire household gathered again around the bed. The nuns asked Old Thad if they might baptize him. He made no objection. One of the Sisters took a glass of water, poured some of it on his head, and pronounced him baptized. Lydia, a Catholic, could now claim him as a member of her church! After the baptism he opened his eyes, once, twice, then closed them for good. It was now nearly midnight. The only sound came from the hooded dusky nuns, chanting their prayers for the dead.[11]

"The prayers of the righteous have at last removed the Congressional curse!" So the *Planters' Banner* of New Orleans announced the news of Stevens' death. "May his new iron works wean him from earth and the fires of his new furnace never go out!" But the carpetbaggers draped the public buildings of the South, even the South Carolina statehouse, in respectful mourning. And in Washington, where two months before the dead Buchanan had been unhonored and unwept, the Republicans put on a display of grief such as the city had not seen in the three years since Lincoln's death. For a few days the body of Stevens, variously puffed and shrunken by his dropsical disease, lay in state in the rotunda of the capitol while gaudily uniformed Negro Zouaves proudly kept watch by day and night. The devoted and the merely curious streamed in and out. "The death of Stevens is an emancipation for the Republican party," James G. Blaine remarked to a companion as the two walked through the rotunda. "He kept the party under his heel."[12]

Many Republicans were glad enough to be rid of the parliamentary despot whose monetary views had become a source of embarrassment to them. Yet none had served the party with a more

---

[11] This account of Stevens' last hours is derived from detailed reports in the *New York Times, Tribune,* and *Herald,* August 12, 1868.

[12] George F. Hoar, *Autobiography of Seventy Years* (3 vols., New York, 1903), 1:239 (Hoar was Blaine's companion on the walk through the capitol rotunda.); *Planters' Banner,* August 15, 1868, quoted in Walter L. Fleming, *Documentary History of Reconstruction* (2 vols., Cleveland, 1906–07), 2:272. The opinion of so-called "liberals" was summed up in the obituary remarks of the distinguished advocate of *laissez-faire,* E. L. Godkin. Stevens, Godkin wrote, had been a success as an antislavery agitator but a complete failure at "working the complicated machinery of government." He had shown his "ignorance of political economy" by his bill (in 1865) to make the greenbacks equal in value to gold and by his proposals of "mild confiscation" to pay off the national debt. He had revealed his ignorance of history when he discovered "a parallel between Charles I and Andrew Johnson." He had demonstrated his belief in the "omnipotence of legislation over human conduct" by his various reconstruction measures. In short, "his failing health, as well as his natural defects," made it very unfortunate for both the party and the country that he should have exercised so much "control over legislation." *Nation,* August 20, 1868. Old Thad's heresies were too many to permit his elevation to full-fledged godhood in the mythology of Republicanism after his death.

wholesouled devotion than he. Republicanism had been his true religion, his all in all. If there had seemed to be inconsistencies in his career, they could all be resolved into a consistent service of partisan interests, as he had interpreted them, and an unwavering determination to maintain and advance his own power within the Radical clique. Nor were his services to the party ended even yet. His soul, like John Brown's, was to go marching on with Republicans, not the least of whom was Blaine, as they waved the bloody shirt in one election after another during the next two decades.

His body, meanwhile, went home to Lancaster. Hundreds of his fellow townsmen, white and black, had stayed up till late at night awaiting the funeral train. Next afternoon they with some of the thousands of visitors stood outside the house on South Queen Street while in the darkened parlor, its shutters closed against the intense August heat, eight Protestant ministers officiated at a simple service. Through crowded streets the funeral procession then moved, by way of the main square, to the unfashionable graveyard on Chestnut Street, the owners of which had long refused to draw the color line. Here, shading their bared heads from the burning sun, a throng of the humble and the famous looked on as the casket was lowered into the ground.

On the tombstone were to be carved the words that Stevens himself had composed for it:

> *I repose in this quiet and secluded spot,*
> *not from any natural preference for solitude,*
> *but finding other cemeteries*
> *limited by charter rules as to race,*
> *I have chosen this that I might illustrate in death*
> *the principles which I advocated through a long life,*
> *Equality of man before his Creator.*

Thus ironical Old Thad perpetuated the irony of his career. Equality of man! None had done more than he to bring on the Age of Big Business, with its concentration of wealth and its diffusion of poverty, its inequalities and its inequities, which were beginning to trouble the nation even before the fresh sod had turned green again upon his unpretentious grave.

BIBLIOGRAPHY
AND INDEX

BIBLIOGRAPHY

MANUSCRIPTS

LIBRARY OF CONGRESS

Benjamin F. Butler Papers
Simon Cameron Papers
Salmon P. Chase Papers
Papers of Gideon and Francis Granger
Andrew Johnson Papers

William D. Lewis Papers
Edward McPherson Papers
Justin S. Morrill Papers
Edwin M. Stanton Papers
Thaddeus Stevens Papers
Israel Washburne Papers

HISTORICAL SOCIETY OF PENNSYLVANIA

Salmon P. Chase Manuscripts
Jay Cooke Manuscripts

The Henry Carey Gardiner Collection
The Society Collection

ADAMS COUNTY COURTHOUSE, GETTYSBURG

Minute Book, giving minutes of trials held before the Circuit Court from 1800 to 1809 and from 1826 to 1834.
Records of Deeds, 20 vols.

HARVARD COLLEGE LIBRARY

Charles Sumner Manuscripts.

CORNELL UNIVERSITY LIBRARY

Justin S. Morrill Manuscripts.

ELSEWHERE

Stevens letters in the possession of the Pennsylvania State Library, Dartmouth College, the Lancaster County Historical Society, Mrs. F. P. McKibben of Black Gap, Pennsylvania, and Mr. T. Fred. Woodley of Bangor, Pennsylvania.

GOVERNMENT DOCUMENTS

AGG, JOHN, and others, reporters. *Proceedings and Debates of the Convention of the Commonwealth of Pennsylvania to Propose Amendments to the Constitution Commenced and Held at Harrisburg on the Second Day of May, 1837.* 13 vols. Harrisburg, 1837–39.
Congressional Globe, 1849–53, 1859–68.
Pennsylvania House Journal, 1833–42.
Pennsylvania Senate Journal, 1838–39.
REED, G. E., ed. *Papers of the Governors, 1832–1845 (Pennsylvania Archives,* fourth series, vol. 6). Harrisburg, 1901.

NEWSPAPERS

Adams Sentinel (Gettysburg), 1828–30, 1838.
Bedford Inquirer, 1842–45.
Chambersburg Whig, 1837–38.
Chicago Tribune, 1863.
Dollar Weekly Pennsylvanian (Philadelphia), 1856.
Gettysburg Star, 1835.
Harpers Weekly (New York), 1865.
Harrisburg Chronicle, 1835, 1838.
Independent Whig (Lancaster), 1851, 1853.
Infidelity Unmasked (Cincinnati), 1831.
Lancaster Examiner, 1848, 1858.
Lancaster Intelligencer, 1842–68.
Lancasterian, 1850–53.
Nation (New York), 1868.
National Enquirer (Philadelphia), 1836.
National Era (Washington), 1850.
National Gazette (Philadelphia), 1836.

National Intelligencer (Washington), 1836.
New York Herald, 1860–68.
New York Times, 1856–68.
New York Tribune, 1856, 1860–68.
New York World, 1860, 1865–66.
Niles Register (Baltimore), 1831–42.
Pennsylvania Freeman (Philadelphia), 1838.
Pennsylvania Reporter (Harrisburg), 1830–38.
Pennsylvania Telegraph (Harrisburg), 1830, 1841.
Philadelphia Daily News, 1850.
Philadelphia Daily Times, 1856.
Philadelphia Press, 1858–68.
Poulson's Daily American Advertiser (Philadelphia), 1832–42.
United States Gazette (Philadelphia), 1841–42.
Vermont Patriot (Montpelier), 1844.
Washington Globe, 1836, 1840–41.

BOOKS, PAMPHLETS, AND ARTICLES

ADAMS FAMILY. A Cycle of Adams Letters, edited by Worthington C. Ford. 2 vols. Boston and New York, 1920.

ADAMS, JOHN QUINCY. Memoirs of John Quincy Adams, edited by Charles Francis Adams. 12 vols. Philadelphia, 1874–77.

AMERICAN ANTI-SLAVERY SOCIETY. Fourth Annual Report. New York, 1837.

BATES, EDWARD. The Diary of Edward Bates, 1859–1866, edited by Howard K. Beale (Annual Report of the American Historical Association, 1930, vol. 4). Washington, 1933.

BATES, SAMUEL P. Martial Deeds of Pennsylvania. Philadelphia, 1875.

[BATES, SAMUEL P., and J. FRAISE RICHARD]. History of Franklin County, Pennsylvania. Chicago, 1887.

BEALE, HOWARD K. The Critical Year: A Study of Andrew Johnson and Reconstruction. New York, 1930.

BEVERIDGE, ALBERT J. Abraham Lincoln, 1809–1858. 2 vols. Boston and New York, 1928.

BIGELOW, JOHN. Retrospections of an Active Life. 5 vols. New York, 1909–13.

BINCKLEY, J. W. "The Leader of the House." Galaxy, 1:493–500 (June 15, 1866).

BLAINE, JAMES G. Twenty Years of Congress: From Lincoln to Garfield. 2 vols. Norwich, Connecticut, 1884.

BOUTWELL, GEORGE S. Reminiscences of Sixty Years in Public Affairs. 2 vols. New York, 1902.

BOWEN, ELI. *The Pictorial Sketch-Book of Pennsylvania.* 8th edition. Philadelphia, 1854.

[BRADSBY, H. C.]. *History of Adams County, Pennsylvania.* Chicago, 1886.

BUTLER, BENJAMIN F. *Private and Official Correspondence of Benjamin F. Butler during the Period of the Civil War.* 5 vols. Norwood, Massachusetts, 1917.

CALLENDER, E. B. *Thaddeus Stevens, Commoner.* Boston, 1882.

COX, SAMUEL S. *Three Decades of Federal Legislation.* Providence, 1885.

CROOK, WILLIAM H. *Through Five Administrations,* edited by M. S. Gerry. New York, 1910.

DEWITT, DAVID M. *The Impeachment and Trial of Andrew Johnson.* New York, 1903.

[DOCK, MIRA L.]. "Thaddeus Stevens as an Ironmaster." *Philadelphia Times,* July 14, 1895.

DUNNING, WILLIAM A. "Paying for Alaska." *Political Science Quarterly,* 27:385–398 (September, 1912).

ELLIS, J. B. *The Sights and Secrets of the National Capital.* New York, 1869.

ERRETT, RUSSELL. "The Republican Nominating Conventions of 1856 and 1860." *Magazine of Western History,* 10:257–265, 360–365 (July, August, 1889).

Estate of Thaddeus Stevens, Deceased. Audit. Notes of Testimony. Lancaster, 1893.

FESSENDEN, FRANCIS. *Life and Public Services of William Pitt Fessenden.* 2 vols. Boston and New York, 1907.

FLEMING, WALTER L. *Documentary History of Reconstruction.* 2 vols. Cleveland, 1906, 1907.

FORNEY, JOHN W. *Anecdotes of Public Men.* 2 vols. New York, 1873, 1881.

Free-Masonry Unmasked; or, Minutes of the Trial of a Suit of Common Pleas of Adams County, Wherein Thaddeus Stevens, Esq., Was Plaintiff, and Jacob Lefever, Defendant, published by R. W. Middleton. Gettysburg, 1835.

GARFIELD, JAMES A. *Life and Letters of James Abram Garfield,* edited by Theodore C. Smith. 2 vols. New Haven, 1925.

GOLDER, F. A. "The Purchase of Alaska." *American Historical Review,* 25:411–425 (April, 1920).

GORDON, T. F. *A Gazetteer of the State of Pennsylvania.* Philadelphia, 1832.

GUROWSKI, ADAM. *Diary, 1863–1864–1865.* Washington, 1866.

HALL, WILLIAM M. *Reminiscences and Sketches, Historical and Biographical.* Harrisburg, 1890.

HAMLIN, C. E. *Life and Times of Hannibal Hamlin.* Boston, 1898.

HARRIS, ALEXANDER. *A Review of the Political Conflict in America ... Comprising Also a Résumé of the Career of Thaddeus Stevens.* New York, 1876.

HARVEY, OSCAR J. *History of Lodge No. 61, F. and A. M.* Wilkes-Barre, 1897.

HAYES, RUTHERFORD B. *Diary and Letters,* edited by C. R. Williams. 5 vols. Columbus, 1922–26.

HAZARD, SAMUEL, ed. *The Register of Pennsylvania.* 16 vols. Philadelphia, 1828–36.

HEMENWAY, ABBY MARIA. *The Vermont Historical Gazetteer: A Magazine Embracing a History of Each Town.* 5 vols. Burlington, 1867–91.

HENSEL, W. U. *The Christiana Riot and the Treason Trials of 1851 (Lancaster County Historical Society Papers*, vol. 15). Lancaster, 1911.

——— "Thaddeus Stevens as a Country Lawyer." *Lancaster County Historical Society Papers*, 10 (1906): 247–290.

HESSELTINE, WILLIAM B. "Some New Aspects of the Pro-Slavery Argument." *Journal of Negro History*, 21 (1936): 1–14.

History of the Rise, Progress and Downfall of Know-Nothingism in Lancaster County, by Two Expelled Members. Lancaster, 1856.

HOAR, GEORGE F. *Autobiography of Seventy Years*. 2 vols. New York, 1903.

HOKE, JACOB. *The Great Invasion of 1863; or, General Lee in Pennsylvania*. Dayton, Ohio, 1887.

HOOD, ALEXANDER H. "Thaddeus Stevens." *A Biographical History of Lancaster County*, edited by Alexander Harris. Lancaster, 1872.

JULIAN, GEORGE W. *Political Recollections, 1840 to 1872*. Chicago, 1884.

KENDRICK, BENJAMIN B. *The Journal of the Joint Committee of Fifteen on Reconstruction (Columbia University Studies in History, Economics, and Public Law*, no. 62). New York, 1914.

LANDIS, CHARLES I. "A Refutation of the Slanderous Stories against the Name of Thaddeus Stevens Placed before the Public by Thomas Dixon." *Lancaster County Historical Society Papers*, 28 (1924): 49–52.

[MCALLISTER, HENRY, JR.]. *Report of the Secretary of the American Iron and Steel Association*. Philadelphia, 1868.

MCCALL, SAMUEL W. *Thaddeus Stevens (American Statesmen* series, edited by John T. Morse, Jr.). Boston and New York, 1899.

MCCARTHY, CHARLES. *The Antimasonic Party (Annual Report of the American Historical Association*, 1902, vol. 2). Washington, 1903.

MCCLURE, ALEXANDER K. *Abraham Lincoln and Men of War-Times*. Philadelphia, 1892.

——— *Old-Time Notes of Pennsylvania*. 2 vols. Philadelphia, 1905.

——— *Our Presidents and How We Make Them*. New York, 1900.

——— *Colonel Alexander K. McClure's Recollections of Half a Century*. Salem, Massachusetts, 1902.

MCGRANE, REGINALD C., ed. *Correspondence of Nicholas Biddle Dealing with National Affairs, 1768–1844*. Boston and New York, 1919.

[MCPHERSON, EDWARD]. "The 'Maria Furnace' Property." *Gettysburg Star and Sentinel*, January 13, 1891.

MCPHERSON, EDWARD. *The Political History of the United States during the Period of Reconstruction*. New York, 1880.

MENEELY, ALEXANDER H. *The War Department, 1861 (Columbia University Studies in History, Economics, and Public Law*, no. 300). New York, 1928.

MILLER, ALPHONSE B. *Thaddeus Stevens*. New York, 1939.

MUELLER, HENRY R. *The Whig Party in Pennsylvania (Columbia University Studies in History, Economics, and Public Law*, no. 230). New York, 1902.

OBERHOLTZER, ELLIS P. *Jay Cooke: Financier of the Civil War*. 2 vols. Philadelphia, 1907.

OWEN, ROBERT DALE. "Political Results from the Varioloid." *Atlantic Monthly*, 35:660–670 (June, 1875).

Pennsylvania State Reports, Containing Cases Adjudged in the Supreme Court, 1845–1868. Philadelphia, 1846–69.

PENROSE, CHARLES, and FRED. WATTS, reporters. *Reports of Cases Adjudged in the Supreme Court of Pennsylvania, 1829–32.* 3 vols. Philadelphia, 1843.

POORE, BEN. PERLEY. *Reminiscences of Sixty Years in the National Metropolis.* 2 vols. New York, 1886.

RAWLE, WILLIAM, JR., reporter. *Reports of Cases Adjudged in the Supreme Court of Pennsylvania, 1828–69.* 5 vols. Philadelphia, 1869.

RIDDLE, ALBERT G. *Benjamin F. Wade.* Cleveland, 1886.

SALTER, WILLIAM. *Life of James W. Grimes.* New York, 1890.

SCHUCKERS, J. W. *Life and Public Services of Salmon Portland Chase.* New York, 1874.

SCHURZ, CARL. *The Reminiscences of Carl Schurz,* edited by Frederic Bancroft and William A. Dunning. 3 vols. New York, 1908.

SCOVEL, J. M. "Thaddeus Stevens." *Lippincott's Magazine,* 61 (1898): 545–550.

SCRUGHAM, MARY. *The Peaceable Americans of 1860–1861 (Columbia University Studies in History, Economics, and Public Law, no. 219).* New York, 1921.

SERGEANT, THOMAS, and WILLIAM RAWLE, JR., reporters. *Reports of Cases Adjudged in the Supreme Court of Pennsylvania, 1814–28.* 17 vols. Philadelphia, 1818–29.

SEWARD, WILLIAM H. *William H. Seward: An Autobiography from 1801 to 1834 with a Memoir of His Life and Selections from His Letters 1831–1846,* edited by Frederick W. Seward. New York, 1891.

SHERMAN, JOHN and W. T. *Sherman Letters,* edited by R. S. Thorndike. New York, 1894.

SMITH, WILLIAM E. *The Francis Preston Blair Family in Politics.* 2 vols. New York, 1933.

SPALDING, E. G. *History of the Legal Tender Paper Money Issued during the Great Rebellion.* Buffalo, 1875.

STERLING, ADA, ed. *A Belle of the 'Fifties: Memoirs of Mrs. Clay of Alabama, Covering Social and Political Life in Washington and the South, 1853–66.* New York, 1904.

STEWART, W. M. *Reminiscences of Senator William M. Stewart of Nevada.* New York, 1908.

SUMNER, CHARLES. *Memoir and Letters of Charles Sumner,* edited by Edward L. Pierce. 4 vols. Boston, 1877–94.

THOMPSON, ZADOCK. *History of Vermont.* Burlington, 1853.

TREGO, C. B. *A Geography of Pennsylvania ... with a Separate Description of Each County.* Philadelphia, 1843.

TURNER, E. R. *The Negro in Pennsylvania: Slavery-Servitude-Freedom: 1639–1861.* Washington, 1911.

WARDEN, ROBERT B. *An Account of the Private Life and Public Services of Salmon Portland Chase.* Cincinnati, 1874.

WASHBURNE, ELIHU B., ed. *The Edwards Papers (Chicago Historical Society Collections,* vol. 3). Chicago, 1884.

WATTS, FRED., reporter. *Reports of Cases Adjudged in the Supreme Court of Pennsylvania, 1832–40.* 8 vols. Philadelphia, 1834–41.

Watts, Fred., and H. J. Sergeant, reporters. *Reports of Cases Adjudged in the Supreme Court of Pennsylvania, 1841–44.* Philadelphia, 1844–46.

Welles, Gideon. *Diary of Gideon Welles, Secretary of the Navy under Lincoln and Johnson,* with an introduction by John T. Morse, Jr. 3 vols. Boston and New York, 1911.

White, Horace. *Life of Lyman Trumbull.* New York, 1913.

[Whitman, Benjamin, and N. W. Russell]. *History of Erie County, Pennsylvania.* Chicago, 1884.

Woodburn, James A. *The Life of Thaddeus Stevens: A Study in American Political History.* Indianapolis, 1913.

Woodley, Thomas F. *Great Leveler: The Life of Thaddeus Stevens.* New York, 1937.

———— *Thaddeus Stevens.* Harrisburg, 1934.

INDEX